THE PHILOSOPHY
OF WILHELM DILTHEY

THE PHILOSOPHY
OF WILHELM DILTHEY

by

H. A. HODGES, M.A., D.Phil.

Professor of Philosophy in the University of Reading

ψυχῆς πείρατα ἰὼν οὐκ ἂν ἐξεύροιο πᾶσαν ἐπιπορευόμενος
ὁδόν· οὕτω βαθὺν λόγον ἔχει.

HERACLITUS

GREENWOOD PRESS, PUBLISHERS
WESTPORT, CONNECTICUT

Library of Congress Cataloging in Publication Data

Hodges, Herbert Arthur, 1905-
 The philosophy of Wilhelm Dilthey.

 Reprint of the 1952 ed. published by Routledge
& Paul, London, in series: International library
of sociology and social reconstruction.
 1. Dilthey, Wilhelm, 1833-1911. I. Title.
B3216.D84H57 1974   193   73-13024
ISBN 0-8371-7112-1

First published in 1952 by Routledge & Kegan Paul Ltd., London

Reprinted with the permission of Routledge & Kegan Paul, Ltd.

Reprinted by Greenwood Press,
a division of Williamhouse-Regency Inc.

First Greenwood Reprinting 1974
Second Greenwood Reprinting 1976

Library of Congress Catalog Card Number 73-13024

ISBN 0-8371-7112-1

Printed in the United States of America

CONTENTS

CHAPTER THREE

CHAPTER FOUR   96

ix

CHAPTER TEN   315

INTRODUCTION

WILHELM DILTHEY, whose philosophy is the subject of the following pages, was born on November 19th, 1833, at Biebrich am Rhein. The son of a pastor of the Reformed Church, he became successively a student at the University of Berlin, Privat-Dozent there in Philosophy (1865), Professor at Basel (1867), Kiel (1868), and Breslau (1871). In 1882 he was recalled to Berlin to occupy the Chair which Lotze, after a brief tenure of one year, had left vacant, and he remained in Berlin, teaching and writing, until his death on October 1st, 1911.

The literary productions of Dilthey's long life extend into several fields of learning, of which philosophy is only one. They include critical and historical studies of literature and music; studies in educational theory and in the history of educational practice, ancient and modern; researches into the history of religious and political as well as philosophical ideas, especially since the Renaissance and Reformation. It was against this background that his specifically philosophical thinking took place. He is one of those philosophers (like Vico, Hegel, Croce, Collingwood) who draw their inspiration from, and find their problems in, aesthetic and historical studies rather than mathematics and natural science. If we turn to his specifically philosophical writings, extending as they do over a long period from 1864 until his death in 1911, we find that amid all their diversity there is one enduring theme which holds them together. That theme is his determination to write a *Critique of Historical Reason*.

Dilthey set himself this task at the outset of his career, and for a long time he had to work at it in isolation. The atmosphere of contemporary thought was not propitious. Later, however, largely owing to Dilthey's own efforts and to those of his younger rivals, Windelband and Rickert, the atmosphere changed, and by the beginning of the present century there was in Germany a strong movement towards a philosophy of history and culture. Dilthey struggled with Windelband and Rickert for the leadership of this movement. His constant polemics against them will be a recurrent theme in the following pages. At first it seemed that Rickert, through the clarity and force of his writing, was gaining the upper hand. For the space of a generation he was able to give his own turn to the problem and impose his solution upon a great part of the German philosophical public. In the long run, however, the qualities of Dilthey's work began to assert themselves. The steady work of his disciples in collating his unpublished MSS. with one another and with his published writings, and the result of their work in the shape of the Teubner edition of his *Gesammelte Schriften*, of which eleven volumes are now available, have combined with a growing recognition of difficulties and inadequacies in Rickert's doctrine to direct attention back from him to Dilthey, who is more and more seen to be the real *fons et origo* of the whole movement. Rickert is a clear and stimulating writer. He gave system and terminological precision to the new philosophy of history and society, a thing which Dilthey was ill qualified to do. But it was Dilthey who gave it and still gives it life, a life for which Rickert's system has proved too cramped.

What was Dilthey trying to do? What is the aim and basis of the movement which he launched? He himself has given us the answer. He points to the dominating position which has been held, in most periods of philosophical history, by the study of the problems presented by mathematics and natural science. The reasons for this predominance are no secret. Pure mathematics in the ancient world, and it and mathematical physics in the modern, have a perennial attraction in that they offer to us exact knowledge, and latterly also a growing power over nature, and it is a matter of deep philosophical interest to enquire how this achievement is possible and what it implies. For a long period this kind of knowledge has held a dominant position among the intellectual interests of the philosopher, and it will always be important. But, says Dilthey, we are now in a position to see that it constitutes only one half of the *globus intellectualis*; the other half is composed of the study of man in society and in history. Here we meet with a different type of study. Instead of observing our object directly, we have to approach it

xiv

indirectly through written testimony and other similar evidence; instead of clearly formulated theories which can be tested by experiment, we have an attempt to analyse and describe the concrete complexities of life; instead of explanation of particular events and processes through general laws, we have an appreciative understanding of the meaning and value of the unique individual. There is no reason why the one sphere of knowledge should not be as thoroughly studied by philosophers as the other. Until recently it was possible to plead the absence of any organised body of research in the historical field, comparable with the scientific study of nature; but the expansion of social and historical researches in the last century and a half has removed that inequality, and confronts us with the spectacle of a large group of interrelated disciplines, all working together to produce a clear and comprehensive picture of the life of mankind. The methods and conclusions of these disciplines, no less than those of the exact sciences, are matter for philosophical investigation, and to carry out this investigation is the province of a *Critique of Historical Reason*.

How is such a *Critique* related to what is known as the 'philosophy of history'? Not very closely; indeed, according to Dilthey, it is part of the task of the *Critique of Historical Reason* to show that a philosophy of history is impossible. That is because he understands by 'philosophy of history' not a critical study of methods and principles, but a speculative construction which claims to find a 'meaning' in the course of events, and to give us understanding of them on a deeper level than historical enquiry itself.

A *theology* of history, making this claim, has existed for over two thousand years; for it grew up in the writings of the Hebrew prophets, and was developed to its full stature under Christian auspices. This Christian doctrine set itself to provide, in the light of revealed truth, a bird's-eye view of world history, past and future. A finite and hierarchically graded universe provided the stage on which was played the drama of the Fall and Redemption of Man. The *philosophy* of history first arose in modern times, when the foundations of this theological view began to be seriously shaken.

They were shaken from the moment that the universe came to be considered as an infinite whole, all the parts of which, albeit in diverse degrees, were ensouled. This new metaphysic was enunciated in its essentials by Bruno, and its ultimate consequences were already suspected both by him and by his judges. In a universe where everything lives, why should mankind be the only, or even the most important, rational species existing? In a world of infinite space, with an endless wealth of diverse existences filling its endless extent, why should the human past be as limited as Christian tradition made it, and why should the human future be limited at all? If the law of existence is not decay and death, as in the fallen universe of Christian belief, but life and development, why should man alone be afflicted by a mysterious inability to rise to perfection? These ideas, which gained currency during the latter half of the seventeenth century, became later, in the hands of Lessing and Herder, the foundation of the new philosophy of history, which was in fact the philosophy of human progress.

The new doctrine was as dogmatic as the old, though it replaced the dogma of Christianity by that of humanism. It is strange that this should have been so. The philosophy of history came into existence about the very time when philosophy was beginning to pass from the dogmatic to the critical standpoint. Vico was contemporary with Locke and Berkeley, and Herder with Kant. Yet the philosophy of history in this period was substantially untouched by the breath of critical thought. At the very time when our knowledge of the physical world was being subjected to careful examination, and the true function of its symbols and conventions was slowly beginning to be seen, the capacity of the historian to know the past substantially as it really happened was tacitly accepted, and philosophers vied with one another in asking the dogmatic question: what is the purpose and meaning of the historical process? If Vico and Herder in their day were thus uncritical, it was not to be expected that Hegel would be any less so. In his hands the philosophy of history became part of a grandiose synthesis, as speculative in its fundamental principles as it was often reckless in its treatment of details.

It was not until the latter half of the nineteenth century, in the widespread reaction of that period against speculative metaphysics, that a more circumspect kind of philosophy was able to arise, whose aim was not to advance any doctrine about historical and social matters which was not already guaranteed by empirical evidence as handled by the historian and the sociologist, but to submit the procedure of the historian and the sociologist themselves to an epistemological examination, as Kant had already examined the procedure of the mathematician and the natural scientist. This is the *Critique of Historical Reason*, of which Dilthey was the founder and (it is hardly too much to say) the only whole-hearted follower. For though Windelband and Rickert in Germany, and after them Croce and Gentile in Italy, have indeed written about the methods and principles of historical research, they have all done so in the framework of an idealist philosophy whose affinity with the post-Kantian systems is only too apparent. Of our own Collingwood I will say nothing here; a detailed discussion of his work in comparison with Dilthey's will be found in Chapter Ten.

There is no tradition of historical philosophy in Britain comparable with that which has long prevailed in Germany and Italy. It is strange that this nation, which has a strong vein of poetry and a strong feeling for tradition, and has produced, in the course of the years, its fair complement of historians, economists, anthropologists, and sociologists, should have let the philosophical problems connected with these studies go so generally unheeded. Even the idealist philosophy, which in Fichte, Hegel, Windelband, Rickert, Croce, Gentile has kept up a vigorous tradition of reflection on these questions, has failed to do so on our soil; the great figures of the movement, Green, Bradley, Bosanquet, have made important contributions to moral and political theory, but not to the philosophy of history. There is, of course, the early essay by Bradley on *The Presuppositions of Critical History*. It is good, but it is short, and deals confessedly with a narrow problem; nor did its author ever return to the subject. Not until Collingwood do we find in this country a philosopher whose mind is penetrated and moulded by historical thinking; and this very fact, coupled with his strong interest in aesthetics, makes him appear more naturally as an outlying disciple of Croce than as a native English growth.[1]

Bradley, Croce, and Collingwood have one important thing in common—their dependence on Hegel. From one point of

[1] Cf. the very appreciative account given of *Speculum Mentis* by de Ruggiero in *Filosofi del Novecento*.

view, this is a pity. British philosophy took a stiff dose of Hegel seventy years ago, made a wry face, and will not soon repeat the experience. It is not to the advantage of historical and aesthetic studies if it comes to be thought that an interest in them is a mark of a crypto-Hegelian. And this is just where Dilthey is important; for in him we find the same range of interest as in Hegel, Croce, Collingwood, but we find it linked with an entirely different philosophy. Dilthey's philosophy does not belong to the idealist family at all. It belongs rather to the progeny of Locke and Hume, to the family of the British empiricists. Other voices are heard in him too: the voice of French positivism, and very notably that of Kant. But at no point does he waver in his twofold determination, (1) to trace all knowledge to experience, recognising no *a priori*, and (2) to have no dealings with metaphysics.

It is worth while to dwell upon this at some length, so as to make clear from the outset what philosophical company Dilthey keeps.

1. *Dilthey and Kantianism*

Dilthey lived in an age when Kantianism was in the air. The return of German philosophy to Kant, after the long interlude of the post-Kantian idealism, was in full swing when Dilthey began his work; and at first it meant a return from speculative system-building to empirical caution, from metaphysics to the critique of knowledge. So far, Dilthey went with the movement. But it was not long before Neo-Kantianism developed into a new version of idealist metaphysics. In the hands of Cohen and Natorp, Windelband and Rickert, it became a philosophy of *a priori* principles, timeless 'meaning-complexes', absolute value-norms and the like. Then Dilthey went into opposition, and remained so to the end of his life. In his theory of knowledge there is no *a priori*. All thought-structures arise out of experience, and derive their meaning from their relation to experience. There is no 'timeless world' of meanings, or essences, or rational principles; there is no clear-cut distinction, such as is drawn by the German Neo-Kantians, or the Italian Neo-idealists, or Collingwood, between the rational level of experience and the irrational, the 'spirit' and the 'psyche'; there is no 'metaphysical subject' or 'transcendental self' such as is found in orthodox

Kantian and post-Kantian theories of knowledge. There is only the human being, the mind-body unit (*psychophysische Einheit*), living his life in interaction with his physical and social environment; and out of this interaction all experience and all thought arise.

2. *Experience and reality*

If all thought draws its meaning from its relation to experience, experience is the foundation of the whole edifice of knowledge. Experience is the only evidence we can have that anything exists; and further, it is only by reference to experience that we can define what we mean by saying that anything 'exists'. Dilthey often speaks of 'reality' (*Realität, Wirklichkeit*), and says that our knowledge of our own minds is knowledge of 'reality' in a sense in which our knowledge of physical things is not. The word 'reality' here has no shadow of a Hegelian meaning. Dilthey does not mean that 'mind' is a 'higher degree of reality' or a 'more explicit expression of the Absolute' than matter, or anything of that kind. He is merely making the well-known point that our own thoughts and feelings are experienced or lived through (*erlebt*) by us immediately and from within, in a sense in which external objects are not. Our own thoughts and feelings are 'real' because we experience them directly. The external world also is 'real', according to Dilthey, because we find it in lived experience; for the not-self also is *given*, along with the self, in the experience of acting and being acted upon, and all our concepts of the external world are built upon, and derive their meaning from, that experience.

Dilthey's empiricism is not of that rigorous type which dismisses all unobservables as meaningless. The unobservable can be conceived on the analogy of the observable, though its existence must of course be for us a matter of more or less precarious inference. The consequences of this are seen in two places in Dilthey's philosophy.

(*a*) Where our modern positivists treat metaphysical questions as nonsense, Dilthey treats them as significant but unanswerable. In this he resembles Kant and the older type of positivism. And because metaphysical questions are significant, philosophy is not debarred from discussing them, though it must not waste time trying to answer them. What it can do is to study their origins, and the motives which lead us to ask them. This study is not, as it would be for a logical positivist, a mere branch of the pathology of language. It is a study of the perfectly natural and healthy process by which we are led on from questions which we can answer to other questions which we shall never be able to answer, not because the questions are irrational, but because the means of answering them, viz. the obtaining of relevant evidence, is for ever beyond our powers.

(b) Within the sphere of the knowable, the thoughts, feelings, and purposes of human beings play a decisive part, above all for a philosopher whose interests lie where Dilthey's lie. Dilthey's philosophy does not confine him to an external and behaviouristic approach to the minds of other people. On the contrary, he has a great deal to say about the way in which, by imaginative reconstruction followed by intellectual analysis and theorising, we can understand not only the behaviour, but the experiences of others. His philosophy would fall to pieces if this part of it dropped out.

3. *The psychological approach*

Dilthey did not live to see the birth of logical positivism; and the tendencies in his own time which were to lead up to it— logical analysis, symbolic logic, the philosophy of mathematics —were outside his range. His thought has more in common with the older positivism of Comte, in its fundamentally historical approach, its readiness to recognise that theological and metaphysical thinking was legitimate and useful in its own day, and its continual emphasis on methodology. Where he goes beyond French positivism, it is not in the direction of logical, but of psychological analysis.

This does not mean that he makes philosophy depend on the experimental science known as 'psychology'. It means that, since all our thoughts are ultimately based on experience, philosophy ought to give us some notion of what experience is like, and how the translation of it into thought-formulae is done. Moreover, it is not enough to let the word 'experience' in the foregoing sentence mean simply sense-experience. The experiential foundations of thought are far wider than that. The very idea of 'objectivity' is a logical symbol for a volitional experience, the experience of frustrated effort; and all value-judgments, as we shall see, are verbal expressions of emotional reactions. Philosophy must examine the 'totality' of experience, emotional and volitional as well as sensory, if it is to find the true foundation on which the edifice of discourse is built.

In making this examination, Dilthey is ready to learn from anyone: from Kant, from Goethe, from Maine de Biran, from William James, from Brentano. In his latest writings there is a good deal about 'acts' and 'contents' which at first sight may suggest an affinity with Husserl. The appearance is deceptive. Dilthey borrowed certain *words* from Husserl at a time when Husserl's *Logische Untersuchungen* were new and influential; but he never borrowed Husserl's doctrines, and he has left his adverse opinion of them on record. Husserl was a 'psychological scholastic', an analyst who multiplied abstractions far beyond necessity; while Dilthey was trying to get away from abstractions to the wholeness of experience.

What is really characteristic of Dilthey in this field may be summed up in two points. (*a*) He believes that we are able, by introspection combined with the interpretation of expressions, to discover in our conscious life a system of sequence-patterns which he calls the 'structural system of mental life'. The successive stages of a mental process are, he says, *experienced* as *belonging together*, as dynamically connected. (*b*) Behind the sequence of states and processes on the surface of consciousness, he claims to discern certain determining factors on a deeper level, which he calls 'attitudes' (*Verhaltungsweisen*). His use of the word 'attitude' here is akin to I. A. Richards' use of it in *Principles of Literary Criticism*. The theory of attitudes makes possible an explanation of certain typical differences of outlook, e.g. between the idealistic and the naturalistic types of thinker. If Dilthey had met the logical positivists, he would have recognised them at once as a splendid example of his 'naturalistic' type.

4. *The status of value-judgments*

Dilthey is an empiricist in ethics as well as in other fields, and he departs from Kantian doctrine in a quite radical way. Not only does he reject the Neo-Kantian philosophy of timeless values; he denies to value-judgments and imperatives any status as cognitive judgments at all. A value-judgment is the expression of an emotional reaction to something; a precept or imperative is the expression of a desire or an act of will. The basis of value-standards and moral principles is therefore not to be sought in 'reason', but in the affective and conative aspects of human nature. It does not follow that there is no sense in speaking of 'objective' standards, or that one value-judgment is as well-grounded as any other. For a reaction is more adequate in proportion as the subject sees his situation more fully; moreover, each of us finds it worth while to try to systematise his reactions, to co-ordinate them with one another and with those of other people in order to find a coherent pattern of life. A great deal of thinking can enter into this co-ordinating process, and from it emerge formulae which represent not the unreflective utterance of a passing feeling, but a settled attitude to life. It is thus possible to distinguish in a significant way between 'subjective' judgments and 'objective' ones, i.e. those which fall within the coherent system. But all this does not alter the fact that what we are dealing with in this whole sphere is emotional and volitional reactions. Nor is it possible to find a single formula which can be relied on to find universal acceptance, and can therefore claim to be an absolute norm. There is no absolute in the moral life except life itself, in its perpetual striving, through perpetually changing forms, to achieve order and satisfaction; and 'life' here means not any 'higher', 'absolute', or 'transcendental' self such as Kant asserts, but individual human beings, mind-body complexes, empirical selves living their lives in the empirical world.

5. *History and the social sciences*

A further point, though less topical than the foregoing, may be added here to complete the picture. In spite of the phrase 'Critique of Historical Reason', the object of Dilthey's concern is not historical knowledge alone. It is something wider than that. What he has in mind is a much more diverse group of studies, including history and biography, but also psychology, anthropology, sociology, economics, jurisprudence, educational theory—a group of studies which vary very much in aim and method, but which find a common subject-matter in the thoughts and activities of men. These studies are known in German as the *Geisteswissenschaften* and in French as *les sciences morales*. There is no generally accepted English name for them, but I have called them the 'human-studies', and I shall use that phrase as an equivalent for *Geisteswissenschaften* throughout this book. It is an essential point with Dilthey that the human studies are an integrated group, comparable with the natural sciences in their ordered diversity, but differing from them in their methods and principles. His object is to analyse the logical structure of this group of studies, the distinctive characteristics of historical enquiry, the continual give and take between history and the social sciences, and of these latter among themselves, the likenesses and differences between social sciences and natural sciences, and the affinities of the human studies with art and philosophy. The phrase *Kritik der historischen Vernunft* is really too narrow for such an enquiry as this, and Dilthey often prefers to call his work a *Grundlegung der Geisteswissenschaften*. This conception of the *Geisteswissenschaften* is as characteristic in his thinking as the conception of history is in that of Croce or Collingwood.

The difference is significant, and what it signifies will become clear in what follows, especially in Chapters One, Seven, and Eight. It is mentioned here simply in order to guard against the idea of Dilthey as a 'philosopher of history' in any narrow or exclusive sense. If he discusses historical knowledge, it is because that is one element, and a predominant element, in the wider system of the human studies; but there are other important elements in that system, and these too must and do receive their proper meed of attention.

Hitherto, so far as I know, there has been no attempt to present Dilthey's philosophy as a whole in the English language, except my own small book (*Wilhelm Dilthey: an Introduction*, Kegan Paul, 1944). That book was not detailed enough to forestall all possible misunderstandings; nor could it make clear what was the intellectual environment in terms of which Dilthey's work is to be interpreted. The present work, being longer, can be more explicit. It gives a fuller account of what Dilthey actually wrote, together with the sources from which he drew inspiration, the development of his views, and some of the controversies in which he became involved.

Dilthey's own philosophical writings are not altogether easy going for the student who comes to them without a guide. One reason for this is their unsystematic character. Their common theme, at all periods, is the project of a *Kritik der historischen*

Vernunft or *Grundlegung der Geisteswissenschaften*: a vast project, involving work in several different, though related, fields of enquiry. Dilthey set about this work in two ways. On the one hand he adopted a piecemeal approach, so that a great deal of his writing consists of separate works on moral theory, on aesthetics, on psychological methods, on the external world, and so on; and some of these cannot be properly understood until we see how they fit into the main scheme. On the other hand, he had always in mind the plan of a comprehensive work which should exhibit the *Kritik* as a whole. Unfortunately, this comprehensive work was never written. He published a first volume of it in 1883 (the *Einleitung in die Geisteswissenschaften*), with the promise of a speedy conclusion; but he was never able to finish it according to the original plan. In the last years of his life he made a fresh start on a different plan, with the *Aufbau der geschichtlichen Welt in den Geisteswissenschaften* (1910); but death overtook him before he could bring this to completion. Fortunately, however, he had assembled a great deal of material for this purpose, some of it mere fragments, but much of it in an advanced state of preparation. With care and patience, and with the aid of his own sketch-plans in the matter of arrangement, it can be pieced together so as to restore the whole work substantially as he meant it to be. This has been done by his literary executors, and the result is available in volume VII of the *Gesammelte Schriften*. Students of Dilthey are very greatly indebted to those who have done this work of restoration, as well as to the author of the Preface to volume V of the *Gesammelte Schriften*, in which many aspects of the development of Dilthey's thought are traced. Nevertheless, Dilthey's failure to complete the *Kritik* himself has led to some inconveniences, and one of them is of a serious nature. His theory of knowledge is presupposed in his writings of all periods from 1883 onwards; but because it was originally meant to come in towards the end of the *magnum opus*, the writing-out of it was continually postponed, and there is no formal and systematic exposition of it earlier than 1905. The epistemological treatises of that and later years have to be allowed to cast a light backwards upon earlier writings if these earlier writings are to be correctly understood.

The plan of exposition which I have adopted is therefore partly systematic and partly historical. In Chapter One I examine the sources of Dilthey's inspiration, and show how, in the years before 1880, the problem of the *Geisteswissenschaften* in its full extent gradually took possession of his mind, and with it the beginnings of a solution. This solution, when fully developed, falls naturally into two parts, one of which is concerned with the most general epistemological issues, while the other refers specifically to the methods and principles of the historical and social studies, their logical relations with one another, with the natural sciences and with philosophy. Accordingly, in the next four chapters I examine Dilthey's views on the wider issues of epistemology. Thus Chapter Two summarises his theory of knowledge, showing how he developed his position in continual controversy with the Neo-Kantian idealists; Chapter Three sets forth briefly Dilthey's view as to the nature of value-judgments and imperatives, together with his reasons for holding that metaphysics, while ineradicable as a tendency of the mind, is impossible as a science; Chapter Four follows him more in detail into moral theory and aesthetics; while in Chapter Five I take up one of the most difficult and important sections of Dilthey's philosophy, viz. his account of the nature of expression, understanding, and interpretation, and the controversy between him and the Neo-Kantians on this subject. The next three chapters take up the other side of Dilthey's philosophy, his logic and methodology of the human studies; and in this a certain development and change of view is to be traced. Thus, Chapter Six summarises the *Einleitung in die Geisteswissenschaften* (1883), in which Dilthey for the first time formulated his problem in full, adumbrated solutions on various points, and laid down a programme for future work; Chapter Seven traces the development of his views on the extremely difficult question of the part to be played by psychology among the human studies; Chapter Eight traces the course of the dispute between Dilthey and the Neo-Kantians about the aims and principles of the human studies, a dispute which occupied the last seventeen years of Dilthey's life, and is not yet laid to rest. (The Neo-Kantian position has much in common with that made familiar to some English readers by Croce and Collingwood.) In Chapter Nine I have reconstructed, so far as the materials printed in *G.S.* VII allow, the final version of the *Kritik der historischen Vernunft* on which Dilthey was working when he died. Chapter Ten rounds off the book with a critical comparison between Dilthey and Collingwood, and an estimate of Dilthey's significance in the development of recent philosophy.

My acknowledgments are due to those friends by whose encouragement and assistance the completion and publication of this book has been brought about; especially to my sometime colleague Mrs. N. M. Bowring, who helped the work forward in many ways, and shared the labour of compiling the index.

Reading, 1952

CHAPTER ONE

THE philosophical work of Wilhelm Dilthey all hinges upon his attempt to write a *Kritik der historischen Vernunft*. This fact tells us two important things about him, viz. that he was deeply interested in historical studies, and that his philosophical thinking was considerably affected by Kant. Something has been said in the Introduction about each of these facts. Let us begin here by giving further consideration to the second —the fact that Dilthey was in some sense a Kantian. In what sense and in what degree was he so?

The heart and soul of his Kantianism lies in the conception of philosophy as a critique of knowledge. The emergence of the critical movement in the eighteenth century, and its gradual victory over the traditional idea of philosophy as metaphysics, appear to him as the great turning-point in philosophical history. From the critical movement he has learned to see in knowledge not merely an apprehension, but a construction, and to recognise that the terms in which we think and speak of objects are determined in large measure by our own cognitive processes. From the same critical movement he has learned that knowledge cannot go beyond the limits of experience, and that therefore metaphysics, as a science of pure being and a reasoned explanation of the world order, is impossible. These are contentions which he could have learned from other sources than Kant— e.g. from some of the British empiricists or from French positivism. Yet in fact it was Kant whom he saw as the great representative of this standpoint, and it was in Kant's footsteps that he wished to follow. Kant had made his critique, ostensibly of human knowledge, but in fact of mathematical and natural-scientific knowledge only. He had not recognised the distinctive character of the historical and social studies, and Dilthey's task was to extend Kant's critique and make it cover these.

Yet, when we come to the details of Kant's teaching, we find that Dilthey departs from him very widely. Imagine a Kantian who does not believe in an *a priori*, and who thinks that the categories of substance and cause are not forms of the understanding, but projections into the outer world of the inner experiences of the will. Imagine a Kantian who rejects the doctrine of the phenomenality of the empirical self, and believes that in introspection we perceive our own mind as it truly is. Imagine a Kantian who says that philosophy must learn from psychology, and who boasts that his ethic is more empirical than utilitarianism. That is the kind of Kantian whom we meet in Dilthey. In fact, when it comes to points of detail, he is plainly not a Kantian at all. Throughout his life he was engaged in controversy with the more orthodox Kantians. He attacked their logic and their theory of knowledge, their moral theory, and their philosophy of history.

He could do this because Kant was not the only formative influence in his thought. There were in fact two others, which on points of detail count for more than Kant. The first is the set of ideas which were current in Germany in the generation after the publication of Kant's writings—the set of ideas which were held more or less in common by poets such as Goethe and the romanticists, and by post-Kantian philosophers such as Schelling and Hegel. I shall refer to this set of ideas as 'romanticism', and this is one of the determinative influences in Dilthey's thinking. The other is the empirical philosophy of the British school and the positivism of Comte. J. S. Mill's *System of Logic* came out when Dilthey was 10, and Herbert Spencer's *First Principles* when he was 30. Present-day philosophers, to whom Mill is a dim memory and Spencer hardly even a name, may yet bear in mind that in their own time these men were symbols of something, and these symbols fired Dilthey's imagination.

The battle between these two strangely assorted influences in Dilthey's mind will be found to be a recurrent theme as we follow the development of his work. Again and again we shall be faced with the spectacle of a positivist trying to do justice to a poet's vision, or a romantic trying to analyse himself in positivist terms. And neither the romantic nor the positivist is a true Kantian, though the romantic at least has his own interpretation of Kant. It is a truism that Kant was one of the influences by which the post-Kantians were moulded; and there must have

2

been something in him to account for what they made of him. What that was, we may dimly see from the ninth chapter of Coleridge's *Biographia Literaria*, if we will not find out for ourselves by reading Fichte and Hegel. Let us begin at this point, and so move on from Kant to his immediate successors, who were the source of so much of Dilthey's inspiration.

What did Kant's philosophy mean to Kant's younger contemporaries, to those men who were students at the time when his three *Critiques* came out? To them, as to Kant himself, it meant a Copernican revolution in thought. It meant the destruction of a great mass of traditional sophistry, and the opening of a new road into the study of the human mind and will. The *Kritik der reinen Vernunft* showed them the power of the mind, by its transcendental activities of synthesis, to give shape and meaning to sense-data and so to build up a world for itself. The *Kritik der praktischen Vernunft* showed that the shaping and legislative power of the understanding is paralleled by an even more deepseated power of self-regulation in the moral will. Indeed, it was here in the will, not in the intellect, that Kant found the true meaning of 'reason', and gained direct access to the ultimate reality of man and the world. Finally the *Kritik der Urteilskraft* showed that there is in nature, in both organic and inorganic phenomena, a shaping power which seems to be akin to what we already know in ourselves. From this point it was a short step to the post-Kantian philosophies, with their insistence on a hidden power, spiritual in character, which manifests itself alike in natural phenomena and in the mind and life of man.

It is important to realise that Kant, for all his greatness, was only one of many voices which were saying new and exciting things at that time. He even stood somewhat apart from the intellectual movement of the day. In that movement, literary and philosophical ideas were inseparably blended. Poets and critics wrote philosophy, and philosophers wrote verses and borrowed ideas from the poets. Many of them were eager students of natural science, though of course from a point of view of their own. Most of them had views on the meaning of history and on the past, present, and future of religion. It was a ferment of new ideas, in which the central and unifying theme was an interest in the nature of man, his place in the universe, and the meaning of his achievements in thought and action. I shall venture to call

3

the whole period of German thought from 1770 to 1830 the 'romantic' period, and the ruling ideas of the period I shall call 'romanticism', in spite of the fact that the 'romantic' movement commonly so called in German literature is only one of many streams which flowed together at this time. It is convenient to have a single word to cover the whole period, and no other seems so appropriate. The outlook of the period does answer pretty well to what we understand by 'romanticism' in the wider sense: a consciousness of hidden depths in human nature and hidden secrets in the natural world and history, and a determination to explore and enjoy them all.

Dilthey showed from his boyhood a keen interest in music and poetry, and early developed a strong enthusiasm for Lessing and Goethe. The humanism of these writers evoked an answer in his own spirit, and quickly obtained an ascendancy over him which was only strengthened when to his literary and musical studies he added an appreciation of Kant and other leading philosophers of that time. Dilthey's interest in the thought of this great period never waned, and he did not a little, in various writings, to interpret its spirit and significance. Of especial value to us is the inaugural lecture which he delivered on being appointed to a Chair at Basel (1867), which has for its main theme a description of what he found valuable in the romanticists, and reveals the basis upon which he was later to build his own philosophy.

He begins by analysing the circumstances in which the romantic movement arose. It was a time when the growth of enlightenment and culture had awakened in Germany a strong patriotic feeling, while the condition of the Empire made it impossible for this feeling to find an outlet through political channels. Hence the spirit of the German people, newly aroused to a sense of its inherent powers, instead of moving outwards in a political and military nationalism, turned inwards upon itself. The problem of human life is always the same—to bring about a satisfactory adjustment between the self and its environment. The German mind, in face of a world which it was powerless to alter, set out to make the adjustment by altering itself, by adopting a new outlook upon the world, a new ideal of life.

Dilthey finds in Lessing the first formulation of such an ideal. According to him, the good life is the life of reason, a free, self-determining life, conscious of inherent worth by virtue of the

4

control exercised by reason over the passions. Goethe took over this ideal and gave it a less narrowly rational form than it had in Lessing. Goethe saw the unity of life on all levels, from the highest to the lowest. He showed that the 'rational' activities of the mind are not distinct from and antithetic to the 'irrational', but are a more explicit development of something which is present even on the 'irrational' level. Logical thinking would be impossible if it had no basis in the life of the senses and the imagination; and here, in the keen sensibility and imaginative 'genius' of the artist, Goethe finds a shaping power at work, which is the same as the power which operates in logical thinking. Art, then, and the senses, no less than science and the understanding, feelings no less than moral maxims, are essential to the completeness of the good life. Even Lessing had recognised that poetry has a function in life; it gives imaginative expression, he said, to the ideal, and this expression is more practically effective than any 'rational' statement of it.

Goethe went further, and applied his principle to the reconstruction of science. Taught by Spinoza and by Shaftesbury, he thought of nature as a living unity, and it was his ambition to make the detailed workings of nature intelligible by intuitive insight into the life of the whole. To this end the same imaginative power which is exercised creatively in art must be applied heuristically in the field of scientific knowledge, and the result is a philosophy of nature which is one of Goethe's most striking achievements. The universe is treated as a living being, whose life develops stage by stage, through inorganic nature, through plant life and animal forms, up to man and his activities, where it attains its end by becoming an object of consciousness to itself. Dilthey emphasises the philosophical originality of this theory. The universe had been treated as a living organism before, by the Stoics, by Bruno, by Spinoza; but no one had taken this thought so seriously as to credit this organism with a life-history, and to seek this life-history in the geological past. That was Goethe's contribution, and it amounted to the creation of a new metaphysical genre, to which Dilthey gives the name of 'evolutionary pantheism' (*entwicklungsgeschichtlicher Pantheismus*). Dilthey also points out how strikingly this half-poetic theorising of Goethe anticipates the growth of evolutionary theories and the expansion of comparative methods in nineteenth-century science.

5

It was with ideas such as these in his mind that Dilthey began his student career. It is therefore not surprising that he soon felt the attraction of historical studies, and devoted himself to them with an ardour which may partly be explained by the circumstances of the time and place. Looking back in later years (*Rede zum 70 Geburtstag, G.S.*, V, 7 ff.), he spoke of the 'inestimable good fortune' which took him to Berlin at a time when he could watch a new historical science being constructed before his eyes. As the seventeenth century had seen a great forward movement in mathematics and natural science, so in the nineteenth a revolution took place in the conceptions and methods of historical study, and this new movement, comparable in its effects with the scientific work of the late Renaissance, was nowhere more active than at Berlin.

Dilthey distinguishes two wings of the movement. (1) One was based on an analysis of culture into its component factors, i.e. language, law, mythology and religion, poetry, philosophy and the like. By comparative research and genetic analysis it was shown how each of these elements of cultural life is governed by an inner law which determines its general structure and the course of its development. Bopp, the Humboldts, Savigny, W. Grimm, and others were the founders of this school. (2) The other wing of the movement studied the life of nations, treating each nation as a cultural unity; it traced their interactions as organised forces, and tried to find laws which determine their rise and fall. Dilthey speaks with praise of the work done in this way for Roman history by Niebuhr, for Greek antiquity by Böckh, for ancient Germanic studies by J. Grimm, and above them all he places Mommsen. What these scholars did for individual nations was gathered up into a whole by Ritter and Ranke, and world history was presented as a self-contained process, coextensive with the inhabited earth and with recorded time. Dilthey confesses an especial debt to the teaching of Ranke (*G.S.*, V, 4, 9).

The significance of the historical movement lay in this, that it extended the dominion of organised knowledge over a region not less rich in content than the physical universe, but of a very different character. After the scientific movement of the seventeenth century had made current a mechanical view of the universe, and the dogma that all scientific knowledge must be

6

mathematical, the historical movement redressed the balance by calling in a new world of experience. This new world was not a mechanical system, but one in which the apprehension of meaning and value by human agents is a determinant force, and in it the enquiring mind finds not an alien object, but its own kin. The attempt to study this new world systematically raised, accordingly, a number of philosophical questions, of which the members of the historical school themselves were not aware, but Dilthey was. What is the nature of those groups of recurrent phenomena which can be abstracted from the historical process as a whole and studied by themselves, such as law, religion, or poetry? What is it that constitutes each of them a unit? By what fundamental concepts must the interpretation of them proceed? And how are they related to those temporally circumscribed but more complex wholes, such as a nation or a cultural period, which are also in some sense units? Is their unity in some way analogous to that of a physical organism or of an individual mind? How far can such an analogy take us, and how must we proceed at the point where it breaks down? Such questions as these, questions at first sight concerning method, but involving deeper epistemological and perhaps even metaphysical issues, arise naturally out of historical study for a mind which is philosophically awake. They arose in Dilthey's mind.

For a solution he looked first to the romantics. After all, it was Lessing who had made current the conception of historical progress as 'the education of the human race'. It was Herder who had laid down that every nation is a cultural unit with a character of its own and an inherent value which is unique. His *Ideen zur Philosophie der Geschichte der Menschheit* met with a welcome from Goethe. And Goethe himself recognised that the highest rung in his ladder of sciences must be the sciences of man, viz. history and anthropology. He saw that the study of man's activities must be based on an understanding of man's nature, and therefore set himself to disengage from the various phenomena of human life and character the structural type to which they all conform. As every animal species is known by the structure which all its individuals have in common, so a similar unity of type or structure betrays itself in the lives and actions of men. In such works as *Faust* and *Wilhelm Meister*, Goethe tried to portray the principles which govern the development of human character. All his writings are instinct with a certain wisdom derived from his insight into the nature of man.

A similar approach to the problem found expression in the writings of Novalis (Friedrich von Hardenberg, 1772–1801), by whom Dilthey was attracted and to whom he devoted a special study (*Novalis*, first published 1865: now printed in *Das Erlebnis u. die Dichtung*, pp. 268 ff.). Novalis had the same encyclopaedic interests as Goethe and Schelling. Like them, he saw in the phenomena of nature the expression of a living power which is akin to the human spirit. In history he saw the expression of the human spirit itself, whose hidden depths he sought to penetrate. He began by seeking in vain to obtain access to the mystery through empirical psychology. He found no help in psychology as his contemporaries practised it. He speaks of it as 'one of the spectres which have taken those places in the temple where genuine images of gods ought to stand'. It is stupid, mechanical, analytical, abstract. In its place Novalis wishes to put a study which is to 'consider man purely as a whole, as a system'. He calls it *reale Psychologie* or *Anthropologie*, and his own contributions to it are fully in the spirit of his age. At the root of human nature he finds the will. 'Every man, at bottom, lives in his will.' And he analysed the life of feeling and will with a penetrating vision. Dilthey ranks him with Spinoza, the philosopher of the *conatus*, and with Kant, Fichte, Schopenhauer, all of whom in various ways held the same view that the fundamental secret of life lies not in thought, but in will. But he sees in the fragments, which were all that Novalis was able to write before his early death, a greater modesty in speculation and a greater respect for positive knowledge than in some of the others. Novalis meant his *Anthropologie* to be the basis of all the studies concerned with human life: history, moral theory, aesthetics, the philosophy of religion. Eight years before Hegel's *Phänomeno-logie*, and twenty years before the *Enzyklopädie*, Novalis had in germ the idea of a grouping of all the human studies on a single basis, which is to be a deep study of human nature.

The reader should keep in mind this *reale Psychologie* or *Anthropologie* of Novalis. We shall find it over and over again, under various names, in Dilthey's writings.

We have mentioned Hegel, and in view of the range of Hegel's interests and the magnitude of his achievement it is natural to

8

ask whether Dilthey could not find in him the guide to follow in his own researches. The question arises very naturally in Britain, since in this country a philosophical interest in history, or in historical methods and principles, has long been associated with adherence to Hegelian doctrine. Some of us have read Croce on the subject, and he and his disciple, Collingwood, make no secret of their Hegelian affinities. It is therefore necessary to say quite distinctly that Dilthey was never a Hegelian in any sense whatever. Certainly he avoided holding Hegel in that uninformed contempt which was the usual attitude eighty years ago, and in his inaugural lecture at Basel, in the very act of proclaiming himself an adherent of Kantianism, he could plead for a better recognition of Hegel's lasting achievement. But his understanding of Hegel was imperfect. He saw him as one who gave a systematic form to Goethe's evolutionary pantheism (in which Dilthey himself did not believe); but he showed no sign of appreciating his work in connection specifically with history, and he distrusted him profoundly as a dogmatic metaphysician.

It was not in Hegel that he found his philosophical guide, but in another thinker of the post-Kantian generation. It was in F. D. E. Schleiermacher (1768–1834), the theologian-philosopher, Hegel's colleague at Berlin, that the various tendencies of Dilthey's thought were able to find a focus of unity. Schleiermacher represented the religious spirit in the closest alliance with philosophy and with literary and historical studies. He was in the full stream of the romantic and post-Kantian movement, in close touch with Fichte and the Schlegels; but it was an added attraction in Dilthey's eyes that, of all the philosophical writers of that time, Schleiermacher stands furthest from metaphysical speculation, and nearest to the critical position of Kant.

Schleiermacher's philosophy is a large system, and I shall describe only those of its contentions which bear upon Dilthey's problem and have influenced his treatment of it. These are to be found in Schleiermacher's moral theory, his philosophy of religion, and his theory of understanding and interpretation.

The governing principle of Schleiermacher's ethic is the high value which he sets upon individuality. He complains that previous writers on moral theory have neglected this aspect of things, and have been content to treat morality as a universal law or principle—as if a man were moral only in what he shares

9

with other men, and not in what is unique and distinctive in him. Schleiermacher himself sees life as a polarity of the universal and the individual, and finds a principle of value in each of these aspects. A common nature and a common environment create common needs and interests among men, and these find expression in the universal principles of law; but physical and psychological differences mould each human being into a unique individual, with his own peculiar interests and his own peculiar way of seeing the world and conducting himself in it. Schleiermacher formulates the moral law as a demand for individuality within the universal. 'Enter into community in such a way as to keep your individuality intact; cultivate individuality in such a way that in so doing you also enter into community.'

Schleiermacher also complains that moralists have neglected the values of the cultural life. Morality is a discipline of the whole personality: not only of the passions and desires, but also of the mind. The good life consists not only in our overt actions towards one another, but also in the activities of the imagination and the intellect, in science which studies the universal laws of nature, and art which presents to us individual forms. And neither the theoretical nor the practical side of the good life can develop as it should unless the whole is pervaded and sustained by the spirit of religion, by which Schleiermacher means the consciousness of the unity of all being.

This consciousness is not in Schleiermacher, as it is in Hegel, a reasoned conviction supported by a dialectical process. In Schleiermacher's *Dialektik* we are shown that human thinking moves perpetually between two poles, viz. the thing in itself, as a reality wholly independent of our thought, and God, as absolute Being, the source of all existence and all knowledge; and we can never attain to reasoned knowledge of either pole. But we have an immediate intuitive awareness (a 'feeling', Schleiermacher calls it) of God as the Whole which is immanent in all its parts; we are aware of the immanence of God in our own thinking and willing, as the common ground of our own spiritual life and the external world in which we have to think and will. This 'feeling' of the presence of God is our bond with one another and with the external world, and in it the deepest secret of our being is disclosed. For it shows how every man is a vehicle, unique and irreplaceable, of the self-manifestation of God. Im-

10

plicit in each individual is 'the divine Idea', the expression of the Whole through this particular part, and the moral and cultural development of the individual is at bottom neither more nor less than the explication of this Idea. It is in the consciousness of this that we find happiness and a sense of personal worth and significance. It is thus that religion is the heart and centre of the good life.

Religion, so conceived, is of course inseparable from morality and culture, and the relation between them is twofold. On the one hand, religion is the inner life and spirit of all human activities. On the other hand, religious feeling would perish if there were not one system of activities specially dedicated to the purpose of cultivating and expressing it; and this special system of activities is what we call 'religion' in the narrower sense. It is not really a distinct form of spiritual activity, it is the adaptation of all forms of such activity for the purpose of evoking and sustaining the religious feeling, on which they all ultimately depend. Thus the creative imagination gives it expression in myths and cult-observances, and the intellect reduces these to a system of conceptions, a theology; the practical activity lays down universal laws and precepts, and also builds up the spiritual life of each individual according to his personal *attrait*. Religion cannot live, says Schleiermacher, without finding expression in traditions and institutions of this kind, though at the same time all such traditions and institutions are historical products, relative to the age and country which produced them. There is no universal religion, no absolute theology, no one true Church. The same principle of relativity applies also, of course, to moral standards, to systems of philosophy, and to all cultural values.

It was from this point that Schleiermacher was led to one of his most characteristic achievements. Interest in the historical development of religious ideas led him to a critical study of St. Paul's Epistles, in which he broke new ground. He saw that in these writings we have to do not with a systematic theology systematically stated, but with a lively mind reacting to particular situations, and the proper way to interpret the Epistles is to set them in their context in the life of their author. Bringing out an edition of the Dialogues of Plato, Schleiermacher found that something very similar has to be said about them. They too are not a considered exposition of a completely coherent philosophy

11

but essays on particular subjects written at different stages in the development of Plato's mind. Meditating on these discoveries, Schleiermacher was led on to raise more general questions about the understanding and interpretation of written texts, about the way in which the interpreter must proceed in order to get behind the printed word to the idea which it expresses, and the mind and personality from which that idea came. He was led on to explore the principles of the art of interpretation, and his conclusions are set forth in his masterly *hermeneutic* theory.

He finds that the understanding of a literary whole has two aspects, both necessary and co-ordinate in status, but different in aims and method, viz. *grammatical* and *psychological* understanding. The aim of grammatical understanding is to remove ambiguities in, and to wring the last drop of meaning from, the words and phrases which constitute the outward appearance of the work. The aim of psychological understanding is to go behind this outward appearance to the 'inner form', the living principle or idea in the author's mind, of which the written text is the expression.

Both processes involve a twofold approach. On the one hand there is the comparative method, which interprets the work in terms of the language, the stylistic principles, and the ideas which prevailed generally in the period and in the circle from which the work proceeded; thus the work and its author are seen in their context and understood in terms of that. On the other hand there is what Schleiermacher calls the 'divinatory' approach, which penetrates intuitively through the written work into the mind of its author; this has not the cogency of a reasoned analysis, and yet it goes deeper than such analysis can. Both ways are necessary and complementary to one another in each department of interpretation, though the comparative method is predominant in grammatical understanding, and the divinatory method in psychological understanding. Even with the two together we can only get approximate results; and the success of the interpreter depends as much upon a personal gift as upon an acquired skill.

Such, in bare outline, is Schleiermacher's hermeneutic theory. It was the result of personal experience in the study of Plato and the New Testament. It was a methodology of interpretation, written by one who was himself a skilled interpreter. But it was more than a methodology; it was a philosophical analysis of the conditions which make understanding possible, and this was the aspect of it which especially interested Dilthey. It was here, too, that Dilthey found a flaw in Schleiermacher's theory.

The assumption behind all Schleiermacher's methodology is that interpretation is complementary to creation, that to understand a work is to retrace the process by which it came to be. We understand because we reconstruct (*nachbilden, nachkonstruiren*), and the comparative method and the divination are merely the tools with which we make this reconstruction. But what then is the original creative process, and how does it arise? From the interplay of a man's environment with his native temper and outlook. Environment, however, which acts alike on all who live in it, accounts only for the common features of their productions, but not for the individuality of each. To find the roots of that, we must go behind the outer form of the work, and behind the 'inner form' or idea of it in its developed form, to the primary synthetic act, or 'germinal determination' (*Keimentschluss*) in the author's mind, in which the character of the developed work was implicitly contained. And, as the details of each individual work are derived from its own inner form, so too the successive works produced by one artist proceed from and express the inner form of his character and outlook, which in turn is only the explicit development of the germinal synthesis made at his birth.

Schleiermacher's hermeneutic attracted Dilthey from his early years, and its influence over him grew continually as time went by. Yet as early as 1860, in a prize essay, *Die Hermeneutik Schleiermachers*, he had put his finger on its weak point, which was the doctrine of the germinal synthesis. If every stage in the development of an individual is predetermined, and all he can do is to show more fully what he really was from the beginning, then all change is merely formal, and time brings no real novelty. The philosopher will therefore be able to forget about the details of the process, and find the clue to the understanding of a man not in his social and historical situation, but in some timeless principle which he embodies. Schleiermacher actually did so. He believed that the personalities of individual men flow from the Absolute by a timeless dialectic, and in his historical studies he leaned more on his notion of the Idea embodied in a

13

person than on the historical evidence as to what that person was and did.

Dilthey reacts strongly against this procedure and the doctrine behind it. In a developed work of art, or an individual human life, we find an intelligible unity; but how, he asks, do we know that this unity, in all its wealth of content, has been produced by linear development from a single germ? Factors affecting its character may come as well from without as from within, and the final unity of form may crystallise at a late stage. (Quoted by Misch in *G.S.*, V, lxxxii.) Only if this in fact happens can we say that something new occurs with the passage of time, and history is something more than the mere shadow of a timeless dialectic. And this cuts deeply into the moral and religious theories of Schleiermacher; for, on this showing, the meaning and value of the individual cannot lie in the explication of a 'divine Idea', nor can his duty lie in fidelity to such an Idea, since his nature is determined by forces which are in part unknown to him, and he has a historical significance which he himself does not understand. 'Man does not merely *possess* the ideas which operate in him to shape his work, he *is possessed* by them' (quoted by Misch in *G.S.*, V, xv). His importance lies rather in the manner in which 'quite disconnected elements of culture, in the workshop of a significant individual mind, are shaped into a whole, which in turn has an effect upon life' (*G.S.*, V, 11). Lines of influence from the past meet in him, intersect, and are directed afresh into the future. The individual so conceived is still for Dilthey, as for Schleiermacher, 'the greatest reality' in history, and therefore the greatest reality we can know; for it is in human life alone that we know reality from within, and it is in the life-history of the individual man that we can see in detail the workings of the life-process (*ibid.*).

No one among Dilthey's contemporaries in Germany had an influence upon him that was comparable with Schleiermacher's. The outstanding figure among them was Lotze, whose *Mikro-kosmus* (1856–64) was confessedly intended to take up the thread of Herder's *Ideen*, was dedicated to the memory of Ritter, and anticipates a good deal of Dilthey's own work. Like Dilthey, Lotze singles out the human mind as the one object of which we have knowledge by acquaintance as well as by description. He sets the free, self-determining life of the mind in contrast with

14

the mechanical processes of nature. He seeks the meaning (*Bedeutung*) or sense (*Sinn*) of history, and finds it in the gradual realisation of timeless values in time through the actions of men; and he works out, as Dilthey was later to do, the part played in the process by physical conditions, racial and other differences, the forces of individual and social will which make for progress, and the cultural forms in which progress is achieved. Yet all this in Lotze was subordinated to a logic and a metaphysic for which Dilthey felt a strong distaste, mingled with contempt.

Lotze's logic is in the Kantian tradition, and we shall see in the following chapter how Dilthey attacks Kantianism in logic. Lotze's metaphysic was an affair of postulates, apologetic and unconvincing; yet, such as it was, it included a doctrine of the phenomenality of time, which served only to undo what its author had done for the human studies. It reduced to an illusion that very experience upon which all historical knowledge rests, and in which alone, as even Lotze had said, we have direct acquaintance with reality.

This was Dilthey's main preoccupation at the time (in 1865) when he gave his first course of lectures (entitled *Einleitung in die Philosophie*) as Privat-Dozent at Berlin. 'It was with the criticism of this doctrine that I began. So arose the principle: behind life, thought cannot go. To regard life as illusion is a contradiction in terms; for it is in the life-process, in the growth out of the past and the reaching-out into the future, that those realities lie which compose the dynamic system and the value of our life. If, behind the life which flows from the past through the present to the future, there were a timeless reality, then this would be an antecedent of life; for it would be, on this showing, something by which the whole ordered process of life was preconditioned; and then this antecedent would be precisely that which we did not directly experience (*was wir nicht erlebten*), and therefore only a realm of shadows' (*G.S.*, V, 5).

Neither Schleiermacher nor Lotze did what Dilthey considered to be justice to time, and therefore to history. Nor was it possible to do so without setting timeless realities and absolute values aside, and considering history in relation to nature and the natural sciences. Dilthey singles out Novalis among the German romantics as the one who was most willing to give natural

15

science its proper weight; but Novalis died young and left behind him only hints and fragments. It was not in Germany that Dilthey found the help he sought. He found it in French positivism and in the British empirical philosophy. Here he found philosophers who were determined to understand the discoveries of natural science, to elicit its methods and principles, and to consider the question of historical knowledge and social studies in the light of all this.

British philosophy in the seventeenth and eighteenth centuries proclaimed three revolutionary changes. (1) The first was announced by Bacon when he hailed the new experimental method in natural science. (2) The second was initiated by Locke when he doubted the capacity of the human mind for metaphysical speculation, and accepted for philosophy the humbler position of an under-labourer clearing the way for the advance of natural science. In his work the shift of emphasis from metaphysics to epistemology is already carried out, and the grander edifice of Kant's critique of reason is only the execution of a plan conceived in its essentials by Locke. (3) The third revolution was proclaimed by Hume in the Preface to his *Treatise of Human Nature*, when he called for a renovation of the human studies by the introduction into them of the empirical methods already approved in natural science. In spite of the general refusal to follow Hume in the more sceptical parts of his philosophy, it remains true that the British empirical school from his time to that of J. S. Mill was in essence doing little more than carry out the programme put forward in his Preface.

Neither Locke's programme nor Hume's could be carried out without giving a prominent place to the study of the human mind; and in fact the British school is well known for its psychological approach to philosophical questions. This is evident not only in the theory of knowledge, but in moral and political theory and in aesthetics. Hume in his Preface not only recognised the central importance of psychological knowledge, but drew striking conclusions from it. He said outright that all other knowledge, if properly considered, will be found to depend on psychological knowledge. 'All the sciences have a relation, greater or less, to human nature.' Mathematics, natural philosophy, and natural religion deal with objects other than ourselves, but our knowledge of these objects is conditioned by the

16

nature of our minds, while in logic, ethics, criticism (i.e. aesthetics), and political theory we are directly studying our own activities, theoretical and practical. Thus all questions of importance refer us to psychology in the end, and conversely the construction of a new psychology amounts to a renovation of the whole edifice of knowledge. Hume's *Treatise* is meant to be such a renovation. Over a century later, in Dilthey's own lifetime, the same principle found expression in the philosophy of J. S. Mill, who, in offering the world a logic and methodology of knowledge, together with an economic, moral, and political theory, based the whole structure on principles drawn from psychology.

To say that psychology is the foundation of all knowledge, but especially of the human studies, sounds reminiscent of Novalis' 'anthropology'. The German romantics and the British empiricists might seem to meet here. In fact, however, if they do meet, it is largely as opponents. The psychology of the British school is precisely that psychology which Novalis denounces as a profane intruder into the temple of learning. Why? Because it is not based on honest observation and self-searching, but on a slavish imitation of physics. This is true in a measure of Hume himself. Hume certainly knew more about the real workings of the mind than some of his successors. He knew in his wiser moments that mental life is not to be explained exclusively in terms of impressions, ideas, and laws of association. But in his less wise moments he wrote as if it could be explained just in those terms, and in his Preface he argued that psychology must be renovated by adopting the methods and principles which have proved so successful in physics—which means analysis into distinct units whose interrelations are governed by a few simple laws. It was the wrong model of explanation, and it could only appear to succeed so long as attention was focused mainly on questions of perception and memory. It could not deal with the deeper levels of the instinctive life, nor yet with the higher intellectual and spiritual activities. That is what Novalis meant by calling it an empty and formal science, and not a *reale Psychologie*.

There is no doubt that, in depth of insight and range of understanding, the German romantics and the post-Kantian philosophers are far in advance of the British empiricists. Nevertheless the British school stood for something which Dilthey would not surrender. It stood for an attempt to integrate psychology with the other empirical sciences, in recognition of the fact that the human mind lives and works in the physical world, whereas the Germans were too apt to run off into metaphysical speculations and to seek in the soul of man the key to the understanding of all that is. Moreover, in Bentham and the other utilitarians the empirical philosophy and psychology were blended with a deep concern for social reform. The understanding of the human mind became, in their hands, a pointer to improvements in the penal code, in education, in political institutions. Fifty years before Marx, the utilitarians understood the unity of theory and practice, and believed that knowledge ought to be a force in social life. Natural-scientific knowledge is such a force inescapably; but surely too a philosophy or a psychology which has not social consequences must be lacking in something essential. So the utilitarians believed, and Dilthey believed it too.

The same combination of a profound respect for science with a strong concern for social welfare was manifest in France in the work of Auguste Comte, the founder of the positive philosophy. He was an original thinker, whose philosophy in its original form has exercised a great influence in France and other European countries. It influenced Dilthey. But Comte had also a considerable influence on J. S. Mill and Herbert Spencer, and through these again, indirectly, upon Dilthey. We must consider what his philosophy was.

Comte claimed to have discovered that the human mind, in developing to maturity, has had to adopt in succession three distinct attitudes to its objects; the third and highest of these is consummated in Comte's own philosophy. The first or *theological* attitude springs from a desire to know the ultimate causes and the inner nature of things, and it leads us to explain things and processes in terms of personal or quasi-personal agents, i.e. gods and spirits. The second or *metaphysical* attitude consists in asking the same question, but answering it in terms of impersonal 'forces' or hypostatised abstractions. The third or *positive* attitude consists in recognising that we cannot know the real nature and the real causes of things at all, that all we can do is to formulate laws which govern the succession of phenomena in our experience; to do this is the task of science. Comte undertook, in the *Cours de philosophie positive* (1830–42), to complete the reduction of all the existing sciences to the positive form, and to apply positive methods to the one realm of phenomena, viz. the phenomena of history and society, which had not yet been treated by anyone from this point of view. He thought that the existing psychology, moral and political theory, and historiography were wholly compounded of theological and metaphysical survivals, and that it was reserved for himself to erect upon their ruins the new positive science of *sociology*, viz. the study of the laws which govern the actions of human beings as members of social groups.

Sociology was to be the latest-born of the sciences, but it was not to be merely one more science added to the rest. Its subject-matter gave it a privileged position. In studying the activities of human societies, in making the community rather than the individual the object of its study, it draws attention to the mutual dependence of all men, and so becomes a force in support of human solidarity and social co-operation. Moreover, in studying the social conditions under which human knowledge develops it lets us see the proper place and function of science in the life of society, and makes possible a deliberate co-ordination of all scientific activities for a social end.

The influence of the positive philosophy has been very great. In France, the land of its origin, it has given rise to a distinguished tradition in sociology and anthropology, such as is represented by Durkheim and Lévy-Bruhl; and it has inspired a whole series of studies in scientific methodology and the history of science. More important for our present purpose is the immediate influence which Comte enjoyed in Great Britain. His work appealed to that section of British thought which hoped for social progress through the steady pressure of an enlightened public opinion. J. S. Mill, the most outstanding representative of this body of opinion, was a sincere admirer of Comte's teaching, accepting both his fundamental conception of positive method and also his demand for a science of sociology.

This is evident in the famous sixth book of Mill's *System of Logic*, entitled *On the Logic of the Moral Sciences*, where it is shown how, first of all, scientific methods may be applied in psychology; how then, on that basis, may arise a science of the laws governing the formation of character and the genesis of national and racial types, which Mill calls 'ethology'; and how, again, on this we may base a sociology which will deal with 'the actions of collective masses of mankind'. Special branches of knowledge with a limited field may be constituted by singling out a particular type of phenomena for study; thus e.g. political economy becomes possible when we determine to ignore for the time being all motives in human action except the pursuit of wealth. But sociology will embrace all such sectional studies, and correct their one-sidedness, by exhibiting each of them as one aspect of a comprehensive enquiry whose object is social life in all its aspects. Finally, on all this knowledge of facts and laws, we can base a system of practical precepts, an art of human conduct, whose principal divisions will be moral and political theory. This 'logic of the moral sciences', with the rest of Mill's logical work, was widely known on the Continent. The writings of Herbert Spencer, especially his *Principles of Sociology* (1876–96), bear witness to its effects in England.

Dilthey shared the preoccupation of the positivists and the empiricists with social problems, even though his own sphere of work was not political. He says in the *Einleitung in die Geisteswissenschaften* that it is 'a vital question for our civilisation' to obtain a correct diagnosis of the growing social instability. Natural science, which can do nothing here, is for that very reason becoming less important in comparison with the social sciences, and the 'reversal of scientific interests' brought about in ancient Greece by the Sophists and Socrates is repeating itself today in a society shaken, like theirs, by violent winds of change (*G.S.*, I, 4). This shift of emphasis in the sciences must find a reflection in philosophy. For 'philosophy stands in a regular relation to the sciences, to art and to society. From this relation its problems arise' (*G.S.*, V, 27). Like every activity of the human mind, it is a historical product and reflects the circumstances of its origin; incapable, like religion and morality, of a finally valid formulation, it readjusts itself with every change in the public outlook, and this is true not merely of the conclusions it advances, but even of the problems it canvasses.

It follows that Dilthey must re-examine his relation to the philosophers of the post-Kantian generation, and in his inaugural lecture at Basel he states the conclusion to which he is driven. He sets out to vindicate the post-Kantians against the neglect into which they had fallen, to show 'what it was in them which so powerfully moved the nation, and rightly moved it'. He finds the answer in their attempt to formulate, in response to the needs of their generation, a distinctively German outlook and ideal of life. It is this which was first adumbrated by Lessing, developed by Goethe and Schiller, and metaphysically grounded by Fichte and Schleiermacher, Schelling and Hegel. But however well their philosophy met the demands of their own time, it is not wholly appropriate to a generation whose problem is very different from theirs. Our concern today (1867) is not to construct an ideal, but to gain control of social processes. For even the romantic ideal itself can only be translated into fact by exercising such control. 'If the end of man is to act, philosophy will be able to guarantee truly fruitful preconditions for active life in its various great spheres, in society, moral action, education and law, only in so far as it discloses the inner nature of man; in so far as it teaches us . . . to be active in the moral world in accordance with clear knowledge of its great order of laws' (*G.S.*, V, 27).

Here Dilthey embraces the ideal of Hume and Mill. Philosophy is to be an empirical study of the mind, an analysis of social forces and laws, a theory of education, morality, and jurisprudence; in short, it embraces nearly the whole compass of the human studies; and it is all to rest upon a scientific psychology. Dilthey has an especial concern to see these methods applied to the reform of educational theory and practice, and his efforts in this direction are reflected in his published works as well as in his correspondence with the Graf Paul Yorck von Wartenburg. In every department of historical and social knowledge, psychological influence is to be paramount. Psychology is to be the basis of all work in the human studies, as mathematics is the basis of all work in natural science;[1] that is, as all explanatory concepts in physical science approximate to a mathematical form, so all formulae of interpretation in the human studies must be drawn from or assimilated to those of psychology. It is the programme of Hume and Mill which Dilthey embraces; but he differs from

[1] A bad analogy; for mathematics is not a natural science, whereas psychology is one of the human studies. The position ascribed by Dilthey to psychology is really analogous to that held in his time by mechanics. The comparison with mechanics is made by Dilthey himself in *G.S.*, VII, 116–17.

them in recognising and facing, to the best of his power, certain obvious difficulties.

The difficulties relate to the function assigned to psychology.

In the first place, if mathematics serves as the basis for natural science, that is because mathematical reasoning leads to conclusions which are certain and beyond the reach of doubt. If psychology is to serve as the basis for the human studies, it too must be able to advance incontrovertible conclusions. Hume supposed that this need would be met by the adoption of a method modelled on the methods of physics, and the British association-psychology was the result. But it was already clear by Dilthey's time that neither this nor any form of experimental psychology then existing could claim the required certitude for its results. Dilthey himself in an early essay quotes the hedonistic principle as a doctrine which Bentham regarded as evident and unchallengeable, and then proceeds to challenge it and repudiate it himself (*G.S.*, V, 43). By 1880 he had come to see that no experimental laws could ever have the authority which the position that he assigns to psychology demands that it should have, and that, if psychology is to do what is required of it, it must become independent of the method of hypothesis and verification. The question whether this can be done, and if so, how, runs through Dilthey's thinking in every period of his life. In Chapter Seven we shall trace the development of his views on the point.

In the second place, Dilthey finds the experimental psychology of his time too narrow, and calls for a widening of its field. (1) He echoes the views and almost the very words of Novalis when he complains that psychology confines itself to a purely formal study of mental processes, whereas there are certain basic elements of content which also form part of human nature and should be recognised. 'Psychological laws are pure laws of form; they have to do not with the content of the human mind, but with its formal behaviour and disposition. We may take the human mind to be a poem, of which they are in a manner the language, syntax, and metre. . . . Human nature, in addition to the laws which govern the modes of the mind's activity and its formal behaviour, includes also fundamental elements of its content' (*G.S.*, VI, 43–4). Dilthey instances the categories as 'fundamental metaphysical presuppositions' discovered by Kant.

(2) But these belong only to the cognitive sphere of experience.

We must go on to recognise fundamental elements of content in other spheres also. 'The meaning of the problem is not seen in its whole range until we recognise that the phenomena of will and the feelings are not reducible to relations between ideas (*Vorstellungen*). When Spinoza begins with self-preservation, when Kant recognises in the moral law a distinctive root of our moral and religious outlook, not explicable in terms of ideas (*aus dem Vorstellungsleben*), we are enabled to give a far more wide-ranging explanation of the content of our soul. Going further in this direction, we come in sight of Schleiermacher, Hegel, Schopenhauer. These are mere beginnings' (*Das Erlebnis u. die Dichtung*, p. 308). In these words Dilthey points forward towards the psychology of instincts and the depth-psychology of the present day, whose full development he did not live to see. He himself speaks of an *Inhaltspsychologie*, or *Realpsychologie*, or *Anthropologie*—the last two of these being terms used by Novalis.

(3) Finally, he complains that psychology, even in the hands of Mill and others who wish to apply it to social studies, takes the individual as a unit prior to, and in essence unaffected by, his union with others in society. In terms of such units it is impossible to give a true account of the social relationships which actually prevail. The fact is that human beings are in their very nature social. It lies in their nature to transcend themselves, to embrace and fulfil tasks for the benefit of others as well as of themselves. They can understand and co-operate with one another. Psychology must bring this aspect of human nature to the fore, and treat man as the social being that he is. Here again Dilthey points forward to the development of social psychology in more recent times.

We have now seen how the two sides of Dilthey's inheritance, the romantic and the empirical or positivist, amplify and correct one another. The romantic tradition gives him a lively sense of the depth and movement of the mind's life, but does not correlate it satisfactorily with the scientific view of nature, or apply it energetically enough for the betterment of society. The empirical and positivist tradition has a sense of social function, and a proper respect for scientific knowledge, but its view of the mind's life is crude and superficial. Each requires the other, and one main strand in Dilthey's thinking will be his unceasing effort to combine what is good and true in both.

We must, however, also ask how these two contending influences relate to the Kantianism whose adherent Dilthey professes to be. The relation is twofold: for the Kantian standpoint enables Dilthey to criticise both sides of his inheritance, while on the other hand each of them is a basis from which Kantianism itself can be criticised.

(1) From the point of view of the Kantian critique, the post-Kantian philosophers and their literary friends on the romantic side were all undisciplined thinkers, who allowed speculative enthusiasm to run far ahead of sober thought. Their idealism, their pantheism, their speculative philosophy of history all come under the critique. Dilthey is altogether Kantian on this point. Though he understands and sympathises with the speculative ideas of the romantics, he does not agree with them. It is noteworthy that the member of the post-Kantian galaxy whom he chooses for his philosophical inspiration is Schleiermacher, the only one who resisted the speculative enthusiasm and retained a truly critical theory of knowledge.

(2) From the Kantian point of view, again, the empiricists are only half-hearted in their critical attempts. Their associationist theory of mental life is crude and superficial; the Kantian account of the unity of apperception and the transcendental syntheses puts it wholly in the shade. The Kantian moral theory, too, opens up depths which empiricism never sees.

(3) From the romantic point of view, Kant has stultified himself by his doctrine of inner sense and the phenomenality of the empirical self. Having opened up the depths in his moral theory, he should have explored them as his successors did. Instead, he wrote off the greater part of our inner experience as merely phenomenal, and reduced time itself to the status of a phenomenon. Therefore he made it impossible for himself to see the problem of historical knowledge, or to write a *Kritik der historischen Vernunft*.

(4) From the empirical and positivist point of view, Kant is a dogmatist in disguise, who spoiled his analysis of the cognitive process and the moral will by his doctrine of *a priori* principles. He took the categories as principles flowing ready-made from the legislative understanding, whereas he should have analysed them and reduced them to their basis in experience. He believed that what makes known objects 'objective' is their conformity

24

with a coherent set of intellectual principles, whereas the true test of reality is lived experience and especially the experiences of the will.

In the next chapter we shall proceed to examine Dilthey's theory of knowledge; and the double critique of Kantianism will be seen at work in detail.

CHAPTER TWO

At the time when Dilthey began to write, German philosophy was in full retreat from the post-Kantian idealism. Hegel had died two years before Dilthey was born; Schelling lived on until 1854 and Schopenhauer until 1860, but after Hegel's death the tide began to flow in another direction. Philosophers began to turn away from speculative metaphysics and system-building, and to look towards mathematics and the physical sciences, in which great advances were being made at that very time. By reflection upon the methods of these disciplines it was hoped that a more modest philosophy might be found which, if less spectacular than that of Hegel, might have the more solid merit of being true. Some borrowed the empirical philosophy of Mill or the positivism of Comte. Others went back behind Hegel to Kant, and began a careful re-examination of his analysis of the cognitive processes. In the 1860s there was a veritable *Kantbewegung*, in which both philosophically minded scientists and critical-minded philosophers were involved.

In the following decade there took shape the influential 'Neo-Kantian' school of Marburg, founded by Hermann Cohen (*Kants Theorie der Erfahrung*, 1871: *Kants Begründung der Ethik*, 1877: *Kants Begründung der Ästhetik*, 1899) and continued by Paul Natorp (*Einleitung in die Psychologie nach kritischer Methode*, 1888: *Die logischen Grundlagen der exakten Wissenschaften*, 1910), and Ernst Cassirer (*Substanzbegriff u. Funktionsbegriff*, 1910: *Philosophie der symbolischen Formen*, 1923, 1924, 1929). The Marburg school was not content to study Kant's writings with care. It made a point of keeping up with contemporary developments in mathematics and mathematical physics, so as to be able to go over Kant's ground afresh with up-to-date information, and to re-do for the mathematics and physical science of the nineteenth century what Kant had done for those of the eighteenth. Thus Natorp, for instance, is not content merely to discuss Kant's

26

doctrine of space and infinity. He discusses space and infinity themselves, in the same spirit as Kant did, but with a knowledge of the work of Dedekind and Cantor, Frege and Russell, to point the way for him. In spite of keeping thus up to date, the Marburg school found that the fundamental principles of Kantianism were still the only satisfactory basis for philosophy, provided that the thing in itself was decently buried and Kant's theory of knowledge given an idealist turn. Kant's great discovery was the transcendental unity of apperception and the transcendental activity of synthesis by which that unity is maintained. Once we understand that to think is to synthesise, we see that there can be no object of knowledge outside the unity of apperception, and that within that unity all objects of knowledge are shaped for us by their relations with other objects in a continually growing whole. The object is not an independently existing reality, and knowledge is not the apprehension of something which is already there to be apprehended. Knowledge does not find and explore its object, but constructs it, and the object is not *gegeben* but *aufgegeben*, not presented to us as a given fact but set before us as an 'endless task'. In fulfilling this task of constructive synthesis the mind is governed by formal principles which are ultimate, irresolvable, unchangeable, and it is these which determine the structure of all possible experience. They include first of all the primary logical relations, among which that of subject and predicate is fundamental. On them is built up a systematic 'logic of relations', which is what we commonly call 'mathematics'. All possible concepts of objects are specifications of these universal *a priori* forms. Similar formal principles govern human action, and constitute an *a priori* system of ethics and jurisprudence. In short, behind all cultural activity, transcendental analysis discloses *a priori* forms, and to make this disclosure is the task of philosophy.

This was a development of Kantianism beyond Kant, but in accordance with his spirit; and from the work of the Marburg school in turn there followed the Baden school, whose founder was Wilhelm Windelband (*Präludien*, 1884: *Einleitung in die Philosophie*, 1914) and whose most influential member was Heinrich Rickert (*Der Gegenstand der Erkenntnis*, 1892: *Die Grenzen der naturwissenschaftlichen Begriffsbildung*, 1896). These became in due course the most serious rivals that Dilthey had to face; for they

27

carried Kantian methods and principles into the sphere of the human studies which Dilthey had marked out for his own. We shall see in several of the following chapters how their teaching clashed with his.

The revival of interest in Kant, and the sustained attempt to carry philosophy on further from the point where Kant had left it, are one of the leading factors in the history of German philosophy during Dilthey's lifetime. In his inaugural lecture at Basel in 1867, Dilthey himself professed adherence to the *Kantbewegung*, at least to the extent of believing that philosophy must turn away from metaphysical speculation and take up again the task of a critique of knowledge. From the very beginning, however, he set himself against the Kantians of his own time, and against Kant himself, on fundamental points of doctrine and method. His spirit was not the Kantian spirit. The positivist in him felt that Kant had not sufficiently criticised his own assumptions. The romantic in him felt that Kant had stayed on the surface of experience and failed to see what forces are wrestling and weaving their pattern of interaction below. Both sides of him found Kantianism 'thin'. He wrote of the Marburg Neo-Kantianism as 'an artificial tissue of logic, . . . floating unsupported in empty air, (*G.S.*, V, 150–51). Dilthey's philosophy retains throughout its development the character of a polemic against Kantianism in the interests of true empiricism, an appeal from thought to life, of which thought is only one aspect.

Yet it is by starting from Kant and subjecting his views to criticism that Dilthey finds his way to the truth. From Kant he learned that the way into philosophy is one which leads from the 'objective empirical point of view' to the 'transcendental point of view', a point of view which is altogether strange to common sense. The plain man and the scientist are at one (1) in taking for granted the independent reality of the physical world, however they may differ in their conceptions of its character. They are at one (2) in thinking of mind as something which appears at certain points in the physical world. They both (3) think of consciousness as an attribute of mind, and therefore as itself an incident in the process of nature. But the transcendental standpoint reverses the perspective. Instead of regarding consciousness as something which is inherent in minds and which therefore occurs, like them, as an incident in nature, transcendental philosophy makes consciousness the primary unity; it regards nature and minds alike as 'facts of consciousness', constituents of human experience; and the relations which it finds between mind and nature are not ontic relations, but epistemological ones, i.e. relations which spring from the unity of apperception. The unity of apperception embraces everything that comes into our experience, whether it be a mental state or process or an object in the physical world, whether it be something that really exists, or an illusion, or a mere fantasy. All these are 'facts of consciousness', whatever else they may be or not be, and philosophy must begin by learning to regard them so.

This is not subjectivism. We are not saying that physical objects are *mental* facts, that they are states of mind or in any way dependent on mind. We are not talking about *mind*, but about *consciousness*. We are saying that whatever else may be true about the physical world, and whatever else may be true of our minds, it is true at any rate that both are things of which we are conscious in some way. The question, how far they are 'real', comes up later, and brings with it the far more fundamental question of what is meant by calling anything 'real'. That is an epistemological question, perhaps the fundamental question in epistemology. But there is a stage of enquiry prior to epistemology, and that is the stage where we survey and describe the various types of 'facts of consciousness' just as they present themselves in consciousness. These are the subject-matter with which epistemology will subsequently have to deal.

Dilthey disagrees with Kant and his followers both in their epistemology and in their description of the facts of consciousness.

(1) Kantianism says that all objects of consciousness are 'phenomena', i.e. that they are constructed by the understanding through the transcendental syntheses, and are subject to the conditions of time, space, and the categories, which are imposed by the knowing mind. Kant and the Neo-Kantians do not agree as to whether there is an independently existing reality behind the phenomena of nature, but they all agree in distinguishing between the 'empirical' and the 'transcendental' self. The empirical self, which is the object of introspection and of psychological study, is phenomenal in the same way as physical objects

are. The transcendental self on the other hand is that which performs the transcendental syntheses by which all experience and all objects of experience, including the empirical self, are made possible. It is that which knows, and can never itself be an object of knowledge.

Dilthey will have no such distinction. According to him there is no justification for speaking of the knowing self as distinct from the self we know. The most we can say is that many of the processes of thought are unconscious, and are therefore no part of what we actually observe in ourselves. But they are only the unconscious aspects of the same mind to which the mental states and processes of which we are conscious belong, and the distinction between conscious and unconscious is not the same as that between phenomenal and noumenal. For Dilthey, as for Bergson, our experience of the life of our own minds is a direct experience of that life as it is, not as some distorting power within us 'constructs' it.

(2) Kantianism makes much of the *a priori*. According to it, the principles on which the understanding constructs the world of objects originate in the understanding itself, and are rational principles, clear and distinct and transparent to the understanding whose laws they are. It is in terms of these principles that the ordered system of nature is to be conceived. All laws of nature and all concepts of objects are specifications of the *a priori* forms. The 'objective reality' of phenomena consists in their conformity to the laws of the system so constituted.

Dilthey recognises no *a priori*. Thought finds order in experience, it does not originate and impose it. There is structure and coherence in prelogical experience, and all that thought does is to elicit this and use it as a clue for exploration. Some of the most important types of order and structure are found not in sense-experience, but in the inner life of the mind, and these cannot be clearly and distinctly formulated; for they represent not logical structures, but the structure of life itself, a many-sided whole in which thought, and cognition generally, is only one component. The 'objective reality' of external objects and of other minds consists not in their conformity to the laws of an intelligible system, but in a vital relationship of action and interaction between ourselves and them. Instead of life and mind being phenomenal objects constructed by the thinking subject,

30

thought itself is merely something that goes on in the course of life, and is governed at every point by the ever-shifting confrontations of the living self and the surrounding world.

(3) It follows from this that a theory of knowledge cannot be constructed in the void, but requires for its basis an understanding of the totality of the mind's life. Dilthey says outright that it requires a good psychology, and in saying this he comes again into conflict with Kantianism. In strict Kantian doctrine psychology and epistemology cannot meet; for psychology is an empirical science dealing with the empirical self as a phenomenon among other phenomena, while epistemology is the science of reason itself, dealing with the *a priori* principles on which the possibility of all phenomena depends. It is psychology that is logically dependent on epistemology, not vice versa; for epistemology sets forth and 'deduces' those principles without which neither psychology nor any other empirical science can proceed.

But if there is no *a priori* and no transcendental self, these conclusions are overthrown. Epistemology becomes an empirical study, the study of how in fact knowledge comes about, and is no longer logically prior to the positive sciences of nature and mind. We do not need a theory of knowledge to assure us that there is such a thing as knowledge, or that a particular group of propositions is knowledge. On the contrary, it is because we have knowledge in the sciences, and know that we have it, that there can be something for a theory of knowledge to discuss. The *Grundlegung* of the sciences depends for its possibility on the existence of the sciences. They do not presuppose it, but it presupposes them, and is judged by its success in elucidating and accounting for their achievements (*G.S.*, I, 415, 417–19).

This granted, there can be no objection in principle to using in epistemology knowledge drawn from the empirical sciences, and in particular from psychology. There has never been a theory of knowledge which did not openly or tacitly do this (*G.S.*, V, 151), and the only real question is whether it is to be done consciously and systematically, or surreptitiously and at haphazard. We must not borrow doubtful conclusions, but we must make use of all that are well-founded; for epistemology 'is infected with error by the failure to apply assured principles, no less than by the application of insecure ones' (*G.S.*, I, 419). If the epistemologist thinks he can get on without this appeal to psychology, that is because he quietly draws upon his own consciousness for such knowledge of the mind's workings as he needs. But then his knowledge is amateurish and untrustworthy. 'He presupposes it. He makes use of it. But he has no control over it' (*G.S.*, V, 149), and is at the mercy of current psychological superstitions. So it is that even the *Kritik der reinen Vernunft* itself is disfigured by a faculty psychology which Kant's own discoveries serve to refute, but which he adopted without criticism, and 'we shall never escape from the arbitrary and piecemeal introduction of psychological views into epistemology unless by placing at its basis, with scientific awareness, a clear conception of the ordered system of mind' (*G.S.*, V, 150).

There can be no objection in principle, we said; but there is a very obvious objection based on the actual state of psychology today. Is its teaching relevant to the questions raised in epistemology? And are its conclusions and its hypotheses adequately verified? Is there not a conflict of views in its field, which casts doubt on them all, and makes it dangerous to build anything on them in philosophy? Dilthey was aware of the objection—he could hardly have failed to be so—and did his best to meet it.

Is psychology relevant to the questions raised in epistemology? A great deal of it, he agrees, is not. The spheres of the two studies do not coincide, they merely overlap at certain points. But the points where they overlap are points of fundamental importance for both, since they relate to the basic pattern of mental functioning, or what Dilthey calls the 'structural system of life' (*Strukturzusammenhang des Lebens*). This is all that the epistemologist needs to know. He does not need a detailed knowledge of psychology over the whole range of its investigations (*G.S.*, V, 146, 150). What he needs is 'the living consciousness and the universally valid description of the mental system', i.e. a 'reflection on self (*Selbstbesinnung*) embracing the whole unmutilated content (*Befund*) of mental life'. We may perhaps say that this is not properly a psychology, but the common root in experience from which both psychology and epistemology grow. 'All detailed psychology is but the scientific completion of that which forms also the basis of epistemology.' Or we may prefer to say that this rudimentary description of mental structure is actually the first stage in a psychology; and in that case epistemology, being an offshoot of it, must be regarded as 'psychology in motion, and in motion towards a definite end'.

Towards what end? Towards an analysis of the meaning of metaphysical and logical terms such as 'real', 'true', 'valid', and the like (*G.S.*, V, 151–2). Psychology, in studying what goes on in the mind, discovers among other things how we draw a distinction between self and not-self, and how in conceiving the not-self we tend to move away from mere fantasy and baseless supposition in search of reasoned beliefs and objective knowledge. Psychology is concerned to show how we come thus to distinguish between self and not-self, and how the quest of reason and objectivity plays a part in building up an integrated personality. What epistemology has to do is to analyse what exactly we are doing when we distinguish self from not-self, what objectivity really means, and under what conditions and to what extent the pursuit of knowledge can be successful (*G.S.*, VII, 7–13).

But has psychology any assured results to offer? Here we come to the crucial point. Towards the end of the foregoing chapter we saw how Dilthey, seeking a psychology which might be to the human studies what mathematics (*sic*) is to natural science, concluded that no experimental psychology could do this, and demanded a psychology which should be independent of the method of hypothesis and verification. The idea of psychology as a basis for epistemology drives him with equal force in the same direction, and it is now time to examine the position which he took up. It is based on a distinction between two kinds of science, viz. *explanatory* and *descriptive*.

All science, he says, observes and analyses, seeking to show how its object can be constructed, on clearly defined principles, out of elements of a clearly defined character; but where does it find these elements and principles? A 'descriptive science' (*beschreibende Wissenschaft*) finds them in the data of experience, distinguishing and cataloguing their simplest components and observing the relations between them. An 'explanatory science' (*erklärende Wissenschaft*) seeks its elements and principles behind the data, helping out its observations by means of hypotheses; by assuming a few simple factors which may be selected from among the data, or may be of a kind not observed at all, it tries to account for the whole wealth of what is observed, and the

33

hypothesis is deemed to be verified if it gives understanding and control of the observable facts. The explanatory method is used e.g. in physics and chemistry, where the visible world is built up out of 'elements which are obtained by a division of external reality, a breaking and splitting up of things, and then only as hypotheses' (*G.S.*, I, 29).

It is evident that explanatory science as here defined is logically dependent upon descriptive science, for the accurate analysis of the data must precede the verification of any hypothesis professing to explain them; further, the mere fact of using hypotheses introduces into explanatory science an uncertainty to which descriptive analysis is not exposed. Accordingly, if psychology is to be the basis for epistemology and the human studies, everything must depend on our finding a psychology which is not a 'psychology of hypotheses' (*G.S.*, V, 151). We must describe and analyse the contents, acts, and processes observable in mental life, but abstain from introducing any which observation cannot verify.

A great deal of Dilthey's energy in his middle years was devoted to the question what form such a psychology might take. He formulated his conclusions in his *Ideen über eine beschreibende u. zergliedernde Psychologie* (1894), and the contents of this work are analysed below (in Chapter Seven). It is made clear in the *Ideen* that the psychology there described is the one which is to serve as a foundation for the theory of knowledge, and that part of it which is to serve this purpose is given in a fair amount of detail, but the application of it to epistemological problems is not made. For that we must look to the first two of Dilthey's *Studien zur Grundlegung der Geisteswissenschaften* (1905), where the relevant psychological analyses are given in greater detail than in the *Ideen*, and their epistemological consequences are indicated. These *Studien* do not contain a complete and systematic account of Dilthey's theory of knowledge. He never wrote such an account. We must put his views together from various sources, but the *Studien* of 1905 will provide the framework into which the evidence of other sources may be fitted.

These two *Studien* show in certain respects the influence of Edmund Husserl, whose *Logische Untersuchungen* had appeared only a few years before (1900–1). Husserl's philosophical interests were quite different from Dilthey's, and his philosophy developed on quite different lines; but here at the beginning, in the *Logische Untersuchungen*, he gave expression to views with which Dilthey had a certain sympathy. Like Dilthey, he demands for epistemology a foundation which shall not be open to doubt, and he finds it in a descriptive analysis of inner and outer experiences, taken purely as experiences, in abstraction from any 'reality' which may be ascribed to them. No statement about 'real, objective' existence, he says, is beyond doubt; but it is certain that we have experiences (*Erlebnisse*), and these are known to us by acquaintance, immediately and intuitively. Philosophy must begin with a 'phenomenological reduction', a suspension of belief (ἐποχή), a bracketing-off (*Einklammerung*) or dismissal from consideration of everything except the observable character of our experiences, purely as experiences. The objective world (including our own empirical self) then becomes not something which exists or does not exist, but something which *we believe* to exist. As such it is an inescapable 'phenomenon of consciousness'. Thus we enter on a branch of study, the 'phenomenology of knowledge' (*Phänomenologie des Erkennens*) which is beyond the possibility of doubt and error.

Dilthey thought it worth while in writing his *Studien* in 1905 to indicate the points of agreement between Husserl and himself. He even adopted the distinction between mental 'acts' (*Akten*) and 'contents' (*Inhalte*), which Husserl had borrowed from Franz Brentano and made fundamental in his phenomenology. It is true that he adopted it in a way of his own, and the use he makes of it has little in common with Husserl's subtle and involved analyses. Dilthey's emphasis lies elsewhere, as we shall see. But when all is said and done it is true that the underlying conception of Husserl's 'phenomenology' is the same as that of Dilthey's 'reflection on self' (*Selbstbesinnung*), and both represent that 'transcendental point of view' which is one of Kant's great gifts to philosophy.

Let us start at this point and follow Dilthey's exposition.

We can fairly ask, he says, of any alleged object of knowledge whether it is 'real'. For it is made known to us by processes of thought, by judgment and inference, and these carry with them the possibility of error. This error however concerns not the data on which our judgments are based, but the way in which the data are connected by our understanding to form an object;

and, whether the objects so built up be real or not, yet the data themselves as facts of consciousness, apart from their objective reference, and the objective reference itself considered merely as a mental act which takes place, are real beyond a doubt. The sensible contents which, when referred to objects, go to characterise an independently existing physical world, may also be taken as facts of consciousness in abstraction from their relation to objects (*G.S.*, VII, 17, 27), and an event of inner experience, which forms part of the history of a self, may be considered apart from its relation to the self, purely as a momentary event. The external object may be phenomenal or even illusory, and the 'self' may prove to be a superstition; yet the sensible content and the momentary conscious event are real as such, irrespective of the reality or unreality of that to which they are referred (*G.S.*, VII, 26).

It is from this point of view that descriptive psychology or 'reflection on self' is called upon to study mental facts. First of all it must describe them as they are in immediate experience, before they are referred either to an object or to a self, or made to *mean* anything other than what they *are*; then it must show how by the mediation of unconscious thought-processes these primary data are raised to the level of perceptual knowledge, and imagination, memory, and abstract conception begin their work; then, how discursive thought arises, and through judgment and inference we build up the 'outer world' of nature and the 'inner world' of mind.

In almost every moment of consciousness we are conscious *of* something, and can distinguish that of which we are conscious from our being conscious of it, or that which we 'mind' from our 'minding' of it. That which is minded, Dilthey calls the content (*Inhalt, Inhaltlichkeit,* and occasionally *Gehalt*). For the minding of the content he has several names, but he seems at a loss for one which begs no questions. Very often he calls it the act (*Akt*). But then he adds that this word must be taken 'in the broader sense' (*G.S.*, VII, 20), and he disowns any interpretation which might give it an activistic or a noegenetic meaning. That is to say, by the 'act' e.g. of perceiving he does not mean an activity or process by which the state of consciousness is in some mysterious way rendered possible. Dilthey is describing, not explaining; and by this word 'act' he means simply and solely

36

the being-aware of the object (*G.S.*, VII, 27). Elsewhere he calls it an 'attitude' (*Verhalten, Verhaltungsweise*); but this term may seem to suggest that in having the attitude we are aware of something, viz. our mind, which takes up the attitude. Now it is true, Dilthey allows, that in certain modes of experience the consciousness of a content is accompanied by that of a self which minds it or assumes an attitude towards it; in the experience especially of wish, desire, or will, the self is experienced as an active whole having commerce with its environment, and adopting towards it the feeling-attitude of love or hate. But in other experiences the consciousness of a self is not present. 'For one who watches Hamlet suffer on the stage, his own self is extinguished. In the effort to finish a task I literally forget myself' (*G.S.*, VII, 21). Awareness of a self is therefore not psychologically primary, and the name 'attitude' applied to the act of minding must not be taken as implying that it is so.

The mental acts or attitudes appearing in consciousness are of many kinds, but fall into three main types, viz. cognitive, affective, and volitional. This trichotomy is contested by those who regard feeling as a mere first stage in volition. In its defence Dilthey urges that feeling has a distinctive character, viz. the contrast of the pleasant and the painful, to which nothing corresponds either in cognition or in volition; for if the contrast between desire and aversion be cited to the contrary, yet these are only border states between feeling and will, and when volition reaches its climax in resolve, even if the content of the resolve is the avoidance of something unpleasant, yet in itself resolve is always positive, in that it tends to bring about the realisation of its content. Further, there are feelings which, however strong they may be, have no tendency to pass into action; such are the feelings aroused by poetry and music, or by natural scenery, or the sympathetic feelings of one who watches others at play (*G.S.*, VII, 56–7). There are also acts of will which do not proceed from pleasant or painful feeling, e.g. those resulting from the recollection of a promise; the resolve to fulfil the promise results not from a feeling-state, but from the volitional relation of being bound (*G.S.*, VII, 67). Therefore feeling and willing, though closely related, are distinct types of conscious attitudes.

Each of the three main types of attitude includes many subordinate species. Thus perceiving, remembering, supposing, doubting, judging are types of cognitive attitudes; being pleased, fearing, hating are types of feeling; approving, wishing, resolving, being obliged are forms of volitional consciousness.

Act and content vary independently. 'I perceive a colour, judge about it, feel pleasure, wish to produce it, thus the same element of content runs through various types of attitude, and yet at the same time each of them can have reference to various colours and also to other objects' (*G.S.*, VII, 325,c f. 20–1, 23).

Act and content are ours by virtue of two different modes of consciousness, which in German are called respectively *Erlebnis* and *Vorstellung*. The content is something *of* which we are conscious. It stands over against us, and we take up an attitude towards it. The 'act' is the attitude which we take towards the content. But in being conscious *of* a content we somehow experience, or consciously have, our attitude towards the content. We are not consc ous *of* this attitude. No attitude is an attitude towards itself, and the act by which I apprehend a content cannot have itself as a part of the content apprehended. This does not mean that the act or attitude is unconscious, but that it is related to consciousness in a different way from a content. The act or attitude is inherently conscious (*bewusst*), but we are not conscious *of* it. We 'live through' (*erleben*) it, and it is therefore described as a 'lived experience' (*Erlebnis*). An act or attitude, besides being *erlebt*, can also be *vorgestellt*, or become an apprehended content, if e.g. we turn our attention upon it in introspection, or if we remember it when it is past; but in that case there will be a second act to which the first act stands as content, and this second act in turn will not be *vorgestellt*, but *erlebt*. In a word, *das Erleben* is the mode in which we experience our own states or psychical acts in the actual having of them, and it differs from all other modes in which we can be conscious of ourselves in that it is an *immediate* experience.

Such experience is not knowledge (*Erkenntnis*) of the self or of its states. For only a content can be an object of knowledge, and even so only when the act is an act of knowing and not e.g. an act of feeling; but the act, as act, is never known, since even the knowing act knows not itself, but only the content which it apprehends. The knowing act can indeed come to be known, viz. by reflection, but then it is known not by itself, but by a

38

further act of knowing, to which it stands as content, and this further act in turn does not know itself. Thus life, as the all-inclusive unity of act and content, is never known as a whole to itself as a whole. There is always something in it which is merely *erlebt*, and this is the fundamental experience which sustains all the rest.

Dilthey himself speaks of *das Erleben* as 'a distinctively charac-terised manner in which reality exists for me' (*G.S.*, VI, 313). This means that, while whatever is *erlebt* is 'conscious' (*bewusst*), the relation between it and consciousness is one peculiar to it-self. It is, indeed, a relation almost of identity. We can, if we choose, distinguish between consciousness and the conscious *Erlebnis* by regarding consciousness as an identical quality which is shared by various kinds of *Erlebnisse*, remaining itself un-affected by their variety (cf. *G.S.*, VII, 26). But it is more im-portant to recognise that, wherever there is an *Erlebnis*, the consciousness is an inseparable and intrinsic quality of the *Erleb-nis* itself, and not a separate psychological factor attached or related, however closely, to it. In particular, it is not something, other than the *Erlebnis*, 'for' which the *Erlebnis* exists, or by which it is apprehended. There is no distinction in *Erlebnis* be-tween apprehension and the apprehended, between observer and observed. The *Erlebnis* 'does not stand as an object over against the observer, its existence for me is not distinguished from that *which* in it exists for me' (*G.S.*, VII, 139, cf. 27). The consciousness which I have in having it is not, strictly speaking, a consciousness *of* it at all, but simply the consciousness which belongs intrinsically to it. It may be described as an 'immediate knowing' (*unmittelbares Wissen*, *G.S.*, I, 118) or as 'aware-ness' (*Innewerden*, *Innesein*).

It should further be noted that *Erleben* or *Innewerden* is not the same as 'inner perception' (*innere Wahrnehmung*); for though inner perception is perceptive knowledge of *Erlebnisse*, yet the *Erlebnis* which is *erlebt* does not, in being *erlebt*, perceive itself. Nor may we speak of it, without qualification, as a *datum*. It is a datum for inner perception, when inner perception occurs and turns the *Erlebnis* into an objectively perceived content; but in and for itself it is not a datum, because a datum, to be 'given,' must stand objectively (*gegenständlich*) over against the subject to whom it is given, and in *das Erleben* as such this overagainstness is absent. '*Erlebnis* does not appear over against me as a percept or an idea (*ein Vorgestelltes*), it is not given to us, but . . . exists for us by virtue of the fact that we are aware of it (*ihrer innewerden*), that I immediately have (*habe*) it as in some sense belonging to me. Only in thought does it become objective' (*G.S.*, VI, 313). In itself, purely as *erlebt*, it is 'not given and not thought' (*G.S.*, VI, 314).

By contrast with the act, which is *erlebt*, the content is always *vorgestellt*; and it cannot be so without there being also an act which apprehends it. This relation to an apprehending act is the only thing which we can know for certain beforehand about any content that may enter our experience. We cannot assume that the content will always be a 'real' being, something that actually 'is' *in rerum natura*. It may just as well be an imaginative figment or an illusion. The question, which of these it is, does not even arise at the stage of descriptive analysis where we are at present. In any case, however that question may be answered when it does arise, whether our content turns out on examination to be a 'reality' or not, at least it is a 'fact of consciousness', it 'exists for me' (*ist für mich da*), and it is intimately related to the act by which we are conscious of it. Dilthey even runs the two together and speaks of the content as 'contained in' the *Erlebnis*. Thus he says (*G.S.*, VII, 19–20) that 'every lived experience (*Erlebnis*) contains (*enthält*) a content', and defines the content as 'a part of what can be distinguished in the lived experience, (*ein Teil von dem am Erlebnis Unterscheidbaren*).

The ordinary use of the word *Erlebnis* gives some justification for this inclusion of the content in the *Erlebnis*, and even for speaking of it as being itself *erlebt*: though this latter is not a usage which Dilthey adopts when writing philosophically. Thus he can write (*G.S.*, VII, 334) of 'the war with France, which I among others have *erlebt*' (*der französische Krieg, den ich miterlebt habe*). This is not the narrow use of *erleben* which we have just been defining, the use in which *erleben=innewerden*. It is a broader use in which any event which has fallen within my conscious history, if thought of as having so fallen, and therefore as in relation to me as the experiencing subject, can be said to have been *erlebt* by me, or to be an *Erlebnis* of mine. Just so in English we can describe a war, or a bereavement, or a journey, or the reading of a book, or any event, great or small, of which a man is conscious as happening to him, as an 'experience' which he has. From a biographical point of view, a man's life can be seen as a series of 'experiences' in this sense. Dilthey would call them *Erlebnisse*; and this wider use of the word plays an important part in his analysis of consciousness.

An *Erlebnis* in the sense here indicated may be, from the biographer's point of view, an ultimate unit of the life-process; but from the psychological point of view it is of course highly complex. It involves many different kinds of mental acts and processes, and it also involves a reference to the contents with which these acts and processes are concerned. All these, taken as 'facts of consciousness', as elements in the experience of some conscious subject, go to make up what Dilthey calls an *Erlebnis*. The next stage in his analysis of consciousness must therefore be to examine the relations which obtain between the elements within a single *Erlebnis*, and also between different *Erlebnisse* in the whole process of life. These relations, taken all together, constitute what he calls the 'structural system of mind' or 'of life' (*psychischer Strukturzusammenhang, Strukturzusammenhang des Lebens*), and the account which he gives of this structural system is both distinctive and fundamental in his philosophy.

He finds three fundamental types of relation which are constitutive of mental structure, and it is now time to examine them.

With regard to the *first* structural relation, Dilthey's position varies. In the *Ideen über eine beschreibende u. zergliedernde Psychologie* (1894) he gives under this rubric the coexistence of cognitive, affective, and volitional acts in every moment of consciousness. For feeling bears conscious reference to some cognised content, and volition involves an idea of what is willed; again, volition is moved by feeling, and cognition gives rise to feeling; again, feeling tends to pass into volition, and cognition is governed by the volitional act of attending. Thus no mental act of any of these three types can exist without at least one of the other two. But there is always one of the three which dominates and gives its name to the whole complex. Thus feeling and volition may be subservient to cognition, operating merely to sustain interest and attention; again, feeling and cognition may subserve volition, operating merely to sustain desire and to guide deliberation. In such cases we speak simply of 'cognising' or 'willing', though in fact in each instance we are doing both and also

41

feeling (*G.S.*, V, 201–4).—But even as he states this view Dilthey confesses a doubt. He is not convinced that every single sensation arouses feeling, and, though he says that all feeling *tends* to pass over into volition, he does not say that all feeling does so pass over, nor is he quite sure that ideas produced by association are in any way dependent upon will (*G.S.*, V, 202–3). Later, as we have seen, he came to recognise feelings with no conscious cognitive basis, feelings which do not even tend to pass into volition, and volitions whose motive is not feeling; thus his generalisation breaks down, and after 1905 he seeks his first structural relation elsewhere.

He finds it in the relation subsisting in consciousness between act and content, a relation which he says is '*sui generis*', and 'occurs only in mental life' (*G.S.*, VII, 22, cf. 16, 325). The relation is of a different character according to the type of act involved. Thus every cognitive act is 'directed upon' (*gerichtet auf*) that which is cognised, i.e. the light of consciousness here falls not upon the act but upon the content. Likewise every volitional act is 'directed upon' a 'fiat', i.e. the realisation of that which is willed. On the other hand, in experiences of feeling, the light of consciousness falls upon the feeling-attitude rather than upon the content arousing it; we look away from what is before us to the response which it evokes in us, so that when feeling dominates our consciousness 'it seems as if every vital relation, every object, every individuality outside ourselves, exists to be enjoyed, endured, and appreciated to the full' (*G.S.*, VII, 48). These characteristic relations between act and content are the first element of structure in mind.

The *second* structural relation is a mutual subservience and hierarchic subordination among the different species of act within each of the three main types. Thus, in the cognitive realm, perceiving, remembering, judging, inferring, are all involved as hierarchically related stages in a single process, viz. the acquiring of knowledge about something; deliberation, choice, resolve, selection of means, are likewise stages in a single conative process, viz. adjustment to a situation. The steps in such a process occur successively, but the process as a whole has a unity of function, which is not broken even though the process may suffer interruption, and the acts occur at considerable intervals of time. 'Engaged in a cognitive process, I am interrupted by news, by a person coming in, or by physical indisposition; it may be long before the cognitive process in which I was engaged is carried further by me; yet these widely separated cognitive experiences are bound together as parts in the whole of my cognitive system' (*G.S.*, VII, 36). Again, 'the decision in which I indicate for myself a plan of life can be structurally bound up with a long series of actions arising in many years and at long intervals from it' (*G.S.*, VII, 325). And further, in each sphere, as particular acts unite to form one process, so particular processes unite to form the comprehensive process of our cognitive, affective, or volitional life. Particular cognitive processes, each based on what has gone before, build up a growing system of knowledge; particular volitional processes, similarly related to one another, build up an increasingly integrated plan of life. As knowledge grows and character crystallises, the living person becomes continually more independent of time and change. 'The flow of life, in which all is swept away into the past, is overcome by memory, and the contingency of events by the coherence of thought' (*G.S.*, VII, 329).

In this way our activities of knowledge, feeling, and will come each to form a comprehensive organised system, and it is between these systems that Dilthey finds his *third* structural relation. For as, in a particular act of knowing, elements of feeling and will are present in subordination to the dominant cognitive attitude, so the whole complex systems of feeling and will play a part in elaborating the complex system of knowledge. 'Knowing is in the researcher a teleological system: here the relation which we call will is bound up with that which we style objective apprehension to form the structural unity of one process, and in this whole teleological system particular functions work together to produce states which somehow have in consciousness the character of values or ends' (*G.S.*, VII, 23). In the same way the whole knowledge-system is at the disposal of the will, to be used as a tool in the working out of a life-purpose; and knowledge and will together can be brought into play to create and maintain an equilibrium in the life of feeling. In short, all three systems combine in one, and work together to preserve and develop the teleological unity of life.

In calling the unity of life 'teleological', Dilthey is careful to safeguard himself against too rigid an interpretation. He does

43

not mean that there is a fixed and definite 'purpose of life' which is laid down for us by God or Nature, and is the same for all men. 'The structural system does not work out a determinate purpose (*Ziel*); it merely contains purposiveness (*Zielstrebigkeit*)', but the determinate content or ideal informing this purposiveness varies with the character and temperament of each individual (*G.S.*, VII, 329–30). The consciousness of the individual sets up definite aims for him to pursue, and the structural system in him 'works purposively in the direction of determinate mental attitudes (*Bewusstseinslagen*)' (*G.S.*, VII,17).

The relations set up between mental events by the structural system must be carefully distinguished from another type of relations, also present in the life of the mind, and formulated in some well-known psychological laws. In the experimental study of stimulus and response, of memory, of association, and similar processes, we are able to make generalisations which we can formulate on the analogy of physical laws, and make the basis of an 'explanatory psychology' (*G.S.*, VII, 324). These psychological laws are certainly valid, for they are established by observation and experiment; but they are dead to us and alien like the laws of physical nature, because we have no inner consciousness of the processes underlying them. They are instances where we do not see into the life of mind, but stand outside and read off inductively the laws of its behaviour. On the other hand, the relations above called 'structural' are known to us through immediate consciousness, from within, and give no impression of being alien. When one mental event by a structural relation 'produces' (*erwirkt*) another, 'the production itself is directly experienced (*erlebt*)' (*G.S.*, VII, 328), and the relation so set up yields a sense of 'affinity and life (*Zusammengehörigkeit, Lebendigkeit*) in the mental system' (*G.S.*, VII, 14). The relations which we observe as from without reveal mind as a system of processes conforming to laws, but those experienced from within reveal it as a living whole of intimately coordinated parts (*G.S.*, VII, 15). Structural relation of this sort is a unique peculiarity of mental life. 'It can only be experienced (*erfahren*) and pointed out, but not defined' (*G.S.*, VII, 16).

Next in importance to the structural unity of mental life is its relation to time. All life is a temporal process, and this process 'is experienced as the unresting advance of the present

44

(*Vorrücken der Gegenwart*), in which what was present continually becomes past, and what was future becomes present'. This perpetually advancing present (*Gegenwart*) is defined as 'the filling of a moment of time with reality (*Realität*)', the term 'reality' signifying that present experience alone is actually lived by us (*erlebt*), while past and future are for us only as remembered, anticipated, or inferred. 'The skiff of our life is carried along as it were on a continually advancing stream, and the present is always and everywhere where on these waves we are, suffer, remember, or hope, in short, where we live in the fullness of our reality. But we pass along ceaselessly on this stream, and in the same moment in which what was future becomes present, it sinks away already into the past.' Nothing is permanent in the process except the fact that there always is a present. 'This filling with reality, or present, remains continually, while that which constitutes the content of living experience perpetually alters' (*G.S.*, VII, 192–3 = 72–3, cf. VI, 315).

If we think of time abstractly, prescinding from the character of the experience which fills it, we obtain the time-picture which is characteristic of physical science; time is as it were a line, a continuous homogeneous manifold of successive parts. This is the time-picture in which Kant rightly found antinomies, and which he relegated to the status of a mere phenomenon. For, in fact, it is impossible to describe real time in terms of this linear picture. In the linear view of time, the present is conceived as a cross-section of the process. But since the manifold is homogeneous, every part of it, however minute, must contain other parts, must in fact be still a line and not a point, and therefore no part of the line can be a true present. For the present, being a cross-section, 'has no extension', and cannot therefore be a real part of the manifold at all. Hence, if time is a successive manifold and experience is in time, it is impossible in experience to encounter a real present. And yet, in fact, in 'concrete time', it is the present which is the sole reality, and past and future have no being except as thought of in the present. Evidently, then, the experiential content of the time-series has characteristics to which the mathematical division of time does less than justice (*ibid.*).

When we turn to ask what these characteristics are, the answer seems to be imposed upon us by the very terms of

45

the question. No part of real time is instantaneous. Therefore the conscious present, if it is a reality occupying a place in time, must embrace a duration. And that is what Dilthey says. 'The present, psychologically regarded (*Gegenwart psychologisch angesehen*),' he writes, 'is a lapse of time whose extension we grasp together as a unit. We grasp together, with the character of the present, that which, by reason of its continuity, is for us not separable' (*G.S.*, VII, 230). Looking at it from the standpoint of the 'cross-section', this amounts to saying that the conscious present includes a surviving consciousness of the immediate past. It is paradoxical to say that the present necessarily includes an element of the past, and that therefore present experience consists to some extent of memory. But the fact is that there is no hard and fast line between immediate experience and memory when the immediate past is in question; and Dilthey is not afraid of the paradox. 'The smallest part of the onward movement of time still includes a time-process in itself. The present never *is*; what we experience (*erleben*) as present always includes memory of what was present a moment ago' (*G.S.*, VII, 194).

This 'memory', which is integral to the lived experience of the present, is of course a different thing from memory in the ordinary sense, which is fully aware of its object as past. But about memory in the ordinary sense, too, Dilthey has interesting things to say. He distinguishes between a more intimate and dynamic kind of memory and a more indirect and distant kind.

The first and more intimate type of memory is one in which the experiences remembered, whether temporally continuous with the conscious present or not, are at any rate dynamically bound up with it. Thus, when I listen to a symphony, my experience of it is successive. Note follows note, theme follows theme, and each theme is worked out at length. But there is also a constant gathering up of the experience into a present whole, and the closing bars of the symphony are not merely the last of a succession of sounds, but the whole of what has gone before is implicit in them. When I contemplate a picture, the experience builds itself up piecemeal over a period of time, and the last moment has in it implicitly all that has gone before. Even if my contemplation of the picture is interrupted, and resumed only after a considerable time, yet I begin again at the point where I left off; the structural unity of the process is preserved, and my last visit to the picture is enriched by the cumulative experience of all my previous visits. So too if I meet, after separation, an intimate friend, it can seem to me that we had never parted, so fully is the structural unity of experience maintained. In such cases elements of experience, which according to the mathematical division of time should be irretrievably buried in the past, are preserved in memory (*Erinnerung*) and 'dovetailed' (*einbezogen*) into the present, forming with it a 'dynamic unity' in which they are experienced as a determining force (*Kraft*), and so acquire the peculiar character of 'presentness' (*Präsenz*)[1] (*G.S.*, VII, 73 = 194, VI, 315–16).

It is to this intimate type of memory that Dilthey seems to confine the use of the name *Erinnerung*, in a brief passage where he distinguishes it from another way in which past experiences may be recalled and have a kind of influence upon the present. When an experience is not merely past, but dead, when I have put it behind me, and the chords of my soul will no longer vibrate to that note, this deeper intimacy of recollection becomes impossible; but I can still know, objectively and impersonally, that I once had such an experience, and this knowledge can arouse in me a feeling which is no part or continuation of the past experience, but is a present reaction to the knowledge that I once had it, and this feeling will then be a factor in determining the present course of my conscious life (*G.S.*, VII, 231).

We are now in a position to understand fully what Dilthey means by a life-unit or lived experience (*Erlebnis*). '*Erlebnis* denotes a part of the life-process . . . which, teleologically regarded, has a unity in itself', i.e. which has unity by virtue of structural relations among its parts, and especially the 'presentness' of the earlier of them in the later. Dilthey instances the hearing of a friend's death, together with the ideas and feelings aroused by it, and their verbal expression or the resolve to which they lead. Here the object apprehended is a unity, and my relation to it is also worked out as a single complex unity. 'In the economy of my life it is an element separable by itself, because it is structurally articulated to perform a function in

---

[1] *Präsenz* is neither the character of presentness as contrasted with pastness or futurity (*Gegenwart*), nor that of presence as contrasted with absence (*Anwesenheit*). What is *präsent* is 'present' in a sense analogous to that in which God is said to be 'a very present help', i.e. dynamically present.

47

this economy' (*G.S.*, VI, 314). If the whole of such a structural complex falls within the conscious present, it is a lived experience in the narrowest sense, the smallest unit of life which is itself life. But several such experiences separated in time, e.g. successive visits to a picture, may be bound together by a similar unity of structure and theme, and these constitute a lived experience in the broader sense. In such a case the whole experience does not fall within the conscious present. In its later stages I am indeed still aware of the 'presentness' of the earlier stages as a determining force; but, in so far as my memory of these is explicit, they are recognised as past.

Thus, a compound lived experience cannot be apprehended as a whole without the conscious recognition that some of what is apprehended is not present (*gegenwärtig*). And even a simple lived experience, which does not transcend the conscious present, may still include some apprehension both of the past and of the future. For it may well include the memory of previous experiences, which, even if they are dynamically *präsent* in the actual *Erlebnis*, are none the less past. Moreover, every lived experience includes a volitional element, and this involves some anticipation, however dim, of the future. But it is now time to ask, if 'nothing exists but what appears in the present', what meaning we are to give to propositions about 'past' or 'future'.

The time-series, past and future, 'exists for us' only 'in' our present experience, i.e. as the form in which the objective content of our present experience is cast. For to say that an experience belongs to the present means only that the mental act or attitude within the experience is taking place in the present; the content, of course, is 'referred' (i.e. taken as belonging) to a date within the objective sequence of events, and this date may be very far from the present. Thus the physical world of past ages 'exists for me' as the objective content of a cognitive experience which I am having now; and as with past physical events, so with past experiences. If I remember a pain which I felt yesterday, then my memory-experience as such is present, while the pain, which is the content of the memory-experience, is taken as belonging to yesterday. Now, a content thus dated in the past or the future may be said in a sense to be 'severed' from the present lived experience, or to 'transcend' it. It does

48

not transcend consciousness altogether, but it transcends 'the present moment of consciousness which is filled by lived experience'. And Dilthey finds here in 'the time-process and the memory which embraces it' the real 'objective basis' of the idea of a 'transcendent' object. Something 'transcendent' does truly exist for us; but it is transcendent not for consciousness altogether, but only 'for the immediately experiencing consciousness (*für das erlebende Bewusstsein*)' (*G.S.*, VII, 29). Dilthey sums up all this in his 'principle of lived experience', viz. that 'all that exists for us exists only as such and such a datum in the present. Even if an experience is past, it exists for us only as a givenness (*Gegebensein*) in the present lived experience' (*G.S.*, VII, 230).[1]

Not every detail of the structural system is consciously enjoyed (*erlebt*), even within the limits of a single lived experience, and still less does any such experience include an apprehension of all the relations in which it stands to other experiences remote from it in the time-series. And yet, by the very nature of life, every experience has connections with other experiences and with physical events of different dates, which are, for it, transcendent; it presupposes the past course and future aims of the individual life in which it is an incident, and that life again depends upon the surrounding society and the natural world. In the lived experience itself there is no awareness of these connections, but yet they are 'contained' (*enthalten*) in it, and every lived experience tends naturally to give rise to a process of 'reflection' whereby they are brought to light. Dilthey gives an example. 'I lie awake at night, I worry over the possibility of completing in my old age works which I have begun, I think over what is to be done. In this experience there is a structural system of consciousness: an objective apprehension forms its basis, on this rests an attitude (*Stellungnahme*) in the shape of worry about and sorrow at the state of things objectively apprehended, and an effort to escape from it. And all that exists for me in this its structural connection. I bring the situation to distinct consciousness. I pick out what is structurally related. I isolate it. All that I thus pick out is contained in the lived experience itself and is hereby merely clarified. But now my apprehension is carried

[1] This may be compared with the 'principle of phenomenality' or 'principle of consciousness' as set forth on p. 53.

49

onward (*fortgezogen*) by the experience itself on the basis of the moments contained in it to experiences which in the process of life, though separated by long periods of time, were structurally bound up with such moments; I know of my works through a previous review of them; in relation with this, further away in the past, stand the processes in which these works came to be. Another moment leads into the future; the material lying to my hand will yet require of me incalculable labour, I am worried about it, I inwardly address myself to the performance of it. All this *about*, *of*, and *to*, all these relations of what is directly experienced (*erlebt*) to what is remembered and to what is future carry me on—backward and forward' (*G.S.*, VII, 139–40, *cf.* 28). Every experience tends to set up such a reflective process, which brings to light the structural relations hidden within it. Dilthey calls this process the 'onward trend' (*das Fortgezogenwerden*) of consciousness (*G.S.*, VII, 140, *cf.* 28).

This 'onward trend' of consciousness brings us up to the frontier of epistemology. For to it we owe our view of that objective world of things and persons, stretching out far beyond our present experience and existing independently of it, whose 'reality' is the matter of epistemological debate. (1) Reflection takes us beyond the lived experience of the moment and 'objectifies' it, showing it to be merely one incident in the history of an enduring centre of structurally ordered mental life. This enduring centre is the 'self' or 'subject' (*G.S.*, VII, 22, 30). (2) In the same way we take the sensible content of present perception, and by reflection recognise it as one of a system of contents which we group together as an 'object', a system of 'objects', and finally an 'external world' (*G.S.*, VII, 32–5). (3) Some of these objects, again, we credit with the possession of a mental life structurally identical with our own, and we interpret their attitudes and movements as expressions of their thoughts and feelings. Thus the world around us comes to be peopled, for us, with other selves whose experiences we more or less understand, and on this basis the edifice of the human studies is built up.

Epistemology according to Dilthey is the branch of enquiry which asks in what sense, and to what degree, the selves and objects thus appearing in our consciousness are 'real' and 'objective'

50

The question about the 'reality' of our own lived experience and of our own self, Dilthey thinks, is easily settled in the affirmative; for, in his view, lived experience is the very paradigm of 'reality'. It is the basis on which imagination, memory, and thought arise, and their sole function, as will appear later, is to clarify and amplify what is ours in lived experience. Lived experience is what it is, and does not carry any 'reference' to anything beyond itself, while all other modes of consciousness in the end 'refer' to it. It is not phenomenal in the sense in which so many philosophers, including Dilthey himself, have held sense-experience to be phenomenal. External objects, he thinks, are apprehended not 'immediately', but through the medium of sensible qualities which are dependent on the sense-organs of the observer. How this perception takes place we shall see later. But lived experience is apprehended not through sense-organs, but 'immediately' in and through itself, and therefore there can be nothing merely phenomenal in our apprehension of it. The question whether a lived experience is 'real' cannot arise in so far as it is lived; it exists in being lived and it is just what is lived; 'its givenness and its reality are not separated from one another' (*G.S.*, VII, 27). Whereas in external perception we have to pass from the perceived quality to the object behind it, 'in lived experience there is only this qualitatively determined reality, and nothing is for us behind it' (*G.S.*, VI, 316). It is 'a reality immediately appearing as such, of which we are aware without abstraction' (*G.S.*, VI, 314). And we gain knowledge of the self not by abstracting from lived experience or trying to go behind it, but simply by accepting it and following its ramifications as they unfold themselves in reflection.

Even Kant's notorious theory of 'inner sense' and the phenomenality of the empirical self does not deny that we experience the life of the self as a fact of consciousness in the sense here laid down; it is merely one of many attempts which have been made to show that there is something else behind what we experience. Such attempts have had various motives, philosophical, scientific, or religious; but they all introduce us to alleged entities and processes which cannot be experienced, and which are not required in order to make sense of what is experienced. For instance, the 'pure subject' of Kantian theory, the transcendental ground of experience, which is not in time but on which time rests, is nowhere found in experience; nor is it required as a hypothesis to give system to lived experience, because lived experience has system in itself. It is therefore beyond the pale of assured knowledge, and at the same time irrelevant to the human studies. Our whole interest there is in the life-process unfolded in lived experience, and so far as we can trace the structure of that, we ask for no other 'reality' beyond it. If there is such a 'reality', we cannot know it; and whether there is or not, the processes of lived experience in any case are what they are, and it is they which are 'reality' to us (*G.S.*, V; 5, VII, 27, 194, 319, 333–4).

When we turn to the question of the 'reality' of the external world, we find it more complicated and difficult. The only work by Dilthey which is wholly devoted to this problem is the *Beiträge zur Lösung der Frage vom Ursprung unseres Glaubens an die Realität der Aussenwelt u. seinem Recht* (1890), but the evidence of this essay can be amplified by reference to numerous passages in his other writings. It must be said at once that this question of the external world, which has seemed so fundamental and so engrossing to many philosophers, was not so to Dilthey. He was concerned mainly to answer it in a way which would be consistent with his general principles and outlook, and would enable him to get on and tackle the question which really did interest him, the question of our knowledge of other selves. It is not clear that his utterances concerning the external world are always consistent. Certainly they are sometimes obscure and elliptical. To us as students of Dilthey's thought, they are of value less for their own sake than as illustrating his method and outlook; and from that point of view they have considerable value.

Dilthey begins by saying that, for three centuries past, the problem has been debated in the form which Descartes gave to it. It is assumed that we have an immediate certitude of the existence of the self, and of its 'ideas'; but whether these 'ideas' are or reveal a reality independent of the self is held to be open to argument, and the argument has not yet issued in any decisive proof of the existence of such a reality. Yet such a proof is needed; for the reality of an external world is presupposed in all positive enquiry, and a philosophy which fails to 'assure the scientist of the reality of his objects' cannot hold his respect

(*G.S.*, V, 77, 90). The conventional theory is that our sole data for knowledge of the world are sensations and images, both of which can only exist in consciousness; but that because many of these are independent of and resistant to our control, we rightly infer an 'external' cause of them, i.e. a cause which lies outside our consciousness. This cause is the 'object', and sensations are 'referred' to it; but because the inferential process by which we are led to the object is unconscious, we mistakenly come to think that the sense-data themselves are a part of the object, and so we believe that an 'external' world, i.e. a world independent of our consciousness of it, is immediately presented to our senses. This, however, on the conventional view, is a mistake, for the sense-data are mind-dependent; further, since we know the external object only through, or in terms of, the sensations which it produces in us, we cannot be sure what it is like in itself. Thus philosophers believe in the existence of a transcendent object while doubting its knowability, and this brings about an estrangement between philosophy and empirical science, while in philosophy itself it opens the door to unchecked speculation about the nature of the transcendent object.

Kantianism after the time of Kant himself has felt bound to get rid of this unknowable object and to insist on finding the object somehow within experience, even at the cost of adopting phenomenalism or idealism. On this first point, that the object must be found within experience, Dilthey agrees with the Kantians. He enunciates what he calls the 'principle of phenomenality' or 'principle of consciousness', viz. that 'everything which exists for me is subject to the most general condition of being a fact of my consciousness; even external things are given to me only as combinations of facts or processes in consciousness; object and thing only exist for a consciousness and in a consciousness' (*G.S.*, V, 90). In particular, the relation between subject and object, if it is to be known to us at all, cannot be a relation between something in consciousness and something outside, but must have both its terms within consciousness and lie itself wholly within consciousness. 'Every object can be resolved into facts of consciousness, viz. into colour-sensation, sensation of resistance, solidity, weight, combination of these impressions into a unity, etc. And it is useless to say that, although sensations

53

and images are only elements in my consciousness, yet these my impressions and ideas refer to an object outside me. For it is only in the act of consciousness that the contrast, the severance of self and object exists' (*G.S.*, V, 91).

This after all is no more than the 'transcendental point of view' which philosophy brings to bear in contrast with the 'objective empirical point of view' of science and common sense. (Cf. *G.S.*, I, 15, 20.) Yet it is enough to overthrow the Cartesian view which thinks of the objective world as something whose existence has to be inferred from subjective data. The question of the 'real existence' of the 'external world' is not primarily a question of inference at all, but of analysis and definition. We have not to begin by defining 'object', 'reality', 'existence', 'external world' as seems best to us, and then trying to prove that an 'external world' in the sense which we have defined 'exists' in the sense which we have defined. If we do that, our definitions will be arbitrary, and we shall find to our discomfort that we cannot prove our point. We should rather begin with the fact that we *know* there is something which we call an 'external world', and then by analysis discover what it is that we call by this name. This is to let experience and common usage define our terms and at the same time exhibit to us that to which they refer. In Dilthey's own words, we must '*describe analytically* what is given in living experience', and 'make known what is meant by the reality of the external world in the proper sense of this experience' (*G.S.*, V, 133). This is what Dilthey calls the 'standpoint of life'; it is the only way, he holds, by which philosophy can avoid building hypotheses into its foundations.

Agreeing with the Kantians on this fundamental point, Dilthey still finds that they have gone wrong in several respects. They take too intellectual a view of the process by which objects are perceived. Kantianism makes us start with sense-data and synthesise them under the categories. The phenomenon resulting from this synthesis is 'objective' because it is constructed in accordance with principles which hold good for all rational beings, and is itself therefore an element in a coherent system of phenomena intelligible to all thinking subjects. This is to make the object a logical construct, and reduce objectivity to universal validity, which is not really the same thing. Against this Dilthey maintains that the roots of objectivity lie not in the

understanding, but in the will, and that the logical constructions which we do undeniably make are inserted into, and
derive their meaning from, a context of volitional experience.
'The processes of perception and thought, which interpose between stimulus and volitional reaction on the higher levels of
life, expand and diversify only in connection with the instinctive
life. . . . It is out of the private life, out of the instincts, feelings,
volitions which compose it, . . . that I consider the separation of
self and object, of inner and outer within our perceptions to
arise' (*G.S.*, V, 96).

If this is true, most modern theories of knowledge stand convicted of a double error. They have misconceived the nature of
the knower, treating him as no more than a cognitive faculty
working in isolation. 'In the veins of the knowing subject constructed by Locke, Hume and Kant runs no real blood, but the
diluted fluid of reason as bare thought-activity' (*G.S.*, I, xviii).
And they have misconceived the nature of the object by supposing it to consist entirely of representational (*vorstellungs-
mässig*) elements, i.e. sensations, impressions, images, and logical
constructions based on these, and leaving out the characteristics which it has by virtue of its relation to our will. A true
theory of knowledge will 'begin with the totality of our being'
(*G.S.*, I, xviii), and show how, from the joint work of all aspects
of the structural system of mind, our consciousness of the objective world grows up.

How does Dilthey's analysis proceed?

He begins by admitting that sense-data are mind-dependent.
'The subjectivity of sensations is an assured result of science; it
was shown by physics, physiology, and philosophical analysis
alike' (*G.S.*, V, 92). But among our sensations are sensations of
movement, and sometimes this movement is initiated and controlled by us, sometimes not. Whenever it is, we are conscious
not only of the movement, but also of ourselves as initiating and
controlling it. Suppose then that I will to execute a certain
physical movement. This volition, says Dilthey, is a mental act,
immediately experienced, and accompanied by an idea of the
physical movement which is desired and expected to follow. It
gives rise to sensations of muscular tension, and may lead to
sensations corresponding to my desire and expectation. This
series of facts of consciousness, from the act of will to the fulfil-

ment of the expected movement, is what we call the perception of voluntary movement. But it may happen that the expected perceptions do not occur, and instead I have sensations of pressure and other sensations which, when compared with the idea of the expected movement, are judged to be unexpected and contrary to my intention. Meanwhile, the volition does not cease, it increases in determination and expends more physical effort, but the only result is to intensify the unwelcome sensations, and to arouse a feeling of surprise and a painful consciousness of limitation. Here is a new type of volitional and affective experience, viz. 'frustration of intention', which, when experienced in combination with the original impulse of will, constitutes the 'experience of resistance' (*G.S.*, V, 98–105).

Out of this complex experience is built up all awareness of self and not-self. For, first of all, a distinction is made between perceived movements directly controllable by our will and accompanied by the sensations of voluntary movement, and others not so controllable, but accompanied by the experience of resistance; the former class of movements are taken as belonging to ourselves, i.e. to our body, and the latter class as falling outside it, and thus the primary duality of self and other arises in consciousness (*G.S.*, V, 106–7).

Dilthey traces this process back to the embryo, appealing to certain observations made by biologists to show that 'before the child is born it possesses in broad outline a dark, perhaps rather dreamlike consciousness of the distinction of its own life from an external something conditioning it on every side' (*G.S.*, V, 100). At this stage, of course, the only sensations are those of touch, but after birth the other senses come into play, and their data are inserted into the pre-existing scheme of self and not-self (*G.S.*, 108–10). Sensible qualities are found to fall into relatively permanent groups, obeying laws of their own and resisting interference; such a quality-group is called an 'object' (*G.S.*, V, 133), and its 'objectivity' lies in its being regularly accompanied by the volitional and affective experience of frustration. 'The explosion is the best evidence to the dumbfounded chemist of the independent nature of the object' (*G.S.*, V, 116).

Here is the experiential basis of the distinction between self and not-self. This 'self' is not the 'pure knowing subject' of Kantianism, by whose synthetic activities all phenomena (including even the empirical mind and its body) are constructed. Dilthey has no use for such a 'pure knowing subject'. He regards it as an abstraction hypostatised. The subject that really knows is the living organism, and the object is anything which, while appearing within experience, proves itself independent of the organism by resisting its control. The knowing subject experiences his own mental life, and can reflect upon it and make it an object of knowledge to himself; he can also perceive and know the body over which he has immediate control, and which he recognises as part of himself. But there are other elements in his experience which cannot by any stretch of terms be counted as parts or attributes of himself, because they are extraneous to his own organic and mental processes, and outside his control. These elements constitute the 'object' or the 'objective world'.

Dilthey sometimes writes as if the object could be resolved without remainder into sense-data resistant to the subject's control. This, however, is not his complete view. He is always conscious that there is more to the object than this. If we ask 'what more?' his answer is not always given in the same terms. Sometimes it seems more positive, sometimes more guarded. Let us see what he says in his most positive mood, in the *Beiträge*.

We are conscious of the object, he says, not merely as having certain observable qualities, but as a force, a centre of energy, exerting influence upon us. This simply means that we treat it as similar in character to ourselves. For 'we experience our self as an active whole' (*G.S.*, V, 114) in which will passes regularly into movement; i.e. the perception of our own voluntary movements is accompanied by the perception of our will as their cause. Hence, by a simple transference, even when we perceive movement of which our will is not the cause, or when we will to move and find that a resistance is offered, we still perceive this as the expression of will or force (*G.S.*, V, 114, 125). But, Dilthey continues, our own will cannot be the force producing those events which frustrate or limit it, for then it would be acting in opposition to itself. 'When the night-worker finds the concentration of his thoughts all at once painfully interrupted by the crackling of the fire or the extinction of his lamp, it would be he who on the one hand is wrapped up in this concentration, and at the same time forcibly breaks through it. The attempt to conceive this produces complete vertigo; this is due to the fact that

57

we are trying to conceive in one mind and at the same moment two mutually conflicting intentions of will. This is as impossible as to think at once the affirmation and the denial of the same thing' (*G.S.*, V, 115–16, cf. 134). Therefore we perceive such events as manifestations of an active force distinct from ourselves, which is the object or at least the dynamic core of the object.

The introduction of this new element into Dilthey's theory serves only to emphasise his opposition to the Neo-Kantians. It is now clearer than ever that, for him, the object is not a logical construction shaped by *a priori* forms, but a 'central living reality' (*G.S.*, V, 104). 'The object has the same centrality (*Kernhaftigkeit*) as the self. For it is not constructed in the void by thought, but has in the lived experience of will its own life and its independent centre' (*G.S.*, V, 132–3). 'There exist two independencies, two volitional unities, and that is the experience underlying the expressions: unity, externality, and plurality of wills or objects in general. . . . Both are conscious facts, and we can say that consciousness embraces both' (*G.S.*, V, 134).

If the Neo-Kantian view which makes the understanding construct the object is wrong, so also is the conventional view which makes us infer the object as the cause of our sense-data. Dilthey tells us that the active force which is the kernel of the object is not inferred, but given. In saying this he is stretching language somewhat; for of course he does not mean that the objective force is actually present and immediately experienced (*erlebt*) by us as we experience (*erleben*) our own acts of will. He means that it is a kind of reflection of ourselves in the not-self, a projection of our own inner life into the world around; but he thinks that this projection is unreflective, immediate, and automatic, and presents the object to us as 'wearing the character of immediacy' (*G.S.*, V, 104). Hence he can say that the force whose sensible manifestations we perceive is 'present to us' in them, and is thus 'given'. 'In the experiences of frustration and resistance the presence of a force is *given*. . . . For frustration and resistance include force as much as impulse does. As the consciousness of impulse includes the experience that I am exerting a force, so the consciousness of frustration and resistance includes (the experience) that a force is acting upon me' (*G.S.*, V, 131–2).

But though we need no causal inference to tell us that an active force is present, we do need one to tell us that this force is other than ourselves. That is where Dilthey's instance of the night-worker comes in. The extinction of his lamp is *given* as the manifestation of an active force, but that this force is other than himself is *inferred* from the fact that it frustrates his will. Inference does play an essential part, but a limited one, in our knowledge of the external world; it assures us of the world's externality, but not of its existence. Before we begin to infer, we already have something given, about which we can infer, something which is not constructed in a void where no experience is, but is itself a datum of experience. As force, its presence is given; its character as external and alien is inferred. And so we can understand the following (at first sight inconsistent) remarks from the *Beiträge*. 'In the sensation of resistance, a reality independent of me is *not given* in an immediate volitional experience. The doctrine of the immediate givenness of the reality of the external world does not prove tenable at this point. But on the other hand—and this is our point—the reality of the external world is *not inferred*, i.e. deduced, by *mere* thought-processes, from the data of consciousness. It is rather the business ·of the said conscious processes *to mediate a volitional experience, the frustration of intention*, which is included in the consciousness of resistance and discloses the central living reality of that which is independent of us' (*G.S.*, V, 104). 'We *do not construct* an outer reality in *thought* by *subsumption* under the conception of *cause*: in the experiences of frustration and resistance the presence of a force is *given*, which force we are then compelled to regard as an external one, separate from us' (*G.S.*, V, 131). The external world, in short, is given, in the sense that the basis of our idea of it is a given force, but also not given, in the sense that our recognition of its externality is due to operations of thought.

Has Dilthey succeeded by this analysis in placing our knowledge of the physical world on a firm basis? In one sense, yes. He sees that the solution of the problem lies in perpetual experience, and can be found by analysing that experience and showing what our words mean in terms of it (*G.S.*, V, 130). Idealist theories, which necessarily involve unobservable entities and processes, vanish when we keep within the empirical realm. But Dilthey's account of perpetual experience itself is not free from difficulty.

Can we be certain, in the end, that our interpretation of perceived movements as manifestations of force or energy is justified? Dilthey says that the unsophisticated human consciousness always does so interpret them, and goes on to show how on this foundation a dynamic view of the universe gets built up not only in common sense, but in poetry and mythology (*G.S.*, V, 126), in philosophy, and even to some extent in science (*G.S.*, V, 134–5, *Bw.D.Y.*,[1] p. 106). The common-sense conceptions of a *thing* and of *power* are derived directly from the experiences of the active and passive self. The Aristotelian conceptions of δύναμις and ἐνέργεια and the traditional philosophical conceptions of *substance* and *cause* are merely sophisticated versions of the same experience. But there are many passages, in writings both earlier and later than the *Beiträge*, which show that Dilthey does not really think much of these concepts as pointers to the truth. He even speaks of them in one place as having been a bar to scientific progress, and calls them 'the hardest form of superstition to analyse scientifically and dispel' (*G.S.*, V, 53). In the *Einleitung in die Geisteswissenschaften* (1883) he argues at length that they add nothing to our knowledge of nature (*G.S.*, I, 359 ff.), and that, derived as they are not from pure thought but from lived experience, they cannot even be unambiguously defined, and fill philosophy with antinomies (*Einl.*, bk 2 *pass.*). He quotes with approval Du Bois-Reymond's argument against Häckel's attempt to credit matter with a rudimentary will. 'A will,' he says, 'which is supposed to will, whether it wills to or not, and this in direct proportion to the product of the masses and in inverse proportion to the square of the distance, is a contradiction in terms' (*G.S.*, I, 14). Something similar is true of other more abstract and impersonal concepts which have played a part in physics and mechanics, e.g. 'impetus', 'momentum', 'live force', 'energy'. The tendency of modern science is to replace these dynamic concepts by others which are purely mathematical in character, and it is significant that in recent philosophy even substance and causality have been redefined, e.g. by Kant, in purely quantitative terms.

Can we then find reality in the concepts of modern physics? Dilthey does not absolutely reject them. He speaks of chemistry as 'gradually approaching juster views about the constitution of matter' (*G.S.*, V, 45 = I, 28). But these concepts are valid

[1] *Briefwechsal zwischen Wilhelm Dilthey u. dam Grafen Paul Yorck v. Wastenburg, 1877–97;* edited by S. V. D. Schulenburg. Hall, 1923.

only for the purposes and within the limits of natural science. They are hypothetical constructions, which go beyond experience in order to 'explain' it, but must not be taken seriously as describing the nature of a reality lying behind the phenomena. As early as the *Einleitung* we are told that 'our picture of all nature turns out to be a mere shadow cast by a reality hidden from us' (*G.S.*, I, xviii), and in Dilthey's latest writings this point of view is increasingly brought out. It is clearly stated in the second of the *Studien* of 1905. 'What is perceived with the character of givenness offers resistance, it cannot be altered, it exerts pressure upon the subject. From these relations in which perceptions stand arises the character of objective necessity with which their content . . . is affirmed in the processes of objective apprehension. Thus, the character of givenness, which is peculiar to sense-perception, is the basis of the necessity of every statement about objects within sensuous apprehension. If their character of givenness refers back to something which is not itself perception, yet this reference is without any content, and the circle of apprehension, which always demands a what, a content, is enclosed within the immanent relations of its positively determined elements' (*G.S.*, VII, 34).

This conclusion, though negative in itself, has great positive importance for Dilthey. It brings to view what Rickert has called 'the limitations of the concepts constructed in natural science' (*die Grenzen der naturwissenschaftlichen Begriffsbildung*). According to this view the concepts of natural science, being valid not absolutely but only for the purposes of natural science itself, have no prescriptive rights in the field of the human studies. Dilthey insists upon this, because he finds in it a charter of freedom. If either metaphysics or natural science could give an account of the physical world which was more than relatively true, it would be incumbent upon the philosopher whose interest lay in the human studies to relate the fundamental presuppositions of the human studies to the truths ascertained elsewhere, and to incorporate his doctrine of history and society in a wider system where the relation between nature and mind should be presented as it really is. He would have to embark, like Fichte, Schelling, Hegel, or Lotze, upon an ontology. But, if metaphysics is silent and natural science speaks only for itself, the human studies may regard the external world in any way they find appropriate for themselves, and their philosopher need only accept and elucidate their attitude, without having to go further and harmonise it with something else.

In this way Dilthey is able to side-track the whole of general metaphysics and natural philosophy, and take into consideration no hypotheses about the external world except such as the human studies themselves may turn out to require. And it turns out that they require none. The external world, in fact, is treated in the human studies only in relation to feeling and willing subjects, sc. as that which affects the behaviour of men, and furthers or hinders human purposes. But this is exactly the view of it which Dilthey has already taken at the beginning of his epistemological analysis. The 'standpoint of life', in fact, which is in any case the starting-point for epistemology in general, turns out also to be an integral element in the special standpoint of the human studies themselves, and therefore to be a point beyond which the *Grundlegung der Geisteswissenschaften* need not try to go. 'External world is a relation of pressure, of relation between impulse and resistance, which is contained in life. Its reality lies only in this vital relation. Its reality means nothing but these relations to the structure of mind in the human studies. Hence it contains nothing of any transcendence over against consciousness. The natural-scientific conception of external objects belongs to a wholly different world of categories. Hypothesis etc.' (*G.S.*, VII, 332).

In a word, Dilthey in the *Beiträge* has made a raid into territory which he finds he need not try to occupy. He has gone into the question of the real nature of the physical world, and his findings are inconclusive. But he has also analysed the way in which the physical world appears in human consciousness; and for the purposes of the human studies, and of a philosophy of the human studies, that really is all that matters, so far as the physical world is concerned. What does matter supremely, however, for a philosophy of the human studies is the way in which we come to know of other human minds, and the extent to which we can understand what goes on in them. All the energy which Dilthey saves by evading the problem of the physical world is poured into the study of this problem instead. The question of our knowledge of other minds will be examined in detail in Chapter Five below, but something must be said here to indicate how Dilthey approaches it, and how his answer fits into the general scheme of his theory of knowledge.

. The fundamental process, on which all our knowledge of other selves depends, is the projection of our own inner life into objects around us, and the attribution to such objects of a mental life similar in structure to our own. We have met this process already. We have seen how we tend automatically and unreflectively to interpret the movements of physical objects as manifesting an inner life, will, or force. We have seen, too, that the attempt to work out this interpretation into a coherent account of the nature of the physical world breaks down. Why? Because we have no information as to what constitutes a real unit of matter or energy, because we have no precise information as to what feelings and impulses may lie behind the physical movements we observe, and because we do not know how the active force which we take to be the core of the object is related to its sensible appearances. When we come to deal with human beings, the case is different. Here we have our unit, the human individual, clearly marked out. Here too we meet an object whose physical structure and behaviour are so like our own as to demand interpretation in terms of a consciousness closely resembling our own. And here we can understand the relation between inner life and outward expression, because we experience the same relation in ourselves.

This is where Dilthey's account begins in the *Beiträge*. Having experience in ourselves of the connection between certain 'inner states' or 'mental processes' and certain types of bodily 'expression' (*Ausdruck, Äusserung*), and then perceiving similar bodily expressions in external objects, we 'swiftly and unnoticeably' pass to a belief in similar mental states as the cause of those expressions (*G.S.*, V, 110). I perceive e.g. in a human body, not my own, the physical expression proper to a certain feeling, and the sight of it automatically induces in me a kind of echo or reverberation of that feeling. I attribute to the human being before me a lived experience of the kind which is indicated by his expression and is now reverberating in my own consciousness. Then, since I know by inner experience that all mental facts stand in a structural context, I look for the structural context of this feeling in him. Consulting further physical expressions of his, which reveal to me further mental facts

63

about him, and piecing all these together, I build up the reflection (*Nachbild*) in my consciousness of a self-contained and self-conditioning structural process of mental life which I attribute to him. The reflection (*Nachbild*) exists only in my consciousness, and coheres by virtue of the structure of my consciousness; but my mind, in constructing it, operates with an altered balance, with 'the emphasis on types of attitude, powers, feelings, strivings, tendencies of thought' differently distributed (*G.S.*, VII, 215); in short, my mind within this process conforms to a rhythm not its own. A structural process so constituted, though existing in my consciousness, is no more a segment of my own life than are the natural forces which interrupt my activities; it 'refers to' the physical body whose expression conveys it to me, I read it into that body by an 'inner amplification' (*innere Ergänzung*), and the mental and bodily factors so linked in my consciousness constitute my idea (*Vorstellung*) of an 'other person'. In building up my consciousness of this other self, I am as it were 'living over' (*nachleben*) a prescribed theme, 'feeling my way' (*nachtasten*) into the given expressions, and the result is a 'reconstruction of another person's inner life' (*Nachbilden des fremden Inneren: G.S.*, V, 111, 113).

In this manner the world of which we are conscious comes to be peopled with our kin, every one a structural unit or independent living centre. New relationships arise: relationships of sympathy and sharing of experience (*Mitfühlen, Mitleiden, Mitleben*); moral relationships, based on the mutual reverence of persons as 'ends in themselves' and the solidarity of mankind; social relationships of leadership and dependence, association and conflict. These relations are the substance of history; in them we live and move, in them to the fullest extent we experience reality, and through this reality alone can we acquire self-knowledge. For the nature of man is not to be read in the secrecy of his own breast, but where it is writ large on the pages of history and society (*G.S.*, V, 111–13, 135).

As with physical objects, so here with human persons, their 'reality' lies in their independence of our will. Persons now living, whom we meet, can show that independence in obvious ways, and can also take the initiative and impose themselves upon us. But even historical characters can do the same; they draw and hold our attention, they resist interpretation on the

64

lines which we should perhaps prefer, they enter into our lives as a living influence. Here, indeed, is the real meaning of historical knowledge and experience. It is not a matter of knowing *about* people who lived and acted in the past, it is a matter of feeling their impact upon us here and now. 'The reality of historical personages does not for us depend exclusively upon interpretative and critical inferences, which e.g. by the thread of causality reach back from the historical narratives of Ranke, Häusser, and innumerable others about Luther to the printing of his works, letters, and table-talk, and to the statements of those who saw him, and then back from these to Luther himself, who added letter to letter, or whose features were seen by a contemporary.... The reality of Luther, Frederick the Great, or Goethe takes on a heightened energy and centrality (*Kernhaftigkeit*) from their constant influence upon our own self, i.e. from the determination of this self by the will of those powerful persons as it moves forward creating wider and wider circles in history. They are realities for us because their great personality acts upon us as a forceful will' (*G.S.*, V, 113–14).

Dilthey sets epistemology two chief problems: the reality of the objects of knowledge and the validity of the principles and processes of thought. We have examined his answer to the first of these questions, and must now turn to the second. At this point again we may recognise his opposition to Kantianism, for the very order in which he takes the two questions is the reverse of the Kantian order. Kantianism begins by 'deducing' the principles of thought as the *a priori* forms of all possible experience, and then declares objects to be 'real' or 'objective' in so far as they form a coherent system within these principles. Dilthey makes lived experience the primary reality, and finds the reality even of the external world in the lived experiences of action and reaction which signalise our dynamic involvement with the not-self. Thought enters in, of course, but only to clarify and integrate what is given in lived experience. As Dilthey himself says, looking back at the end of his life, his aim throughout was to establish 'a theory of knowledge on realist or critically objective lines'; and in so doing, 'in contrast with the idealistic doctrine of reason, I did not go back to an *a priori* of the theoretical understanding or of practical reason, founded on a pure self, but to the structural relations in the mental system, which can be actually pointed to (*die aufzeigbar sind*)' (*G.S.*, VII, 13 n.). Thought is thus purged of its Kantian megalomania and brought back to its proper place as the interpreter of lived experience. It remains now to round off our account of Dilthey's theory of knowledge by examining directly the functions of thought and the foundations on which its validity rests.

There is one essay by Dilthey which is devoted entirely to this question, viz. *Erfahren u. Denken* (1892). It is a direct attack on the coherence theory of truth in the form given to it by Sigwart and Lotze. At the head of it stands the motto: *amicus Socrates, amicus Plato, magis amica veritas*. From this and from numerous references elsewhere, especially in writings of Dilthey's latest years, his standpoint emerges clearly.

But is there really a problem? Lotze argues that there is not: for we cannot argue whether the principles of thought are objectively valid or not without using these principles in the very argument which is supposed to enquire into them, and thus the argument will move in a circle. It is impossible to go behind thought. If we are not to stop thinking altogether, we must make up our minds to trust thought, and make its validity an absolute presupposition.

Dilthey has no difficulty in showing that this is beside the point. Unquestionably we cannot go behind thought in the sense of arguing whether it is valid or not. But we can ask what makes it valid, and this is a useful enquiry; for it reveals that thought is not a self-contained self-based system, containing its own validity and objectivity in itself, as Kantianism supposes, but is based on experience, and has its meaning and its objectivity wholly in that relation (*G.S.*, V, 82–3). There is indeed a kind of 'circle in thought' (*G.S.*, I, 419 *et pass.*), but it is not a vicious circle. It only means that we cannot wait for logic and epistemology to provide us with a criterion of truth before we begin to think; we possess our criterion and use it in building up the empirical sciences, and afterwards logic and epistemology come in to reveal to us the nature and significance of the criterion which we have been using all along. Empirical science and epistemology reciprocally support one another, and their coherence with one another and their common dependence on lived experience is the sufficient vindication of both.

The common function of all thought-processes, says Dilthey,

is to 'represent' (*repräsentiren*) in a clear light to cognition the characters, contents, and structural relations of lived experiences. The word *repräsentiren*, signifying etymologically to bring something before someone's notice, as in 'making representations', or again in 'representing' a character on the stage, is frequently used by Dilthey in various connections from 1883 onwards, but is used in the *Studien* of 1905 and in later writings to cover all the forms and processes of thought, from the simplest up to the most complex. Within this general conception he distinguishes various ways in which thought fulfils its function.

Fundamental among these is the work of 'clarifying' (*aufklären*) the data of experience. This is done by the 'elementary logical operations' which Dilthey calls 'silent thought'—i.e. thought in its prediscursive stage, whose operation, inseparable from sensation and lived experience, raises these to the level of perception. In sensation or in lived experience as such we are aware of 'qualitatively determined reality', but it is silent thought which makes us perceive relations between the qualitative determinations of it. Thus we perceive, e.g. not merely colour, but colours of different hues and tones; not merely pleasure, but pleasures of varying kinds and degrees. These relations are as truly given as the terms they relate, though without the process of comparison they would not be noticeable (*merklich*); but when this silent comparison is made, then they are observed as aspects of the given, themselves given in it, and needing no explicit reflection to make us conscious of them. This leads us on further to the process of separation, whereby we hold apart in consciousness the elements of the given; and when we separate in idea what is inseparable in fact, considering e.g. colour apart from any extension, this process is called abstraction. But elements so separated or abstracted can be recombined and perceived as wholes; thus we can perceive series of visible contents in space and time, or sound-complexes such as a harmony or a melody (*G.S.*, VII, 122–4, cf. 300–1).

The processes here described are an elementary form of thought; for they apprehend relations. They do not make these relations, or impose them on the data. They find them there, and all that we do in silent thought is to explore what is given. But, since comparison and abstraction lead to the discovery of universals and the exploration of logical relations, it is evident that silent thought contains the germ of all the more complex forms of discursive thought, which are thus shown to be continuous with perception itself (*G.S.*, VII, 42, 122–4, 300–2). The actual data of perception are fragmentary and full of gaps. Memory and creative imagination come in to fill the gaps and build up a *Totalvorstellung*. Imaginative reproduction, taken a stage further, makes possible the framing of general ideas (*G.S.*, VII, 33–5, 124, 39 = 128). Then we advance to discursive thought, and to language, which is its necessary vehicle. At this point Dilthey draws largely upon the second volume of Husserl's *Logische Untersuchungen* (*G.S.*, VII, 39–41). He goes on to describe briefly how, by more and more abstract conceptions, by more and more complex systems of inference, by methods increasingly adapted to the subject-matter in each sphere of enquiry, the edifice of human knowledge is gradually built up. The whole system is like a pyramid, where bodies of scientific doctrine rest on empirical generalisations and hypothetical constructions, and these rest on judgments of perception, and these in turn rest on the data of experience. Even the most general laws of thought are found in the end to be the expression of relations which can be observed in every thought-experience as such (*G.S.*, VII, 125–7). In short, the truth, and even the meaningfulness, of any logical structure depends on its referability to some datum or data of experience (*G.S.*, VII, 38, 126 *et pass.*).

Is Kant then wholly set aside and refuted? Was he quite wrong in saying that connection cannot be given, but must be made? Are we to say, for example, that the causal relation is *found* by *observation* in the data of external perception? Not altogether. This is not what Dilthey means. All forms of connection, including what Kant calls the 'categories', are indeed known to us from experience, but not all from outer experience. We must now follow Dilthey in his account of how the categories are obtained.

He begins by saying that the data of experience are not so utterly formless as Kant says they are. Certain formal relationships must necessarily be present in any qualitatively differentiated manifold as such, and can be elicited from it by simple analysis. They constitute what Dilthey calls the 'formal categories': unity and multiplicity, likeness and difference, whole and part, degree, and other elementary concepts of that kind. All the forms of discursive thought, as analysed in formal logic, and all the fundamental concepts of mathematics, can be reduced to these formal categories. They are a network within which all thought about any subject-matter must be enclosed. They are applicable to all possible objects of thought, but they express the peculiar nature of none of them; and, as without them nothing can be understood, so nothing can be understood with them alone (*G.S.*, VII, 192, 196–7, 302).

But the formal aspect of experience is richer than this. Each realm of experience has formal characteristics, peculiar to itself, which distinguish it from the rest of experience and are the basis of its ordered unity. The physical world has space, substance, causal interaction, and so on; the world of mind has duration, creative freedom, value, significance, and the like. These categories express the distinctive structure of a particular world of objects, and are the basis of all real understanding of it. Dilthey calls them the 'real categories' (*loc. cit.*). And it is just these which Kant says are imposed by the experiencing subject. Is he right? Dilthey thinks he is obviously wrong. After all, when we find that two colours cannot be seen together except side by side, while we cannot put tones side by side at all, but only combine them in a chord, it should be obvious that the nature of the sensations has in itself the formal characteristic which forces upon us these modes of synthesis (*G.S.*, V, 77–9, 149–50). Similarly the data of inner experience are instinct with form— in this case the structural system which we have already analysed —and all that thought has to do is to elicit this structural system and pursue its ramifications as far as it can.

The structural system is the key not only to the understanding of mental life, but also to the formation of a coherent conception of nature. The formal aspects of sense-data do not by themselves suffice for that purpose. Dilthey may have found, in the perception of colours and sounds, a formal element which is not imposed upon the data, but is inherent in their character; but this alone does not enable us to construct a world. For that we need unity of structure, regularity, permanence amid change, and the like, and Dilthey himself allows that these are not given in sense-data, but are read into them by the interpreting mind. 'The senses give only coexistence and succession, without a causal order in this simultaneous or consecutive existence, and therefore causal order arises, in our apprehension of nature, only by amplification' (*G.S.*, V, 140). If this regular order is not to be derived from a transcendentally legislative intellect, whence can Dilthey derive it? From our experience of the structural system in our own inner life. The mind, in attempting to discover the nature of the external world, ascribes to it by transference the same structural unity of which it is conscious in itself.

We have seen above how this happens, and how the concept of a thing, and the more sophisticated concepts of substance and causality, are formed. 'Nature' herself, when personified as she used to be in the older philosophy and science, is a projection of the same inner life upon the stage of the physical world as a whole. The categories of substance and cause, therefore, though not built up from our sensory experience of the external world, are not *a priori* forms of the understanding. They are abstracted from our experience of inner life, and projected into the physical world. What happens to them afterwards, when physical science formulates its methods and presuppositions, and the dynamic concepts begin to be edged out of physics in favour of purely mathematical ones—all that is another story. But it is the story of physics, not of common human reason. It is the error of Kant and his followers to have mistaken the abstract formulae of modern science for the full-blooded concepts of common sense, and treated what is no more than a methodological convenience as the precondition of all possible experience.

We have now examined Dilthey's conception of the structural system in lived experience, and seen how he makes it the key to knowledge both of the natural world and of the world of mind. With this the first stage in his theory of knowledge is complete. But it is only the first stage. If knowledge is to be made the object of a descriptive analysis, we cannot do less than analyse all the branches of knowledge that we have. Hitherto we have discussed our knowledge of the external world and of our own minds, as if there were nothing else to know. But our knowledge also embraces values, and besides these, imperatives and rules of conduct; here are two ordered branches of knowledge which cannot be resolved into knowledge of fact, physical or mental, but stand as independent systems side by side with it. The task of epistemology cannot be completed without an analysis of these systems; such an analysis is 'the condition to which the success of a theory of knowledge is bound' (*G.S.*, VII, 11). It remains, therefore, to examine how this enquiry is conducted by Dilthey himself; and this demands another chapter.

CHAPTER THREE

DILTHEY's theory of value-judgments may be dealt with much more briefly than his theory of our knowledge of existing things; not because it is less important, but because it is comparatively simple, underwent little change, and is moreover only another application of principles which we have met before. In this field, as elsewhere, his main antagonism is to orthodox Kantianism, though other doctrines also come in for criticism. His appeal, again, here as elsewhere, is to a descriptive analysis of experience.

The Kantianism which Dilthey has chiefly in mind is not that of Kant himself, but that of the Kantian schools of his own day. In discussing our knowledge of the existing world, he criticises Kantianism in the form given to it first of all by Lotze and Sigwart, and later by the 'Neo-Kantian' school of Marburg, under the guidance of Cohen and Natorp. When he turns to discuss our knowledge of values and principles of conduct, the place of these opponents is taken by the younger branch of the Neo-Kantian school, the Baden school of Windelband and Rickert.

The doctrines of these philosophers have grown out of those of the Marburg school very much as the philosophy of Fichte grew out of that of Kant. For this reason, the Baden philosophy has also been called Neo-Fichteanism. They agree with the Marburg Neo-Kantians that the object of knowledge has no existence apart from consciousness, but is created by the transcendental ego through the act of judgment. But they try to avoid a merely subjective idealism, and to make their theory do justice to the realist convictions of the plain man, who believes that, however active his mind may be in knowing, there is a reality transcending his mind, to which, on pain of error, his thinking must conform. The Baden philosophers admit that the individual thinking subject is checked and controlled by the necessity of conforming to something beyond himself, something which he neither makes by his own activity nor finds given in his sensations. Here the plain man is right. But he is wrong when he regards this something-beyond-himself as an independently existing thing. Properly understood, it is simply a logical necessity, the necessity of interpreting phenomena coherently. It is this which compels the mind to build up out of its sense-data a world of permanent objects, governed by physical laws, and deriving its ultimate structure from the categories of the understanding. This world of objects is wholly a mental construct, though the individual thinking subject is not its maker, and feels himself under an external constraint in building up his knowledge of it. The individual thinker *is* constrained. It is from the transcendental self that the initial data, the categories, and the actual order of nature really flow. The transcendental self is a reality which transcends the individual self, not in the sense of being a separate entity, but in the sense that it is the common ground of all such individual selves and also of the external world which they share, the ground of all facts which enter into the experience of such individual selves and also of all norms of value by which their activities are directed. All their thinking and willing is the transcendental self thinking and willing in and through them. It is by this, not by any independently existing external world, that our empirical thinking is conditioned. The categories which give structure to the experienced world are not the reflection in consciousness of an independent reality, but the transcendental norm of truth. From this transcendental norm, in the last resort, all concepts of 'reality' and 'objectivity' are derived. 'Reality' and 'objectivity' signify not a pre-existing object which thought is to explore, but an 'infinite task' for thought to execute.

This means, continue the Baden philosophers, that behind the many obvious differences between cognitive and practical experience there lurks an important likeness. Practical experience, as Kant in his ethical writings made clear, is dominated by an *a priori* norm of conduct, the moral law, whose demands transcend all possibilities of empirical action, but to which all agents are under a moral necessity to conform. But cognitive experience is also a branch of activity, a constructing of objects of consciousness, and it is governed by an *a priori* norm of truth, viz. the system of categories, which sets empirical thinking subjects a task which transcends their powers, though they are under a logical necessity to keep on working at it. In both instances we have an activity of the mind, giving rise to a distinctive realm of experience, and governed by an *a priori* norm which transcends all empirical realisations of it. Need we add that (to complete the list of Kant's *Critiques*) aesthetic experience also is found to be based upon a mental activity, with an *a priori* norm of beauty to which it ought to conform? All experience is summed up in these three spheres, each of them presided over by a norm. These norms are what the Baden school call *values*: abstract, universal, *a priori*, having no actual existence (*Wirklichkeit*), but possessing validity (*Geltung*), they are the objects of a pure rational knowledge which is philosophy. Philosophy accordingly consists of three *a priori* sciences of value: logic, ethics, and aesthetics.

Philosophy, however, is not the only study which has to do with values. Although in their *a priori* majesty the values stand high above experience, yet there can be no experience which does not in some degree embody them; for there can be no experience without the various activities of the mind, which follow the values as their guiding principles. All that we know can be resolved into a complex of particular truths, each of them an embodiment of the *a priori* value of truth, all our conduct can be resolved into a succession of moral actions, and all aesthetic and artistic experience is a pursuit of beauty, whether in nature or in the works of men's hands. Particular truths, moral actions, or beautiful objects are alike in being empirical embodiments of the *a priori* values, and may themselves be called values. Practical reason lays upon humanity the endless task of generating and appreciating particular values of these three types, criticising and amending them perpetually to bring them into closer accord with their transcendental archetypes. The task is fulfilled in and through a multitude of closely interrelated activities such as science and scholarship, philosophy, private and public morality, economic, legal, and political systems, art and religion: and these activities taken all together as the fulfilment of a single task are what we mean by *culture* (*Kultur*).

The realisation of cultural values in the course of time, the various forms which they assume, the historical circumstances

74

of their realisation—these are the object of that group of studies which in common German usage are called the *Geisteswissenschaften*. Windelband and Rickert and their followers find this name unsatisfactory. They prefer to speak of the group of studies in question as the historical studies (*Geschichtswissenschaften*) or the cultural studies (*Kulturwissenschaften*).[1] Unlike philosophy which studies the absolute values in their purity, without reference to time or place, the cultural and historical studies are concerned with the empirical realisation of the values in the temporally conditioned life of men.

Now, say Windelband and Rickert, the method of the cultural studies is radically different from that of natural science, and it is a task for philosophy, a task too long neglected, to work out the logic of the cultural studies and set it in its proper relation to that of the natural sciences. The work of the cultural studies is to describe and classify all products of cultural activity, to elicit the underlying principles to which the mind has conformed in producing them, and to exhibit each particular cultural achievement as a contribution to a wider system such as the development of a science, a movement in art or religion or politics, or in the last resort the development of a whole civilisation. It is by relation to such wider systems that the merit and importance of particular works or actions can be judged.

But here a difficulty arises. It is impossible, with the methods of historical scholarship employed in the cultural studies, to discover principles or norms which have more than an empirical generality, circumscribed by time and place; principles which are unquestioned throughout one culture-area or period may be wholly unrecognised in another. The historical and cultural studies as such, therefore, know of no standards by which to judge of historical events and cultural achievements, except those standards which were recognised by the agents responsible for the events and achievements, or by observers who have watched and judged their actions; and all these standards are historically limited and relative. If the historian ventures to judge the past by his own standards, these are relative too. And yet on the other hand the study of history and culture is not

---

[1] The equivalence of these terms is not exact, because the *Kulturwissenschaften* or *Geschichtswissenschaften* of the Baden school do not include psychology, whereas Dilthey's *Geisteswissenschaften* do. See below, pp. 211–2, 226.

complete until we rise to absolute standards, viz. the *a priori* norms of value, and interpret history in a universally valid way in the light of these. This interpretation, which cannot be made by the historical and cultural studies themselves, is made by the philosophy of history, which is thus neither more nor less than the application of the rational principles laid down in logic, ethics, and aesthetics, to the interpretation and evaluation of the cultural activities and products which the cultural studies describe. In the philosophy of history, our value-judgments upon the facts of historical experience acquire absolute validity, while philosophy, passing from the universal to the particular, achieves concreteness.

Windelband and Rickert claim that their philosophy is the inevitable outcome of the work of Kant, taken as a whole in the light of his three *Critiques*. To an outside observer it will probably seem that they have done to Neo-Kantianism what Fichte did to the original Kantianism. It is a fact that their influence told strongly in favour of the revival of Hegelian ideas in Germany in the first third of this century.

It will be seen that the main line of thought is the same in this general doctrine of values as it was in the logic and epistemology of the Marburg school. Dilthey's objection to it also follows the same lines; that is, he says it is a theoretical construction which does not answer to the realities of life. The transcendental self with its apparatus of *a priori* norms is not a fact of experience, but a hypothesis introduced in order to explain the facts of experience. This it fails to do. A better account can be given without it, by an empirical analysis and description which 'understands life in terms of itself'.

For example, if we apply such a descriptive method to the phenomena of the moral life, it yields a quite un-Kantian result. The driving force in human life is not 'pure reason'; it is our 'bundle' of basic instincts. When Kant speaks of 'reason' as a power heterogeneous from the instincts and capable of controlling them in the light of a principle of its own, he is referring to something real, but is wholly misconceiving its nature. 'Reason' in the moral sphere is not a distinct faculty, independent of our instinctive nature and able to dictate to it. 'Reason' here is merely a name for the self-developing and self-organising power which is inherent in the structure of the mind. It is this which controls and disciplines the impulses and desires of each moment. The structural system, when functioning healthily, tends always towards greater coherence. When we reflect on moral issues at large, the ideal which we set before ourselves is this coherent development of the mind and character. When we act on intuitive judgments inspired by 'moral feeling', it is a dim inchoate recognition of this same ideal which finds expression in these judgments and this feeling.[1]

If the transcendental self and pure reason are thus set aside, there is only one source from which our value-judgments can come, viz. lived experience; and the problem for a philosophy of values will be to show how they arise from this source. It is not merely a question of accounting for a momentary liking or dislike which we may feel for some perceived object, or for a momentary desire or aspiration or sense of moral constraint. Our value-consciousness does not consist of isolated moments of feeling or isolated intuitive judgments like these. There is a complex system of verbal utterances relating to values, ideals, and duties. Not only in philosophy is there such a system, but in ordinary life. Kant is right in remarking what a subtle casuist the plain man can be at times. Dilthey himself is clear that our judgments in these spheres are not merely personal and temperamental. They have a certain 'objectivity', they can 'become objects of universally valid knowledge (*Wissen*)' (*G.S.*, VII, 297) if they are properly analysed and co-ordinated. They can be 'expressed in universal form and referred to tenable grounds' (*ibid.*). If it were not so, the Kantian philosophy of rational principles would not even be plausible. There are indeed general principles running through our values and our moral decisions, and these can be elicited and expressed in a way which commands general (though not strictly universal) agreement. The problem for Dilthey is to show how this can be so, if the Kantian explanation of it is not true. What precisely is the basis in experience from which value-judgments and moral precepts arise? How do they come to be generalised and systematised as we see they are in ordinary human thinking? What is the basis of these general formulae and principles, what is their 'validity' or claim on us, if they are not pronouncements of an *a priori* legislative reason?

[1] See the fuller account of Dilthey's moral theory in the following chapter.

Dilthey answers the first of these questions by going back to his analysis of the structural system in mental life. We saw in the previous chapter how he distinguishes three types of attitude which the conscious subject can take towards the content of which he is conscious. In his theory of knowledge he explored in detail the structure of the cognitive attitude, describing the various acts and processes in which it finds expression and the manner in which they work together to build up our knowledge of self and world. Now we must follow him in a similar, though briefer, analysis of the structure of the attitudes of feeling and will. For Dilthey's contention is that value-judgments and precepts are not the expression of cognitive experiences and activities, but of emotions and volitions. They are not 'judgments' (*Urteile*), but emotive and volitional utterances.

It is of course possible to make 'judgments' about our inner experiences, whether they be cognitive or affective or conational experiences. Any experience can be made an object of inner perception, and on this we can base a proposition which asserts as a fact that I have the experience in question. I can say 'I know this', 'I like this', or 'I am resolved upon this'. Autobiography, biography, the general science of psychology, in short a very great deal of our knowledge in the human studies, is based on propositions of this kind. But there is another kind of verbal expression which does not *assert that I have* a certain experience, but *gives direct utterance to* that experience. The proposition itself is such an expression, if we consider it for a moment not as asserting that which it asserts, but as giving evidence of, or expressing (*not* asserting) my own state of mind in believing that which it asserts. That is the natural form of expression for a cognitive experience; by *talking overtly about* the object which I cognise, it also *gives expression to* my mental state in cognising it. There are corresponding verbal forms for the affective and volitional types of act or attitude. Dilthey says in one place that the natural expression of a feeling is an exclamation, and that of an act of will is a precept or imperative[1] (*G.S.*, VII, 296). And he

---

[1] Not exclusively; for a few sentences later he says that the words 'I shall act according to my convictions' are 'not a judgment' (*kein Urteil*) (*ibid.*), because, or in so far as, they are not a statement of something about myself which I have learned by self-scrutiny. What are they then? The direct expression of a volitional act, a resolve.

holds that value-judgments are expressions of feeling, while precepts, maxims, imperatives are expressions of acts of will.

Such expressions of feeling or will are often clothed in a grammatical form which conceals their real sense; for ostensibly they are descriptions of the object, and assert that it possesses some quality such as 'beauty' or 'goodness' or 'rightness'. These qualities, however, are really pseudo-qualities, fictitious attributes, reflections back into the object of the affective or volitional responses which it evokes, or is capable of evoking, in us. 'A value is for me what I have experienced in feeling as valuable or what I can relive. A good in the strict sense is merely that which my will can set itself as an end' (*G.S.*, VII, 297). Obligation, too, is something about me who am bound, not something about the act to whose performance I am bound. 'Obligation, with the content enjoined, is not a predicate. If I take the statement (*Satz*) in that sense, I destroy what was to have been expressed in it, viz. the being bound to a prescript, rule, or norm' (*G.S.*, VII, 299). A precept or norm is not something which exists, but something which 'holds good' or 'is valid' (*gilt*), and to give it utterance is not to refer a predicate to a subject under the categories of knowledge which apply to existing things, but to give expression to a will-attitude.

Yet such experiences and attitudes and their verbal expressions can be subjected, like perception and its verbal expressions, to the clarifying and generalising work of thought. Indeed, the building up of our feelings and resolves into a coherent world of value-judgments and principles of conduct is a necessary consequence of the way in which our perceptions get built up into a coherent world of objects. A passing sensation may evoke a feeling-response which is as transient as itself; but as memory and imagination come into play, building up the *Totalvorstellung* of an enduring object, they bring with them memories and imaginative constructions of feeling-responses relating to aspects of the object which are not immediately present to the senses. Gradually our attitude to the object, and our value-judgment upon it, come to be independent of passing feelings, and of the momentary impact of the object upon us. They become part of a system of stable or 'objective' value-determinations which ultimately embraces not only this one object, but the whole world with which we are acquainted (*G.S.*, VII, 48–9, 242).

On the basis of this system we can determine the comparative values of things, and so, with a view to action, make choice of the greater goods. Here too, in the first instance, we choose with reference to the immediate situation only; and here again, as our horizon broadens, our choices become emancipated from the desires and pressing needs of the moment, and we can judge a thing to be good or bad, even if our will is not actively engaged with it when we judge (*G.S.*, VII, 242).

Many of the values and ends thus laid down, though 'objective' in the sense of being stable throughout the life of one individual, may be private and personal to him. Others may be shared by a smaller or larger number of individuals; these will be 'objective' in the further sense of being public. It is natural to suppose that there will be some valuations which express neither individual peculiarities, nor even the common outlook of some limited portion of mankind, but aspects of human nature itself, and are therefore valid for all men. This would be a universal validity based not on necessities of pure reason, but on the identity of mental structure in all mankind. In this sense and on this basis Dilthey believes that there are universally valid valuations and precepts. 'History itself throws up principles, but their validity arises from the explication of the relations contained in life. Such a principle is the obligation involved in a contract, and the recognition of the worth and the value of each individual, considered as a human being. These truths are universally valid, because they make possible a guidance (*Regelung*) at every point in the historical world' (*G.S.*, VII, 262). In so far as these principles dominate our feeling and willing, we escape from the limitations of a subjective outlook into a world of objective 'ideal' standards, a 'life on a higher level' (*Bw. D.T.*, p. 90).

It is on this level that social co-operation becomes possible. Groups of individuals appreciating common values, and therefore pursuing common ends, join forces for the attainment of these common ends. Organised societies spring up, in which the human will enters into structural relations of a new and complex character. Such is the power of compulsion, on which all authority and government are based. Such, again, is the relation of obligation, into which an agent can enter by virtue of work done, contracts made, or principles adopted; 'these bindings pervade the whole of life, partly as supports, partly as hindrances to life' (*G.S.*, VII, 64–6, 69).

From time to time our cultural activities and social organisations get into difficulties. It is then that we begin to reflect upon our aims and activities, and build up theories about them. Such theories take shape first of all in separate studies, each one dealing with a particular branch of human activity; e.g. jurisprudence, studying law, paedagogy, studying educational methods, or criticism, studying artistic practice. These sectional studies, and the explanations which they give of our activities, serve well enough for a time, until a widening of the social and historical horizon shows us that they have only a local and temporary validity. Then, out of the clash of principles and standpoints, is born the attempt to go behind their diversity and discover more ultimate principles, which are exemplified in them all. This is the work of philosophy, and it culminates in the production of theories about an absolute beauty, a supreme good, and an unconditional moral law or categorical imperative. These are alleged to follow from principles of pure reason, and to provide a ground of explanation for all that is (*G.S.*, VII, 66, 299–300).

This, says Dilthey, is where we fall into error. The quest of the unconditioned, the belief that it can be found by reason, is inveterate in human thinking, but it is an inveterate illusion. There are really no absolute values and no unconditional norms of conduct.

This bald statement requires elaboration. What does Dilthey mean by it? For he does recognise that there are principles which are universally valid within particular spheres of activity. In his aesthetic writings he lays down principles of poetic composition. He recognises certain principles by which educational practice should always be governed. His moral theory recognises three fundamental principles of morality which are universally valid because they are grounded in human nature as such. What does he mean then by denying that they are absolute and unconditional norms?

We must understand the denial in the light of his campaign against Kantianism, and against the traditional metaphysics, of which Kantianism is merely a shamefaced continuation. These are philosophies of reason. They believe that principles can be found which, when properly formulated, constrain assent; they say that these principles flow from a Supreme Reason which is the ground of all existence. Dilthey does not believe in this Supreme Reason. His principles do not flow from it, but from the structure of the human mind, which is merely one among many existing things, though to us it is the one most intimately known. His principles are not self-luminous, nor are they known to us by rational analysis. They are known by induction from experience, and express what life itself teaches us. For that reason they may not even be capable of a particular verbal formulation which will always command assent; for future experience and the interpretation of it are not bound to our present formulae. Certainly their meaning changes as the growing historical experience of mankind enables us to read more into them. And a further reason why they cannot be called absolute or unconditional is that they all belong to limited spheres of activity, and express the conditions which must be fulfilled if those particular activities are to succeed. It is the whole structural system, or life itself, which is absolute, at least in the sense that nothing can be known to us, or appreciated or desired or willed by us, except by entering into relation with lived experience.

Why then should not Dilthey regard life itself as an ultimate value and highest good? In effect, that is what he does, but he does not like to say so. He is conscious that life contains infinite and inexhaustibly various possibilities, all of which are in some degree valuable; and the relations of mutual subordination and co-operation among its parts and functions are so variously adjustable without loss of value in the whole that no set of formulae that had any definite content at all could cover them all. It is not enough to say, as some have said, that the good for man is to be a good specimen of humanity; for 'humanity is only an indeterminate type' (*G.S.*, VII, 159). 'Life cannot be brought before the tribunal of reason' (*G.S.*, VII, 261, cf. V, 170, etc.). Therefore, since life is nothing definite, it cannot be regarded as a primary or absolute value or end from which all the rest are derived. It is something which stands behind and beyond all values and ends, as the condition of their possibility, manifested in all, but unconditionally manifested in none.

Everything in Dilthey's philosophy comes back at last to the concept of *life* (*das Leben*), or lived experience (*das Erlebnis*), and the structural system which he finds in lived experience. It is here, and not in abstract logical principles, that he finds reality and truth. It is here, too, and not in abstract principles, that he finds goodness and rightness and beauty. The Neo-Kantian coherence theory is as wrong in the one case as in the other. Objects are not objective because they conform to the principles of thought, but thought is objective because it 'clarifies' and 'represents' what is contained in our experience of objects. So too, although our value-judgments and imperatives work out as a coherent system, it is not their systematic coherence which gives them their 'validity' or their claim on us. They claim our attention because they express the response of our feelings and our will to the impact of the world upon us, and because they help us to see a situation more clearly and judge for ourselves more confidently than we could if guided by inarticulate feeling. The sole function of formulae and theories in this sphere is to extend our horizon in order that, cognisant of more facts and with more considerations in mind, we may respond more adequately to the demands of the situation (*G.S.*, VII, 299). They make possible an appeal from Philip blind to Philip open-eyed. But still it is by his own feelings when open-eyed that Philip must be guided. 'The sureness of a resolve and its rightness for the given person lie in the possibility of verification by feeling-experiences. Many mistakes occur by the substitution of other people's feeling-experiences, likes and dislikes etc.' (*G.S.*, VII, 68). The cycle of thought arises from lived experience, and returns for its verification to lived experience again.

With this conclusion Dilthey's theory of knowledge, in the broadest sense of the word 'knowledge', might seem to be completed and rounded off. He has examined, interpreted, and vindicated the things we say about facts and laws of nature, about values and ends and duties. He has given us a firm hold on the cognitive, affective, and volitional branches of our experience alike. But he has not yet correlated these three branches. He has left us with a world of facts and laws, a world of values, and a world of goods or norms of conduct, standing each on its own basis, side by side in consciousness. Life, however, is not thus parcelled out, and it remains for us to consider how the unity of the structural system finds its reflection in a subtle unity and interpenetration of the three worlds of experience, so that they become for us one world and one experience.

Here we are no longer dealing with facts, or values, or norms as such, in their distinctive characters. We are regarding them as all alike members of a comprehensive system which is our total experience of reality. Our enquiry is no longer about the objective existence of the facts, or the validity of the value-judgments and imperatives; it concerns the question, how these three types of content are related to one another. How do we conceive the relation between facts and value? Is our outlook in this matter naturalistic or Platonic? Do we think that facts are primary and alone ultimately real, and that values are merely a by-product or epiphenomenon of psychological and social facts? Or do we think that values are in some way the source and ground of existence, that the world of facts is in the last resort a reflection of value-archetypes? Abstruse as these questions may seem when formulated thus, everyone really answers them in one way or another; his answer is implicit in the correlation between knowledge, feeling, and will which he brings about in himself, and in the view of the 'meaning' of the world (*Weltan-schauung*) which results from this correlation. A true *Selbstbe-sinnung*, or reflective study of experience, is not complete until this process of unification has been brought under discussion, and the truth or validity of its results in the forming of *Weltan-schauungen* has been critically tested.

This apprehension of a unity and a 'meaning' in things, which, for all its vagueness, is powerful enough to colour a man's whole outlook and determine his choices, is called by Dilthey the *meta-physical consciousness*. With a half-serious glance at etymology, he explains that it is a consciousness of something meta-physical, i.e. beyond nature, and the reasoned theory of it is called *meta-physics*, the science of what lies beyond nature. For, in spite of the abstract and dogmatic methods pursued by some of its practitioners, even metaphysics is not merely a construction of empty forms in the void; like every other branch of thought, it is the 'representation' in logical terms of something which experience (in this case the 'metaphysical consciousness') brings before us.

One question for *Selbstbesinnung* to answer is therefore: how far can the 'metaphysical meaning' of things be expressed in concepts, and how far can such an expression of it be empirically grounded and logically water-tight? But metaphysical concepts are not the only expression of the 'metaphysical consciousness'. The Neo-Kantians, for example, regard the formulation of a *Weltanschauung* as the proper function of religion, while Dilthey himself, following here the richer Hegelian tradition, makes it the common concern of religion, art, and philosophy (i.e. metaphysics).[1] And so his problem takes a fuller form: how far can the expression of the metaphysical consciousness through religion, art, or philosophy, but especially through philosophy, which claims logical rigour, be either adequate to the metaphysical consciousness itself, or true in relation to the real?

Dilthey's views on this subject engaged much of his attention, especially in later years. The reader may find them in detail in the second book of his *Einleitung in die Geisteswissenschaften* (*G.S.*, I, 123 *seq.*), in *Das Wesen der Philosophie* (*G.S.*, V, 339 *seq.*), and in *G.S.*, VIII *passim*. Here it will suffice to give a brief account of their tendency.

He describes first of all how, through the co-operation and interpenetration of the three modes of experience, every content presented to the mind in cognition can be made the object of an affective and a volitional attitude as well. In this way there grows up a many-sided and yet coherent system of experience, in the building up of which we draw not only upon our own observations and reactions, but also upon the accumulated wisdom of mankind, expressed in custom and tradition. Reflecting upon this living and growing body of experience, we elicit from it a *Weltanschauung*; and, since this embodies the response of our whole mind to our experience as a whole, it necessarily displays in itself the triple structure of the mind which creates it. Thus, (1) at its basis we find a *Weltbild*, i.e. a body of knowledge and belief about the real world; (2) on this is reared a structure of

[1] Not that Dilthey is prepared, like Hegel, to define any of these three activities in terms of the formulation of *Weltanschauungen*, or find in that their origin and prime motive. The prime motive of religion is to regulate our relations with 'the invisible' (see below, p. 87), that of art is to refine and organise the life of feeling, and that of philosophy is, at least in part, to trace the presuppositions of the sciences back to indubitable principles. But all three can become vehicles of the *Weltanschauung*, and this is the highest function they can come to perform in the economy of the mind. That is where Dilthey agrees with Hegel.

value-judgments, expressing the relation of the subject to his world, and the meaning (*Bedeutung*) which he finds in it; (3) this in turn supports a system of ends, ideals, and principles of conduct, which are the point of contact between the *Weltanschauung* and practical life, making it a force in the development of the individual and, through him, of society at large.

The growth of the *Weltanschauung* is conditioned in some way or other by everything that enters into our experience; but it is dominated by our ceaseless attempt to find a solution for what Dilthey calls the 'riddle of life'. By this he means the mystery that surrounds the great crises of birth and death, the round of the seasons and the crops, the endless battle of human freedom against natural forces and necessities, the inexhaustible task of satisfying with limited means a capacity for appetition which has no limit—in fine, the whole mystery of the situation of mankind in the world. From the most primitive societies upward, men busy themselves to read this riddle. What is unknown is guessed at on the analogy of the known; what is unintelligible is explained by analogy from the intelligible. Language itself is full of relics of such attempts, in the shape of personifications and metaphors; and systematic *Weltanschauungen* are deliberately worked out, where, by the same method of personification and analogy, a full interpretation of the universe is set forth (*G.S.*, VIII, 78–84, V, 372–5).

The *Weltanschauungen* so formed differ as the experiences underlying them differ, in a manner determined by climatic, racial, and national conditions and by the temperament and surroundings of the individual. As a result of these causes, numberless forms of *Weltanschauungen* arise and become involved in a kind of struggle for existence, whereby the most viable of them are selected to receive detailed development at the hands of successive generations. Historical and social changes, and the steady progress of knowledge, turn men's interest continually upon different problems, and thus particular nations and particular periods in history each become dominated and characterised by a distinctive *Weltanschauung*. On a broad view, however, it becomes clear that there are a few fundamental types under which all *Weltanschauungen* can be classified, which types form a group of recurrent themes running through the bewildering multiplicity of *Weltanschauungen* recorded in history, and

86

offering a basis for a comparative study of them, or *Weltan-schauungslehre*.

Every *Weltanschauung*, since it is an interpretation of all ex-perience, must be formulated in terms of some system of rela-tions which pervades all experience. There are three such systems of relations, which it is the business of religion, of art, and of philosophy to make explicit; and every view of ex-perience can be expressed in terms of each of these three, so that we may say every type of *Weltanschauung* can take either a reli-gious, an aesthetic, or a philosophical form. Therefore, before Dilthey proceeds to the actual classification of *Weltanschauungen*, he turns to examine the differences between religion, art, and philosophy (*G.S.*, VIII, 84–7, cf. V, 378–81 *et al.*).

The ground of *religion* lies in reflection partly upon the regular and uncontrollable processes of nature, and partly upon those mysterious accidents by which our lives are sometimes so power-fully affected. Regular processes and chance accidents are both alike regarded as due to the agency of unseen superhuman powers, and the idea of these powers is gradually elaborated with all the resources of mythological fantasy. The question at once arises, how we are to order our relations with the unseen world, and religion is the answer to this question. In primitive societies it appears as a system of symbolic ideas and practices, centring in an organised cultus under the control of a priestly class. At a later stage we find the individual of genius, the prophet or the mystic, who brings to the fore the experiences of the inner life; hence arise various forms of religious ascesis, and the traditional mythology and cultus are reinterpreted and re-assembled as elements in a reasoned and comprehensive system of doctrine. Such a system finds the meaning and value of every-thing in its relation to the unseen world; the origin of the exist-ing universe, the attitude of the individual towards it, and the mutual relations and duties of individuals, are all determined by reference to the unseen supernatural order (*G.S.*, VIII, 88–9, V, 381–7).

The *artistic* point of view is different from and indeed anti-thetic to this. The artist differs from the religious man precisely in that he tries 'to understand life in terms of itself' rather than in terms of the supernatural; he finds the meaning of life not in a relation between the seen and the unseen, but in the thoughts and passions and purposes of human beings, and in the relationships into which they enter with one another and with the natural world. His view of the meaning of life is not theoretically elaborated in his works; they are not a contribution to philosophy. And yet his *Weltanschauung* does find expression indirectly by their means. It reveals itself in their style; it is symbolised in their content; and occasionally in poetry or novel the writer inserts, in his own person or through the mouth of a character in the piece, some reflective generalisation which lights up the significance of his work, though still without reducing it to a theory. The reader, while not mistaking the work of art for a reality, yet treats it as a type or 'representation' of reality, comparing it with the rest of his experience and reflecting upon its meaning, and thus the writer's *Weltanschauung* is conveyed to the reflective consciousness of the reader; the process is the same, *mutatis mutandis*, in the other arts as it is in literature (*G.S.*, VIII, 91–3, V, 392–8).

The *philosopher* differs both from the religious man and from the artist. He seeks to elicit from experience a system of concepts and universal truths, bound together by a chain of mutual implication; his desire is to know, if it were possible, all that is to be known, and to find for his knowledge a logically exact and universally valid basis. To this end he engages in an endless criticism, reducing every experience to its constituent factors and tracing every proposition to its logical grounds, never resting until he has related all fact to an ultimate reality, all knowledge to a highest truth, and all value to a supreme good. He draws ideas from every available source, from religion and art as well as from empirical science; but the reasoned whole in which he combines these data has its own distinctive structure. It represents the world as an intelligible system, whose composition and structure can be made the object of a demonstrative science. This science is metaphysics (*G.S.*, VIII, 94–5, V, 400–2).

These, then, are the three media of expression for every *Weltanschauung*. Returning now to his main project of a comparative study and classification of *Weltanschauungen*, Dilthey finds that they fall easily into three types, which he proceeds to characterise.

(1) The first type is based on a view of human nature which gives primacy to its animal side; and it tends to see the criterion

88

of the good life either in pleasure or in power. In the field of religion this outlook shows itself as a revolt against other-worldliness, and sometimes against religion itself on account of its otherworldliness, and an assertion of the claims of the world and the flesh. In art it takes the form of so-called 'realism', bringing to view by preference the dark forces of passion, and exposing the illusory character of the higher ideals and principles. The corresponding movement in philosophy, viz. *naturalism*, sees the world as a mechanical system composed of elements all of which are clear and distinct, i.e. mathematically determinable. This view may be held either as a doctrine of the nature of reality (materialism) or, more cautiously, as a methodological principle (positivism). It is associated with sensationalism in epistemology; in ethics it is either hedonist, or preaches libera-tion through enlightenment and the destruction of illusion. As representatives of this philosophy, Dilthey names Democritus, Protagoras, Epicurus, Hume, and Comte.

(2) The second type of *Weltanschauung* is based on our inner experience of free will, and interprets the world in terms of per-sonality, conducting at all points a bitter and relentless cam-paign against naturalism. Its fundamental premiss is the existence in man of a moral will which we can know to be free from physical causation; this will is bound, not physically, but morally, and therefore freely, to other wills in a society of moral persons, and the relations between these persons depend ulti-mately upon an absolute, free, personal agent, viz. God. In religion this *Weltanschauung* appears as theism, in particular Christian theism, where the fundamental premiss of naturalism, that *ex nihilo nihil fit*, is contradicted by the doctrine of creation *ex nihilo*. In art it appears in the conception of the world as a 'theatre of heroic action', e.g. in Corneille or Schiller. In philo-sophy it has developed from the conception of reason as a forma-tive power in Anaxagoras, Plato, and Aristotle, to the mediaeval conception of a world governed by the personal providence of God, and thence in Kant and Fichte to the idea of a super-sensible world of values, which are real only in and for the infinite will which posits them. Dilthey calls this philosophy the *idealism of freedom*, and finds its modern representatives in Berg-son, the Neo-Kantians, and the pragmatists.

(3) The third type of *Weltanschauung* is based on a contempla-

tive and affective attitude to experience. We read our own feelings and mental activities into the external world, regarding it as a living whole which continually realises and enjoys itself in the harmony of its parts; we find the divine life of the Whole immanent in every part, and rejoice to feel ourselves in sympathy with this life. This *Weltanschauung* emerges in the panentheism of Indian and Chinese religion; in art its most notable exponent is Goethe. In philosophy it leads to the conception of the universe as an 'organic' individual, whose parts are themselves individuals reflecting the character of the whole; this leads to a kind of determinism, but the determining principle is 'organic' and purposive, not blind and mechanical as it is in naturalistic theories. The epistemology of this third type of philosophy gives an important place to what it calls 'intellectual intuition'—the intuitive grasp of the wholeness of things. Dilthey finds this philosophy in Stoicism, in Averroes, Bruno, Spinoza, Leibniz, Shaftesbury, Schelling, Hegel, Schleiermacher; and he calls it *objective idealism* (*G.S.*, VIII, 100–18, V, 402–4).

In *Die Drei Grundformen der Systeme in der ersten Hälfte des 19 Jahrhunderts* (*G.S.*, IV, 528–54), Dilthey shows how the history of recent philosophy can be described and elucidated in terms of a conflict between the three types. The revolt against the naturalism of Hume and the Encyclopaedists, conducted by Kant and Fichte, Maine de Biran and Cousin, Hamilton and Mansel, is an instance of the idealism of freedom, for it depended in the last resort upon an appeal to the experience of free will. Against this movement naturalism was defended by the Mills, Comte, and Spencer, and the reply to these in turn, which Dilthey traces in the works of Lotze, Renouvier, Martineau, Green, and Bradley, is a form of objective idealism influenced by Leibniz and Hegel.

Of course, Dilthey adds, the types of *Weltanschauungen* are not always found pure, and every classification must be approximate. In particular, it is not unusual for the apparent irreconcilables, naturalism and the idealism of freedom, to come together as complementary aspects of a single system. In a fanciful review of the three types of *Weltanschauungen*, entitled *Traum* (*G.S.*, VIII, 218 *seq.*), Dilthey instances Descartes as one who attempted this synthesis, and Kant as 'the great man who raised the idealism of freedom to critical consciousness, and thereby reconciled it with the empirical sciences'.

The philosopher is under a natural temptation to believe that there is one universally valid system of metaphysics; every metaphysician intends to contribute to the discovery of this one system, and the history of philosophy is often represented as a gradual approximation to this goal (*G.S.*, VIII, 96 *et pass.*). The facts refute this optimism; not only has no particular system ever secured general assent, but there is no sign that the different points of view in this field are nearer to a reconciliation now than they were two thousand years ago (*G.S.*, VIII, 86–7 *et pass.*). This suggests that the problem which metaphysics has set itself is insoluble, and Dilthey has various epistemological reasons for holding that it is so. He nowhere gives a comprehensive argued statement of these reasons; regarding the collapse of metaphysics as evident and the reasons for it as obvious, he only alludes to them as occasion serves, to point this or that argument. They may, however, be summarised as follows.

In the first place, all human experience is fragmentary, and we have to try to fill the gaps. This is achieved in the empirical sciences by inference from empirical data. The inference leads us either to new facts analogous to those already observed, and capable in principle of being themselves observed, or to entities and relations which are not observable, but can be verified indirectly through deduction and experiment. In this way an ordered system of facts and processes is brought to our knowledge, both in nature and in the historical world. But the unity established by the sciences covers only particular segments of experience, and metaphysics, attempting to conceive the whole as a compact logical system, finds gaps which the empirical sciences cannot fill. In particular, the relation between mind and matter, which neither natural science nor the human studies as such can disclose, is of prime importance for metaphysics; and again, while every experienced fact and value is conditioned and relative, a metaphysical system requires for its centre an unconditioned reality and an absolute value. To satisfy these demands, metaphysics must transgress the limits of possible experience; this step is so inevitable in metaphysics that Dilthey can describe it as a 'science of the transcendent' (*G.S.*, I, 129 n.).

But such a science is impossible, precisely because it has no experience from which to draw its concepts. We can have no experience of the relation between mind and body, because mind is perceived from within and the body from without; in no moment of consciousness do we obtain a view of both side by side, so as to observe the relation between them, and though psychological experimentation discloses a correlation between events in the one and events in the other, the real process underlying this correlation is dark to us (*G.S.*, I, 15–16, V, 135). Similarly, we have no experience of a reality which is not temporally and causally conditioned, or of a value which is not relative to a particular subject or subjects (*G.S.*, V, 405). It may be urged that, although we have no actual experience of these things, we can still conceive them on the analogy of what we do experience. But we cannot conceive a mind-matter relation on the analogy of relations between elements of matter or between elements of mind, or an absolute on the analogy of a relative; the matter of the analogy contradicts its form, and no definite conception emerges from it (*G.S.*, I, 279–91, 318–28, VIII, 117–18).

In the second place, we have seen how the structural system in mind is the basis of all experience; not only are all mental facts understood in terms of it, but from it are derived the 'real categories' by which coherence is read into nature. Now, the structural system is *lived* (*erlebt*), and 'what we live (*erleben*) we can never make clear before the bar of the understanding (*Verstand*)' (*G.S.*, V, 170); for the clarity of the understanding lies wholly in the 'formal categories' which reflect the analytical and generalising processes of thought, whereas lived experience is a concrete reality, and though thought may analyse and 'clarify' it indefinitely, there is always a remainder which resists such 'clarification'. What applies to the lived experience naturally applies also to the 'real categories' derived from it. And thus metaphysics is in a dilemma. Naturalism, by working only with the 'formal categories' and applied mathematics, can obtain a clear and distinct idea of the world, but at the cost of misconceiving life and mind and mutilating the 'real categories'. On the other hand, idealism, both forms of which interpret the world in terms of life, sacrifices thereby the metaphysician's ambition of logical precision. For the relations between fact and value, and the fundamental conceptions of thing, substance, cause, power, God, though 'intelligible' in one sense in terms of the structural system in experience, defy analysis by the logical understanding. The attempt to define them clearly and to build them into a universally valid system of truths has led to innumerable ambiguities and antinomies, whose persistence through system after system for two thousand years has brought metaphysics into discredit. For every possibility in this field has now been tried in vain, and no one who understands the lesson of history will make the attempt again (*G.S.*, I, 201–11, 386–408, V, 405 *et al.*):

Thus we are left with a succession of metaphysical systems, all of them too full of paralogisms and antinomies to be true, and yet so ambiguous that no refutation is accepted as final, since there is always a possibility of restatement and reinterpretation. There is a natural temptation to conclude that relativism is the last word in philosophy, and that nothing can be known about any meaning in experience. But this is so only if the evidential value of metaphysics depends wholly upon its truth as a science, and Dilthey denies that it does so. Once more he brings to bear his method of *Selbstbesinnung* or 'reflection on self'. By studying metaphysical systems and *Weltanschauungen* simply as intellectual phenomena, in abstraction from their claim to be true, he undertakes to show that they perform a necessary function in life which is unaffected by the fate of their truth-claim.

Every metaphysical system, he says, claims to be derived by logical processes from empirical facts and/or self-evident truths. It claims to be a purely cognitive achievement, an intellectual product, in line with the positive sciences and mathematics. In fact, however, it rests upon a mode of the metaphysical consciousness, a *Weltanschauung*, a way of looking at life and the world, in which cognitive, affective, and volitional elements are bound up together and are alike primary. The elaborate logical structure of definitions and inferences, which characterises a metaphysical system as distinct from a religious or artistic one, appears at first sight to be the evidence on which the underlying *Weltanschauung* is based; but in fact it serves only to render its content explicit, and to defend it against possible objections. The failure of this argumentative superstructure to attain logical precision and universal validity therefore leaves the significance of the *Weltanschauung* itself untouched (*G.S.*, VIII, 98–9). For a *Weltanschauung* is simply a form in which the structural unity of experience comes to conscious expression; the structural system of the mind, in its continual commerce with the outer world, is therefore the ultimate fact, by reference to which the significance of metaphysics, as well as of religion and art, is to be determined. Whatever religion, art, and philosophy may say in their effort to discover an objective world order, their true function is not to reveal such an order, but to give expression to the various ways in which human minds endeavour to unify their experience of the world (*G.S.*, V, 413–16).

The specific character of philosophy lies in its use of logical analysis to this end. Thus, it strikes root first in logic and epistemology; from thence it branches out into the philosophy of nature, of art, of law, of religion—all those enquiries, in short, by which our knowledge of fact and value in its several departments is dissected and referred to its basis in experience (*G.S.*, V, 406–13); then, last of all, in what Dilthey calls *Weltanschauungslehre*, or 'philosophy of philosophy', it traces the genesis of *Weltanschauungen* and their formulation in metaphysical systems, exposes the flimsiness of these systems, and finally refers them also to their true basis in the experience which they express and defend (*G.S.*, V, 405–6, VIII *passim*).

It is easy to find here a parallel to Kant's transcendental dialectic; for, as Kant solved his four antinomies by going behind them to the mind in which they arise, and showing that thesis and antithesis really represent not actual knowledge about reality, but complementary methods and tendencies in our endless search for such knowledge, so Dilthey breaks the deadlock between the types of *Weltanschauungen* by going behind them to the structural system which they 'represent', and showing that they embody the various ways in which that structural system may be experienced in its relations with the universe (*G.S.*, VIII, 7–9). The mind is hereby set free from each particular *Weltanschauung*, i.e. from the illusion of its absolute validity, but it is at the same time made free to dispose of all the *Weltanschauungen* and to judge them from an absolute point of view. For the structural system at any rate is absolute, in that it does not change and that all change is relative to it, and in this system are stored up infinite possible ways in which man may have experience of himself and of his world. It is for philosophy as *Weltanschauungslehre* to make visible the full extent of these possibilities, and so reveal to mind its own infinite freedom. 'The last word of the mind which has run through all the *Weltanschauungen* is not the relativity of them all, but the sovereignty of mind in relation to each single one of them, and also the positive consciousness of how, in the different forms of mental attitudes (*Verhaltungsweisen des Geistes*), the one reality of the world exists for us' (*G.S.*, V, 406).

In this conclusion Dilthey is faithful to the two traditions, romantic and empiricist, which together determine all his thought. For the conception of philosophy as a *Weltanschauungslehre*, whose subject-matter is mind with its infinite possibilities of experience, has evident affinities with the dialectic of Schleiermacher (see above, pp. 10–1,); while on the other hand, rejecting as it does all thought of apriorism, and resting on an empirical epistemology, a descriptive psychology, and a comparative study of religious, aesthetic, and metaphysical ideas, it conforms to the programme which Dilthey laid down as early as 1867 at Basel. 'Philosophy', he said, 'enters the circle of the empirical sciences whose object is the regular order of phenomena. It is allied with the other sciences of mind in the great task of founding an empirical study of mental phenomena' (*G.S.*, V, 12–13).

CHAPTER FOUR

Now that we have seen what Dilthey says in general terms about value-judgments and imperatives, and have taken the measure of his relativism, we may turn to consider his specifically moral theory, with which his aesthetic may conveniently be linked. In both these spheres we shall find that his teaching accords with his general theory of values. It is psychologistic and anti-metaphysical, though it insists on the wealth and variety of the inner life, which orthodox empiricism or positivism neglects. And it is relativistic. Three fundamental and irreducible attitudes to life are found to express themselves in three distinct moral principles, and there is no objective order of precedence among them.

We do not possess any formal treatise in which Dilthey sets forth his mature views on moral philosophy. The only formal treatise on the subject which he has left us belongs to the very beginning of his career. It is his *Habilitationsschrift*. The date is 1864, and the title *Versuch einer Analyse des moralischen Bewusstseins*. Its manner betrays the hand of a young man, anxious to cover, and to be seen to cover, all the ground. Unnecessary space is given to discussions of Herbart and Schopenhauer, who were not among the writers by whom Dilthey was lastingly influenced. The terminology is still that which Dilthey inherits, not one which he has found for himself. The essay is ostensibly a prolegomenon: it does not profess to touch upon the really fundamental questions of ethics.

In spite of all this, the work is interesting and useful. It makes Dilthey's approach to the study of ethics very clear, and it is a distinctive approach. The contentions set forth in the essay stood essentially unchanged for the rest of Dilthey's life, though the development of his philosophy led to certain changes in the mode of expression, and to slight enrichments of detail. Amplified by certain passages in a later essay, *Über das Studium der*

Geschichte der Wissenschaften vom Menschen, der Gesellschaft u. dem Staat (1875) and in the *Einleitung in die Geisteswissenschaften* (1883), the *Habilitationsschrift* is something more than a mere prolegomenon. It gives us an all-round view of Dilthey's moral theory, though it does not give us the whole of it.

The *Habilitationsschrift* was written soon after Dilthey had conceived his project of a *Kritik der historischen Vernunft*, and is meant as a partial contribution to that enterprise. In the last chapter we saw what method Dilthey follows in dealing with our consciousness of values and norms of conduct. He appeals to psychology for a descriptive analysis of the structure of the human mind; in particular, for an account of all the factors involved in judging something to be valuable, and the function of such judgments in mental life. The validity of value-judgments, i.e. their claim upon our acceptance, is defended by an appeal to their function; value and norm are shown to be grounded on psychological fact. Dilthey himself, in the *Habilitationsschrift*, describes his aim in these very terms. 'Alike the demand of moral theory for influence upon life and the disinterested pure stimulus of enquiry drive us to an examination of *what is* as the basis of all imperatives and all ideals' (*G.S.*, VI, 2).

He begins his enquiry by urging that moral philosophy is obviously in need of reform. Hitherto it has aimed at acquiring influence over society, and has largely succeeded by allying itself with religion and making the pulpit its channel of diffusion. This practical interest has affected the method of moral philosophy; it has set itself to discover with demonstrative certainty and in full detail what actions are right and what are wrong, and has put forward its conclusions as unconditionally binding. But today the religious support of moral teaching is cut away from under it, while a growing realisation of the diversity of moral opinion in the human race past and present, near and far, contrasts ominously with the dogmatism of moral theories. Hence 'moral philosophy at present drags out its remaining existence only in professorial chairs, and begins even here to die out' (*G.S.*, V, 33, cf. VI, 2).

But this is only because moral philosophy has put the cart before the horse, i.e. has advanced conclusions without going through the labour of empirical research. For ethics, like jurisprudence or economics, is really an empirical study, and is concerned with the facts of the moral life, 'the world and history of morals' (*G.S.*, V, 66). Its first step should therefore be to analyse and describe the type of behaviour known as 'moral' and the structure of the moral consciousness; then it should advance to the 'metaphysical and psychological groundwork of ethics' (*G.S.*, VI, 4), plunging into those mysterious depths of the soul from which the moral consciousness emerges; when this ground-work is complete, and not until then, ethics may approach the morphology of moral codes and ideals, knowing now in what sense and to what extent they can be 'valid'. By this procedure ethics might escape at last from dogmatism; but hitherto it has never begun even that structural analysis of the moral consciousness upon which all the rest depends. 'Therefore, even to-day, moral scepticism . . . is still in the right against a study which has not so much as developed a comparative review of the facts which compose its domain. . . . Accordingly, the prime condition for the restoration of moral philosophy from its downfall is the introduction of the historical facts and their utilisation by the comparative method' (*G.S.*, V, 33–4). It is to this preliminary task alone that Dilthey in the *Habilitationsschrift* addresses himself.

By the 'moral consciousness' is meant first of all the awareness of obligation which arises in the course of deliberation, and which ought to issue in moral action. An analysis of the moral consciousness might then seem to involve an analysis of the moral act. Unfortunately, the deeper our acquaintance with human nature becomes, and the more we recognise the limitations of our insight into human character, the more impossible it appears to single out any specific action for study on the ground that it is moral (*G.S.*, VI, 10 = V, 68, cf. I, 62). We need not deny that moral motives are at work, but the attempt to separate them from the non-moral motives presents 'extraordinary difficulties'. In consequence, 'enquiry into the actions of men . . . is quite valueless as a foundation for ethics. No bridge leads from the vision of human characters and their complicated conduct to duty and the ideal' (*G.S.*, V, 67).

But the moral consciousness does not appear only in deliberation before the act, it also manifests itself afterwards in moral judgment, i.e. the judgment made upon an action by a disinterested spectator, and here the specifically moral element is 'ready separated, in pure form'. The moral consciousness is the same in both its manifestations, and moral theories can be built upon either; upon the awareness of obligation, as by Kant and Fichte, or upon the judgment of the observer, as by the British moralists and Herbart. A thorough treatment of this subject must combine both points of view, but the approach through moral judgment is the more important, because there the facts are clearer (*G.S.*, VI, 11 = V, 69 = I, 61-2).

Every moral judgment may be presented as the conclusion of a practical syllogism, whose major premiss is a moral maxim, and whose minor subsumes a particular action under the maxim. But what is the status of the major premiss? Is it a principle, universally valid and known *a priori*, the knowledge of which is presupposed in every judgment or action that is truly moral? Or is it a generalisation from moral feeling, so that feeling is the real basis of moral judgment, and the syllogism a mere inductive expansion of it? This is the point at issue between Kant and Hume, and is to be decided by a criticism of Kant (*G.S.*, VI, 9–12).

The name of Kant is often associated with the doctrine that the essence of morality is obedience to a law, and that the only moral motive is respect for the form of law; but Dilthey undertakes to show that it is not upon this that Kant's theory really hinges. In his *Untersuchung über die Deutlichkeit der Grundsätze der natürlichen Theologie u. der Moral* (pub. 1764) Kant lays down that the good will has unconditional value for its own sake, irrespective of consequences; but he does not at this date hold that the motive of the good will is respect for a universal law. On the contrary, he holds that it is the appetition of a particular good, perceived in the particular situation, and the medium whereby it is perceived is an 'unanalysable feeling'. Later, in the *Grundlegung der Metaphysik der Sitten*, Kant again begins by asserting the unconditional value of the good will; and it is only then, when he goes on to ask how the good will gets its motive, that he introduces the doctrine of the universal law. Man, he says, is distinguished by his power of acting according to principles, which are enunciated by practical reason; some principles are valid hypothetically and as means to an end, but moral principles constitute a law which is valid for its own sake alone and in all possible circumstances. How can practical reason lay down such a law? Because, says Kant, personality, or the capacity for rational conduct, has unconditional value for the rational will, i.e. the good will wills itself as a universal law for all rational agents. Kant never explains why the good will should be its own content in this way; and the theory that it is so is no part of his original insight. It is only an inference, forced upon Kant by his assumption that moral action is directed by practical *reason*, coupled with his complete severance of reason from feeling; and it is an inference which contradicts experience. 'Practical reason, conceived in isolation (*für sich*) as the subject which makes moral judgments, renders the universal and conscious the starting-point of all moral life, which is against all experience and psychology' (*G.S.*, VI, 19).

Kant's earlier theory of an 'unanalysable feeling' is nearer the truth. And yet this in turn presents difficulties of its own. For 'feeling' as Hume and Kant conceive it is the passive response of the subject to an external stimulus, whereas will is active, and proceeds from the whole personality of the agent. Again, feeling is of the moment and is relative to a particular instinct which is moving us to action at the moment, whereas a judgment of good and evil belongs to an objective value-system, recognised by the whole self when in a state of recollection; and this is only possible through thought. 'Through it alone is the whole will present in each individual action. And so also through it alone is a judgment of good and bad possible' (*ibid.*).

Thus, while moral judgment is immediately based upon feeling and not upon a principle, yet the feeling in turn must somehow embody a principle if the judgment based upon it is to be objectively valid. Reason and moral feeling must therefore have a 'point of coincidence', and each must be so understood as to render this coincidence possible. It *is* possible if by 'reason' we understand not the intellectual faculty by which we apprehend general principles, but a formative purpose (*gestaltender Zweck*) immanent in life, which expresses itself in the form of desires and feelings; and if by 'moral feeling' we mean not a chaotic aggregate of passive impressions, but a 'purposive system', 'not heterogeneous from reason', which 'springs from the end of our being (*Zweck unseres Wesens*)' and expresses to our consciousness in intuitive form the immanent teleology of our nature. Acting under the guidance of such a 'feeling', even without explicit reflection on laws and principles, 'we can take up into our will the inner purpose of our existence'; and this is the primary form of moral action. Subsequent reflection can make explicit the rationality inherent in moral feeling, until at last 'with complete insight into the structure of the world it will arrive at complete clarity' (G.S., VI, 20–1).

The moral consciousness, then, is the inner teleology of human life, expressed in 'feeling' and in value-judgments, and working as a motive to determine the moral will. Dilthey goes on to analyse this teleology, showing what types of ends the moral judgment approves and the good will feels bound to pursue. This, he says, is where most moral theories go wrong; for they assume that there is one discoverable principle upon which the moral life is based, e.g. prudence, benevolence, duty for duty's sake, or pleasure, and they reduce all moral values to their one principle, doing violence thereby to the moral life as actually experienced. An empirical study of it reveals three types of moral judgment and obligation, based upon three distinct principles. *First*, there is 'obligation taken in the strict sense', or *Verpflichtung*; here the will is bound by the law of its own consistency to the fulfilment of an undertaking which it has openly or tacitly assumed. This type of obligation finds organised sanctions in law; the type of character built upon it has the distinguishing virtue of rectitude (*Rechtschaffenheit*). *Second*, there is 'the form of ought in which benevolence expresses itself', which is based upon human sympathy, and yet is no mere indulgence of kind feeling; it is a recognition that the action suggested by such feeling is right and ought to be performed. *Third*, there is the type of ought which is conceived as a universally valid ideal. It is based upon 'the striving after inner worth'; the ideal is conceived as the 'significance and perfection of our existence' (*Bedeutung und Vollkommenheit unseres Daseins*), and Dilthey observes that it often receives a speculative interpretation through some theory of the universe and of our place in it (G.S., VI, 25–7, 46–7).

These three principles are irreducible to common terms, but they are all alike principles from which flow actions that are felt to be obligatory. Dilthey calls them 'practical attitudes of our will in so far as it is moral'; they constitute the inner structure of the moral will, irrespective of its empirical content, and 'might be styled practical categories' (G.S., VI, 43). Every moral life embodies all three, and no moral theory is adequate which ignores any of them; but in life there are individuals in whom one or other of them predominates, and in ethics there are theories which build exclusively upon one or other of them. This is responsible for much confusion in ethics and for the consequent scepticism, which will vanish when the moral life is analysed in a truly empirical manner.

Having thus analysed morality as it appears in the normal individual, Dilthey further traces its workings in the community; for it is not a private activity of the individual, it is a social force, and a system of relations between agents in the historical process. It acts, as was seen, in the 'double form' of motive and of judgment. As motive, it issues freely from the conscience of the agent; as moral judgment, it is a force which others exert upon him, and the sum of moral judgments constitutes a group opinion through which society as a whole controls its members. The opinion of the group affects the individual partly through prudential motives; but it is also the means whereby a true moral consciousness is awakened in the child, and it guides the doubting conscience of the adult. Thus by several channels, over an ever-widening range of social life, the moral consciousness exercises a determinative influence (G.S., V, 70–1 = I, 62–3).

The range of life so affected is called 'the moral system', and is the empirical subject-matter of ethics. It appears first of all in the guise of custom; for, although much of what is customary in any society is due to mere convenience, yet there is always a residual ideal element which is due to moral feeling. From this the moral system slowly evolves into widely different forms, and two principles govern its evolution. First, usage interpreted by reflection becomes public opinion and a code of honour; from this are abstracted concepts, maxims, ideals, and finally moral theories. So the moral consciousness develops out of feeling into philosophic self-consciousness. Second, the influence of moral feeling over conduct spreads from the narrow circle of custom to the utmost confines of human activity. The individual, in pursuit of inner worth, exalts his ideal more and more as civilisation progresses. Benevolence widens his horizon to embrace the physical and moral welfare of others. Rectitude recognises in all persons a natural right to equal treatment. The last stage is reached when the 'rights of man' are given legal recognition, and through this extension of law into the domain of morality 'the moral world fulfils itself objectively'. The process is never complete, and Dilthey quotes from Lotze (*Mikrokosmus*, II, 378) to the effect that the real system of values and duties is something which 'we learn first by a long course of education, and never learn to the full' (*G.S.*, VI, 46–8, V, 70–2, I, 61).

The analysis of moral experience here given is offered by Dilthey not as an ethical theory, but as the prolegomena to any adequate ethical theory. The real study of ethics cannot confine itself to empirical observation and analysis, but must go below the surface of experience to the principle of 'reason' which is active in the human mind. The empirical analysis ends with an unresolved triplicity of 'practical categories', and it is for the *Grundlegung* of ethics to exhibit the significance and meaning (*Bedeutung und Sinn*) of these categories and their ultimate unity in the 'end of our being'; this end, which is implicit in moral feeling and is realised in practice through the good will, will thus be brought into explicit self-consciousness. But where, then, is the 'end of our being' to be found? Many theories seek it in the individual; but this, says Dilthey, means in the end reducing all human action to self-love; and the experience which we have of unselfish motives cannot thus be explained away. 'Rather it is that the moral organisation of man serves the end of the species. Not we ourselves, each in isolation, are its sufficient ground, but the end which nature has set before herself in the human race' (*G.S.*, VI, 52).

What this end may be, Dilthey does not tell us. Writing at this early date, with the romantic and the positivist elements in his outlook not yet really reconciled, he might have found the question hard to answer; however, the issue belongs to the 'metaphysical and psychological *Grundlegung* of ethics' rather than to a preliminary enquiry, so that Dilthey in his *Habilitationsschrift* can safely let it go. We are entitled, however, to demand an answer in due course, and in the writings of his more mature years some answer should surely be found. As a matter of fact, there is none in his published writings. The essay of 1875 is the last which treats of moral issues at any length. But Dilthey did proceed to the *Grundlegung* of ethics, and the views which he adopted may be found informally stated in several letters to von Wartenburg between 1888 and 1890.

Among the marks of immaturity in the *Habilitationsschrift* is its unquestioning use of Kantian or post-Kantian phraseology. The three principles of morality are called 'practical categories' without any explanation or qualification of the meaning of the term; they are said to be 'universally valid', again without qualification; the living unity of our mind, from which they proceed, is called 'reason' (*Vernunft*); the *Grundlegung* which enquires into it is called 'metaphysical' as well as 'psychological'. If Dilthey had attempted the *Grundlegung* at this date, we may guess that it would have shown very much the influence of Schleiermacher.[1] In 1867, however, the year of the inaugural lecture at Basel, came Dilthey's decisive breach with metaphysics, and the influence of the empirical philosophy in his thought became stronger. It is very clear in the essay of 1875 (see below, pp. 162 ff.), in the *Einleitung in die Geisteswissenschaften* (1883), in *Die Einbildungskraft des Dichters* (1887), and in *Über die Möglichkeit einer allgemeingültigen pädogogischen Wissenschaft* (1888), and we may note that in this last treatise the three moral principles of the *Habilitationsschrift*, reappearing under the names of 'sympathy', 'striving after perfection and happiness', and 'the feeling of obligation', are called no longer 'categories' but 'living impulses and instincts' (*G.S.*, VI, 57). This is the very time at which the ethical discussions begin to appear in Dilthey's letters to von Wartenburg, and there too we find a strong naturalistic vein.

There is one form of naturalistic ethics which has no attraction for Dilthey, viz. the utilitarianism of Bentham and the Mills. He takes a malicious delight in hoisting these writers with their own petard, i.e. proving that their doctrine has no empirical grounding, but is an abstract theoretical construction.[2] They try to bring all moral ends under a single formula,

---

[1] In the year of the *Habilitationsschrift*, Dilthey was already at work upon his great *Leben Schleiermachers*. He had previously written a dissertation *De principiis ethicis Schleiermacheri*.

[2] Cf. Dilthey's gleeful attempt to shock his devout Lutheran friend by showing how empirical he is becoming—more empirical even than Mill! 'Over my ethic you would at once rejoice and cross yourself! I trump utilitarianism! Show that it is a construction from above downward. . . . I defend the concrete realities of the moral impulses against abstract principles, and a manly morality which feels itself in them against the sentimental altruistic, utilitarian, etc.' (*Bw.D.Y.*, p. 106.)

a featureless 'good' or 'utility', ignoring the rich variety of volitional experience and the many diverse ends which we do in fact pursue (*Bw.D.Y.*, p. 106). Again, they fail to analyse the real relation between the pursuit of private and that of social welfare, falling back upon the dogma of a pre-established harmony between the two. This is the incurious attitude of a ruling class, who readily think that what is well for them is well for the community. Dilthey calls their philosophy a 'fat, full-fed, genial' doctrine, a 'rentier-philosophy', and speculates sarcastically on the reception that extracts from Bentham and the Mills might find among the proletariate (*Bw.D.Y.*, p. 76).

For Dilthey's positive doctrine, almost the only authority is a letter written in January 1890 (*Bw.D.Y.*, p. 89 *seq.*), in which he explains to his friend the outline of a long lecture on ethics, covering the whole subject, which he means to give later in the year.

He begins by looking for a 'firm standing-ground' in the 'stream of evolution and its vague possibilities, which have the up-to-date moralists of today at their mercy', and he finds this firm ground in the structural system of mental life. From here his exposition can proceed by first describing the form of the structural system, and the position of instinct and feeling in it, and then singling out the instincts and describing them in detail. As he says in another letter, so long as the instincts are really as he describes them, it does not matter if any subtler psychologist finds that he can reduce them to simpler terms; the ethic built upon Dilthey's description of them will be unaffected (*Bw.D.Y.*, p. 106).

Then he goes on to describe how three volitional principles emerge as the basis of a 'life on a higher level'. They are not quite the same three as in the *Habilitationsschrift* and the educational treatise of 1888. The first is 'a heightening of inner life, operative in every state, which corresponds to the false abstraction of a striving after development or perfection, and operates from the feelings upon all ideas, images, impulses'. The second, 'very complex in its origin', is the fact that 'we, being not atoms, have in all particular impulses a supervenient tendency to impart, to receive, to share, etc.' The third is 'that we find our-

105

selves in our mental constitution compelled to respect others as ends in themselves'.[1]

The working out of these three principles is accomplished in the 'moral process', by which Dilthey means a kind of struggle for survival among all the volitional impulses in human nature, in which these three come out victorious. 'Moral process: that of course is only an abstract expression for a new group of real processes which are specifically ethical. Since the manifestations of instinct in pugnacity, hatred, exclusion of others from one's own sphere of interests, oppression of others for one's own advantage, altogether diminish the satisfaction of individuals and society, they are involved in a gradual decline (if we abstract from intrusive factors which bring about periods here). Because inclinations of a certain kind produce lasting satisfaction, they are preferred.'[2] In due course an ideal of life springs up and operates as a force determining subsequent growth, and religion, mythology, and art are brought to bear in support of it. The three moral principles, variously combined and glossed, become the basis of a succession of moral ideals and standards, whose history and morphology are a theme for the human studies.

Dilthey's *Grundlegung* of ethics is all contained in this letter, and here, as elsewhere, his breach with the Kantian and other metaphysical traditions is complete. The active principle of 'reason' in the mind is replaced by the structural system. The unity underlying the three practical principles (no longer 'categories') is found in their common tendency to further the development of human capacities and to heighten the satisfactions of life. The 'end of our being' is not any determinate and

---

[1] The original formulation reappears in the second *Studie zur Grundlegung der Geisteswissenschaften* (1905), where we have 'duties of perfection' based on the 'striving for perfection', 'duties of love' based on 'love of God or man', and 'the binding in an obligation', with 'the sincerity and rectitude based upon it' (*G.S.*, VII, 67).

[2] Cf. again the second *Studie zur Grundlegung der Geisteswissenschaften*, where the sanction for the three principles is found in the fact that persistent neglect of any of them will involve exclusion from a rich vein of human intercourse. Neglect of the duty to strive after perfection shuts a man out from the community of cultural effort, neglect of the duties of benevolence shuts him out from the sphere of human sympathy, and neglect of the duties of rectitude shuts him out from any share in the life of an organised society (*loc. cit.*).

formulable good, from which the necessity of the principles might be deduced; it is simply the effort of the structural system to unfold its inherent possibilities in any way that, under the conditions of our world, may prove to make for freedom and happiness. Morality, in short, appears not as a metaphysically grounded formative principle with *a priori* rights over all our practical activities, but as merely one among several groups of guiding rules which gradually disengage themselves from the chaos of practical life, and extend their influence over such fields and with such authority as experience permits.

One of the crucial factors in the growth of the 'moral system' is the work of the imagination. Since the primary form of the moral consciousness is intuitive, and abstract principles are only generalisations from intuitive perceptions, anything which can influence the way in which we perceive a situation and size it up will influence the development of the moral consciousness. This makes a natural transition from moral theory to the philosophy of imagination and the arts—in a word, to aesthetics.

For English readers, the most obvious parallel to Dilthey's position in aesthetics is that of I. A. Richards. Both writers are moved by a fundamentally romantic inspiration: Dilthey's dependence on Goethe and Novalis is parallel to the fascination exercised over Richards by Coleridge. Both have forsworn metaphysics, and are trying to keep alive the romantic vision and find adequate expression for it in a positivistic universe. Both seek help from psychology, and consider that a sound aesthetic cannot be written without a psychological underpinning: thus Richards inserts a series of psychological chapters into his *Principles of Literary Criticism*, while Dilthey in *Die Einbildungskraft des Dichters* begins with a detailed exposition of a psychological theory, and goes on to deduce aesthetic and critical conclusions from that. Both, in the detail of their psychology, give a fundamental place to basic 'attitudes' (*Verhaltungsweisen* in Dilthey), though it is not in aesthetics that Dilthey makes his chief use of this concept. Both find the function of art to lie, at least partly, in the creation of balance and harmony in what would otherwise be the unintegrated minds and souls of men.

Dilthey's views on the subject find expression in many places. They find practical application in his literary criticism, whose volume is considerable and whose value as criticism is high.

They find theoretical expression to some extent in his *Weltan-schauungslehre*, where, as we have seen, the aim and function of art is compared with those of religion and philosophy. They find expression in various passages of his writings on the logic of the human studies; for it is a point of his doctrine that the understanding of life, which is fundamental in the human studies, is greatly furthered by the work of the arts, and that poetry can sometimes give valuable insights to a historian. But besides all this, there are two considerable treatises directly devoted to aesthetics, viz. *Die Einbildungskraft des Dichters: Bausteine für eine Poetik* (1887) and *Die Drei Epochen der modernen Ästhetik u. ihre heutige Aufgabe* (1892). To these we must now turn.

In both essays, in different ways, Dilthey gives his view of the history of aesthetics in modern times, and its present condition and prospects. He describes how the two chief pre-Kantian schools of philosophy applied their respective principles to it. The rationalists (Descartes and Leibniz and their followers) studied the beautiful object, asked what makes it beautiful, and answered that beauty is symmetry of form. The British empiricists (e.g. Lord Kames) studied rather the impression made by the beautiful object on the mind, and laid the foundations of the psychology of beauty which has since been worked out by Fechner (*G.S.*, VI, 248–62). Dilthey's sympathies are naturally with the empirical and psychological school, but none the less he finds their standpoint inadequate. Without dwelling upon Kant's contribution, he passes on to consider the work of Goethe, Schiller, and other German writers of the romantic period. It was they who called attention to the relation between the inner life of the mind and its outward expression in a visible form (*Gestalt*). By so doing they called attention away from the beautiful object and the aesthetic impression which it makes on the observer, and focused it rather on the creative process in the artist's mind. Beauty, on this view, can be defined in terms of expression: that form is beautiful which adequately expresses the inner life behind it (*G.S.*, VI, 116–17). But the same conception opens up vistas in philology, the study of language, and in hermeneutics, the study of interpretation (*G.S.*, VI, 122). It also leads on to a study of the creative process whereby the inner life finds its outward expression, and this again, by forcing attention upon the conditions under which the creative process works, paves the way for the application of the historical method and the comparative study of periods and schools of art (*G.S.*, VI, 266–70). Thus aesthetics links up with the wider movement of thought in the human studies in the post-Kantian generation.

Dilthey's own aesthetic is fundamentally that of the romantics, but with an important difference. The romantics allied themselves with the speculative metaphysics of their time, and lost their hold upon concrete fact. Cut loose from its proper empirical basis in the study of medium, technique, and historical conditions, their conception of art degenerated into that of a world of ideal forms, 'the romantic world of beautiful illusion', having no positive relevance to experience, while the history and comparative study of art was left to be transmuted by Hegel into an abstract dialectic (*G.S.*, VI, 122–3, 269). Dilthey shows that the underlying truth of romanticism can only be saved if the neglected factors are restored to view; the analysis of the creative process, the comparative study of the different genres of art, and the interpretation of their history, must all be made to rest upon knowledge of the technical conditions imposed by the artist's medium, and of the historical conditions which affect him and his public. Dilthey goes on to say that the work cannot be carried through without the aid of psychology. He very frankly owns that the psychology prevailing in his time is incapable of explaining or even correctly describing the process of artistic creation; but the conclusion he draws from this is merely that there will have to be sweeping changes in psychological methods and doctrines. In the meantime, we must not strain ourselves to keep within the terms of contemporary psychological theories; we must describe and analyse without preconceptions, and so contribute towards the psychology of tomorrow.

Accordingly, in *Die Einbildungskraft des Dichters*, Dilthey sets himself to analyse the mental constitution of the poet. He finds that it does not differ in kind, but only in degree, from that of the ordinary man.

We have seen in previous chapters how experience is built up from its primary data and organised into a coherent whole. Sense-data and lived experiences, as they arise in consciousness, are clarified by silent thought, amplified by elements drawn from memory and imagination, and made the basis of a system of general ideas. It is thus that, in the sphere of cognition, we build up a system of organised knowledge. In the sphere of volition, similar processes lead to the formation of habits, customs, laws, moral and religious disciplines, and finally to the reasoned formulation of ideals and principles. Now, it is the same process which, in the sphere of feeling, gives rise to poetry. The basic function of poetry, as of all the arts, is to bring order and harmony into our emotional life, to create and maintain in us a balance of prevailingly pleasant feeling. The poet is one who can do this for himself and for others, because his experiences are richer in content and clearer in detail than those of other men. His imagination is prolific in invention. He can understand other people, and can express himself, more adequately than most. And so. he is able to play upon our imagination and evoke in us what emotional responses he will. He invents persons and characters, and brings them together in a dramatic situation; around them he evokes, assembles, and controls emotional attitudes of various kinds; and so he leads us, through anticipation, discord, and suspense, to the final reconciliation in a harmonious balance of feeling (*G.S.*, VI, 131–63).

If this were all, it would be no small thing. The poet would then be to our emotional life what the scholar is to our intellectual life or the prophet to our religious consciousness. But his function, important as it would be, would relate wholly to the emotional life, and not at all to the intellectual or the moral. He would be a master of invention and illusion, which would be none the less invention and illusion because they would be beneficial. But this is not in fact the whole story. The images used by the poet, and the experiences which they convey to us, are more than mere works of fantasy. They are, as truly as scientific statements, a 'representation' of reality. Individual themselves, they yet convey universal truths. And Dilthey sets as a motto, at the head of *Die Drei Epochen u.s.w.*, the words of Schiller: 'Would that at last the demand for beauty might be given up, and wholly and entirely replaced by the demand for truth.'

In trying to understand what this means, we must first of all avoid the error of thinking of the poet as a man with a message, who has an idea clearly formulated in his mind and writes his poem with intent to give it expression; so that the poem is to be understood by unearthing this hidden idea. There is no 'underlying idea' in that sense. What underlies e.g. *Hamlet* is an imaginative process which took place in Shakespeare's mind. Various thoughts and feelings, arising out of his personal experience and attitudes to life, found a focus in the Hamlet saga. Under their influence the saga was altered and shaped into the complex story which is the existing play. All that Shakespeare had in mind to do when he wrote it was to give expression to this imaginative and emotional complex which had grown up in his mind. 'The action put forward . . . in play and counter-play admits of various interpretations. But this much can clearly be seen, that here in the poet's lived experience and in the moving symbols of it there lies a kernel of the drama which cannot be uttered in a set of propositions. In the mind of the deeply moved spectator the whole is fused in a merely imaged and felt unity of the deepest experiences of life, and it is this that the poetry has to say to him' (*G.S.*, VI, 207–8).

And yet, even in and through this complex of feelings and images, *Hamlet* does convey truth to the reader. It can do so because the characters and situations out of which the play is built up are, severally and collectively, *significant* and *typical*. What does Dilthey mean by this, and what does it involve?

He leads up to his point by telling us a great deal about the way in which knowledge and true value-judgment depend on past experience. A child, who has present perceptions but little experience by which to interpret them, reacts artlessly and unreflectively to each present stimulus, and has no great power of criticism or self-control. With advancing maturity there slowly comes into existence a deposit of past experience which Dilthey calls the 'acquired system of mental life' (*erworbener Zusammenhang des Seelenlebens*). He dwells at great length upon the functions of this 'acquired system'. It is the organ by which true perception is distinguished from illusion, and reality from fantasy. It is the organ by which judgment is guided aright in matters alike of fact, of value, and of duty. It provides the material for theories and for plans, together with sound judgment to make them wise and true. 'Propositions owe to it their certitude; concepts derive from it their sharp delimitation; . . . feelings likewise receive from it their measure for the system of life. Our will, which is mostly occupied with means, by virtue of the same system remains conscious throughout of the complex of ends on which the means are based' (*G.S.*, VI, 143–4, cf. 167–8 *et pass.*).

If, through some lesion of the brain or other cause, the acquired system fails to operate efficiently, then the subject, without losing the power of imagination or of logical inference, loses the power to correlate his imaginations and his inferences with common sense, and becomes unable to distinguish fact from fancy. That is what happens in dreams, and again in madness. The dreamer and the madman have a free flow of imagery, without the power to discriminate between their imaginations and reality. The poet too has a free flow of imagery, but he is not deceived by it. His acquired system prevents such error, and shows him the difference between what he perceives and what he merely imagines. But it does more than this; it enters into his imaginations too, and imparts to them a subtle meaning and relevance to the world of reality (*G.S.*, VI, 165–72; and cf. *Dichterische Einbildungskraft u. Wahnsinn, G.S.*, VI, 90–102). It is in this relation that we shall find the means by which poetry conveys truth.

The poet, we saw, is a man whose sensations, images, and lived experiences are unusually vivid and detailed, and who has an unusual power both of expression and of understanding. It follows that his acquired system is richly stored with experience, especially with experience of human life; and by virtue of this he is able to discount what is accidental or contingent in any character, event, or aspect of life, to single out what is *essential* (*wesenhaft*) in it, and to give clear imaginative expression to this. 'The essential, thus singled out from the actual, we designate as the *typical*,' and the image which embodies or expresses it is called a *type*. Such is the account which Dilthey gives, somewhat haltingly, in *Die Einbildungskraft des Dichters* (*G.S.*, VI, 185–8).

He returns to the subject three years later in *Über vergleichende Psychologie*, and here he treats it at greater length. He tells us that the *type* or the *typical* individual, in the proper sense of the word, embodies a *norm* or standard of value; it is not merely the common or ordinary, but the ideal. The *typical* in the sense of the usual, without the implication of value, is a secondary conception, arrived at by abstraction. 'I observe a skater or a dancer. The aptness of the movements is for me inseparably bound up with the perception of them. . . . Only by effort and practice can I here sever my ideas of fact from those of value. In this way, for every department of the manifestations of human life, there arises a type of their apt fulfilment. It denotes their norm, lying between variations on both sides. One typical manifestation of life thus represents a whole class. This is the primary sense in which we apply the concept of the typical. But if I emphasise, or sketch as it were in heavier lines, those traits in such a type which express the regular element in the whole group, I can also speak of what is brought out in these heavier lines as a type. The concept of the type then denotes the emphasised common element. . . . It is thus that we commonly speak of a typical course of events. It is in this sense that Shakespeare presents types of the passions.' The power to see what is typical is present in all men, but more highly developed in the poet, and is an essential part of his equipment (*G.S.*, V, 279–80).

We can now say precisely wherein consists the revealing power of art. The characters and situations presented to us in a poem, and the feeling-responses evoked by them in us, are *typical* of a segment of possible human experience, and of its value or significance for us. By contemplation of the type, our acquaintance with what it represents is widened, and our power to see its true significance is heightened. Art therefore, no less than science, but in a very different way, is a vehicle of truth. 'Thought produces concepts, artistic creation produces types. These . . . embody a heightening (*Steigerung*) of experience, not in the sense of an empty idealisation, but in the sense of a representation of the manifold in one image, whose strong, clear structure makes the lesser, confused experiences of life intelligible (*verständlich*) in accordance with their meaning (*Bedeutung*)' (*G.S.*, VI, 186).

If a poem conveys truth, there must be something in it which holds good for all men. Dilthey ascribes to it, in fact, two of the formal characteristics of scientific propositions, viz. universal validity and necessity, though not in the same sense in which these terms apply to propositions. 'Universal validity means that every feeling heart can reconstruct (*nachbilden*) and enjoy the work.' 'Necessity means that the system present in a poem is as cogent for the reader as it was for the creative artist.' 'The persons act with necessity if the reader or spectator feels that he too would act so' (*G.S.*, VI, 186–7).

This does not mean that there is not also a strong element of subjectivity in the artist's work. There always is and must be such an element. It is not that what the artist sees is false or unreal; on the contrary, it is true and real in the sense which has just been defined. But he sees it in his own way, and only he could ever have seen it in just that way. This element of personal perspective is of course not peculiar to the artist's vision. It is common to all of us. Suppose I am perceiving an object—say, a human face. Among the features composing it, some one will stand out in my consciousness as central; Dilthey calls it the 'point of impression' (*Eindruckspunkt*). The point of impression will not necessarily be the same for me as for another man; the selection of it will depend on my experience, aptitudes, and character. Once determined, the point of impression then becomes the centre round which I arrange the rest of my data, stressing some and slurring over others by virtue of the structural relations which radiate from the central point. 'It is from here that structure and form become intelligible and significant' (*G.S.*, VI, 283). What happens to me happens to the artist also. He also selects and modifies according to his personal standpoint, in spite of himself, even when he talks of 'naturalism' and aims at faithful recording of facts. 'Every effort to see without apperceiving, as it were to resolve the sensuous image into colours on a palette, must fail. . . . Poetry too cannot merely transcribe what goes on. . . . Such an attempt to transcribe will always be conditioned by the subjectivity of the poet who hears, remembers, reproduces (*nachbildet*), because all these processes are influenced by the system of acquired concepts and images.' It is natural, therefore, that the various characters and situations depicted by the same artist should show a 'family likeness' (*G.S.*, V, 280–3, cf. VI, 282–4). And, since the artist's acquired system is historically conditioned, and mirrors the society in which he moves, his work as a whole becomes typical of his age and country, and is not the least important of the factors which make possible the understanding of the past (*G.S.*, VI, 230–1).

It is characteristic of Dilthey's work in aesthetics that we can never go far in it without being brought up against the conception of understanding (*das Verstehen*). This is the more striking because he draws so much of his inspiration from the romantics, whose main emphasis was laid upon the expressive and creative activity of the artist. It is worthy of note how in the aesthetic writings of Croce and Collingwood, and even of Coleridge, the artist as creator has first place, and the way in which we come to understand him is dealt with casually, as if no problem arose there. Dilthey too is interested in the artist. He praises the post-Kantians for having turned our attention in that direction. But he is at least equally interested in the artist's public, in what he means to them, and how they understand him. It is perhaps the positivist again, with his insistence on the public good and his demand that cultural activities shall be of benefit to the community, who speaks here. But it is also the historian and the critic, accustomed to reading and interpreting texts, and asking themselves how the interpreting is done. At any rate, throughout Dilthey's aesthetic there runs an emphasis on understanding: on the artist as himself possessing the power to understand life, and on the understanding of the artist's work by others, by critics and interpreters, by historians, and by the general public, as the consummation and fulfilment of his function.

This points us beyond the present chapter. The nature of understanding, as Dilthey opens it up, is a vast subject, and to it our next chapter shall be dedicated.

CHAPTER FIVE

I N the foregoing discussion of Dilthey's theory of knowledge, very little has been said about his conception of the process whereby we come to know other minds. This is an issue which writers on epistemology have too much neglected; so much so that there is not even a tradition of discussion on the point, or a sequence of outstanding works dealing with it, comparable with the classic sequence of theories, from Descartes to our own day, dealing with our knowledge of physical objects. Dilthey himself has a good deal to say upon the question. His conception of the relation between lived experience, its expression, and the understanding of it (*Erlebnis, Ausdruck, Verstehen*) is deservedly prominent in most expositions of his philosophy, because it holds a central place in his final synthesis, and is an important issue in the psychological and philosophical controversies which have arisen from his writings. Hence it has seemed advisable to devote a separate chapter to this part of Dilthey's philosophy. This course has the further advantage of enabling us to examine it in relation to his peculiar conception of *meaning (Bedeutung)*, which is not, as might be supposed, a conception belonging to epistemology or to pure logic, but one which leads us directly over to the question of the methods and subject-matter of the human studies, with which we shall be concerned in subsequent chapters.

It is obvious that our earliest acquaintance with other minds is obtained through experience of living human bodies, in whose behaviour the life of the mind which informs them is manifested; and this source of knowledge remains fundamental and indispensable, no matter what more subtle modes of communication and understanding may later be added to it. How then, according to Dilthey, do we pass from the perception of people's bodies to the understanding of their minds? We need not repeat the account of how we pass from sensations to the

116

perception of a physical object. That was dealt with in Chapter Two. The question now is, how we pass from the perception of a particular kind of physical object, viz. a human body, to an understanding of the mental life which inhabits and informs it.

There are really two questions. First: how do we pass from the physical expression, perceived by the senses, to the recognition that there is a mental life behind it? And second: granted that there is such a mental life in another person, how do we explore it and come to understand it coherently and in detail? Dilthey answers both questions with one and the same contention, viz. that we understand others by transference from our own inner life. Confronted with a body which resembles our own, and behaves in ways which resemble our own behaviour, we credit it with having a mental life as we have, and we also credit it with having the same sort of mental life as we have. What we impute to others is not merely occasional flashes of consciousness, isolated thoughts or feelings, but a structural system like our own, a wealth of inner life which forms a self-organising complex like our own. That is why, from the fragmentary data which must be our starting-point, we can in favourable conditions build up a wide and intimate knowledge of other minds. Because we assume that their structure is like our own, we can pass from particular facts about them to a picture of the whole of which those facts are part.

Dilthey says that this double process is, in both its parts, equivalent to an inference by analogy (*G.S.*, V, 110, 277, VII, 207). But he is clear that it is not in its own nature an inferential process. We shall come near to the heart of the matter if we examine his reasons for this. He has two reasons, of which the first concerns only the first part of the process—the passage from expressions to what lies behind them—while the second concerns both.

In the first place, an inference involves a distinction between the premisses and the conclusion, and a process by which we go from the one to the other. In this instance the premiss would be that X's body is like mine and behaves like mine, and the conclusion would be that therefore X has a mental life like mine; or, more specifically, the premiss would be that X is in a certain physical state, e.g. weeping, and the conclusion would be that he is sorrowful. In real life we do not draw this explicit distinction between bodily and mental states, and argue from the one to the other, any more than in reading a printed page we explicitly distinguish the words from their meaning and argue from the one to the other. It is only if the language is unknown, or the grammar or spelling or printing at fault, that we stop to notice the printed word as an entity in itself. In the same way, it is only in the presence of some eccentricity that we stop to notice the bodily expression of a mental fact, and then only because we do not at the moment know what it expresses. Where we do know, the expression and the expressed are fused in one perception. As Dilthey himself puts it, 'the mental activity which governs all understanding', in its 'drive (*Zug*) towards the mental fact expressed', 'places its goal in the latter, and yet the expressions presented to the senses do not disappear in the mental fact. Through the fundamental relation between the expression and the mental fact it comes about that e.g. the look on the face and the terror are not two coexisting things (*nicht ein Nebeneinander*), but a unity' (*G.S.*, VII, 208).

In the second place, an inference is an intellectual process, a succession of judgments linked with one another by logical relations; whereas our understanding of other minds, in both its aspects, is primarily a work of imagination. To understand another person is not merely to know that he is having a certain experience, but to feel the reverberation of that experience in myself, to relive it (*nacherleben*) or reconstruct it imaginatively (*nachbilden*). I may then form a judgment to the effect that 'X is having such and such an experience'; but such a judgment depends for its evidence on the imaginative reconstruction (*Nachbild*), and never succeeds-in saying verbally as much as I have relived imaginatively. Dilthey puts the point in his own way as follows. 'The understanding of someone else's state can be conceived *prima facie* as an analogical inference, proceeding from an *external physical* process, by virtue of its *likeness* to *similar* processes which we have found connected with certain *inner* states, to an *inner* state *like* these. But this account gives only a rough and schematic description of what is contained in the result of the reconstructive process (*die Nachbildung*). For this idea of it in the form of an inference severs the inner states, both that from which we infer and the other which is added by inference, from the complex of mental life at the time when each occurs, whereas it is only by its relation to this that the reconstruction obtains its certainty and its closer definition of detail. This can be confirmed by the following facts. The interpretation of other men's utterances (*Äusserungen*) varies very much according to our knowledge of the complex to which such an utterance belongs, or according to the type of mental life which in most cases is, quite unreflectively, laid at their basis. And the limit of our understanding always lies at the point where we can no longer reconstruct on the basis of the complex. But the elements in the reconstructive process are bound together not at all by logical operations, e.g. an analogical inference. To reconstruct is to relive (*Nachbilden ist eben ein Nacherleben*)' (*G.S.*, V, 277).

This is the process which Dilthey calls understanding (*das Verstehen*), and the passage quoted, in spite of its clumsy wording, takes us near to the heart of his doctrine about it. The structural system appears in a double capacity. As the structural system of another mind, it is the object which I understand; and as my own structural system, it is the organ by whose means I understand. The task of understanding, says Dilthey, is 'to discover a living system (*Lebenszusammenhang*) in the given'; and 'this is only possible because the system which exists in my own lived experience, and is experienced in numberless instances, with all its inherent possibilities is always present and available (*gegenwärtig und bereit*)' (*G.S.*, VII, 213–14). Again he says that understanding is 'a rediscovery of the I in the Thou' (*das Verstehen ist ein Wiederfinden des Ich im Du: G.S.*, VII, 191); but this is only possible because I read myself into the Thou. Dilthey speaks of a 'transposition' of my own life into the object (*Übertragung des eigenen Selbst: Transposition: Sichhineinversetzen*). It is not enough merely to 'transpose' isolated experiences, a passing feeling or desire, into the other person. If I am to see him as a person, to understand his mental life in its continuity and coherence, I must trace in his experience the lines of connection with which I am familiar in my own. I can do this in proportion as the consciousness of my own mental structure is present (*präsent*) in and governs my understanding of his. 'The soul travels the accustomed paths, on which of old, in similar conditions of life, she enjoyed and struggled, desired and acted' (*G.S.*, VII, 214).

Dilthey remarks that the two parts of the process of understanding are differently related to the order of events in the life-process which is understood. (1) Lived experience gives rise to an expression; and when we pass from this to the experience behind it, we are moving back from effect to cause. The expression, which is mental life crystallised and as it were congealed in a physical form, is 'turned back into life' when it is understood. Again, when we move from a particular mental event to the whole complex from which it proceeds, and in the light of which it is to be understood, we move from effect to cause. But (2) understanding reaches its crown when, by virtue of my grasp of the other person's experience as a self-differentiating unitary process, I become able to let the whole course of it unroll itself in my consciousness in the order in which it actually took place, and so not merely understand, but even share or relive, the life of another person. 'On the basis of this *Hineinversetzen*, this transposition, arises the highest form in which the totality of the life of the mind is operative in understanding—the process of reconstructing or reliving.[1] Understanding is in itself an operation inverse to the causal process (*Wirkungsverlauf*) itself. A perfect sharing of life (*ein vollkommenes Mitleben*)[2] depends on the

[1] In the late essay from which I am quoting, Dilthey seems to confine the term *nachbilden* or *nacherleben* to this final stage in understanding. We may ignore this change of usage, because there is no trace of it before 1910, and then it is not important.

[2] It is important to distinguish between *nach* and *mit*, as in *nacherleben* and *miterleben*, *nachfühlen* and *mitfühlen*, etc. When I understand an expression of feeling in some other person, the first thing is that I have in my mind a reproduction, or *Nachbild*, of his feeling; i.e. a feeling of the same kind as he has. This is *das Nachfühlen*. The second thing is that I have a feeling about his feeling; i.e. I feel in a certain way about the fact that he has the feeling which he has. This second feeling is called *Sympathie* or *Mitgefühl*, and takes the form of rejoicing because of his joy (*Mitfreude*) or sorrowing because of his sorrow (*Mitleid*). Sympathy is an inevitable accompaniment of the understanding of persons, whether the persons understood be people in real life, or characters on the stage or in a novel, and the extent to which we can sympathise defines also the extent to which we can understand. We can sympathise profoundly with characters on the stage, because, no private interests of ours being affected by their fortunes, no private feelings can distort our sympathy; and Dilthey regards the drama as the field where we have also the clearest and deepest understanding. Where we cannot sympathise with a man at all, we cannot understand him either. 'How impatiently we listen to many an exposition; we notice only one point in it, which has practical importance for us, without having any interest in the inner life of the speaker. Whereas in other cases we strive persistently to pierce through every look, every word, into the inner life of a speaker.' There are

condition that our understanding shall move forward in the line of history itself. Continually advancing, it moves on with the course of life itself. Thus the process of *Sichhineinversetzen* or transposition is widened. To relive is to create along the line of history. So we move forward with the history of time' (*G.S.*, VII, 214).[1]

two spheres where we have a *Nachgefühl* without *Mitgefühl*. The first is instrumental music. 'No one will condole with Beethoven over the expression of grief in one of his adagios, and no one can rejoice with the unruffled cheerfulness of an allegro by Haydn.' The second is the empathic experience, in which we ascribe feelings to nature (*die Einfühlung*). Finally, when our understanding grows from a momentary *Nachfühlen* to a fully developed *Nacherleben*, so that we follow sympathetically a continuous process in another person's life, while our own reaction to the *Nacherlebtes* widens from a mere feeling of sympathy to include admiration, esteem, contempt, etc., and finally becomes the basis of a whole structural complex of thoughts, feelings, and volitions in us—then we have *das Leben im Anderen*, or *das Mitleben* (*G.S.*, V, 111, 277–8, 319, VII, 51–2).

[1] It is of some interest to compare these statements with those of Gentile on the same subject. 'It is common knowledge that, whenever we are to understand (*intendere*) something which has spiritual value and can be called a *spiritual fact*, we need to regard such an object of our research not as something set over against us who seek to understand it, but as something which becomes identical (*s'immedesimi*) with our spiritual activity. . . . It is a fundamental condition of understanding others, that we should penetrate into their spiritual reality. . . . Without the consensus (*il consenso*), without the unification of our spirit, this thinking activity of ours which is to strive to understand, with the other mind with which it desires to enter into relation, it is not possible to have any understanding, nor even to begin to observe or discover anything which goes on in another mind. Every spiritual relation, every communication between our inner reality and someone else's, is essentially unity. . . . We need to unify ourselves with the mind which we desire to know, because the reality of that mind consists in our very own mind; and that mind cannot be met with even in our own mind, except as its own proper subjectivity: life of our life, there where, within our mind, we distinguish nothing in opposition to it' (*Teoria generale dello spirito come atto puro*, pp. 6–8). Gentile's metaphors are different from Dilthey's, but it seems clear that his 'identification', 'penetration', 'consensus', 'unification' represent the same thing as Dilthey's *Übertragung* or *Sichhineinversetzen*.— 'This deep unity we feel every time that we can say we comprehend our neighbour: in all those moments when we are no longer simple intelligence, and have need to love; we are not content with that abstract activity which is called mind (*mente*), but we need, as it is said, a good disposition of spirit, which is commonly called heart, good will, charity, sympathy, openness of mind, warmth of affection' (*op. cit.*, p. 7). Here we may recognise Dilthey's contention, that understanding is a function not of thought

At first sight this is a large claim, and it must be read in the light of things which Dilthey says elsewhere. He is not so naïve as to think that we understand by having in our minds an exact replica of another person's mental processes. Apart from other considerations, the time factor alone makes this impossible; for how can we relive a long process, such as we meet with in a historical narrative or a novel or a play, in the short time which we take to read it? And would it help if we could? Surely to understand something must involve grasping it as a whole; and if we did relive a long mental process in detail, would that bring us any nearer to this total grasp of it? Would not the mass of detail be even a difficulty?

Dilthey himself raises this point and deals with it. A detailed retracing of the course of history, he says, is out of the question, if only because the historical process, being temporal, is like

alone, but of the whole structural system; though Gentile seems not to distinguish, as Dilthey does, between sympathy and understanding, *mit* and *nach*. And when Gentile sees it as a limitation of the psychologist's insight that he does not actually *become* the mind which he studies, e.g. 'the anthropologist working at criminal anthropology does not wish to become even for a moment the criminal, and so resolve the object into the subject', we may equate this 'becoming the criminal' with what Dilthey would call the reliving (*Nacherleben*) of the criminal's experience; and indeed Gentile, in a neighbouring sentence, uses the term *rivivere*, which is obviously *nachleben* or *nacherleben* (*op. cit.*, pp. 21–2). It is unfortunate that Gentile, after formulating these conclusions which come so near to Dilthey's, goes on to make them appear to lead up to metaphysical propositions about the unity of all minds in one mind. If I am to understand you, I must have, and recognise that I have, the same structural character as you, and in that sense we must be 'unified' or 'identical', I must 'penetrate' you and find your subjectivity in my own, just as Gentile says. Dilthey says, in similar language, that 'understanding is a rediscovery of the I in the Thou', and that 'the subject of knowledge is here one with its object', and speaks of the 'identity of mind in the I and the Thou' (*G.S.*, VII, 191). But the conception of this identity of structure has nothing whatever to do with the conception of a transcendental self, a self-conscious self-actualising subject, a 'person which has no plural', 'immultiplicable' and infinite, in which all empirical selves are one (*op. cit.*, pp. 4–5, 13–15, 25–7, *et pass.*). Gentile's desire to bring the two conceptions into close relation has had a bad effect upon his analysis of understanding; for the only way to make this analysis appear to support his metaphysic is to express them both in vague and ambiguous terminology. Dilthey's account of understanding gains by being made without any speculative *arrière-pensée*. It is hard to say as much for any idealist account of the matter.

time itself infinitely divisible, and therefore infinitely rich in detail; and it is a problem how such a series of events can be intuitably portrayed at all (*G.S.*, VII, 252). Even the short duration of a dramatic performance, or the reading of a play, exceeds the limits of our intuitive grasp, and we can only grasp the whole by considering the plot or general framework of it in abstraction from the details. 'When I read a play, it is the same as with life itself. I move onward, and the past loses its clarity and distinctness. So the scenes fade. Principle: only by holding on to the plot (*Zusammenhang*) do I obtain a unitary survey of the scenes, but then I have only an outline' (*G.S.*, VII, 226–7). In the wider field of history, the outline must become more general still, while the details of the process have to be telescoped into a few pregnant incidents which 'represent', i.e. symbolise or typify, a multitude of their kind. In this way we can apprehend, not the separate details of the process, but its structure, and the intelligible sequence of its stages (*G.S.*, VII, 255).

The intelligible order is not necessarily the same as the temporal order. In the relation between end and means, for example, what is last in order of happening is first in order of understanding. Dilthey speaks of mental attitudes (*Stellungen*) which lie deeper than the surface series of psychological events, and control it in the interests of wider purposes. 'In the life-attitude, significance supervenes upon the causal system as a relation between its members which goes deeper than the lived experience of efficient causality (*des Erwirkens*), and connects the members in an order independent of their causal origination. Causal processes indeed constitute everything that comes to the surface in life. Life contains for an observer nothing but effects (*Erwirktes*); for the causal action of the self is unknown. But attitude (*Verhalten, Stellung*) is the deeper factor, which determines the manner in which life produces effects' (*G.S.*, VII, 239). If this is so, then obviously the deeper our understanding goes, the more it will be emancipated from the temporal order of events, and the less it will resemble a mere replica of what went on in someone else's mind.

Of course all this abstracting, symbolising, and selecting, without which understanding is impossible, requires more than mere lived experience, and more than mere imaginative reconstruction. It is a work of thought. As my acquaintance with my own mental life is mediated by 'silent thought', which raises lived experience to the level of inner perception, so too my *Nachbilder* of other people's mental life are penetrated, illuminated and moulded by these elementary thought-processes. By virtue of this, as Dilthey says, 'understanding becomes an intellectual process involving the highest concentration, and yet never fully realisable' (*G.S.*, VII, 227).

Such is Dilthey's analysis of the process of understanding. The outstanding characteristic of the process, in this account of it, is that it interprets the details of mental life in terms of our experience of the whole. A particular expression is perceived, and a particular elementary *Nachbild* is generated; at once the whole structural system, experienced by us as a totality, is 'transposed' to form a background for this. Under the guidance of our experience of the whole, we fill in the details which the perceived expression does not reveal, until at last the particular mental fact with which we began is exhibited in its place as part of a system.

In all his writings down to 1895, or later, this is the aspect of understanding which interests Dilthey most. He uses it to enforce the contrast between the experiential foundations of the human studies and those of the natural sciences. The natural sciences begin with sense-data and cannot find any principle of unity in them; the unity of the physical world has to be supplied by hypothesis. But the human studies can rest upon a direct apprehension of their object as a living unity; the enquirer finds it given in himself by inner perception, and rediscovers it from moment to moment in his understanding of others (cf. *G.S.*, V, 60–2 = I, 36 and 29). When Dilthey wrote his *Ideen über eine beschreibende u. zergliedernde Psychologie* (1894), to show that psychology will never fulfil its true function unless it adopts a new method, it was on the basis of lived experience and understanding as the apprehension of a whole that he constructed this method. It was to be a method of understanding, in place of the prevailing method of explanation. 'We explain by means of purely intellectual processes, but we understand by means of the combined activity of all the mental powers in apprehension. And, in understanding, we proceed from the system of the whole, which is given to us in living experience (*lebendig gegeben*), to make the particular intelligible to ourselves in terms of it. It is the fact that we live in the consciousness of the system of the whole which enables us to understand a particular sentence, a particular gesture, or a particular action. All psychological thought has this fundamental trait, that the apprehension of the whole makes possible and determines the interpretation of the detail. Even the theoretical reconstruction (*die Nachkonstruktion*) of human nature in general in psychology must hold fast to the original procedure of understanding, if it is to remain sound, vital, informed, fruitful for the understanding of life' (*G.S.*, V, 172).

The usefulness of the method is not exhausted in giving us an understanding of others. It can also be made to reinforce the experience which we have of ourselves (*ibid.*). There are gaps in our own lived experience as well as in our reconstructions of other people; and if we will stand as it were outside ourselves, and treat our own experience as an object for understanding like anyone else's, our self-acquaintance can be enriched and clarified. 'We adopt an attitude of understanding in face of our own life as well as of other people's' (*G.S.*, VII, 196), and the process goes on refining itself until it finds its climax in autobiography. 'Autobiography is an understanding of oneself' (*G.S.*, VII, 248). And here too, in self-understanding and autobiography, the essential is that we see ourselves, our past lives, as a whole, and interpret the details by that.[1]

Thus lived experience and understanding, though theoretically separable, are in practice bound up with one another. We are present to ourselves in lived experience, but this experience needs to be clarified by understanding. We understand others, but understanding after all is only a transference of lived experience. It is not merely that the content of my experience of myself enables me to understand others, while the content of my understanding of others gives light upon myself; though that

[1] In one place Dilthey writes 'we do not understand ourselves' (*G.S.*, VII, 225). But the context shows his meaning to be only that, whereas the remote past is dead to us until understanding brings it within our experience, our experience of ourselves is not thus based on the process of understanding. In other words, we do not *in the first instance* understand, but *erleben*, ourselves. Elsewhere he says that 'the apprehension of our own states is called understanding only in an improper sense' (*G.S.*, V, 318). The context here shows that by 'understanding' Dilthey means a process to which the mediation of a physical expression is essential. He is not found making this a part of the definition before 1900. See below, pp. 129 ff.

is of course true and important.[1] But further, the understanding of others would be essentially impossible, as a process, without the living movement and intimacy of lived experience; while the experience of myself could never reveal the true wholeness of my life, unless the objectivity and the wide range of understanding were added to it. Lived experience gives my experience reality and life; understanding gives it comprehensiveness and objectivity. The two are thus inseparable, and together form the basis of all our commerce with the world of mind.

We do not, of course, stop at lived experience and understanding. We advance beyond them to abstract and discursive thought. Dilthey has a great deal to say about this when he comes to deal with the human studies, and in the following chapters we shall examine what he says about their methods and principles. But there is one point of high principle involved, which can appropriately be dealt with now: to what extent can lived experience and understanding be translated into terms of thought without being mutilated and distorted? It is here that Dilthey parts company with Bergson, of whom so much that we have hitherto been saying is reminiscent. The two writers move on parallel lines while they are describing lived experience, but they draw apart when it is a question of the relation between thought and life. It will help to show up Dilthey's position clearly if we develop this contrast.

Bergson sees clearly that the process of mental life (*la durée*) is more than a mere succession of states, distinct from and external to one another, and related only by the blind nexus of causality. It is a continuous flux of mental processes, melting indivisibly into one another in an active self-developing unity. It cannot be truly interpreted in mathematical concepts, but it can be enjoyed in an immediate awareness or *intuition*. It is clear that, in important respects, Bergson's *durée* is Dilthey's *Lebenslauf,* and *intuition* is *Innewerden* or *Erleben*. Bergson goes on, however, to make two mistakes. (1) He has no clear account of how I can grasp the durational process of someone else's mind, i.e. he has no doctrine of understanding. (2) He holds that the passage from intuition to concept is always a distortion of the

[1] Cf. Schiller's lines:

> *Willst du dich selber erkennen, so sieh, wie die andern es treiben;*
> *Willst du die andern verstehn, blick' in dein eigenes Herz.*

reality. Dilthey does not fall into either of these errors. He recognises and carefully analyses the extension of lived experience into understanding; and he goes on to show how both these modes of experience are enriched, refined, illuminated by the thought-process which supervenes upon them. The thought-process is continuous with lived experience through the immanence in the latter of 'silent thought', and therefore even the more abstract forms of thought can still be, in their own way, a true reflection of mental reality. Bergson's dualism is 'a chimera' (*G.S.*, V, cvi).

This does not mean that Dilthey is conscious of no danger in thinking discursively about life. It is a chief concern with him to point to the possible errors, and to argue that all natural scientists, all psychologists and sociologists, and most philosophers fall into them. But he holds that the cure for wrong thinking is not to stop thinking, but to think better. Thought has never misrepresented life except in so far as it has mistaken its own true function. The manifold errors which disfigure the human studies are due to the importation into this sphere of methods and ideas which are appropriate only in another sphere. If we will apply to mind concepts which arose in dealing with matter, of course the movement of life will freeze in our hands, and its unity fall to pieces. But if we let our concepts arise naturally out of experience, we shall discover concepts, 'categories of life' (*Kategorien des Lebens*), which are adequate to the task of expressing life, unity, and change. Dilthey points to Fichte as the first man who grasped the function and necessity of such categories, and to Hegel as one who was most successful in formulating them. 'The categories receive from Hegel's experience and historical understanding a peculiar profundity.' 'He makes arrangements of concepts point back to a state of mind; it is as if, along with the concepts, an overtone in the soul made itself heard. Through all his thinking goes the consciousness of the affinity between categories and states of mind' (*G.S.*, IV, 139–40). Such categories may even bear the same names as categories of the abstract understanding (*Verstand*); e.g. 'whole and part' can be taken in an abstract sense, and must be so taken in mathematics or natural science; but it can also be taken with a deeper meaning as the expression of a living relation (*ibid.*). If we are to understand the categories in this

127

sense, 'we must translate these words back out of the language of reflection into that of life, to grasp the meaning in them' (*G.S.*, IV, 147).

In this way and under these conditions, we can without vicious abstraction form general concepts of types of men and societies, of living relations and processes, and even of laws operating in history and society, out of which we can build up a structure of genuine knowledge in the human studies. But it is essential that these concepts be derived from, and used and interpreted always in close dependence upon, the concrete experience of life in inner enjoyment and understanding. The object must be understood before it can be known (*das Objekt verstanden ist, noch bevor es erkannt wird: G.S.*, I, 119–20). Knowledge can widen experience by a train of inferences far beyond the range of our personal acquaintance in the here and now; but wherever knowledge advances, it must take understanding with it, and there can never be more in thought than there is in understanding. Indeed, there can never be as much. For, although thought with its general ideas can truly express mental life, it does not follow that it can comprehend or exhaust it. The 'totality' of life is 'inexhaustible', and the combined data of lived experience and understanding, accordingly, present to the human studies an 'infinite task'. 'We always understand more than we know' (quoted by A. Stein, *Der Begriff des Verstehens bei Dilthey*, p. 55). 'There is no scientific process which could leave this living reproduction behind it as a subordinate moment. Here is the mother earth to which even the most abstract operations in the human studies must constantly return to draw their strength. Understanding here can never be transmuted (*aufgehoben*) into rational conception. It is vain to try to make the hero or the man of genius intelligible by appeal to all kinds of circumstantialities. The most proper approach to him is the most subjective. For the highest possibility of grasping what was powerful in him lies in the lived experience of his effects upon ourselves, in the permanent conditioning of our own life by him. Ranke's Luther, Goethe's Winkelmann, the Pericles of Thucydides, proceeded from such a relation to the living power of a hero' (*G.S.*, V, 278).

In the last fifteen years of Dilthey's life, another element, present from the beginning in his theory of understanding, came to the fore. This was the recognition of the dependence of all understanding of mental life upon a physical expression, 'something external' (*ein Äusserliches*), by which it is mediated. So important is the expression to the whole process, that Dilthey in the end defines understanding by reference primarily to the expression. 'Understanding is our name for the process in which mental life comes to be known through expressions of it which are given to the senses' (*G.S.*, V, 332, cf. also V, 318, VII, 309). If we now turn to consider the many forms that such expression can take, including e.g. speech and writing as well as physical action or gesture, we shall find that the study of understanding melts insensibly into a theory of the logical or semi-logical process of interpretation, i.e. a hermeneutic theory. Dilthey has given us an interesting analysis of understanding from this point of view in his essay *Das Verstehen anderer Personen u. ihrer Lebensäusserungen* (1910) and in certain MSS., most of them probably of the same period, which are published in *G.S.*, V, with his essay *Die Entstehung der Hermeneutik* (1900). I shall summarise the contents of this analysis.

The 'expressions' or 'manifestations of life' (*Ausdrücke, Lebensäusserungen*), according to Dilthey, may be divided into three classes, differing not only in their nature, but also in the degree of completeness and certitude with which they reveal mental reality. Let us take the three in order.

In defining the *first* class, he seems at first sight to depart from his view of the expression as something external and given to the senses. For he makes the first class of expressions consist of 'concepts, judgments, and greater thought-constructions' (*G.S.*, VII, 205); now, Dilthey regards these as mental facts, distinct on the one side from the linguistic or other symbols by which they may be communicated, and on the other from the reality about which they enable us to think. The inconsistency is, however, only apparent. Dilthey believes that concepts and judgments cannot function unless they are focused in a linguistic or quasi-linguistic symbol; he even speaks sometimes of judgment as if it were a process of combining words. Now, it is of the essence of linguistic symbols that they are, or at least can be, externalised as physical facts. In effect, therefore, Dilthey's first class of expressions consists of words, sentences, and written treatises, whose business is to express 'concepts, judgments, and greater thought-constructions'.

This interpretation is confirmed by a parallel account elsewhere, in which the first class of expressions is made to embrace all external facts which 'are the expression of an inner reality by virtue of arbitrary convention'. Dilthey points out that this covers many instances where one external fact seems to be the sign, not of a mental reality, but of another external fact. 'Here too in reality a process of understanding takes place, viz. through the sign a piece of knowledge about a fact, contained in consciousness A, is brought to the knowledge of consciousness B on the basis of an arbitrary convention. The approach of a train to a station and the giving of a signal are two external facts, but the convention about their combination brings a communicating consciousness into an inner relation with an understanding consciousness, and it is only by virtue of this that the one external process becomes a sign of the other process' (*G.S.*, VII, 320).

Expressions belonging to this first class convey the thoughts which they express from one mind to another with great accuracy. Their meaning is independent of the place, the time, or the particular person's consciousness in which they appear. 'Thus, the judgment is the same in the mind which makes as in that which understands it; it passes over, by a kind of transportation, unchanged from the possession of the one which pronounces it into the possession of the one which understands it. . . . Understanding here is directed upon the pure thought-content, the content is identical in every context, and so understanding is more complete here than in relation to any other manifestation of life.' At the same time, the judgment tells us nothing of the episode of mental life in the course of which it came to be made. It tells us what idea someone has, but not how he comes to have it. Our understanding here is precise, but it is not deep (*G.S.*, VII, 205–6).

The *second* class of expressions consists of human acts. Every act is the execution of a purpose, and, since the relation between act and purpose is regular and intimate, the purpose can be read in the act. The act was not done in order to express the purpose, but to fulfil it; nevertheless, to an outside observer, it does in fact express what it fulfils. This applies not merely to isolated acts belonging to the agent's private life, but also to the public acts of legislators, and the customary behaviour of multitudes of men in the ambit of public institutions. 'The [Prussian] *Landrecht* came into being to regulate by legal enactments the life of a particular period, but the student of the age of Frederick uses it as a means of understanding the spirit of that age; he goes back from the legal rules to the intention of the legislator, and from this to its mental conditions. So from institutions in general we understand the value set upon living relations, the choice of ends, the consciousness of obligation, as all these things existed at a particular time and in a particular place as an inner reality which expresses itself for us in this external fact. Expresses itself for us—without purpose or will to do so; the deeds were done in the stress of will, to effect something, not to communicate something to contemporaries or successors. Now they stand there as signs of an inner reality which once existed, as the relic which is left of it' (*G.S.*, VII, 320). This kind of expression must, however, be interpreted with caution. An act reveals with high probability the purpose which inspired it, and the agent's response to certain particular circumstances, which crystallised into this purpose; but it shows us little of his underlying character and outlook, in which are contained endless possibilities of action, though the circumstances allow only one to be actualised. The one possibility which was actualised does not tell us what the others were, how the man would have acted in other circumstances, i.e. what manner of man he really is (*G.S.*, VII, 206).

That could only be learned from Dilthey's *third* class of expressions, which he calls 'vital expressions' or 'expressions of lived experience' (*Erlebnisausdrücke*). What are these? Since the first two classes comprise expressions of ideas and of purposes respectively, we might expect the third class to consist of expressions of emotion. In fact, however, Dilthey never calls them *Gefühlsausdrücke*; and though some of them can fairly be called so, others hardly seem to fit such a definition. What Dilthey has in mind has been dealt with in his own way by Collingwood in *The Principles of Art*. There he distinguishes, in addition to intellectual expressions or expressions of ideas, two other kinds of expression which he calls 'psychic' and 'imaginative' expressions. Psychic expressions are those spontaneous expressions by exclamation, tone of voice, gesture, bodily attitude and the like, which are in essence common to all mankind. These do in fact express emotions. Imaginative expressions are conscious, controlled, reflective expressions, and the most outstanding examples

131

of them are works of art. These too express emotions, but also a great deal more. At their highest point of development we might say that they lay bare the 'soul' of the artist. Collingwood does not use this phrase, nor does Dilthey adopt it officially, though he once speaks of these expressions as 'welling up immediately out of the soul' (*der Ausdruck quillt aus der Seele unmittelbar: G.S.*, VII, 328–9). At any rate, this is what he means, and he groups Collingwood's 'psychic' and 'imaginative' expressions together under one head, ascribing to them this soul-revealing power.

The simpler kind of *Erlebnisausdrücke*, exclamations, gestures, and the like, arise spontaneously, without premeditation. Works of art are consciously produced, they 'proceed from the need to bring the inner experience somehow to expression, somehow to set it out before one's own eyes or communicate it to others' (*G.S.*, VII, 320). Yet they too are *Erlebnisausdrücke*. Even a scholarly treatise, which is an expression of Dilthey's first class, can belong to his third class also in so far as it gives evidence not merely of the author's thought, but of his mind and outlook. 'It may be the copies which still give us a feeble intuition of the Zeus of Pheidias, or Dürer's Apocalypse or the Ninth Symphony, a drama or a philosophical system, a poem by Goethe or Newton's *magnum opus* in mathematical physics; whether it be an individual creation, or a relation between concepts which gives expression to some matter of fact—in all these cases there is an external fact which arose as the expression of an inner reality and thus brings this reality to understanding' (*G.S.*, VII, 320–1). Emerging as they do from the depths of the soul, such expressions reveal more about us than we ourselves know. 'The expression can contain (*enthalten*) more of the mental system than any introspection can discern. It draws it from depths which consciousness does not illuminate' (*G.S.*, VII, 206). 'I set before myself the sum of Goethe's artistic, literary, and scientific publications, and what is found in his remains. . . . Here the problem can be solved of understanding the inner reality, in a certain sense better than Goethe understood himself' (*G.S.*, VII, 321).

The drawback with expressions of this class is that they can easily be suppressed, distorted, or counterfeited. 'What arises out of daily life stands under the power of its interests. What is continually falling away into the past has its interpretation also determined by the hour. There is something disquieting in the fact that, in the battle of practical interests, every expression may deceive, and also the interpretation alters as our attitude changes.' There is, however, just one kind of vital expression which cannot deceive. This is the work of art;[1] for the artist in producing it is not moved by any private interests, and has no motive for deceit or concealment, but is given up to the task of finding an adequate expression for his experience. The work 'comes apart from its author', or stands outside his private life. Therefore 'no really great work of art can . . . try to put forward a mental content (*Gehalt*) foreign to its author. It offers no information about the author at all. Genuine in itself it stands there fixed, visible, enduring, and thus a trained and assured understanding of it becomes possible. So there arises in the confines between knowledge and action a circle in which life discloses itself at a depth inaccessible to observation, reflection, and theory' (*G.S.*, VII, 207, cf. V, 319–20).

The possibility of understanding expressions of any kind depends upon two important facts; first, that human nature is everywhere the same, i.e. that the elementary components of mental life are common to all men, and second, that every expression is constantly connected according to a rule with one such common element. On this double basis is erected a constant and regular system of recurrent expressions, which is the medium of all understanding and communication. The child is introduced to this expression-system from its earliest days. 'Before it learns to speak, it is already thoroughly soaked in the medium of common factors (*Gemeinsamkeiten*). And it only learns to understand mien and countenance, movements and exclamations, words and sentences, because it meets them constantly in the same shapes and in the same relation to what they mean (*bedeuten*) and express.' Further, every branch of human activity, such as art, science, religion, and every social organisation, has a peculiar structure according to which its constituent factors are articulated; it has a general type-character, and in subordination to this various sub-types can be distinguished. Now, with every such type and sub-type of activity is associated a peculiar set of expressions, e.g. tools with industrial activity and

[1] In another passage Dilthey mentions also the work of "the religious genius or the genuine philosopher."

particular kinds of tool with particular kinds of such activity, special forms of greeting with relations of rank in a particular type of social order, and so on. In this way expressions come to be grouped together according to the relations between the mental facts which they express, and the informativeness of each particular expression is in consequence amplified by its relation to the group in which it stands. The relation between the expression and the type to which it belongs is present (*präsent*) in our apprehension of the expression, and determines the interpretation given to it (*G.S.*, VII, 208–9).

Dilthey goes on to distinguish the 'elementary' or simple forms of understanding from its 'higher' or more complex forms.

Elementary understanding is that in which a particular expression is interpreted in isolation as expressing a particular mental fact, without any attempt to see that mental fact in relation to the whole life of the subject in whom it occurs. 'A series of letters combined into words which form a sentence is the expression for an affirmation. A look betokens to us joy or sorrow. The elementary acts of which complex actions are composed, such as the lifting up of an object, the letting fall of a hammer, the sawing of wood, betoken for us the presence of certain purposes' (*G.S.*, VII, 207).

The *higher* forms of understanding are those in which we take not one expression, but a group of expressions, and interpret them as proceeding from a complex process or segment of mental life. Various reasons lead us to do this. (1) The elementary forms of understanding are themselves not always trustworthy; if the perceived expression is unfamiliar to us, or what it conveys is in conflict with other knowledge in our possession, we have to reckon with the possibility that it is deceptive. Then we check our present observation by calling in other observations, and finally we may come to weighing up the entire character and outlook of the person before us, so far as we can discover it, as a means of interpreting a single expression of his. (2) Again, in practical life we continually need to know how far we can count on our associates to help or hinder our plans. For this too we are driven to scrutinise everything that in any way expresses their mind, so as to obtain an understanding of their character, and a forecast of their probable behaviour in various circumstances.

The process of understanding here becomes more complicated. (1) We have now before us a number of particular expressions, each of which, taken by itself, can be made the object of an act of elementary understanding. In this way we obtain a view of many particular mental facts, which are directly revealed by the expressions. (2) Then, when we find that the mental facts behind several different expressions all belong to one structurally coherent group, the expressions themselves can be taken together, like letters combined in a word, as a single complex expression for a single complex fact. But the possibility of this kind of grouping is limited, and the view of the mental system which is obtainable in this way is fragmentary. To piece it out, (3) we finally have resort to inference, taking all the mental facts that we directly understand as an effect (*die Wirkung, das Erwirkte*), and arguing inductively to a coherent mental system as their cause (*das Wirkende*); from this again we can deduce the effects which this same mental system might probably have under other conditions (*G.S.*, VII, 210–12).

It is clear that neither this deduction, nor the previous induction on which it is based, can give more than a probable conclusion, the evidence being at best not exhaustive. This is especially so when the evidence is found in expressions of the second class; for, as all men's actions are determined by the circumstances in which they have to live, it is always possible that the side of a man's character which his actions reveal is disproportionately emphasised, and that the aspect most important for a balanced understanding of him is just that which finds no chance to express itself in action. The actions available for our study are 'never more than sections, vistas, which show parts of a landscape, we never survey the actual articulation of it' (*G.S.*, VII, 321).

From this uncertainty only one of the higher forms of understanding is free, because it is free from the inference which occasions it; this is the understanding of works of creative genius. Here the experience expressed is a self-contained whole, and the expression itself is one which has been elaborated precisely for the sake of completeness and adequacy. Therefore the direct perception of the inner in the outer, made easy by art, is enough without any added inference to reveal to us a coherent living whole. 'A play is performed. It is not only the non-literary spectator who lives wholly in the action, without thinking of the author of the piece; the instructed person too can live wholly under the spell of what here takes place. His understanding then moves towards the systematic unity of the action, the characters of the persons, the interweaving of the moments which determine the turn of fortune. Only then will he enjoy the full reality of the section from life which is displayed. Only then will there be fully carried out in him a process of understanding and reliving, such as the poet intends to produce in him. And in the whole field of such understanding of mental creations, the only relation prevailing is that between expressions and the world of mind expressed in them.' The spectator may, of course, go on to recognise that this experience, in which he has been absorbed, has been consciously and systematically worked out in a poet's mind, and may draw conclusions about the poet. Here comes in inference, and with it uncertainty. This, however, is a distinct step in the process, and need not be taken (*G.S.*, VII, 211–12).

The highest achievements of understanding come about through the process of reliving (*Nacherleben*) in the strictest sense of that word, viz. the process in which we 'go forward with the history of time', and follow stage by stage, in its true temporal and causal order, the experience of another mind. We can do this most fully when the experience has already 'passed through the consciousness of the poet, artist, or historian', and been expressed by him in a lasting work. The author begins by indicating an outward situation or milieu, in which the action is to take place; in this way he tunes our mind to a particular key of feeling, and lays us open to a particular type of suggestion. Then he tells his story. Every particular expression that he uses may call up in us, by an elementary understanding-process, some one of the infinite possibilities of experience which reside, mostly unrealised, or seen only through dreams, in the structure of our minds. 'Numberless ways are open in the past and in dreams of the future; from the words we read run numberless trains of thought.' Through the combination of many particular expressions in a long and complex work we are led at last to reconstruct imaginatively a whole system of events, which may belong to a world of experience far removed from our own. 'The curtain rises. Richard appears, and a lively mind, following his words, looks, and movements, can relive something which lies outside any possibility of the spectator's real actual life. The fantastic forest in *As You Like It* puts us into a mood fancifully to reconstruct any eccentricity.' Thus in drama and novel and in historiography a few chosen incidents, presented to us within a short time, enable us to follow, it may be over months and years, the sweep of a living process. 'The lyric poem in the succession of its lines enables us to relive a complex experience: not the actual experience which inspired the poet, but that which the poet bases on it and puts into the mouth of an ideal person. The sequence of the scenes in a play enables us to relive the fragments from the lives of the characters who appear. The narrative of the novelist or historian, which follows the course of events, produces a reliving process (*ein Nacherleben*) in us. It is the triumph of *das Nacherleben* that, in it, the fragments of a process are so filled out that we think we have a continuity before us' (*G.S.*, VII, 213–15, cf. 255).

Some expressions are momentary and fleeting, and on these no reasoned and methodical understanding can be built. But many expressions are fixed in a relatively permanent form, and while these endure we can return again and again to the study of them, working out in this way a coherent and well-tested interpretation. 'The skilled understanding of permanently fixed manifestations of life is what we call exposition (*Auslegung*)' (*G.S.*, VII, 217 = 309 = V, 319 = 332). 'And since mental life finds in language alone a complete and exhaustive expression, making possible an objective apprehension of it, therefore exposition finds its perfection in the interpretation of the relics of human existence which are contained in writing. This art is the foundation of philology. And the science of this art is hermeneutics' (*G.S.*, VII, 217, cf. V, 319–20). Dilthey emphasises the importance of this science for any *Grundlegung der Geisteswissenschaften*. Its practical value is not great, for it is not the learning of rules, but innate capacity improved by practice, which makes a skilled interpreter. But then, that is not the main purpose of hermeneutics. 'Its business is to furnish, in opposition to the continual inroads of romantic arbitrariness and sceptical subjectivity into the field of history, a theoretical vindication of the universal validity of interpretation, upon which all security in history depends. Taken up into the system of epistemology, logic, and methodology of the human studies, this doctrine of interpretation becomes an important link between philosophy and the historical studies, a principal element in the *Grundlegung der Geisteswissenschaften*' (*G.S.*, V, 331, cf. VII, 217–18). Dilthey gives a few hints, largely based on Schleiermacher, as to the content of this science, i.e. the outlines of an analysis of the systematic interpretation of written sources.

All such interpretation involves a logical circle. For, in the first place, every part of a literary work requires the whole to make it intelligible, and the whole work in turn requires interpretation in the light of the whole mind of its author, the purpose for which and the circumstances in which he writes, the movement or school to which he belongs, and so on; only by such an appeal to the whole can the precise significance of each detail, e.g. of speeches in a dialogue, be determined. Yet the whole by which we interpret the parts must itself be built up by study of the parts. Again, the understanding of any mental state involves a reference to a stimulus which arouses that state, and to that extent understanding presupposes explanation. But explanation in its turn presupposes understanding of that which is to be explained (*G.S.*, V, 334). This circle is theoretically irresolvable, but there are methods of exposition which resolve it in practice, and it is these which are to be described in hermeneutics.

The interpreter must first of all become familiar with the language used by the writer whose work he studies, and the circumstances, the ideas and customs, in fine the kind of society, in which he lived and thought. Part of this task is fulfilled by historical, and part by grammatical research. All languages have a certain rudimentary structure in common, they are all built up from a single ground-plan, and this plan can be made known by a comparative study of language. On this basis can then proceed the grammatical analysis of particular languages, and the interpretation of particular works in these languages can only begin when this knowledge has been applied to these works, and has elicited the precise grammatical meaning of each of the written words and phrases composing them (*G.S.*, V, 335, VII, 219). The process of thought here is at first analogical, a word or phrase being taken to mean in this case what it has been found to mean in many previous cases; though we pass insensibly into a stage where we formulate general principles on an inductive basis, and apply these to new cases as they arise. 'The analogical inference passes over into the inductive inference with reference to a new instance. The distinction between these two forms of inference in the process of understanding has only a relative validity' (*G.S.*, VII, 219–20).

After these preliminaries comes the process of understanding proper. A literary work lies before us. It differs from any datum of natural science in that every part of it is *prima facie* indeterminate. When the scientist observes a natural process or an experiment, he finds sensible images (*Bilder*) which he can treat as given quantities, can measure exactly, and make the basis of a rigorous inference as to the nature of the enduring object to which they bear witness. But in philological exposition the perceived images, i.e. the words composing the work we are expounding, are not amenable to measurement, and we cannot reach the reality behind them by mathematical inference. We have to depend on the relation between expression and the expressed. Now, the meaning of all verbal expressions is in some degree indeterminate; while confined within a certain range of possibilities, it can move freely within that range. The meaning of any word, phrase, or sentence is specifically determined, on every occasion of its use, only by the context in which it functions, viz. the logical structure of the discourse of which it is a part, and the purpose which this discourse is meant to subserve, whether scientific, oratorical, eristic, or what not. This fact determines the way in which interpretation must proceed.

We begin with the 'indeterminately-determinate parts' of the discourse, and, from their general character and the manner in which they are combined, obtain a preliminary idea of the 'sense' of the whole. Then we use this 'sense' of the whole to determine more precisely the significance of the parts. This in turn serves to test and correct our idea of the whole, which must, if possible, be so conceived that all the parts can be understood without violence in terms of it. We can claim to understand the work when behind the words of every sentence we can read its sense, and behind the succession of sentences we can discern the structure or 'inner form' or the whole. All this is an inductive process of a somewhat peculiar kind; starting with a particular group of data, it sets out to discover not a universal law, but a principle of structure immanent in these particular data, which makes them a coherent individual whole. This type of induction is not peculiar to the human studies; it was by its means that e.g. Kepler, from a few observations of Mars, discovered the elliptical form of the orbit of that planet. But in the human studies this form of inference has a fundamental importance, and the higher forms of understanding are impossible without it. By its means alone we can pass from the parts of a work to the sense of the whole, and by reference to the whole again determine the precise significance of every part (*G.S.*, VII, 220, 227).

But understanding does not halt here. Behind the inner form of that particular work it sees the creative mind from which it sprang; the particular work is seen in relation to the life, outlook, and circumstances of its author, and to the condition of his art at the time when he was active; so that it appears no longer as a self-contained unit, but as one moment in the living process which is the history of the art. This way of regarding the work makes a difference to our estimate of the author's originality and power. 'The question is, what place a writer occupies in the development of the genre. So long as the genre is in process of elaboration, the writer makes a creative contribution to the genre from his individual powers. He needs a greater individual strength. But if he comes to the work after its genre has been perfected, then the genre helps him and carries him onward.' More generally, this means that interpretation and history cannot be kept apart. 'Connection between philology and the highest form of historical understanding. Exposition and historical portrayal only two sides of the enthusiastic penetration' (*G.S.*, VII, 226, V, 335).

Finally, since all cognition carries with it a feeling of value, understanding and exposition are inseparable from critical appreciation. For every type of work we recognise a norm, by which we judge the authenticity (philological criticism) or the value (literary criticism) of any work or part of a work. Side by side with these moves historical criticism, in which the form and content of the particular work are accounted for or explained by its antecedents; for 'between exposition and explanation there is only a difference of degree, no firm boundary'. In the end, of course, philological criticism finds its consummation in literary history, literary criticism in aesthetics, and historical criticism melts into actual historiography (*G.S.*, V, 336).

Although the procedure of exposition can be thus described in logical terms, we must not suppose that understanding itself is a purely logical operation which can be reduced to rule. As every lived experience involves cognition, feeling, and volition, so the process of reliving brings all these aspects of life into play; and as no lived experience can be fully analysed by logical categories, so it is impossible by logical inference to construct an adequate picture of another person's life. 'In all understanding there is something irrational, even as life itself is irrational; it cannot be represented (*repräsentiert*) by any formulae of logical functions' (*G.S.*, VII, 218). Dilthey, following Schleiermacher, often speaks of the process as one of 'divination'. The art of it cannot be taught, it can only be obtained 'in personal contact with the great master of exposition or with his work' (*G.S.*, V, 320). It has in it something of 'creative genius' (*G.S.*, V, 335). 'In consequence of these relations, scientific exposition or interpretation, as an understanding which reproduces [its object] in accordance with an art (*das kunstmässig nachbildende Verstehen*), has always something of genius in it, i.e. only through inner affinity and sympathy does it attain a high degree of perfection. . . . This inner relation, which makes transposition possible, forms therefore the presupposition of all hermeneutic rules' (*G.S.*, V, 278).

It follows that the results reached in interpretation can never have demonstrative certitude (*G.S.*, VII, 226), though the process carries with it a conviction of its own, for which any chain of inferences, into which we may pretend to resolve the process, presents no adequate substitute (*G.S.*, VII, 218). And, since understanding is not the work of logical reflection, it is free from the limitations of logical reflection, and, operating with the same creative imagination from which the literary work originally proceeded, can relive factors which were not present to the explicit consciousness even of the writer himself, but which his finished expression has made accessible, i.e. *nacherlebbar*. The bold paradox of Schleiermacher, that the aim of interpretation is to understand the author better than he understood himself, is true (*G.S.*, VII, 217). At the root of every poem is an 'idea'; not, of course, a *concept* or *set of propositions* consciously held by the writer and deliberately embodied in his work, but a *form of unity in experience*, which his creative imagination has brought about without reflecting upon it, and proceeds, still without reflection, to express. 'The idea (not as an abstract concept, but) in the sense of an unconscious system, active in the organisation of the work and understood from its inner form, is really present; a poet need not be, or rather, never will entirely be conscious of it; the interpreter elicits it, and that is perhaps the highest triumph of hermeneutics' (*G.S.*, V, 335).

Such is Dilthey's doctrine of understanding and his outline of a hermeneutic theory. From it we shall pass at once to consider his conception of *meaning (Bedeutung)*. This may seem a natural and indeed inevitable transition; but here at the very beginning must come a warning. The *meaning*, the study of which follows most naturally from that of understanding and interpretation, is of course *meaning* in the sense of *signification*, a relation between a sign and a thing signified, whereby the sign indicates or expresses or 'means' the thing signified. But we have already examined all that Dilthey has to say about this relation. There remains, however, another kind of *meaning*, the conception of which plays a great part in his philosophy; and it is to this that we must now turn our attention.

We may begin by recognising and dismissing yet another sense of the word 'meaning', the sense in which it equals 'importance'. 'This means a great deal to me', or 'this means a great deal for the progress of philosophy' = 'this is important for me' or 'for the progress of philosophy'. *Bedeuten* is used in a like manner in German. Again, *bedeutend* = significant = important. De Ruggiero, in his account of Dilthey's philosophy, asserts that *Bedeutung* in Dilthey always equals importance (*Filosofi del Novecento*, p. 245). This is not so. There are indeed a few passages in which Dilthey uses *Bedeutung* in a way which will bear this interpretation, though there are none, I think, which absolutely demand it. In any case such passages are rare and unrepresentative. *Bedeutung* in Dilthey does not mean 'importance', but something more subtle and profound.

He gives it a high place among the 'categories of life', the concepts in which the nature of life as process and as self-developing unity is brought out. Life is unity in diversity, a whole whose parts are not merely included in it in a mathematical or physical sense, but stand in an intimate relation with one another and the whole. Now, Dilthey tells us that *Bedeutung* is the category in which this relation between whole and part, which is characteristic of life, is most fully expressed. 'Meaning is the category for the unanalysed system of life (*Lebenszusammenhang*)' (*G.S.*, VII, 237). 'The category of meaning designates the relation of parts of life to the whole, which is grounded in the nature of life' (*G.S.*, VII, 233). This is the primary sense of the term in Dilthey's philosophy, and the sense of 'signification' is subordinate to it. Dilthey even makes the point that in grammatical interpretation itself, where we are concerned with the 'meaning' of words and sentences, the relation of part and whole has a decisive part to play.

The simplest case, he says, in which meaning is to be found is the understanding of a sentence, where the meanings of the words and the sense of the whole[1] reciprocally determine one another. What does Dilthey mean by this? He knows, of course, that the words and sentence are signs, and that their meaning as·signs lies in their relation to something behind themselves, which they mean (*meinen, bedeuten*) or betoken (*bezeichnen*), or to which they refer (*hindeuten*). This, however, is not the aspect of the matter which he chooses to emphasise. Rather he is reminding us that the meaning of a word, taken in isolation, is indeterminate within a certain range of possibilities, and is made precise only by being given a specific place in the sentence as a whole. The words give precision to one another by being related in this particular way, by coming before and after each other as they do. Each word receives light from what has gone before and casts light back upon it. Each word suggests other words which may follow, but also limits the range of possibilities there. Dilthey says that the meaning of the words is determined, like the meaning of episodes in life, 'by virtue of memories and future possibilities' (*G.S.*, VII, 234–5).

It is the same when we pass from understanding a written text to understanding a piece of history. Here we work not only from words, but from all available forms of expression; and all of these have meaning in the sense that they are outward signs,

---

[1] Dilthey sometimes distinguishes the *Bedeutung* or meaning of the part as *Bedeutsamkeit* or significance, and the meaning of the whole as *Sinn* or sense. Very often he uses *Bedeutung* for the part and *Sinn* for the whole.

referring to an inner reality behind themselves. But here again this is not the aspect which Dilthey emphasises. What matters is that the meaning of each expression is only to be understood by reference to the whole, including the past, so far as we remember it, and the future, so far as we can foresee it. The expressions are thus interrelated because the experiences which they express are also interrelated in this way. Indeed, the expressions, or 'objectifications' (*Objektivationen*) of life, are not really separate from the life-process, but arise from it and remain part of it. They are themselves historical events, parts of the process whose meaning we are able to read in them. The relations between them are not abstract logical relations, like the relations between the words and sentences of a scientific treatise, nor impersonal causal relations, like those between events in the physical world, but living relations, which we understand by reliving them in ourselves. 'The inner relation is given in the possibility of recreating or reliving (*des Nacherzeugens*,[1] *Nacherlebens*). This is uniformly the method, as soon as understanding leaves the sphere of words and their sense, and looks not for a sense of signs, but for the much deeper sense of a manifestation of life. It is the method first glimpsed by Fichte. Life is like a melody in which it is not sounds that appear as the expression of the real realities (*der realen Realitäten*) residing in life. The melody lies in life itself' (*G.S.*, VII, 234).

This is the heart of the matter. Life is a whole, whose parts have meaning in so far as they condition and illuminate one another within the whole. There is no question here of any relation between signs and things signified. We obtain access to life by reading its signs, but when we come to life itself, the true object of understanding, that relation is left behind. 'Every manifestation of life has a meaning in so far as it is a sign which expresses something, and, as an expression, refers to something which belongs to life. But life itself does not mean anything else. There is in it no separation by virtue of which it could mean anything but itself' (*G.S.*, VII, 234). The meaning of life lies entirely in the relations between parts and whole within it.

Some of these relations are independent of time. For instance, Dilthey speaks of art as showing the meaning of characters,

[1] The verb *erzeugen*, and the doctrine that to understand an experience we must create or evoke (*erzeugen*) it in ourselves, are characteristic of Fichte.

events, or experiences, by bringing out what is essential or typical in them (above, p. 112–3). Similarly he speaks of historical records having meaning for the historian when the personality or process which they record is typical or 'representative' of a certain range of human possibilities. Most of the relations, however, are time-relations, e.g. causal relations, means-and-end relations and the like. 'The essence of meaning-relations lies in the relations which, in the time-process, are contained in the gradual shaping of a life (*Gestaltung eines Lebenslaufes*) on the basis of the structure of life under conditions of the milieu' (*G.S.*, VII, 234). 'We grasp the meaning of a moment of the past. It is significant in so far as in it, by a deed or by an external event, we became bound for the future. Or in so far as a plan for the future conduct of life was conceived. Or in so far as such a plan was carried towards its fulfilment. Or it is significant for the life of the community in so far as it embodies the individual's intervention in this life' (*G.S.*, VII, 233).

What have all these time-relations in common? Causality? Yes, but that is not all. It is not enough to think of meaning or significance as causal efficacy. That is the standpoint taken by the historian Eduard Meyer, who holds that the significant event is the event which has had a wide influence. This is to measure the significance of past events by their dynamic relation to the present; that event is significant which has left a mark on the world of to-day. But this, as Dilthey sees, is not enough. On this showing, 'everything would be significant which had a part in causing the endless multitude of present facts'; a view which we do not normally take. We must rather say that that is significant which had a part in causing something which is itself significant in the present. But then there must be a criterion of the significance of present facts; and this criterion, says Dilthey, is value.

There are two ways, however, of estimating value and so meaning. If we take the practical point of view, we shall fix our eyes on the future, and see in the present only the possibilities which it holds out of future achievement. The values which we recognise will appear to us as ends or projects, and we shall 'find that significant in the present which is fruitful for the future' (*G.S.*, VII, 288–9). But we need not always take this practical point of view. We can forget the future in the enjoyment of the present. Then values will appear to us in the form of present satisfactions, and the past will appear significant in the degree in which it has contributed to these present satisfactions. 'If we step quietly aside from the hunt after ends, and look back into our life, then its moments etc. appear significant. *This is the natural aspect* of life' (*G.S.*, VI, 319).

Dilthey goes on to draw out in an interesting way the relation between the pragmatic and the contemplative attitudes to life. 'In the poet this [i.e. the contemplative] mode of apprehension presents itself in a heightened form. He apprehends the significance of life. Because the poet is not stimulated to action by what he perceives, the world of men becomes meaningful for him. The meaning of an event lies in the fact that its causal concatenation is also the generation of a value. For the active man the value lies in an end, for the poetic man it lies in each moment of life. In youth, life and poetic apprehension coincide, youth can still be planless. Later, when coherent action enters in, the two things come apart. Then the poetic power mostly disappears. In Goethe it becomes stronger in the form of a contemplation severed from action. Hence he has to withdraw from life in order to write poetry. But then the significance of each moment of life appears all the more strongly in contemplation. He who only writes poetry remains a phantast (*Schwärmer*). In him who acts, poetry becomes restricted' (*ibid.*).

Elsewhere Dilthey glances at the obvious truth that the contemplative attitude, which sees and enjoys the present, and the practical attitude, which strains forward towards the future, affect one another. Our plans for the future are a reflection of what we have already found good and desirable in the present, while on the other hand our plans, once formulated and adopted, react upon our judgment of the significance of past and present (*G.S.*, VII, 233). Both the autobiographer, looking back over his own personal past, and the historian, engaged with the past of nations, must balance the two points of view. We shall see in a later chapter how the concentration of a writer's chief interest on past, present, or future can affect the way in which he remembers and sets forth the events of his own life (below, p. 272). It is also obvious that as time moves on, as the past becomes richer and the future presents to us a changing face, our views of the meaning of events will also change. No final judgment can be made on the meaning of events in a man's life until he has died, nor on the meaning of historical events before the end of history (*G.S.*, VII, 233). In real life, in short, all judgments of meaning are provisional. Life as we know it is always building itself into an intelligible whole; but it is a whole that is never complete, perpetually *in fieri*. The key to it is not to be found in the values which we now recognise, or the ends which we now pursue; the pursuit of values and ends is something which happens in the course of life, but life itself, embracing and transcending each and every end-seeking, means-taking activity, works itself out purposively indeed, but without any specific purpose which we can define. In this it resembles music, with which Dilthey so often compares it.

The attempt is sometimes made by religious thinkers, and by a certain kind of philosophers, to discover 'the meaning of life' and express it in one universally valid formula. Such formulae tend to be alike in assuming *one* type of life and character to be the norm for mankind, and they describe a series of stages through which we must pass on the way to it. 'The meaning of life' lies therefore in the ideal type, and the meaning of particular aspects or episodes in life lies in their relation to our growth towards perfection. 'The Neo-Platonic type, the mystical type of the Middle Age, the grades in Spinoza. In these schemata a realisation of the meaning of life takes place' (*G.S.*, VII, 240). Dilthey himself is interested in this way of looking at life, but his *Weltanschauungslehre* shows how he differs from the writers and schools mentioned above. He does not believe that there is one 'meaning of life' which is the same for all mankind; he believes that there are infinite possibilities of variation in meaning. It is an error to tie down what life leaves free.

These doctrines of Dilthey about understanding and meaning have come under criticism from Rickert and the Baden school, whose Neo-Kantian theory of knowledge naturally leads them to take a different view of these matters. Let us now examine their criticism and try to assess its value.

Rickert begins, in the true Neo-Kantian spirit, by distinguishing between the matter and the form of human experience. The 'matter' is the stream of psychological events, which arise in the minded organism in response to the stimuli reaching it from its surroundings, and are related to one another in accordance with psychological laws. This is the 'psychical' realm (*das Psychische, Seelische*). Psychological events as such can be 'explained' by the methods of natural science, but cannot be 'understood', because they are a mere sequence of events without any sense (*Sinn*) in it. Sense or meaning comes into experience from another source, to which scientific psychology has no clue. Sense-data are synthesised under the categories, a world of objects is constructed, moral and cultural values are pursued and progressively realised in real life. These values do not arise out of the life of the psyche. They come upon it as form upon matter, and their source is the transcendental self. Man belongs to two worlds, the real (*wirklich, real*) world of temporal becoming and the unreal (*unwirklich, irreal*) or ideal (*ideel*) world of rational principles. His psychological processes belong to the real world, but all meaning belongs to the ideal world. And, as psychical fact and ideal meaning differ, so do the processes by which they are apprehended. The one is known to us by the psychological process of *Erleben* and *Nacherleben*, and the other by the pure rational process of *Verstehen*.

Rickert illustrates the difference by considering what is involved in understanding Goethe's *Faust*. The meaning of *Faust* is something that Goethe himself understood. In understanding it, therefore, I am reproducing in myself an experience (an act of rational apprehension) which Goethe had. But though the understanding of *Faust* did occur in Goethe's mind, as it does now in mine, it was far from being just an episode in his mental history. *Faust* was and is a work of art, an individual embodiment of aesthetic value, obeying its own inherent laws, which are the laws of reason and creative imagination. All the doubts and hesitations, the false starts, the extraneous motives, which enter into the psychological process of writing *Faust*, are irrelevant to the understanding of it. But if, as Dilthey says, to understand is to *nacherleben*, that can only mean that the whole psychological process is to be relived. Does not Dilthey expressly say that the higher forms of understanding try to go behind the finished work to its genesis, and so merge at last into biography and history? The psychological process as such, however, obeys no rational principle, but only the laws of psychological causality. The *Nachbild* of it cannot be illuminated by any act of understanding, it can only be accounted for, with more or less probability, by scientific explanation. That is the true *Nacherleben*, and to define understanding in terms of it is a gross error.

So then, to understand anything is to grasp a rational principle in it. The primary object of understanding is the ideal principle, the sense-content (*Sinngehalt*) or meaning-complex (*Sinngebilde*) or cultural value (*Kulturwert*) itself. In a secondary sense we may be said to understand, in terms of the principle, the mental activity through which it is realised. Where there is no recognition of a rational principle, we do not understand, though we may relive (*nacherleben*).

The highest understanding is therefore attained in philosophy, where logic, ethics, and aesthetics exhibit the ideal norms in their pure form, and the philosophy of history applies them in order to obtain an absolutely valid interpretation of the meaning or sense of human life and history.

Next to this comes the understanding of empirically discovered principles, and the use of them with a view to an interpretation of history and culture from an 'immanent' and relative standpoint. This is the work of history and the cultural studies; the cultural studies describe, classify, interpret, and criticise cultural achievements, while history examines the time-process in which these achievements come to be and pass away.

In history, however, as distinct from the cultural studies, we try to go behind the value-complexes which we understand, to glance at the psychological background against which they stand out, and to trace the circumstances of their genesis. Here, then, we pass from understanding to reliving; and be it noted that understanding comes first, and acts throughout as a control upon the reliving. We find that a certain person once actualised in his experience a certain ideal value, and we ask ourselves what must have been going on in a mind where such a value as this came to birth. In answer to this question, we build up a picture of that person's mental life by analogy with our own, and try to relive his experience, just as Dilthey says; only, this reliving is not the understanding of that person, nor even a basis for the understanding of him, but something generically different, which moreover can only begin when we have already understood him.

Finally, says Rickert, in psychology, which is a natural science in method and in spirit, and cares nothing for ideal values or principles, there is naturally no place for understanding. Psychology studies the psychical processes as such, in abstraction from any ideal meaning which may enter into them; and for this purpose *das Nacherleben* is its necessary and sufficient tool.

Rickert and his school are not backward in praise of Dilthey as a historian, biographer, and critic. He has, they say, a quite peculiar power of insight, both into individual personalities and into great meaning-complexes such as the *Aufklärung* or the post-Kantian philosophy. He can see, and he can make us see. Further, he understands well enough in a practical way the difference between a psychological process and a meaning-complex, and in his later writings he has said quite clearly that the meaning-complex is the primary object of enquiry in the human studies. Where he fails, say the Baden school, is in explaining how a meaning-complex is apprehended. Because he follows an empiricist theory of knowledge, and ignores the sharp antithesis which exists between psychic experience and rational apprehension, he cannot distinguish *Verstehen* from *Nacherleben* in his theory of knowledge, even though he keeps them properly apart in his historical and critical practice.

Is this criticism sound?

It is true that Dilthey adheres to a radical empiricism, and will have nothing to do with the Neo-Kantians' ideal world or with their conception of reason. He recognises as well as they do that there can be no understanding without thinking; in accordance, however, with his general theory of knowledge he does not conceive this thinking as a transcendental synthesis imposing form on experiential matter, but as 'silent thought' eliciting the formal unity which is ready given in lived experience. This is the core of his quarrel with them, and it shows itself in many ways. When Dilthey insists on speaking of *Geisteswissenschaften* instead of *Kulturwissenschaften*, and uses the word *Geist* in a way which straddles the Kantian dichotomy of psyche and reason, he is not being careless or obtuse. He knows what he is doing. He is saying that lived experience is, of its own nature, instinct with form and meaning. He says so expressly in words whose edge is directed against Kantian teaching. 'The significance which the fact acquires, as the determination imparted by a meaningful whole to its parts, is a living connéction and not an intellectual relation (*ein Lebensbezug und kein intellektuelles Verhältnis*), not an insertion (*Hineinlegen*) of reason or thought into that part of the process. Significance is extracted (*herausgeholt*) from life itself' (*G.S.*, VII, 240). He even defines an *Erlebnis*, or unit of experience, in terms of meaning. 'That which, in the flow of time, forms a unity in presentness (*Präsenz*), because it has a unitary meaning, is the smallest unit which we can designate as an *Erlebnis*' (*G.S.*, VII, 194 = 73). Finally, it is the same conviction which leads Dilthey in another context to disagree with the Kantians when they distinguish philosophy so rigidly from psychology. In their view, psychology is the natural science of the psyche, which cannot be made an object of understanding because it has in it no ideal meaning, and it is to philosophy that we must go for a rational science of the self. But Dilthey believes that the intelligible order which characterises the rational self is homogeneous with, only more fully developed and integrated than, the order which prevails in the smallest unit-experience.

It may be said that this is to exaggerate the intelligibility and meaningfulness of lived experience. Is there *no* element of the irrational in it, no element which calls for explanation in terms of psychological laws while refusing to be interpreted in terms of meaning? The answer is that Dilthey recognises a breach in the meaningful unity of mental life at two points. (1) He draws, as we have seen, a distinction between those relations and processes which are 'structural' and intelligible, and others which are not; the latter including casual associations, some phenomena connected with forgetfulness and recall, and other psychological mechanisms which we discover inductively from observation, but do not experience understandingly from within. (2) For all his insistence on the activity of the mind in understanding, he has also a keen sense of the impact which the mind receives from external sources. The mind is continually receiving stimuli from without, and these continually modify its line of thought and action. Yet here it is true to add that the mind is continually reasserting its unity and self-organising power, and the intrusive elements are either rejected or else accepted into the stream of its life. Everything here is meaningful, except the actual moment of passivity to external influences;

it is these alone which present an element of brute fact which we can explain but not understand. Life, in short, is a coherent system of activities, constantly disturbed by stimuli from without, but constantly self-restoring, and as such it can be understood.

If Dilthey is right in this, the Kantians are convicted of underestimating the inherent intelligibility of lived experience. It becomes reasonable to say with Dilthey that we can understand not only the great works of the past, but also (in a measure) the process of their origin, and the background in human life from which they proceed. Instead of keeping the two apart, and pretending to understand the one while merely explaining the other, we may reasonably claim to understand both, and to understand them properly only when seen thus together. A work of art or literature, or a philosophical or scientific theory, is not merely a self-contained unit or monad, a complex of images and concepts which together form an intelligible whole. It is that, but only because it is something more. It is the result of someone's imaginative and intellectual labour. It is a record of imaginative and intellectual acts which someone has performed, not in isolation, not in a mental void, but as part of the whole business of living his life among his fellow-men. In understanding the work, therefore, in reperforming these imaginative and intellectual acts, we enter into relation with the life of its author, and through him with the life of his times. That is why Dilthey says that all understanding, if pushed to its limits, becomes historical understanding. What we understand in the last resort is not poems and operas and theories, but people. The works of men are interesting to us not merely for what they are in themselves, but also for what they tell us about their makers; though on the other hand it is equally true that the most interesting thing about human beings is that they can produce poems and theories, buildings, legal and political systems, religious disciplines and the like.

Thus it is not into a Neo-Kantian heaven of rational meaning-complexes that understanding takes us, but into the heart of the time-process, the dynamic system of historical life. It shows us men caught in historical situations and summoning their powers to deal with them, feeling the impact of one another's thoughts and deeds, influencing and being influenced; it shows us the fruitful marriage of kindred minds, and the unresolved clash of opposing standpoints. All the many-sided splendour of human history comes thus to be reflected in our consciousness as we watch and understand and sympathise, and, in Dilthey's phrase, 'life embraces life'.

The Neo-Kantian philosophy, he says, goes the wrong way about explaining how we can understand one another. Instead of finding the ground of understanding in experience as we actually live it, Neo-Kantianism argues to 'a super-empirical subject which manifests itself in the individual consciousness. . . . The creation of this transcendental method is the death of history, because the alleged realities are such that we cannot dig ourselves into them by fruitful historical concepts' (*G.S.*, VII, 285). 'We must move out of the pure, fine air of the Kantian critique of reason, in order to do justice to the wholly different nature of historical objects.' That which really lies behind historical phenomena, and is the object of historical study, is not the transcendental self, but man, with his complex mind-body structure and his bundle of instincts; and we can make him an object of study because we are ourselves also men. The experiences of other individuals are intelligible to me because they are the realisation of possibilities which are present also in me; transpersonal systems can be understood, because they proceed from that same human nature which I observe in myself and in others. 'So the first significant moment for the solution of the problem of historical knowledge appears: the first condition for the possibility of historical knowledge lies in the fact that I myself am a historical being, that he who enquires into history is the same as he who makes history' (*G.S.*, VII, 278).

But I am a historical being in another sense as well. I am a point of intersection for many social traditions and institutions, and all the experience of the race, stored up in these objective systems, has gone to the making of my mind. 'The language in which I think has arisen in time, my concepts have grown up within it. Thus I am, down to inscrutable depths of myself, a historical being' (*ibid.*) Hence I can understand the past, because it still lives in me, and operates in my present experience as a force conditioning my knowledge of itself. 'The individual, as bearer and representative of the common traditions woven together in him, enjoys and comprehends the history in which they arose. He understands history because he is himself a historical being' (*G.S.*, VII, 151).

In short, the affinity between historical fact and myself, which makes historical knowledge possible for me, is twofold. (1) On the one hand, the instincts and structural relations which I experience in myself are the same which produced all past events in history; and (2) on the other hand, the experience accumulated by mankind in the course of past history is the same force which, through education and social influences, has moulded my own character and outlook. 'We are historical beings first, before we are students of history, and it is only because we are the first that we become the second' (*G.S.*, VII, 278).

Such at least is Dilthey's view of the matter. But before we can acquiesce in it we have still to see how he meets a final challenge. Is it really true that 'life embraces life' except in a quite superficial sense? Do we really find our way to the ideas and motives of historical agents, so as to reconstruct the inwardness of the process of events? Have we enough evidence to guide us in this, and to overcome what must always be the historian's temptation, to over-simplify? For if he is to reconstruct the past at all, he can only do so along the lines of an intelligible meaning; this he will trace as far as his sources take him, and carry further by inference, while any element of irrationality which is not actually recorded is likely to remain unsuspected. How many things there must be lurking, unrevealed and perhaps never to be revealed, whose detection would overthrow the facile reasonableness of the accepted histories! It is never easy to show that any action has a rational motive; but the sway of passion, prejudice, and all irrational forces over human life is inexhaustibly wide. Sometimes we can risk a guess at a person's character, and in some such cases the character seems to be ruled by rational motives; yet even here we have no clear right to argue from general indications of this kind to a firm conclusion about the motives of a particular act. And if everyone is thus under suspicion, the doubt must also include our sources. They may be ignorant, prejudiced, or tendentious; in any case they are selective, and often fail to tell us just the things which we wish to know. Thus, in fine, we can doubt both the intrinsic intelligibility of the historical process, and the adequacy of our sources to reveal it.

Dilthey himself, in his final sketch of the *Kritik der historischen Vernunft*, faces the doubt on both points, and his answer to 'historical scepticism' must now be considered.

First of all, in the *Aufbau der geschichtlichen Welt in den Geisteswissenschaften* (1910), he deals with difficulties arising from the logical form of historical enquiry. The historian's work, he says, begins with philology, which comprises the study of the languages in which the sources are written, together with the textual criticism and chronological arrangement of the sources themselves. Then follows the interpretation of the sources, the full understanding of what they are meant to convey. Then comes the reflection upon this information, collation of various sources, and the attempt to produce a coherent and intelligible account of the processes described in them. These various stages in historical enquiry do not form a linear sequence, but are carried out *pari passu*, and stand to one another in a relation of reciprocal dependence. That is why Dilthey says in one passage that philology is not a mere aid to the historian, but is actually an integral part of his procedure, 'the ground-science of history' (*G.S.*, VII, 261).

But, says the objector, this 'reciprocal dependence' is only a fine name for logical circularity. Consider Niebuhr's work on early Roman history. He had to examine the origin and, from that, to judge the worth of the existing ancient tradition; he had to deduce from general probabilities what must have been, in outline, the real course of events; and any conclusion which he reached on either of these lines of enquiry was bound to react upon the other. He tried, indeed, to support his results by the analogy of similar developments elsewhere; but our knowledge of these other developments is itself circular, and for the same reasons. The circle must arise, if we once allow that the sources are not an absolute datum, but themselves need revision in the light of the history of their time, for which they themselves are the evidence. And what sources do not need criticism? Even contemporary accounts may suffer, if not from actual fraud, yet from the writer's ignorance, his misunderstanding, his prejudices.

Dilthey meets this objection in the obvious common-sense way. Safety lies, he suggests, in a circumspect use of inscriptions, for ancient history, and in free access to written and printed archives, for more modern times; these have given history a secure framework of knowledge about political and social events, within which the evidence of our other sources, critically checked, can be confidently used to build up a structure of historical probabilities 'whose fitness for use only ingenious but unscientific minds can deny' (*G.S.*, VII, 161–2).

But then we meet the second and really serious form of historical scepticism. The facts, it will be said, as to what men actually did on various occasions are fairly well made out; but what is the use of that unless we know *why* men acted as they did? And this we cannot know. The individual is largely in the dark even as to his own motives, and those who report his actions from without are even less in a position to judge. 'What influence of private interest, ambition, lust of power, pride enters into decisive actions, can be decided only within modest limits. Even verbal or epistolary statements on this point remain questionable. But just here lies the peculiar field of what readers of men and men of the world (*Menschenkenner und Weltleute*) regard as real history. The French especially display their clear-sightedness, their superiority over things and men, by assigning to great achievements small and selfish motives.' This is the natural result of the so-called 'pragmatic method' in historiography, which makes the search for motives one of its chief aims (*G.S.*, VII, 259–60).

Dilthey's answer here is at first sight surprising. 'Historical scepticism', he says, 'can only be overcome if our method has no need to count on the discovery of motives.' How is this possible? 'Historical scepticism is only overcome when psychological refinement gives place to the understanding of spiritual complexes (*Gebilde*). These lie before us as an outward objectification, and so can be made the object of skilled understanding (*kunstmässigen Verstehens*)' (*G.S.*, VII, 260). This sounds at first like an admission of Rickert's point, that a meaning-complex (*Sinngebilde*) can be understood, but not a motivation-process. But that is not what Dilthey means. He proceeds to recall his distinction between three kinds of expressions (above, p. 129 ff.), and to show how all three can be understood. The first kind comprises scientific treatises; these can be understood and expounded with complete certainty. Then there are the productions of art, religion, or philosophy, where the author has tried to express some truth about life, but has also in so doing given expression to his own life; interpretation here is harder, but is not impossible. Finally, there are human actions; and these, says Dilthey, we can consider and understand in a way which makes the question of motives irrelevant. This we can do by taking them in relation to the cultural conditions and social institutions of their time.

A person resolves to bring about a certain thing, he takes what means he can, he achieves his end. What end he had immediately in view is not doubtful; his action reveals it in the process of achieving it. What wider purpose, not recognisably expressed in this or perhaps in any of his actions, may lie behind it, what deep motives may have driven him on, we do not know. But we do know, with respect to the limited end achieved, that it falls within the sphere of at least one branch of cultural life, or of some social organisation, that the very possibility of his conceiving it, and of his finding these particular means available for achieving it, is conditioned by the contemporary state of the social and cultural system according to necessary laws, and that the effects of his action will in turn be felt in that system in a way strictly determined by the laws which govern the system itself. In this way, while leaving the question of motives on one side, we can still discover in history a coherent and intelligible sequence of events, and scepticism is overcome (*G.S.*, VII, 260–1).

We may compare a passage in the *Einleitung in die Geisteswissenschaften* (1883), where Dilthey discusses the controversy between the pragmatic historians and Hegel. "The interaction of individuals seems contingent and incoherent; birth and death and all the accidents of fate, the passions and the narrow egotism which fill so large a space in the foreground of life's stage: all these things seem to confirm the view of those readers of men (*Menschenkenner*) who see in the life of society only a play and counterplay of individual interests under the influence of chance, the view of the pragmatic historian, for whom also the course of history resolves itself into the play of personal forces. But, in reality, it is just *by means of this interaction of the separate individuals*, their passions, their pride, their interests, that *the necessary teleological system of human history realises itself*. The pragmatic historian and Hegel do not understand one another, because the one speaks as it were from the firm ground and the other from an airy height. Yet each of them has one part of the truth. For everything that is brought about, in this historical and social reality of man, is set in motion by the action of will: but, in this will, the end acts as motive. It is the character of the end, it is the universally valid element in it, which reaches out beyond the individual life, whatever formula we may apply to it, which is the basis of the teleological system that pervades the wills of men. In this teleological system the commonplace activity of men, which is concerned only with itself, yet brings to pass what it must. And even in the actions of its heroes, history allows every element which does not fit this teleological system to fall away without effect' (*G.S.*, I, 53).

The meaning of this passage is clear. We saw in the previous chapter (pp. 102–3, 105–7), how Dilthey traces, amid the turmoil of human passions and even in consequence of their interaction, a 'life on a higher level' or a 'moral system' emerging. This system constitutes an order of ends to which, whether we will or no, all our actions are relative; we may will to conform to it, or to transgress it, or we may ignore it in our conscious decision, but one way or another, in all three cases, consciously or unconsciously our purposes are informed by it. It is a structural system running through all history; for it determines all action as a *vis a tergo*, a necessity laid upon the agent by his social environment and training; and where he is free, in the creative recesses of his mind and will, even there it enters in and shapes his resolves. This is the system of relations which Dilthey, in the passages quoted above, declares we can understand, while the 'motives', the understanding of which we are to renounce, are the lower impulses and all private ends, in so far as they do not fit into the intelligible system. The reference to Hegel is obviously not made at random; for this conception of an intelligible system overriding private motives, and forming the proper object of historical understanding, is the same as Hegel's conception expounded in the *Philosophy of History*, only taken out of Hegel's idealistic terminology and reconciled with Dilthey's empiricism.

The close of our discussion of understanding is at the same time the close of the first section of our work. The problem which Dilthey set himself at the outset of his career was twofold: *first*, a problem about the nature and extent of our knowledge in the human studies, and especially of the power of understanding which is so important there—this was the Kantian problem, the problem of the *Kritik der reinen Vernunft* extended to take in a new realm of knowledge; and *second*, a problem about the methods and fundamental concepts of the human studies, the number and nature of the enquiries comprised under that heading, and their relation to natural science and to philosophy —this was the equivalent of Mill's problem about the 'logic of the moral sciences'. Dilthey's philosophy therefore falls easily into two sections, one for each of these two problems, and so far we have been following Dilthey's own lead and the proper logical order by considering the epistemological problem first. This part of our work is now complete. All that Dilthey says in answer to the epistemological question has been examined, his *erkenntnistheoretische Grundlegung der Geisteswissenschaften* has been reconstructed and examined in relation to certain criticisms. There remains his second problem, and we must turn in the following chapters to a different group of his writings, which bear affinity no longer to the epistemology of Hume or Kant, but to the logical analysis and architectonic of Comte and Mill.

CHAPTER SIX

W HEN Kant made his study of the natural sciences, he did it on grounds of high principle. He formulated their fundamental presuppositions and examined their logical foundations. He did not enlarge on their methods and their relations with one another. For Dilthey, in his critique of the human studies, such a way of treatment was not enough. He was not content to analyse the foundations of knowledge and of value-judgment, and to show how knowledge of the self, and of other selves, is possible. He combined this with a careful enquiry into the methodology and architectonic of the human studies.

Why did he do this? To begin with, the empirical tradition which draws its inspiration from Bacon has always shown a tendency towards methodological enquiries. In a work like Whewell's *Philosophy of Discovery* it almost seems as if philosophy is resolved into methodology. Comte and Mill, in Dilthey's early years, made a revealing study of the methods and inter-relations of the natural sciences, and it was natural that Dilthey should ask himself whether they had been equally successful with the human studies. There was, moreover, a further reason why he should go this way. In his time the natural sciences were a coherent body of thought, self-conscious, self-confident, working as a team. Their methods and interrelations were, in principle, generally understood. By contrast the human studies were a scene of strife: strife of methods and strife of aims. If a philosopher was to make a study of this group of disciplines, he must first make clear what they were. Is psychology one of them? Is sociology? Do their methods and principles reflect those of the natural sciences, or are they different? Are they homogeneous throughout the group? Not only Dilthey, but others who followed him in dealing with the human studies, such as Windelband and Rickert, had to face questions like these.

Dilthey discusses these questions in a series of writings which run through his entire career. In these writings a slow development can be traced, due partly to the progress of his own thinking, and partly to changes in the world around him. When he began, it was relevant to quote Comte and Mill, and it was necessary to reach a decision about them. In his latest years, it was the Neo-Kantians with whom he had to reckon. In the meantime certain particular problems had asserted themselves and claimed special attention, notably a group of problems relating to psychology, on which Dilthey never finally cleared his mind. The present chapter and the three following will be concerned with this aspect of Dilthey's work. We shall follow him to the point at which he first attempted a comprehensive survey of the field, in the *Einleitung in die Geisteswissenschaften* (1883). Then we shall see how difficulties and controversies on particular points delayed the completion of his plan by more than twenty-five years, and drove him along unexpected paths (Chapters Seven and Eight). Finally we shall see how in his last years he tried to complete his comprehensive plan (Chapter Nine).

Dilthey tells us more than once that he came to philosophy from history (*G.S.*, V, 10, VIII, 180); it was in terms of history that he saw the great problems of life and thought, and it was by engaging in historical research that he was brought up against the problems of aim and method in history. We find him so engaged from his early years. His chosen field was, in his own words, 'the history of literary and philosophical movements', and he approached it both through the history of theories and general principles and through the study of individual thinkers.

His first considerable undertaking was a biography, a *Leben Schleiermachers*, based upon a thorough examination of unpublished papers. It showed the philosophy and theology of Schleiermacher as the point of convergence of several religious and philosophical movements, and as the starting-point for their further diffusion in the nineteenth century. Dilthey was at work on this as early as 1864, and in 1870 a large first volume appeared, which covered in two books the story of Schleiermacher's life to the year 1802. It was hailed at once as a masterpiece of interpretative biography, and put Dilthey's reputation as a historian of ideas on a high plane where his later writings fully maintained it. The second volume, which Dilthey had planned, was eagerly awaited, as well as a new revised edition of the first volume, which speedily ran out of print; but his enquiries ranged so far afield, and took him so deep into the subtler problems of philosophy and theology, that in spite of several later efforts the revision was never finished, and the second volume remained an empty cadre.[1]

Another of Dilthey's early interests led more directly to philosophy, and specifically to the problem of the human studies. From 1866 onwards, he began to work at the history of political theory, and especially of the doctrine of natural law, whose growth he traced first of all in the Greek Sophists, and then in those seventeenth-century writers, such as Hobbes and Spinoza, who are in effect the heirs and disciples of the Sophists. From this he was led on to raise a logical question. The history of ethics and political theory can only be understood in the light of the conditions which govern their progress, and Dilthey was bound to ask what are these determining conditions. But in this enquiry he had been anticipated by Comte and by Mill. Accordingly, his first task was to define his attitude to these writers. This he did in an essay *Über das Studium der Geschichte der Wissenschaften vom Menschen, der Gesellschaft u. dem Staat* (1875), which will repay a brief study. The spirit and aim of the enquiry is positivist or empiricist; but in the outcome the actually prevailing positivist or empiricist logic is subjected to damaging criticism.

It is the great achievement of Comte to have revealed, in his analysis of the natural sciences, the relations of logical dependence in which they stand to one another. (1) Every science is defined by the phenomena which it studies. The phenomena studied by the various sciences arrange themselves naturally in a scale of increasing complexity, the complex phenomena being subject to all the laws which govern the simpler, but also obey-. ing further laws of their own. Parallel with this scale, the sciences themselves form a logical hierarchy, those which deal with the simpler phenomena being presupposed by those which deal with the more complex; e.g. physics and chemistry are pre-

---

[1] Since his death, the first volume has been reissued, enriched by much of Dilthey's revision-material: *Leben Schleiermachers, Ier Band, 2te Auflage*, herausgeg. v. H. Mulert; W. de Gruyter, Berlin and Leipzig, 1922.

supposed by biology. (2) Each science must conform to Comte's great law of development, passing from the theological stage, through the metaphysical, to the positive, and the historical order in which they reach positivity follows the logical order of their mutual dependence; for the simpler and more fundamental sciences must have made considerable headway before those which presuppose them can begin to advance. Thus it was that pure mathematics came to maturity first, then mechanics, astronomy, physics, and chemistry. Physiology, the science of organic bodies, was not yet, in Comte's opinion, free from metaphysical conceptions, but it was progressing. (3) But then he added that the science of human life, which it was his own peculiar mission to establish, would be found to be only one more rung in the ladder of the natural sciences, continuous with and presupposing physiology, as physiology is continuous with and presupposes chemistry. Finally, in reliance upon a dogmatic epiphenomenalism, he declared introspection impossible, concluded that therefore the alleged science of psychology was impossible, and parcelled out its functions between physiology and sociology. The latter is accordingly the only science dealing with historical and social phenomena, and depends directly upon physiology.

Mill accepted Comte's account of the hierarchy of natural sciences, with the explanation of their historical development which follows from it; but he could not accept Comte's table of sciences in detail. The scientific study of history and society presupposes an acquaintance with the laws of mental phenomena in general, and this acquaintance is surely not a part of sociology itself, but belongs to a prior science, viz. psychology. Mill, the heir of the British tradition, accordingly restored psychology to the place assigned to it by Hume. But he further saw that psychology differs in two important respects from the natural sciences. Its data are not obtained in the same way as theirs, for it rests on introspection where they rest on outer perception. Again, its fundamental hypotheses are not cast in the same terms as theirs. Therefore psychology and the other studies which depend upon it are not, as Comte pretended, a linear continuation of the natural sciences, but an independent group of enquiries standing beside them, with data and grounds of explanation peculiar to themselves. Mill called them the 'moral sciences', and agreed with Comte that they were in a backward state, from which they could only be rescued by the transference to them of the methods already worked out in the natural sciences.

Dilthey, in 1875, agreed with Comte about the hierarchy of the natural sciences, and with Mill about the independent position of psychology and its function as the basis of the 'moral and political sciences' (he had not yet begun to call them *Geisteswissenschaften*). But, in the essay which we have now to consider, he questions whether the relation between the various 'moral and political sciences' is hierarchic, like the relation between the natural sciences; if it is not, the history of the moral and political sciences will be governed by different conditions from that of the natural sciences, and will call for different principles of interpretation.

His mode of procedure is epistemological. 'Presupposing the enquiries of logic about knowledge in general, I ask what are the special circumstances distinguishing the relation of the intelligence to its object in this field from the relation prevailing in other fields, and what consequences follow from this difference in respect of the order in which the truths of the moral and political sciences are discovered' (*G.S.*, V, 44, cf. 49).

(1) In the first place, he says, the facts of moral and political experience have come into existence slowly, they have been growing throughout the whole time that they have been studied, and their range is still 'very restricted'. Here the moral and political sciences are less fortunate than the natural sciences, whose object stood complete before them from the first (*G.S.*, V, 44–5 = I, 216–17). (2) Against this may be set the fact that, whereas the datum for natural science is only a 'sensuous appearance of bodies', and it has taken long to discover the real unit of matter, the unit for moral and political science, viz. the individual mind, is actually 'given in perception'. The advance of the moral and political sciences to a state of 'classical perfection' at a relatively early date is due to the 'transparency and intuitive clarity' of these units, the motives which bind them together, and the ways in which they affect one another (*G.S.*, V, 45–6 = I, 28). (3) To offset this advantage, our knowledge of historical and social phenomena has a peculiar limitation; we can understand, but we cannot explain. Natural science,

which works with abstract, homogeneous, and therefore clearly defined units, can express the relations between them in exactly formulated laws; but of the individuals which are the units in moral and political science, no two are alike, and each is a self-contained world of experience. Analysis here presents great difficulties, and has made hardly any progress. The forces at work in society are intelligible (*verständlich*) to us, because we can reconstruct (*nachbilden*) them in our own experience; but of the laws which govern them we are almost wholly ignorant (*G.S.*, V, 60–2 = I, 29, 36). (4) We may add that the relative strengths of the motives controlling men's conduct may change in the course of generations, so that the experience of the modern man is an unsafe guide to the interpretation of the past (*G.S.*, V, 62, cf. I, 37).

In consequence of all this, our knowledge of history and society must be differently constituted from our knowledge of nature. The natural-scientific hierarchy of laws, where the knowledge of the simpler must condition the knowledge of the more complex, cannot be reproduced in the moral and political sciences; and therefore the principles of their development cannot be those which Comte lays down.

The first step towards a solution lies in recognising that historical and social processes are not brought about by the kind of causation which we find in nature, but by the operation of motives and the pursuit of ends. Instead of necessary laws, we have here to do with free agents, and instead of quantities of energy we have relations of significance and value. 'The water-fall is composed of homogeneous falling particles of water; but a single sentence, which is but a noise in the mouth, shakes the whole living society of a continent through a play of motives in absolutely individual units, none of whom is comparable with the rest; so different is the ideal motive from any other kind of cause' (*G.S.*, V, 63 = I, 37–8).

What is more, the observers who study this social world are themselves agents in it; they are caught up into the historical process, their theoretical enquiries subserve practical ends. And it is here that Dilthey finds the principle which rules the progress of the moral and political sciences. Each of these sciences is concerned with some coherent system of human activity, e.g. language, law, or the State. Whatever may be the origin of such systems of activity, there comes a time for each of them when those who practise it find it necessary to reflect, to organise, to reform; and it is in this stage that the fundamental conceptions for the understanding of each field are hammered out. Then, at a later stage, when practical problems have been mastered and there is time for disinterested scientific enquiry, this enquiry in turn finds its basis in the conceptions handed down from the earlier stage (G.S., V, 64–5 = I, 59). Thus political theory, which arose in the time of the Sophists and the Socratic school, was able to draw upon the practical analysis of political affairs which had been made in preceding generations (G.S., V, 65); on the other hand, the moral reflections of the Pythagorean and Socratic schools were themselves only an element in the practical effort to establish a moral system, and a really scientific moral theory has hardly yet emerged (G.S., V, 72). Accordingly, the moral and political sciences do not form a hierarchy in which some are presupposed by others; they develop side by side, each arising gradually out of experience, and presupposing only so much preliminary reflection as arises in the practical effort to control those activities which are its subject-matter.

Finally, we must own that, when an ostensibly independent study of these activities has at last arisen, it may still be affected by practical motives. Political theories, for example, are often political programmes. But this is an advantage as well as a disadvantage, and by reason of it the history of political theory is of great value to political theory itself. For the theories current at a given date indicate the conflicting interests, the ideals, the social movements of the time, and thus indirectly enlarge our acquaintance with the very facts which it is their function to analyse (G.S., V, 32).

The essay of 1875 has a capital importance in the development of Dilthey's philosophy. Not only did it give him a view of his own about the logical structure and historical origins of the human studies, emancipating him in spirit at once from romantic and from positivist orthodoxy; but it also gave him the ποῦ στῶ for his *Kritik der historischen Vernunft*.

Dilthey himself, many years later, in trying to explain his method of approach to the problem, lets us see how this came about. The fact about the human studies which shows itself most unmistakably in their history is their dependence upon practical needs as their stimulus, and the infection of their conclusions by ignorance and prejudice. Here, as in the natural sciences, but to a far greater degree, knowledge is seen to reflect the historical situation of the knower. We see at once the need of an impartial *Grundlegung der Geisteswissenschaften*, which should stand, if possible, above the sources of illusion, and prescribe for all possible enquiry in the human studies its proper scope and method. And yet, such as they are, the human studies themselves are the only possible evidence for conclusions as to their scope and method. For, if we think to go behind them to their subject-matter, the historical world, and determine their range and procedure by that, this historical world is after all only known to us in and through the human studies themselves. Accordingly, the only way to obtain real insight into their structure and possible future development is to follow the history of their past growth, regarding them not as a body of knowledge achieved, but as an endless search for knowledge, noting where and how the search has best succeeded, and why.

In this way we can watch the gradual application of the various logical processes, and their combination to form distinctive methods; the advance from the study of historical fact to the study of its physical conditions, on the one hand, and of normative principles on the other; the slow separation of particular groups of phenomena as distinct spheres of enquiry, and the coining of methodological concepts found fruitful in each sphere; and the gradual approach by these means to more objective judgments, and to a clearer view of the human studies and their subject-matter as a whole. We can also see how in every stage of their development the human studies have been inspired by the spirit of contemporary culture, and have sought their *Grundlegung* in the philosophy which is the expression of that spirit, and how the philosophies which have successively been pressed into service for this purpose have uniformly failed, until in recent times 'the illusion of a metaphysic binding together the forms of being and value in the world order with their final cause, which has lain so long like a cloud between the relevant objects and the human mind', has begun to dissolve (*G.S.*, I, 411–17).

This is the basis on which Dilthey planned his *Kritik der*

historischen Vernunft. It was to open with a history of the human studies, and by studying their development, like that of a living organism, it was to obtain an insight into their morphology, which in turn would enable him to write their logic and epistemology, and do for them what had already been done for the natural sciences by Comte in the *Cours de philosophie positive.*

When Dilthey went in 1882 as Lotze's successor to Berlin, he had already drawn up the plan for this great work. It was to be in five books. The first was to describe the present condition of the human studies and show their need of an epistemological *Grundlegung.* The second was to show historically how the attempt to provide a *Grundlegung* by means of metaphysics broke down. The third was to continue the history until the time when the sciences became independent of philosophy, and philosophy itself abandoned metaphysics for the Kantian critique of knowledge. The fourth and fifth books would then give Dilthey's own *Grundlegung der Geisteswissenschaften,* which was to take its stand upon inner experience, departing, however, from Kantian prin-. ciples by appealing not to the alleged *a priori* presuppositions of knowledge, but to a descriptive analysis of the structural system, or *Selbstbesinnung* (*G.S.,* I, xv–xx). Of this comprehensive scheme, the first two books were published in 1883 under the title *Einleitung in die Geisteswissenschaften: Versuch einer Grundlegung für das Studium der Gesellschaft u. der Geschichte: Erster Band.* This volume is important, as being the earliest systematic statement of Dilthey's position; and I shall now proceed to summarise its contents.

Dilthey begins by explaining his distinction between *Naturwissenschaften* and *Geisteswissenschaften*; it is based on the difference between outer experience, in which we apprehend nature as an order of causal necessity, and inner experience, where we are conscious of ourselves as free and responsible agents. These two realms of experience were in ancient and mediaeval times interpreted as two orders of substances, viz. the material and the spiritual. Dilthey shows how the Thomist philosophy, the high point of mediaeval speculation, worked out their interrelations within the hierarchic system of created being. With the coming of the mechanistic Cartesian view of nature, however, this theory of two kinds of substance became a source of insoluble antinomies, and was clearly unworkable. Then, to the rescue, came the critique of knowledge, which for the two orders of substances substituted the two disparate orders of 'outer' and 'inner' experience. Looking at the matter from this point of view, we must say that the characteristic marks of outer experience, viz. spatial extension and mechanical determinism, are wholly incommensurable with the synthetic unity of consciousness, the moral responsibility and freedom, which we find in inner experience; from this we may infer the limits of natural science, and the necessity of other methods for dealing with other fields of experience (*G.S.*, I, 6–14).

This does not mean that the human studies are wholly unconnected with the natural sciences. Man is a 'psychophysical unity', conditioned at every point by his physical organism and environment; and though he is free to react upon the environment, this reaction in turn is conditioned by the physical tools at his disposal. Hence the line of division between the two groups of studies is not rigid, and several branches of enquiry have a footing in both realms. Thus the laws of sound-formation are a presupposition of grammar and musical theory. The study of warfare requires knowledge of the physical resources of the belligerents. The human organism has to be studied in the light of biology, and the distribution of population depends partly upon geographical and climatic conditions. Dilthey adds that the precise relation between the two realms of knowledge can only be decided by a deeper epistemological enquiry, upon which he does not enter (*G.S.*, I, 14–21).

Every branch of knowledge is based upon an abstraction, attending to some elements in experience and ignoring others; even historiography, with its interest in the concrete, is only possible through selection of material. The human studies are constituted by abstracting now one, now another aspect of the inner life, and accordingly their logical structure is determined by the real structure of their subject-matter (*G.S.*, I, 27–8). They do not form a hierarchy like the natural sciences; instead, their mutual relations follow from and reflect the relations of reciprocal dependence between the functions in mental life which they severally study. Nor are they concerned only, like the natural sciences, with establishing laws by which to explain events. They have a threefold aim: to describe the historical *facts*, to discover *laws* and regularities among them, and to formulate *standards* of value and imperatives (*G.S.*, I, 26–7). Recognition of this fact enables us at the outset to refute positivism, which, misled by the analogy of natural science, has tried 'to transform into factual knowledge those studies which have their basis not in statements of fact at all, but in imperatives' (*G.S.*, I, 5).

Society is composed of individuals, and the question arises, how is the individual related to the group? One theory, as old as the Sophists, regards the individual as the prior reality, and society as a quasi-mechanical combination of individuals. Another theory, as old as Plato, regards the community as an organic whole which is prior to its parts, and some adherents of this view have credited the group with a 'communal mind' (*Volksgeist*). Dilthey rejects both these views. For the alleged group 'mind' is no mind at all, because it has no apperceptive unity; while the 'organic' theory casts no light upon society, because we know even less about organisms than we do about society (*G.S.*, I, 30–1 = V, 62 n.). What is true is that we never observe an individual apart from society, and cannot even infer what an individual so abstracted would be like. Individual and group are essentially relative to one another, though the relation between them cannot be elucidated by analogies from physics or biology. And yet, so long as we keep this caution in mind, we can still safely say that the unit of society is the individual; and in that case the most fundamental of the human studies will be those which deal with the individual, of which psychology is the chief.

We saw in Chapter One that Dilthey's conception of psychology is the result of influences from more than one source, and that in order to fit psychology for the task he assigns to it he is forced to demand changes in its aims and methods. In the *Einleitung* he makes three demands.

(1) Psychology deals with the human individual, but not with the individual as something apart from society. The individual apart from society is an abstraction which, if pressed, becomes a sheer fiction. The individual is a social and historical product. 'His organisation shows him receiving influences from without and reacting outwards; his whole content is only a transient particular form (*Gestalt*) arising amid the encircling content of

mind in history and society; the highest trait in his nature is that whereby he lives in something not himself' (*G.S.*, I, 30). A psychology which is to be really empirical must examine the social relations which affect the individual so deeply. 'Man as a fact prior to history and society is a fiction of genetic explanation; the man whom sound analytical study has for its object is the individual as an element in society. The hard problem which psychology has to solve is that of obtaining analytical knowledge of the universal characteristics of man so conceived' (*G.S.*, I, 31–2). Only so can it 'unfold universal propositions whose subject is the individual unit and whose predicates are all assertions about him which can bear fruit in the understanding of society and history' (*ibid.*).

(2) When we have gained some knowledge of human nature in general, we shall be able to advance to the study of specific human types; and this will close the gap which exists at present between psychology on the one hand and aesthetics, moral and political theory, and history on the other. For all these studies require, for the interpretation of their data, a typology of human character. 'A type of human nature stands always between the historian and his sources, whence he desires to awaken figures to throbbing life; it stands no less between the political thinker and the reality of society, for whose development he desires to lay down rules. The aim of science is only to render this subjective type correct and fruitful. . . . Away beyond the research hitherto conducted into the regularities of mental life, it must recognise typical distinctions within it, must subject to description and analysis the imaginative power of the artist, the genius of the man of action, and must complete the study of the forms of mental life by adding to it the description of the reality of its process and its content.' At present the human studies have to depend on an *ad hoc* typology derived from the generalities of worldly wisdom and the revealing power of poetry, but psychology could and should be so developed as to furnish a scientific typology (*G.S.*, I, 32).

(3) Dilthey goes on to say that psychology can only do this if it 'remains within the limits of a descriptive science'. This is a contention of which more will be heard later. For the moment Dilthey is content to define the issue in a few short phrases, and pass on. We may do the same. Suffice it to say that a 'descrip-

tive' science is one which confines itself to formulating observable regularities, introducing no entities or processes which observation cannot verify, while an 'explanatory' (*erklärende*) science is one which constructs a theory in terms of unobservables in order to account for what is observed. Such theoretical constructions are of course hypothetical, and therefore subject to an element of doubt. A psychology constructed on this model cannot be a fit foundation for the edifice of the human studies. As Dilthey himself says, 'Psychology can solve the problems of such a fundamental science only if it remains within the limits of a descriptive science, which records facts and likenesses between facts, whereas explanatory psychology, which endeavours to make the whole system of mental life deducible by means of certain assumptions, is clearly distinguished from it. . . . Only so can the special sciences of mind be placed on a foundation which is itself secure, whereas at present even the best expositions of psychology build hypotheses on hypotheses' (*G.S.*, I, 32–3).

Dilthey reserves the further elucidation of this for a later occasion, viz. the projected fourth and fifth books of the *Einleitung*. These were in fact never written, but the whole question of descriptive psychology is gone into at length in the *Ideen über eine beschreibende u. zergliedernde Psychologie* (1894). The same work resumes and carries further the demand for a 'comparative psychology' which will describe and classify human types. The *Ideen*, and the whole question of Dilthey's views on psychology, will be examined in Chapter Seven.

From psychology we may pass to biography; this should not be a mere superficial account of a man's life, but an interpretation of him in the light of his own moments of clearest insight, when he saw himself, and we too can see him, *sub specie aeterni*. Biography so written, revealing the inner life of the individual as a living unit, is the true basis of historiography, rather than the study of mere archives. For the historian gets from archives little but 'dead abstractions'; but in biography he finds the key to an understanding of the mind of classes, social groups, and whole generations, of which the individual is a type or 'representation' (*Repräsentation*). And if the historian has the advantage in breadth of view, the biographer excels him in depth and accuracy of analysis. Biography draws its methods and categories from psychology, but conversely psychology derives much of its material from case-histories, i.e. from biography. Finally, on the frontier between psychology and natural science stands psychophysics, studying the physiology of sensation, the relations between thought and the nervous system, and the development of motor reactions from simple reflexes up to the organised and deliberate movement. This completes the sum of the studies concerned with the individual (*G.S.*, I, 33–5).

We advance to the study of the social and historical process as a whole; and here, as in the study of the individual, we find a fruitful alternation of scientific analysis with historical description of the facts. The scientific function of psychology is taken over here by the 'special' or 'systematic' human studies, of which more anon; the recording function of biography falls to historiography. From the earliest times, in various ways, such a record has been kept. 'From the time when, gathered round the camp-fire, tribesmen and fellow-soldiers told of the deeds of their heroes and the divine origin of their race, the strong interest of contemporaries has lifted facts out of the dim stream of commonplace human life, and preserved them.' But the interest which preserves one fact lets many more fall into oblivion; and, even of these imperfect records, not all survive. Only a short period of human history, over a small area of the earth's surface, viz. modern Europe, can be said to be really well documented. Accordingly, the first requisite for a coherent description of the historical and social world is a critical study of the sources, in order to determine such facts as they put beyond reasonable doubt. This is the work of philology, which has won its spurs in the study of ancient history, and continues to apply its methods there and elsewhere. Gradually, as the material is sifted out, we give it definite character and clarity of outline by means of accurate placing and dating. 'The system of this pure description of historical and social reality, as it takes its stand on geophysics, supported by geography, in order to describe the distribution of mental life and its differentiations on the earth's surface in time and space, can only obtain intuitable form by reduction to clear spatial proportions, numerical relations, determinations of time, through the aid of graphic present-ment'[1] (*G.S.*, I, 24–6).

In this manner we pass insensibly from the preliminary work

[1] Sc. maps, time-charts, and the like.

of philology to the art of historiography. We may call it an art, for the primary business of the historian is to portray, and not, as 'certain recent English and French writers' would have it, to explain and generalise. 'In this world of moral forces, the unique and individual has a quite different significance (*Bedeutung*) from what it has in external nature. The apprehension of it is not a means, but an end in itself.' That, indeed, is the reason why history has so long tended to pass by the occurrences which are common to all places and times, the events of daily life, and to fasten upon the extraordinary. 'It needed the philanthropic motives of the eighteenth century to bring back into clear view the everyday life, the life common to all men in a period, *les mœurs*, as Voltaire expresses it, and the changes which take place in respect of this, side by side with the extraordinary, the actions of kings and the fortunes of States. And the background of things which are the same at all times, in human nature and the life of the world, never enters at all into the historical picture.' For, in the first place, the historical individual is the only point in experience where reality appears to us as it is in itself, and has therefore a unique theoretical interest for us. And, in the second place, there is also a moral interest, 'an interest not of thought alone, but of the soul, of sympathetic feeling (*der Mitempfindung*), of enthusiasm, in which Goethe rightly saw the fairest fruit of historical enquiry. . . . When we sympathise with (*miterleben*) a past life, through the art of historical presentation, we are taught as by the scene of life itself; our being is widened, and mental forces more powerful than our own intensify our existence' (*G.S.*, I, 91). It follows that the historian, like the dramatist, must portray first and foremost, and comment or explain, if at all, only in passing. 'The particular here is merely saturated and informed by the idea (*Idee*) in the historian's mind, and where a generalisation appears, it only throws a flash of light upon the facts, and releases abstract thought for one moment. It is thus that the poet too uses generalisation, to lift the mind of his audience for an instant out of the turmoil, the sorrows and emotions which he portrays, into the free region of thought' (*G.S.*, I, 40).

Yet it is impossible to be content with historical portrayal alone. The material described to us in history must after all be subjected to analysis and explanation. Now, it is for this that the French and British positivists bring forward their plan of a comprehensive science, *sociology*, which shall embrace together all the laws which govern the historical process. We shall see in due course how Dilthey tries to show that this science is a chimera. At present, however, he confines himself to pointing out that it is a novel invention, and that the ground which it is to occupy is already held by a number of independent studies of considerable antiquity, which have arisen naturally out of the practical needs of mankind in the way described in his essay of 1875 (*G.S.*, I, 35–9). It is natural to examine first of all the claims of these studies, to which he adds one other, not derived from practical needs and not mentioned in 1875, but closely connected with historiography itself, viz. 'ethnology or comparative anthropology'.

There is not much to be said about ethnology. The human race is naturally divided into concentric groups on the basis of descent; such groups are the race, the tribe, the family. Each of these groups and sub-groups has distinguishing characteristics, by which the members of a given race, or tribe, or family can be known. Ethnology begins with the question of the unity, the place of origin, and the antiquity of the human race, passes on to the differentiation of the great races and their subordinate groups, studies and explains their migrations and their present distribution and acquired characteristics in terms of the governing geographical conditions. But these racial and subracial divisions of mankind, though important as forming the background of the historical process, play only a small part in that process itself. It is not the race, but the political and social group, the nation, which is the vehicle of historical processes; and although the nation is itself based on common descent, and is often represented by a strikingly stable physical type, yet it is held together as a nation and specifically characterised not so much by blood-affinities as by the ties of economic interest, cultural tradition, and political allegiance. By virtue of these, nations whose physical type is closely akin may come to differ profoundly in spirit. Such differences are not to be explained 'mystically' by metaphysical doctrines about a 'national organism' or a 'national soul', but by detailed analysis of the ties which hold the members of the nation together. Nations are 'living and relatively independent centres of civilisation in the social system of a period, vehicles of the movement of history'. They are to be understood only through the study of the closely interwoven activities of civilised man (*G.S.*, I, 40–2).

These activities themselves offer a basis for such a study in the practical reflection by which they seek self-knowledge and self-control. Grammar, rhetoric, logic, aesthetics, ethics, jurisprudence, political theory all arose from the desire to provide a professional training for persons engaged in cultural and political activities, and thereby to systematise these activities themselves; not until later, when practical training was found to need a theoretical grounding, did these studies advance from the status of technical rules to that of scientific analysis. It is in them that the real understanding of a nation's life must be sought (*G.S.*, I, 21–2, 38–9).

Individuals are not self-sufficing; most of their ends can only be secured in so far as they are willing to co-operate with one another in carrying out present tasks, and, while so doing, build upon the traditions and achievements of their predecessors. The activities in which they co-operate are broadly the same in all ages; they are dictated by abiding tendencies in human nature itself, which always seek satisfaction in the pursuit of the same general ends. Thus, at all places and times, men will freely combine for the production, distribution, and accumulation of economic goods; but also for the furtherance of higher ends such as the increase of knowledge, the maintenance of religious cult and teaching, the creation and preservation of works of art, and the like. In each of these spheres a system of human relations is set up, into which the individual must enter if he is either to receive the tradition of the past, or to work fruitfully for himself and others in the present; a system of relations determined by the nature of the end pursued and the means available for its attainment, and remaining the same in different ages and countries though the individuals at work within it may change.

Such a web of human relations Dilthey calls a cultural system (*Kultursystem*), and he sees, in the general failure to make an adequate study of such cultural systems, one powerful factor militating against progress in the human studies. 'The student of the phenomena of history and society is everywhere confronted by abstract entities such as art, science, . . . religion. They are like masses of cloud, which prevent our vision from reaching reality, and yet are themselves intangible. As once the substantial forms,

176

the spirits of the stars, and the essences stood between the eye of the investigator and the laws which prevail among atoms and molecules, so these entities shroud the reality of historical and social life, the interaction of the psychophysical units under the conditions of the natural world and their native genealogical articulation. My object is to show how to see this reality—an art which needs long practice, like that of the intuitive apprehension of spatial forms—and to dispel these mists and phantoms' (*G.S.*, I, 42–4).

To attain this object in full is of course the business of logic, aesthetics, comparative religion, and similar studies, and elsewhere Dilthey has followed the enquiry into these fields; but all that he says in the *Einleitung* about cultural systems may be summed up in three points. (1) Every cultural system is based on a permanent element or complex of elements in human nature, which remains from generation to generation, the same in different individuals, so that the cultural system itself remains the same though the agents at work in it may change. (2) In every cultural system, the achievements of each generation can be embodied in lasting productions, e.g. systems of ideas, books, paintings, buildings, and the like, which stand firm in the midst of time and change, and are the vehicles of tradition. By virtue of these, the cultural system acquires an 'outward permanence independent of the actual individuals, and a character of massive objectivity'. The individual is born into it, he sees it as a mighty reality which existed before him and will outlive him, and under whose shadow he must work; and it offers itself as a 'self-supporting objectivity' to the historical or scientific investigator. (3) Each individual is many-sided, and is active in several cultural systems at once; nay, a single act may be the point of intersection between two or three cultural systems. 'When a scholar writes a book, this process may be a link in the chain of truths which constitutes science; at the same time it is the most important link in the economic process which culminates in the preparation and sale of copies of the work; it has also a legal side, as the fulfilment of a contract, and it may be an element in the professional functions of the scholar as laid down by the administrative system. The writing down of each and every letter of this work is thus an element in all these systems' (*G.S.*, I, 49–51).

177

It is characteristic of a cultural system that our co-operation within it is *free*; all who take part in it do so because they share the common purpose, and there is thus a deep-lying ground of unity between them. But there are other kinds of human relations, in which we find ourselves in various ways *bound*, constrained, perhaps, by the common will of a social group, or dominated by some personal power or authority. Here we have a different type of human relations, not less widespread or important than the cultural systems; and these also call for analysis.

Their psychological basis is twofold. *First* of all, there is what may be called a 'sense of community' or 'social instinct' (*Gemeinsinn, Geselligkeitstrieb*), i.e. a powerful impulse or complex of impulses (the precise psychological analysis of it into its simplest factors need not concern us) by which people of kindred blood, or people occupying the same territory, or people associated together in cultural enterprises, are drawn together to form a social whole with a spirit and life of its own. In the *second* place, there is a volitional relation, in which a stronger will or personality tends to acquire a position of leadership and to impose itself upon the weaker, with or without the aid of physical force. These two factors, always working together though in various proportions, cause men to be divided into blood-groups held together by feelings of racial affinity or of clannishness, territorial groups upheld by national or local patriotism or by sheer neighbourliness, social and occupational groups with the most varied kinds of sentimental ties and loyalties. All these can, and sometimes do, exist, even without the support of any visible organisation, based simply upon the two psychological forces named above; and in each there is a common spirit and a group will, by which the individual is bound.

But it happens, more often than not, that these social groupings find expression in organised institutions such as the family, the State or municipality, the Church, the corporation. This may come about from no other cause than the social consciousness itself, which seeks to reflect itself in an objective system or organisation. Or it may be imposed from above, by a masterful will, as an individual can found a State, or a government can force men into corporative or professional organisations. Or the organisation may be formed in response to common needs and

178

interests, or (like the professional organisations which tend to grow up freely around every cultural system) in defence of a common ideal against the effects of selfishness or unruly passion. All these causes, acting now separately, now in combination, together produce that intricate web of social institutions, called by Dilthey the 'outer organisation of society', by which the life of the individual down to its smallest details is circumscribed and controlled. Some of these associations are short-lived, societies formed for a specific purpose, and dissolved when that is carried out, perhaps within the lifetime of the first members. Others, like the Church and the State, may count their age in centuries. But all are capable, like the cultural systems, of remaining the same while their individual members change. And here, too, the individual is a point of intersection of many different associations. In some of them he may hold authority, while in others he is subject to it; and thus there will be set up in his consciousness an alternation between being free, or exercising power, and being bound, or yielding to control, which will constitute a reflection in inner experience of his social standing and affiliations[1] (*G.S.*, I, 46–8, 52–4, 64–70).

What constitutes an association, or how many different types of association are to be distinguished, cannot be defined in a universally valid manner; it can only be settled within the limits and for the purposes of a juridical system, and not all such

---

[1] It should be noted, in passing, that Dilthey is far from supposing that the individual can be resolved into a mere complex of social functions, or that the cultural systems and social organisations of which he is a member can collectively exhaust his being. He expressly denies this in more than one passage. 'There is in every individual a point where he simply does not fall into any such co-ordination of his activities with others. That in the full life of the individual which is conditioned from this point enters into none of the systems of social life' (*G.S.*, I, 49). Even the family, 'the most concentrated form of volitional unity among individuals', has not full sway over its members. 'The individuals of whom it is composed do not entirely enter into it; the individual in his ultimate depth is for himself' (*G.S.*, I, 74, cf. 82). 'That which our intuition is constrained to mark off in space as a country, people, and State, and so sees as a full reality under the name of Germany or France, is not the State, is not the object of the political sciences. However deep the strong hand of the State may reach into the unity of the living individual, drawing him to itself, the State unites and subdues the individuals only in part, only relatively; there is something in them which is only in the hand of God' (*G.S.*, I, 82).

systems agree. But we can see from history that the earliest of all associations, and the richest in content, is the family, in which the diverse functions of economic organisation, law, government, and religion subsist without separation, side by side. By the union of families, wider and wider racial and territorial groups arise, and the smaller units are taken up into larger ones; while the widest group of all comes to be invested with what is the distinguishing attribute of the State, viz. sovereign power. Family, tribe, and State alike have their roots deep in human nature, and persist through the whole course of history. Their governing purpose can never be adequately defined, they take up this or that function, or again surrender it, according as social and historical circumstances change; and in this they differ from those artificial associations which, on the higher levels of civilisation, are formed for the furtherance of definitely stated and strictly limited ends, e.g. a joint-stock company. But in all associations alike is to be remarked a characteristic relation between the end or ends pursued, the consequent differentiation of function in pursuit of them, and the outer structure of the society. This relation between end, function, and structure is a matter of direct historical and social experience; and it is from here that biology has borrowed it as a key to the interpretation of organic phenomena (*G.S.*, I, 70–5).

When we turn to examine the relations between cultural systems and the outer organisations of society, we find that they vary with the particular cultural systems and organisations involved. The closest relation of all is that between law and the State; for law is neither altogether a cultural system nor altogether a political institution, but seems to partake of both characters at once.

Thus, on the one hand, law is always enunciated by the 'communal will' (*Gesamtwille*) of an organised society, i.e. in the last resort of the State. For man's most vital interest is security for himself and his property, and this can only be assured through an organisation strong enough to prevent all encroachments; but the only organisation which is strong enough to do this is the sovereign State, which is therefore a presupposition of all human co-operation, in cultural systems and in organised societies alike. The State, however, guards against foreign aggression by means of military defence, and against internal disorder by means of law; and thus law appears as one of the functions of the State. By the same token, it always determines the powers, privileges, and liberties of individuals and groups by reference primarily to their social function; and, however much the modern mind may dwell upon the rights of the individual as such, the recognition accorded to such rights is 'never more than relative', and remains within the social framework. Not that the State is the only vehicle of a communal will in society; associations subordinate to the State, and even in one sense embraced within it, can also lay down, and within limits enforce, laws of their own. What is impossible is that law should exist, as a social fact, with no organisation at all to enunciate and uphold it.

And yet, on the other hand, the organisation which promulgates the law is not free to follow its own devices, but must legislate in conformity with the principles of equity enunciated by the 'consciousness of right' (*Rechtsbewusstsein*). By this is meant the recognition, which we all share, that the power of individuals and small groups to pursue their private interest ought to be circumscribed according to principles which protect the general good. The belief in such principles, often supported by the religious appeal to a 'higher ordinance', or divine will which lays down laws for society, persists from generation to generation in a multitude of individuals, and their mutual understanding and co-operation in support of it constitutes a kind of public conscience. Every social organisation, in legislating, is bound to conform its enactments to this consciousness of right, and if it fails to do so, then the public conscience stands out in opposition to positive law. This truth that 'law is not made, but found', was recognised in the ancient theory of a 'natural law'; but that theory forgot the complementary truth that the individual consciousness of right is nothing apart from the will to enforce the principles of right, and that this can only find expression through sanctions imposed by an organisation, and ultimately by the State. So then, in so far as law is based upon the consciousness of right and the public conscience, it is a cultural system, while, in so far as it finds expression through the common will of a society, it is a matter of outer organisation. Law and the State, though distinct, are inseparable, and neither can exist without the other (*G.S.*, I, 54–7, 76–81).

At no other point is the relation between cultural system and outer organisation so close. Economic life, though much affected by State action, does not depend for its actualisation upon the fiat of the State. Religion, morality, language, art, science are affected by social and historical, but hardly in particular by political conditions. And, although religion cannot exist wholly without a Church, yet religion and the Church are distinct entities; while the associations connected with art and science are quite insignificant[1] (*G.S.*, I, 57–8, 81).

From these facts we can infer the logical structure of the 'special' or 'systematic human studies', i.e. those which analyse the various branches of civilised activity. They fall into two groups. The first group is concerned with the cultural systems, formulating laws to express the general character of each, comparing and accounting for the specific forms which they take in concrete instances; and Dilthey maintains that all these studies are dependent upon psychology. It is true that men have attempted to subject cultural systems to a philosophical study without any infusion of positive science. But, in the long run, every cultural system must be interpreted in terms of certain

[1] In Dilthey's account as summarised above, all social organisations are grouped together in contrast with the cultural systems. They are said to be psychologically grounded on the 'sense of community' and on the volitional relation of command and obedience; and this description is applied both to many-sided political and social forms like the family, the tribe, the State, and to associations with a single cultural purpose, like scientific societies, religious sects, and so on. This seems to be a confusion. To begin with, relations of authority and obedience play a more subordinate part in a religious or scientific society than in the tribe or State; such societies are more closely bound up with a specific function, and depend much less upon force. Again, while a sect or a scientific society exists merely to uphold a cultural system, the function of the family, tribe, or State is obviously different from and much wider than this. In Dilthey's *Aufbau der geschichtlichen Welt in den Geisteswissenschaften* (1910) and various MSS. of similar date, the standpoint of the *Einleitung* is so modified that these objections are met. The organisations which exist merely to serve a cultural system are there taken as forming a part of the cultural system and are treated under that head; nothing is said in relation to them of an authority based on force. On the other hand, those institutions which are more properly described as social and political are treated as a homogeneous group, centring in the State; their unity and authority are based on force, and their primary function is to express the 'common mind' of a social group. See below, pp. 293–5.

primary concepts, e.g. *certitude* in epistemology, *demand* and *value* in economics, which, though they refer not to human activity as a whole, but to specific branches of it, and are therefore not actually included in psychology, are yet not clearly definable without the aid of psychology, and must be regarded, in relation to psychological concepts, as 'concepts of the second order'. Thus e.g. the question of the origin of law is really a question about the part played by thought in that branch of human activity; it can therefore only be settled, as Jhering saw, by an appeal to psychology, and only when it is so settled can the fundamental concepts in the theory of law be clearly defined. Every analysis of a cultural system in this way presupposes psychology (*G.S.*, I, 44–6, 58–60).

This principle applies not only to economics, jurisprudence, the theory of education, or comparative religion, which no one regards as branches of philosophy, but also and in equal measure to certain branches of study which are so regarded, viz. aesthetics, political theory, and even ethics. These too, in Dilthey's view, are really empirical sciences dealing with branches of human activity. The relation between aesthetics and the cultural system of art is indeed obvious, and so is that between political theory and the outer organisation of society. About ethics, on the other hand, Dilthey himself expects to find his view strongly challenged. The tradition of ethical enquiry has always been to regard morality not as a social fact or process, but as a private affair of the individual conscience. Even Herbert Spencer, for all the positivism in his thought and his interest in sociology, regards the moral consciousness essentially in this way, and treats ethics as a different enquiry from sociology. Dilthey, however, as we saw in Chapter Four, proclaims the bankruptcy of moral theory both in the transcendental and in the empirical tradition, and bases his own ethic upon the study of morality as a social fact. And it is undeniable that the system of social and historical facts which Dilthey calls the 'moral system' conforms to his definition of a 'cultural system'. Like art, or religion, or science, morality as he describes it is a system of human relations and activities which arise in the pursuit of certain common ends, and maintain themselves in various places and at varying times, however the individuals who come within this system may change. It is a cultural system regulating human conduct from within, as law regulates it from without, and the study of it is accordingly neither more nor less than one of the 'systematic human studies' which analyse the cultural systems. 'Moral theory has its place among the human studies not as a mere group of imperatives governing the life of the individual, its object is one of the great systems which have their function in the life of society' (*G.S.*, I, 60–63).

In a letter to von Wartenburg, Dilthey describes how moral theory can develop along these lines as a comprehensive study of the moral system in history and society. First of all it must analyse the three fundamental impulses of the moral consciousness. Then it must describe the differentiation of society into cultural systems and outer organisations, and proceed to show how, under these conditions, the moral impulses gradually rise to clear consciousness, and are embodied in ideal standards which art and religion help to set forth and maintain. 'In this way, step by step, we can deduce the origin of the leading moral ideas in active human society: the heroic or active ideal of life, the recognition of man as an end in himself, and of his spheres, in law and (Stoic) philosophy etc., brotherly love and the Kingdom of God, the natural rights of the individual (moral kernel of natural law) etc.' These 'leading ideas' can combine in various ways, and their changing combinations give rise to distinctive periods in moral history, which we must describe and explain. 'They have the volitional impulses, norms, and ideas as their material, and are to be likened to the periods of artistic technique. The philosophical moral systems are only the reflective and fragmentary expression of them.' And if, in the end, moral theory enables us to take sides in present-day moral controversies, and to judge the relative worth of rival ideals, that is simply the practical application which can be made of the empirical researches that are the staple of its enquiry (*Bw.D.Y.*, pp. 90–1).

The second group of 'systematic human studies', which deals with the outer organisation of society, gives rise to another question. Have we really the right to speak of a 'group' of studies in this field? We can certainly distinguish between political theory and jurisprudence; but then, as the social phenomenon of law itself is only in part a visible institution and partly also a cultural system, so jurisprudence belongs as much to the cultural sciences as to the science of social organisation. If, however, we dismiss jurisprudence as a special case, and look for studies which concern themselves exclusively with the outer organisations of society, political theory seems to be the only one.

It is true that there are many organisations in society besides the State, comprising both natural groupings such as the family or clan, and artificial associations of various kinds; and, although these are all sheltered by the State and in various ways dependent upon it, it may be held that the State in turn presupposes and is continually affected by them. This view is especially plausible today, when, owing to the industrial revolution, there is a rapidly growing international proletariate, self-conscious and self-organised in opposition to the whole machinery of law and the State; and in general it is true that the transition from the individual to the State is mediated through a complex hierarchy of associations which are not included in the State, however dependent they may be upon it. 'Individuals confront the State not as isolated atoms, but as a system.' This complex of organisations and associations, distinct from the State, and more closely related to the lives of ordinary people, is sometimes called 'society' (*die Gesellschaft*) in distinction from the State; and the idea naturally arises that there may be a branch of knowledge which studies 'society' in this sense, independently of political theory. Dilthey is not very partial to this idea. He thinks rather that the scope of political theory should be widened to take in all this variety of social relationships, which it has so often ignored. A science, after all, he says, is constituted not by defining an area to be covered by it, but by discovering important truths in that area, and about 'society' in abstraction from the State no important truths have been discovered. The social system cannot exist in fact without law and the State, and nothing is gained by severing it from them in theory (*G.S.*, I, 48, 83–6).

Of course, the study of social organisations depends upon psychology in the same way, and for the same reasons, as the study of the cultural systems.

Such is the logical structure of the special human studies, the body of enquiries by which the historical process is analysed into its constituent elements, and each of these elements is

185

referred to its psychological and social basis. Taken all together, these studies cover the whole field of historical reality. On the other hand, they only cover this field by dividing it into distinct areas, and considering each in at least partial abstraction from the rest. We cannot but reflect that the cultural systems and social organisations, which we separate for the purpose of study, are really parts of a living whole, and the question must then arise, how their various functions combine in the unity of this whole. The problem is all the greater because of the comprehensive standpoint of the human studies, according to which every product of civilised activity is studied from three distinct points of view—as a fact, as a case of a causal law, and as subject to a norm. Dilthey instances the study of poetry; for that involves at once the historical and social conditions which determine the production and content of any given poem, the psychological laws which govern its genesis in the poet's mind and also the appreciation of it by a reader, and the critical canons by which alone it can be judged important enough to be studied at all. The three lines of enquiry proceed side by side, but we never reach the point, within the sphere of poetics, at which the deep-lying unity between historical fact, causal law, and critical norms can be made explicit. Is there a further branch of knowledge in which these abstractions are overcome, and the reality of life made visible as a whole? (*G.S.*, I, 86–9).

A claim to do this is made by the 'philosophy of history', as developed in modern times by Vico, Lessing, Herder, Humboldt, Hegel, and others; these writers all assume that history can be understood as the fulfilment of some simple though comprehensive idea, a law of progress or a divine plan. The claim is also made by 'sociology', in the sense given to that term by Condorcet, Saint-Simon, Comte, Mill, and Spencer; these writers not only believe in a law which governs historical changes, but further expect, by understanding this law, to be able to control the future development of society.

Both begin by accepting the account of past events which has been drawn up by the historian; and they try, by taking a comprehensive view of this, to elicit from the historian's facts a formula which will explain why things happen as they do. In this crude way, says Dilthey, it is indeed possible to obtain a general idea; but it will be that vague and confused kind of idea which in all branches of knowledge precedes and invites the real scientific analysis. It will be sketchy, inadequate, and one-sided. Yet it is from such generalisations that sociology pretends to deduce the causal connection of events, and the philosophy of history claims to find their meaning (*Sinn*), the value or end which history realises (*G.S.*, I, 95–6).

Dilthey will not recognise either the philosophy of history or sociology as a genuine branch of knowledge. He undertakes to show that both have attempted an impossible task, that their methods are ineffective, and that they spring from a failure to recognise the true relation between historiography and the special human studies. His discussion of these points is lengthy and diffuse, and much of it refers to doctrines and standpoints with which the present-day reader will not be familiar. It further suffers from his attempt to deal with the speculative philosophy of history and the positive science of sociology in one and the same argument. It will probably be better to separate these two sides of the discussion and examine them successively. Let us begin with sociology.

What Dilthey says about this is very largely a criticism of certain particular sociologists. He begins with Comte, the self-appointed founder of sociological science, the professed enemy of metaphysics and believer in empirical research; and he convicts him of vague use of language, unscientific dogmatism, and 'crass naturalistic metaphysics'. He goes on to deal with J. S. Mill, who thought that the study of mental and social phenomena would be furthered by transferring into that field the methods and techniques of physical science; and Dilthey rehearses all the reasons which show that the human studies have a structure of their own, and the transference of natural-scientific methods into them is as groundless in theory as it is barren in practice (*G.S.*, I, 105–9). All this tends to show that Comte and Mill were not very good sociologists, but it does not prove that no such science as sociology is possible at all. Dilthey's argument in support of this latter contention is simple. It is that the task is too great, that a scientific examination of the facts of social life cannot be made by a single science, but requires a group of distinct though related studies which will divide the ground between them.

A scientific examination of historical and social life, says Dilthey, must investigate two kinds of relations: the relations between one state of society and another which comes before or after it in time, i.e. the laws of historical change; and the relations between the different branches of social life and activity at any one moment in time. The former problem could only be solved within a single science if we could devise a formula which should express the whole complex of social conditions at a particular moment, or sum up in one all the causal influences which operate in society; and it need hardly be said that such comprehensive formulae are beyond our contrivance. We must therefore imitate natural science by dividing our great problem into smaller problems, and this the human studies have in fact done. Not one science of history and society, but psychology, ethnology, and the studies of cultural systems and social organisations together are the proper channels of enquiry, and every 'exact and fruitful law' hitherto discovered in *Geisteswissenschaft* has been within some such sectional study: e.g. Grimm's law in philology, Comte's law of the successive development of the natural sciences, and various laws in aesthetics and political economy. In the same way, the relations between the different branches of social life at any particular date cannot be profitably studied without a separate examination of these branches, each by itself. As a matter of fact, the men who have advanced our knowledge of history and society have always been men who were acquainted with several of the special human studies, and it was the combination of these special branches of knowledge which gave their work its value (*G.S.*, I, 109–12).

Some readers may wonder whether Dilthey's dismissal of sociology on these grounds is not a little cavalier. It may even be urged that he departs from his own principles at one point where he uses the impossibility of one all-inclusive science of nature as an argument against the possibility of one all-inclusive science of society. If historical and social reality differs from the physical world as much as he says it does, and if this difference is reflected in the structure of the empirical sciences dealing with each, it is dangerous to argue by analogy from the one group of sciences to the other. If the hierarchic structure of the natural sciences precludes any all-comprehending science, may not the relation of parallelism and mutual dependence, which characterises the human studies, permit or even demand such a science? No one thinks that sociology can replace or absorb the sectional human studies. But if we can distinguish the various cultural systems and social organisations from one another, we can also ask how they interact with one another, and what pattern they make as a whole. The modern concept of a 'culture-pattern' is concerned with precisely this. It may be hard to reach clarity in these matters, but that is not a sufficient reason for dismissing the enquiry out of hand.

It should be remembered that Dilthey was not here discussing sociology as we know it today. Writing in 1883, he had in mind primarily Comte, Mill, and Spencer, and not only his criticisms on specific points, but his more general argument too must be seen as a criticism of them. What they had in common was the assumption that all events in social history can be accounted for as parts of a single homogeneous process with a single ground of explanation. The facts and forces of social organisation, with their alleged inherent tendency to encourage social and political progress, were used as a ground of explanation also for the cultural life of mankind. Returning to the question more than twenty years later, Dilthey emphasises this common assumption of the early sociologists, and says that it is a metaphysical dogma unsupported by the facts. He argues that there is much, both in the life of the individual and in the cultural systems, which cannot be accounted for in terms of social causes. But then he goes on to discuss the 'sociology' of a more recent writer, Georg Simmel, and this, he says, is a very different thing. It is 'a theory of the forms assumed by mental life under the conditions of the social relations between individuals'; that is, Simmel abstracts altogether from the cultural systems, and studies only the ties which bind men together in social groups, the relations of rank, influence, division of labour, competition, group spirit, representation, party loyalty, etc. which arise in such groups. These relations he classifies, describes, and reduces to their psychological grounds. But this is the same as Dilthey's 'study of the external organisation of society', except that Dilthey includes ties of family and race, and geographical conditions, along with the individual-psychological forces to which he appeals. Accordingly, he welcomes Simmel's work as a partial fulfilment of his own programme (*G.S.*, I, 420–3). If he had seen a 'sociology' which covered the cultural systems also, but which studied their relations empirically, describing what can be found in each age, society, or culture-area, without pretending to reduce the whole to a single formula, it is an open question what he would have said of it.

The philosophy of history differs from Comte's sociology in that it seeks not a causal law, but a meaning and a purpose in history. The attempt to find such a meaning has in the past been closely associated with theology, from the time of St. Augustine, who is its first great representative, down to Lotze in the nineteenth century. But, says Dilthey, a critical philosophy, which has set aside theology and all speculative metaphysics, can recognise no values or norms except such as are set up by human feeling and will. The meaning of history is therefore the meaning which human agents themselves read into it, and to study the meaning of history is to analyse the human value-consciousness. That is the work of sectional enquiries like moral and political philosophy, aesthetics, and the philosophy of religion, but not of a 'philosophy of history' which takes everything together in unanalysed confusion (*G.S.*, I, 95–104). As with sociology, so here we must recognise that the philosophy of history is attempting single-handed a task which only a group of distinct but related studies can fulfil. Those philosophical writers who have made real discoveries in the study of history and society have done so by virtue of their acquaintance with one or more of the sectional studies, not by virtue of their philosophy. Vico was a jurist and a philologist, Herder a naturalist and a historian, Turgot an economist, a natural scientist, and a historian. When these writers pass from questions of detail, in which they are well informed and strong, to try to formulate the meaning of history as a whole, their work dissolves into a 'metaphysical nebulosity' whose only value lies in such propositions about particular peoples, cultural systems, or States as may be held in solution in it. 'These statements about the life of the branches and systems of humanity are the elements of every more precise picture whereby any philosophy of history endows its shadowy fundamental idea with some semblance of flesh and blood' (*G.S.*, I, 109–12).

Summing up, we may say that any attempt to obtain a general

view of the historical process by abstraction from the results of historiography must fail. There is no alchemy by which the material of historical fact may be transmuted into 'the pure gold of abstraction', no magic word to be discovered which could unlock the secret meaning (*Sinn*) of history. The only way to obtain a general view of history which is also a true view is to be a historian oneself. 'The thinker who has the historical world for his object must master history and all its methods in direct contact with the immediate raw material. He must subject himself to the same law of hard work at the raw materials to which the historian is subject.' His philosophy will then appear in the use which he makes of this raw material and these methods, and the degree of critical reflection which he brings to bear. 'If we speak of a philosophy of history, this can be nothing but historical enquiry from a philosophical standpoint and with philosophical aids' (*G.S.*, I, 92). And if we ask what is this philosophical standpoint, it consists in just that spirit of analysis and criticism which leads to the constitution of the special human studies, and then, to put them on a firm basis, goes beyond them to a careful analysis of human consciousness in general, or *Selbstbesinnung*.

There is 'no conceivable sense' in speaking of a systematic explanation of history except by means of the special human studies; for 'to know this system means to resolve it, an immensely complicated whole, into its elements, to look for uniformities in the simpler material, and then by means of them to approach the more complex'. Such a use of the systematic human studies is more and more forced upon the historian; for that objectivity of view, which Ranke in a famous phrase declared to be his aim,[1] is to be obtained not by merely looking at the facts, but by recognising among them the units of which the whole is built up, and the forms of interaction in which they are necessarily drawn together. 'The knowledge of the whole of historical and social reality . . . realises itself gradually in a system of truths, based on epistemological reflection (*erkenntnistheoretische Selbstbesinnung*), wherein, on the basis of the theory of man, the special theories of social reality are built up, and these are applied in a true progressive historical science to explain more and more of the factual historical reality which is

[1] '*Ich möchte mich selbst auslöschen, um die Dinge zu sehen, wie sie gewesen sind.*'

191

bound up in the interactions of individuals. . . . World history (*Universalgeschichte*), in so far as it is not beyond human power altogether, would form the colophon of this whole of the human studies' (*G.S.*, I, 92–5).

The foregoing analysis of the human studies has raised, as it went along, numerous logical and epistemological problems. At the end of this first book of the *Einleitung*, Dilthey calls these problems to mind, and points forward to the *Grundlegung der Geisteswissenschaften* by which they must be solved. The *Grundlegung*, he says, must be something deeper than a merely logical study such as we had from Mill. It must bring to light the relation between thought and its foundations in lived experience. It must further recognise the peculiar character of the epistemological problem in connection with the human studies. Some of the hardest problems raised by natural science, such as those relating to space and motion, are irrelevant in this field, because here we consider space and motion (when we refer to them at all) not as they reveal themselves to a scientific analysis, but as they appear in the consciousness of an ordinary human agent. The priority (in this field) of understanding to analysis, the presence of feeling and will as determinant factors in understanding, the interest we take in the individual for his own sake —all these contribute to give the human studies a distinctive logical structure. And finally, the relation between fact, causal law, value and imperative is peculiar to this field of experience, and can only be made clear by finding the common ground of all three in lived experience. A *Grundlegung der Geisteswissenschaften*, or *Kritik der historischen Vernunft*, which should do real justice to these facts, would free the study of history and society from the tyranny exercised over it by the methods of natural science since Descartes, Spinoza, and Hobbes (*G.S.*, I, 116–20).

The second book of the *Einleitung* seems at first sight to be a turning aside from this task. It is occupied with a history of philosophy from Thales to Hume, in which the ambiguities and antinomies inherent in all metaphysics are brought to light. In Chapter Three I have summarised Dilthey's reasons for rejecting metaphysics. Some of them are taken from this second book of the *Einleitung*, and I shall not repeat them here. But there is another side to this second book. It not only writes the obituary notice of metaphysics, but also shows how, while metaphysical thinking prevailed, its influence on the human studies was a hindrance to them rather than a help.

For instance, social theory among the Greeks never reached a proper understanding of the relation between the individual and the State. It failed because the cultural systems and social organisations, which stand between the individual and the State and bridge this gulf, had not at that time been recognised for what they are and made the object of serious study. Instead of this, the Greeks applied formulae drawn from contemporary metaphysics. The Sophists adopted a kind of social atomism, recognising no political motive or social bond but private interest; but out of this they could not conjure a living community. The Socratic school considered the people at large as an irrational mass upon which the State must impose order, as form is imposed on matter; but this left no positive affinity between the matter and the form, and the power of the State therefore remained an external compulsion.

The mediaevals had the advantage over the ancients of living in a richly diversified and highly sophisticated social order, and so their concepts have more empirical backing. But, in the first place, instead of analysing this complex of institutions in a methodical way, they tried to take it as a whole and elaborate its meaning in the light of the Christian philosophy of history. This meant, among other things, that Church and State were both held to rest upon a divine authority, which comes to men from above. Then, when the later mediaevals attempted, after Aristotle and the Stoics, to base law and the State on a 'natural law' inherent in the human mind itself, the two doctrines came into irreconcilable conflict.

Since the Renaissance our empirical material has vastly increased, and slowly, at last, a really scientific method has grown up, which takes as its basis a theory of the nature of man ('anthropology'), and builds up the edifice of the human studies from that.

Here the *Einleitung* breaks off, and the later books were never written. We know what they would have contained. There would have been a critical study of the Kantian and post-Kantian philosophy, which promised for a moment to fill the place previously held by metaphysics as the foundation of all possible knowledge, but which breaks down under the weight of its abstractness and its apriorism. Parallel with this Dilthey would have traced the history of the human studies in the eighteenth century, when the belief in abstract principles was prevalent and historical variations were regarded as regrettable departures from the rational norm. This would have led on to an account of the nineteenth-century movement in the human studies against abstract principles, and towards a study of historical facts and processes in all their concrete diversity. Dilthey's own theory of knowledge, inspired by this movement, and at the same time giving it the philosophical groundwork which it needed and could not provide for itself, would have completed the work.

Dilthey spent the last thirty years of his life in constantly renewed attempts to finish the *Einleitung*. He never did finish it according to the original plan, summarised above, in spite of an attempt to do so during a sabbatical semester in the winter of 1895–6. The internal development of his own thought, and the external pressure of criticisms and rival views, forced him to depart from the plans he had laid down for the work. His original solution of the problem proved to be inadequate, and the problem itself was found to need restatement. The *Einleitung*, too, was seen in retrospect to be unsatisfactory in certain respects. In the end, instead of taking up the work where he had left it and bringing it to a conclusion, Dilthey began all over again with the writings which were to be his *Kritik der historischen Vernunft*. In Chapter Nine this final statement of his conclusions will be summarised, as we have already summarised the *Einleitung*. The two intervening chapters will describe the processes of thought which led Dilthey from the earlier work to the later, showing by what inherent tendencies and by what external pressures his thought was shaped.

What were the problems with which the *Grundlegung* was to deal? They fall under three heads.

(1) There were the epistemological problems. The *Grundlegung* is meant to perform the same task as Kant undertook in the *Kritik der reinen Vernunft*, though by no means after his manner, and with proper allowance for the human studies which Kant ignored. That is, it must describe the processes of lived experience and understanding upon which the human studies depend, and show how these experiences can be made the basis

of a system of objective knowledge. Dilthey's views on this aspect of the problem were not formulated fully and systematically until the last five or six years of his life, and the solution which he then put forward has already been stated and examined in Chapters Two, Three, and Five. There is no need to go over that ground again.

(2) It is made clear in the *Einleitung* that no one can interpret evidence and reach coherent conclusions in the human studies without being guided by some conception of human nature, which gives meaning to the evidence and determines the weight which he assigns to different kinds of evidence. Dilthey crystallises this conception of human nature in the idea of a typology, and further demands that it be furnished by psychology, which is to be reformed and specially developed for the purpose. Is he right in this? The problems involved, and the position which Dilthey finally reached, are analysed in Chapter Seven.

(3) The *Einleitung* does not merely describe the human studies in general terms, or in a casual order, but professes to exhibit their logical relations with one another and with the natural sciences. The human studies are defined as a group by their possession of a common subject-matter, and from their concern with this subject-matter their principles and methods are said to follow. Is Dilthey right on these points? These are the questions raised before his time by Comte, Mill, and Spencer, and we have seen how he deals with these writers. But in Dilthey's later years the same questions were raised again in a very different way by the Kantians, Windelband and Rickert, with whom Dilthey became involved in serious controversy. This new development is examined in Chapter Eight.

CHAPTER SEVEN

A T various points in the preceding chapters we have found Dilthey proclaiming that the human studies, and even philosophy itself, are in some way dependent on psychology. We have constantly deferred consideration of this part of his teaching, but the time has now come to take it up and reach some conclusion about it. First of all it will be necessary to see what he actually says and why he says it.

We shall find the two sides of him, the romantic and the positivist, in evidence here as elsewhere. But whereas in other parts of his philosophy he brings the two sides together in a fairly harmonious synthesis, he failed to do this in the group of questions relating to psychology. The very word 'psychology' means something different in his writings, according as it belongs to a romantic or a positivist line of argument. Here more than ever, therefore, it is important to learn to see the two sides separately and assess their value independently, before going on to watch his unsuccessful attempts to unite them. We shall find, moreover, that Dilthey himself was aware of the tension, and that his view changed more than once. The Dilthey of the last years is a trenchant critic of his own earlier position.

To most readers in the twentieth century, 'psychology' means primarily the experimental science of that name. It means this in Dilthey when he is writing in his positivist strain. Now, to ascribe to experimental psychology a central position in the scheme of human thought is to offend against all Kantian principles. Dilthey's Kantian contemporaries were not slow to tell him so, and to give their reasons why psychology cannot be a foundation for philosophy or for the human studies. In a similar way Collingwood, from his Hegelian point of view, conducts a campaign against those who would allow psychology to invade the territory of philosophy and history. In *The Idea of History* he brings Dilthey's views on the role of psychology (which he misrepresents) as a main point of criticism against Dilthey.

On the other hand it must be remembered that Kant and Hegel themselves, and their followers, have a great deal to say about the nature and operations of the human mind. They claim to have a better insight into it than Hume or Mill, and they make their insight into the transcendental unity of apperception the focal point of their philosophies. It is true that what they write about the mind is not 'psychology', if that word means the experimental science so called. But it has a great deal to do with 'psychology' as Dilthey means it when writing in his post-Kantian and romantic vein. Collingwood's analysis of the relations between feeling, imagination, and thought in *The Principles of Art* is a typical example of the kind of 'psychology' that Dilthey has in mind.

'Psychology' in this sense is in fact unavoidable in philosophy. No one can write on the theory of knowledge as (distinct from pure formal logic) without committing himself consciously or unconsciously to some view of what we do when we cognise. Even Cook Wilson, who objected to the intrusion of 'psychology' into logic, had no objection to describing the difference between knowing and opining as he thought he found it in experience. All philosophers of all periods have done the same kind of thing. No one can go far into ethics without adopting some view about desire and will and similar questions. Nor can we go far into aesthetics without discussing imagination, expression, understanding, and the like. In all these cases we form opinions about what goes on in the mind and will, and these opinions are built into our philosophy and become integral to it.

Some philosophers have codified their views on the mind and made them into a separate treatise περὶ ψυχῆς. Aristotle's work with that title is well known. We may compare the second, third, and fourth books of Spinoza's *Ethics*, and the *subjektiver Geist* section of Hegel's *Enzyklopädie*. Other philosophers, the majority, have let their 'psychology' remain as it were in solution in their writings on properly philosophical subjects. What Dilthey says is that it makes for clarity if we do separate out our 'psychology', and make it a subject for consideration by itself; for it affects our conclusions in other more strictly philosophical fields.

What has been said of philosophy is equally true of history, or literary criticism, or any other of the human studies. In them too it is impossible to go far without using as a clue some conception of human nature, of the motives which prompt men to action, of the part played by principles and ideals in shaping conduct, and so on. The historian or critic does not always feel a need to work out his views on these points systematically, and it is better that he should not do so than that he should run the risk of becoming tied to a doctrine or a school. He should keep his views flexible and open to modification by the progress of his studies. Nevertheless he has these views, and they govern his interpretation of the evidence. It is a fact that one historian or critic judges differently from another because he holds, consciously or unconsciously, a different view of human nature.

This conception of human nature, sometimes openly professed, but often held in solution in the historian's writings, is what Dilthey calls his 'anthropology'. This is what Dilthey is studying in his essays on the history of 'anthropological' ideas in the Renaissance and early modern period. This is the *Anthropologie* (or *reale Psychologie*) of Novalis; and one of the things which attracted Dilthey to that author was his clear recognition that the human studies, as well as philosophy, rest on this basis. He even speaks of history as 'applied anthropology'.

This is the heart and substance of what Dilthey means when he says that 'psychology' is fundamental to philosophy and the human studies. But then, it will be asked, what has all this to do with the experimental science of psychology? That is just the question which exercised Dilthey himself throughout his life; and we must now trace the development of his views on the point. From the beginning he was disposed, through the influence of Hume and Mill, backed up by psychologists such as Wundt, to suppose that experimental psychology could do what was wanted for the human studies and philosophy. We shall see how he struggled in vain to overcome the difficulties involved in this view, and had finally to abandon it.

We can distinguish three periods, which may be dated 1860–80, 1880–1907, and 1907–11.

About the first period there is little to say. It was the formative period, during which Dilthey slowly took the measure of the problem. In his essays on the moral consciousness (1864) and on Novalis (1865) he made clear that what was wanted was a *Realpsychologie*, or *Inhaltspsychologie*, and that experimental psychology could not provide this unless it widened its aims very considerably. It must cease to be a purely formal study; it must take in other aspects of mental life besides perception and thought; it must learn to see man as a social being. At this early stage Dilthey did not yet call for a change in psychological method. As late as the essay of 1875 we find him reckoning with the possibility that associationism may have a fruitful future before it (*G.S.*, V, 55). In the following five years, however, his view changed, and in the *Einleitung* (1883) he declares that psychology cannot achieve the solid and reliable results which the other human studies expect from it unless it changes its method and principles of procedure, and becomes a 'descriptive' instead of an 'explanatory' science.

This new contention introduces our second period, during which Dilthey's thinking about psychology is dominated by the question of method. In the *Einleitung* the problem was merely stated, the solution being reserved for the promised sequel to that work. In various essays during the following years we find Dilthey feeling his way towards the solution, and he finally gave it to the world in the *Ideen über eine beschreibende u. zergliedernde Psychologie* (1894). This work is the key to Dilthey's position in the second period of his development, and will repay study.

It begins by setting in the foreground the criticism of prevailing methods in psychology, and it is interesting to see that both sides of Dilthey, the romantic and the positivist, have something to contribute to this discussion.

(1) When he says, as he so often does, that psychology must drop 'explanatory' methods and become purely 'descriptive', this is a summons to psychology to assert its independence. He thinks it leans too heavily on natural science, both in detail and in principle. In detail, he thinks, psychologists are too ready to accept physiological causes, even sometimes purely hypothetical ones, for mental events and processes, when they ought to be looking for psychological causes. And in principle, psychologists have taken their very idea of causality and their model of explanation from physics and chemistry. In saying this Dilthey is referring especially though not exclusively to sensationalism and

associationism, the doctrine brought into psychology by the British school, by Hume, Hartley, and Mill. Hume makes no secret of the fact that he is imitating physics. As in physics the object is broken up into many small independent units and put together again out of these, so the mind is to be broken up into many small units—sensations, ideas, and feelings—and its processes explained in terms of these. Hume apparently thinks that these unit sensations and ideas can be found in introspection. In this he is wrong, and Dilthey emphasises that he is wrong. As in physics, so in this kind of psychology, the units are not found by observation. The atom is a theoretical construction, nd so is the atomic sensation or idea. This procedure, Dilthey contends, is justified in physics, because there the object is not presented to perception as a coherent system, and order has to be read into it by this method of theoretical construction. But it is not justified in psychology, because the mind is given in inner perception as a system having its own unity in itself. The structural system of the mind, in fact, is a causal system and the source of all our ideas of causality. To go behind this perceived unity to a purely hypothetical unity, and to import a model of explanation from physics, where coherence is not perceived, into psychology, where coherence is given in perception, is simply absurd (*G.S.*, V, 139–45, 158–68).

Dilthey's position here was strengthened by the growth of the 'descriptive theory' of science in general, which was beginning to be popular in his time. The roots of the descriptive theory go back into Berkeley, who treats the concepts of physics as merely so many ciphers which enable us to codify and predict our perceptions. Matter, according to him, is nothing in itself, it is merely a convenient abstraction, and all statements expressed in terms of it must be translated into terms of perception before their real meaning can appear. Physical laws do not describe the operation of real physical causes, but are merely generalised expressions of the way our perceptions are related to one another. This Berkeleian view of science became a European power with the spread of positivism. It found a welcome from scientist-philosophers such as Avenarius (*Kritik der reinen Erfahrung*, 1888–90) and Mach. It was adopted and used for their own purposes by the various idealist schools. Now, if physical explanation is not to be taken literally even in physics itself, if even in the natural sciences our real purpose is not to go behind the phenomena, but merely to codify and predict them, then *a fortiori* in psychology, where the facts of experience have an inherent order and coherence, our aim must be to describe them without going behind them. The process by which experimental psychology ultimately threw off sensationalism and associationism, and took courage to describe the unities of lived experience as they really are, was assisted by this undermining of theoretical physics on its own ground, and Dilthey in 1894 was aware of this.

(2) It is the positivist Dilthey, therefore, who discusses the function of theories and hypotheses in psychology, and calls for the adoption of a descriptive method. But he is no positivist when he actually describes the structure of mental life. Positivism, as much as scientific realism, thought in terms of events and laws. The paradigm of intelligibility, for it, was to bring many particular instances under a general formula. Its procedure, even in psychology, was always to abstract and isolate, to single out a particular process in mental life for special study, and then build up the whole out of the pieces. This is not Dilthey's way. Dilthey is concerned with the whole man rather than with particular aspects of his mental processes and the laws which govern them; and he sees the whole man not from without, like an impersonal observer, but from within, as the man sees and feels himself. This is the view of life which finds expression in lyric poetry, or in autobiography, or in religious meditations, and it is to these and similar sources that Dilthey calls our attention. He says in the *Ideen*, and often elsewhere, that contemporary psychology must be judged by its failure to describe the higher intellectual and moral processes as we know them in our own experience, and by its failure to account for the various forms of genius in the poet, the saint, the teacher, and their like. Such phenomena as these have often been well described in a peculiar type of reflective literature, of which Seneca, St. Augustine, and Montaigne are notable representatives, and this literary study of man covers a far wider range of the facts of life than does explanatory psychology; but, unhappily, it lacks method and system. Poetry, too, enlarges our acquaintance with life through the portrayal of characters and events, lit up by appropriate generalisations here and there; and we have all

heard it said that the works of the poets are full of psychology. Of course, if psychology means an abstract scientific statement of laws governing mental life, poetry contains none of it; but at the very least it does offer to psychology 'a problem and a subject-matter'. It is now time that those facts which hitherto have been revealed to us only through literary description should be brought within the range of a more systematic study (*G.S.*, V, 152–3, 156).

If we draw upon these sources, and upon the source which lies behind them all, viz. lived experience, we shall *first* of all discover that living dynamic unity of the mind in all its operations, which Dilthey calls its 'structure'. Unlike Hume, to whom introspection never revealed anything more than 'a particular perception', Dilthey finds the whole life and movement of the mind focussed and reflected in every moment of experience. He calls upon psychology to become aware of this and to find ways of expressing it. *Secondly*, we shall find that the mind not only lives, but grows. Past experience, stored in memory, throws light on the present; attitudes and habits, once acquired, remain to shape our reactions for the future. As we grow older, our views become wider, our thinking clearer, our purposes firmer and more coherent. This process of development is the theme of novels like *Wilhelm Meister* and poems like *Faust*. And *thirdly*, we shall see how no two people develop in the same way, and the growth of character is also a growth of individuality. Here, in the supreme value and significance which Dilthey ascribes to the individual in his uniqueness, the influence of Schleiermacher becomes manifest. Yet at the same time a firm protest is made against the speculative metaphysical way in which Schleiermacher gave expression to his insight. To talk of a divine dialectic, and to pretend to explain the origin and the significance of individual character in terms of that, is abstract and unreal. We must look to psychology to show how individual character is built up gradually by the convergence of factors belonging to the natural and historical order, in accordance with laws which can be discovered empirically (*G.S.*, V, 226–8).

Thus the positivist and the romantic unite, here as elsewhere, in an intimate co-operation. It is the romantic, the lover of Goethe and Schleiermacher, who contributes the vision and the aim, but it is the positivist who seeks the means of fulfilling it.

In the light of this analysis let us now glance briefly at the *Ideen* as a whole.

The essay begins by defining the distinction between explanatory and descriptive psychology. A little later comes a section which traces the history of explanatory psychology, showing how at every stage of its development it was governed by the influence of mathematics and natural science. The roots of it are found in Spinoza and Leibniz, but the decisive influence in its growth is shown to have been the British school: Hume and Hartley, the two Mills, and Herbert Spencer. The mathematical side of it owes much to Herbart, and the experimental technique was perfected by Fechner and Helmholz. By their time the assimilation of psychology to a natural science was complete, and the discovery of fundamental psychological laws was confidently expected. It was a vain hope. Experimental psychology has made a masterly analysis of sensation and perception. 'It proved to be the indispensable instrument of the psychologists for the establishment of an accurate description of inner mental processes, like the limitation of consciousness, the rapidity of mental processes, the factors involved in memory and in the sense of time, and the skill and patience of the experimenters will certainly succeed in finding *points d'appui* for enquiries into other relations in the inner life of mind. But to knowledge of laws in the inner domain of mind it simply has not led' (*G.S.*, V, 158–65). And the reason is plain. It is because 'explanatory psychology can only attain its end through a combination of hypotheses' (*G.S.*, V, 140).

Hypothesis is a necessary element in all thought, in so far as thought goes beyond the immediate given; but in natural science the role of hypothesis is peculiarly important. For the aim of science is to exhibit systematic connection in its subject-matter; and, since no such connection can be given through the senses, it must be added by a theory which goes beyond the data, i.e. a hypothesis. Hypothesis is therefore a condition of the possibility of natural science. We often find the data compatible with two or three alternative hypotheses; then we proceed by deduction and observation to exclude and to verify, and when a hypothesis is so well verified that no further thought need be given to alternatives, it is accepted as a law. All scientific knowledge of the physical world has been obtained in this way; the units in terms of which we interpret phenomena and the laws which they are said to obey are all alike hypotheses more or less verified by experiment. Now, explanatory psychology too seeks its causal system through hypotheses, but, unlike natural science, it has not been able to decide between conflicting possibilities. 'A war of all against all rages over its domain, not less fiercely than over the field of metaphysics. Nowhere yet, even on the farthest horizon, is anything in sight which might avail to decide this war.' A decision is made possible in natural science by the relative permanence of the objects studied, the unrestricted scope for experiment, and the possibility of exact measurement. Psychology, except in the borderland realm of psychophysics, has none of these advantages, and is further distressed by the insoluble metaphysical problem of the relation between mind and body. 'Therefore no one can say whether this war of hypotheses in explanatory psychology will ever end, or when that may happen' (*G.S.*, V, 140–5).

In various parts of the *Ideen* Dilthey gives reasons for thinking that explanatory methods must ultimately be abandoned in psychology, and are already on the decline. He shows how Wundt and James, among others, have moved away from the crude sensationalist position and recognised the synthetic and creative character of mental processes. 'In proportion as this movement advances, the influence of explanatory and constructive psychology must wane' (*G.S.*, V, 165–7). And it is necessary that it should wane, for explanatory and constructive methods can never do justice to the instinctive life on the one hand, or to the higher life of the spirit in thought and moral action on the other (*G.S.*, V, 156).

Nor can the old methods achieve that certainty which psychology must achieve if it is to serve as the basis for philosophy and the human studies. Dilthey's reasons for making epistemology dependent on psychology have been stated above and need not be repeated here; but he thinks the case is even clearer in respect of the human studies. 'As the systems of culture, viz. economic life, law, religion, art and science, and the outer organisation of society in such groups as the family, the community, Church and State, have arisen out of the living system of the human mind, so also in the end they can only be understood in terms of it.' It can be shown for each individual human study that its fundamental concepts, unless illuminated by psychological analysis, are 'dark and lifeless', and obviously the relations between the various human studies themselves must be determined by the relations between the mental facts which they study. 'Without reference to the mental system on which their relations are grounded, the human studies are an aggregate, a bundle, not a system' (*G.S.*, V, 147–8).

It is no use to try to counter these arguments by pointing to instances where psychology has had a bad effect on historians, or on the administration of criminal law, on economic and political theories, on aesthetics and so on. Dilthey himself gives a list of instances where writers and practical men have been led astray by 'the one-sided theories of the explanatory psychologist'; but he insists that this was because the psychology was bad psychology. The cure for bad psychology is better psychology, a psychology which throws its hypotheses to the winds and describes and analyses life as it really is (*G.S.*, V, 145–6, 163, 191–2).

To find how this is possible, we must examine the conditions under which mental facts are known.

That it is possible to perceive mental facts is obvious. 'Every one of us knows what a feeling of pleasure, a volitional impulse, or an act of thought is. No one is in danger of confusing these with one another. Since such knowledge exists, it must be possible.' Its basis is an 'awareness' (*Innewerden*) of mental facts in which there is no distinction between subject and object; the mental fact, e.g. a feeling, is not an object for me, but 'exists for me' by virtue of being 'conscious' (*bewusst*). This 'awareness' can be raised to the level of 'inner perception' through an act of attention. This process, however, is surrounded by difficulties. Attention can only turn where volition (i.e. interest) directs it, and therefore mental facts outside our range of interest cannot be perceived, though they may become known in retrospect; further, those mental facts which we can perceive are hard to observe with accuracy, because they are in constant flux, and largely incapable of being measured. We can indeed check and amplify our introspective knowledge by comparison with what we know of the inner life of other persons; but this knowledge in turn is subject to serious limitations. For it depends upon a 'transposition of our own mental life' into the other person, and we cannot thus form an idea of any experience differing from our own except in mere quantity, i.e. in the relative intensity of the factors composing it; confronted by an experience containing an element not present in our own life, or lacking an important element which we have, we could recognise the presence of something alien, but could form no idea of what it was. That is why we find it so hard to understand the minds of animals (*G.S.*, V, 197–9).

All these difficulties, however, are outweighed by two advantages. (1) Our experience of physical objects is mediated by sense-data, and the systematic unity of the physical world is not given in these, but has to be imposed upon them by thought. But we enjoy mental facts immediately, 'in their reality, as they are', and that means that their systematic unity is present to us in the lived experience itself. Every process or group of processes in mental life is an indivisible whole constituted by unity of function, and is enjoyed as such. True, we never enjoy the whole system of mind at once, but only changing segments of it; silent thought, however, enables us to detect the permanent form of the system, to recognise and to name its various parts as we experience them. The awareness of the system is a prime factor in our understanding (*Verstehen*) of its parts, and carries with it an 'immediate consciousness of the value of particular functions for the whole', whereby we can distinguish what is essential (*wesentlich*) in mind and what is not (*G.S.*, V, 169–73).

(2) Besides the direct observation of ourselves and others, we have a further source of knowledge in the cultural systems and organisations of society, the 'creations of the common mind in which, to use Hegel's phrase, human consciousness has become objective and so abides analysis' (*G.S.*, V, 180). In contrast with the endless flux of the individual mind, these systems present 'permanent forms with firm outlines' from which analysis can take its bearings (*G.S.*, V, 200). Moreover, they are almost our only means of obtaining knowledge of the acquired system in our minds. That system is 'the primary object of psychological description and analysis', because it is the principal factor in the shaping of individual character, as well as of social ideas and institutions; yet introspection and direct observation of others reveal the merest fragments of it, and the only way to full comprehension of it is through the analysis and the historical

study of these objective manifestations in which the acquired system of a whole society is expressed. 'What man is, he learns not by rummaging about in himself, nor yet by psychological experiments, but by means of history' (*G.S.*, V, 180, cf. VII, 279).

Dilthey can now infer the true method of psychology. Since all systematic unity in our experience is a reflection of the structural unity which we experience in our own minds, it follows that this structural unity, just as we experience it, is the sole basis of psychological understanding. For if we go behind it, as does explanatory psychology, to a system of abstract elements combining in accordance with causal laws, it remains true that our conception of causality is itself obtained by abstraction from our lived experience of the structural system; that system, therefore, is surreptitiously assumed by the very theory which is to explain it, so that the explanation is circular. 'We cannot make a system outside the one which is given to us. . . . Consciousness cannot go behind itself.' In any case the concepts of natural science, being conditioned by the sensuous character and spatio-temporal form of outer perception, cannot apply to the facts of inner experience; in that experience there is no distinction between substance and quality, no system of clearly defined units, no mathematical equation of cause and effect, but 'life, historicity, freedom, and development' (*G.S.*, V, 194–6, cf. 143–4). Indeed, it is impossible exhaustively to analyse lived experience in the categories of the formal understanding (*ratio*); there is a permanent disparity between thought and its object, which Dilthey calls the 'immanent antinomy' in this sphere (*G.S.*, V, 175, 196).

We cannot therefore seek knowledge of the structural system anywhere but in itself. But then there is no need to do so; for the silent thought which accompanies lived experience, raising it to the level of inner perception, of its own accord develops further into judgment and into reflection on self, and so insensibly passes into psychology, in the same way as reflection on law passes into jurisprudence and reflection on trade into economics. Psychology therefore finds its data already worked over and concepts formed for its use in common sense, and all it has to do is to extend and deepen this pre-existing knowledge by the intensive and methodical application of the same process which gave it birth. This means an analysis of the structural system, so conducted that 'every problem which it raises and every conception which it forms is conditioned by this system and receives its place there'. 'Psychological thought articulates and distinguishes on the basis of the given system', and its analysis 'always retains something of the living, artistic process of understanding (*Verstehen*)'. From this analysis will emerge a morphological description of the structure of mind, and because this structure is 'immediately and objectively given', therefore 'description in this field has an indubitable, universally valid foundation' (*G.S.*, V, 173–5).

After this description has been completed, and only then, psychology may indulge in hypotheses. For Dilthey allows that the formation and experimental verification of hypotheses is the proper method of extending knowledge, even in psychology, into those regions where direct experience of the structural system fails us; only, the hypotheses must be controlled by our pre-existing descriptive knowledge of the structural system, and must not presume to 'explain' mental facts in terms of any other fundamental system but that. Descriptive psychology can thus absorb all that is good in experimental psychology, without overestimating its significance or impairing the universal validity of its own foundations (*G.S.*, V, 175, 191). Such a psychology will be equal to the task which its own nature and its relation to other studies impose upon it. 'It will be the foundation of the human studies as mathematics[1] is of the natural sciences' (*G.S.*, V, 193).

Dilthey proceeds to outline the contents of this psychology. It will begin by describing the *structure of mind*, showing how from cognition we pass to feeling and from feeling again to volition. All these three elements coexist in every moment of consciousness, forming an indivisible unity; and the whole state of consciousness at any moment is called cognitive, affective, or volitional according as this or that element is the dominant factor. In each of the three departments of experience, states and processes of mind can be arranged in an order of increasing complexity and refinement, ranging e.g. in the cognitive sphere from sensation up to abstract thought, or in the volitional from momentary impulses to a coherent system of ends. The central problem in psychology is to discover the connection between

[1] On this analogy, see above, p. 21 n.

these two spheres of thought and will. Dilthey finds the connection in feeling, but adds that feeling itself is based on instinct; the instincts, therefore, are the real kernel of mental life. 'A bundle of instincts and feelings, that is the centre of our mental structure.' The whole system has an immanent teleology, which may be considered both from a subjective and from an objective point of view. Subjectively, it lies in the way in which mental processes work together to bring about the satisfaction of our instincts, or 'happiness'; objectively, it lies in the way in which they work to secure the survival of the individual and the species. But Dilthey adds that the subjective teleology is the only indubitable one, being seen in lived experience; the objective teleology is only a plausible hypothesis, borrowed from biology (*G.S.*, V, 200–13).

This structural analysis constitutes as it were a cross-section of the mind, and must be amplified by a longitudinal section, or analysis of *mental development*. The structural system works towards satisfaction; and since satisfaction is best assured by the more complex and refined of our activities, the structural system itself launches the mind upon the path towards increasing refinement and perfection. This leads to a better adaptation of the subject to his physical and cultural environment, and an increasing freedom and enrichment of all his activities; and the appreciation of all this in feeling is what constitutes the 'worth of life'. The first disorderly mass of sense-data, feelings, and impulses becomes an articulated whole of experience, resting upon an 'acquired system' whose control over life increases continually, and under its guidance new points of view, new values, new principles of conduct come to be adopted (*G.S.*, V, 213–20).

The controlling influence of the 'acquired system' is the guiding factor in the growth and development of the mind, whose crown is reached in the attainment of individual character and personality. This process of development cannot be accounted for by metaphysical principles, nor yet by an appeal to biology, if only because mental development, unlike physical growth, follows an unpredictable course. Psychological development must be described in psychological terms, in terms of the structural system, behind which psychology cannot go. We must translate into these terms, and so treat scientifically, what has so well been portrayed by poetry and the novel, autobiography and biography (*G.S.*, V, 220–5).

Finally, since all men share the same mental structure and the same external world, it follows that not merely the process of mental development, but also its results, must show common features in all men. This is in fact so. In the cognitive sphere there is only one space and time, one numerical series, one mode of causal explanation; in the sphere of feeling, the relations between feelings, the ways in which they are expressed, and the structure of the value-system are constant; in volitional experience the relation between means and end, the fundamental types of ends, and the forms of social co-operation are always the same. Psychology must study these uniformities, and Dilthey argues in detail that explanatory or 'constructive' methods are not satisfactory here. We must seek these constants in their most highly developed form, viz. in the cultural systems and the organisations of society, and subject them there to descriptive analysis (*G.S.*, V, 180–90, 225–6).

This study of uniformities demands as its complement a study of individuality. Here too we must not appeal to a metaphysical principle, as Schleiermacher does, but to what we know of the structural system of the mind. All qualitative differences between individuals depend ultimately upon quantitative differences. The structure of life and the fundamental instincts are the same in all men, but they differ in the intensity of the various functions, the readiness of their response to stimuli, the depth and permanence of impressions received, and the power to pass from impressions to reasoned judgment. These innate differences do not themselves constitute individual character: before that can arise they must be modified and stabilised by the immanent teleology of the structural system. The mental system in every man takes up the factors provided by his birth and surroundings and develops them, moderating some and encouraging others, so as to form a coherent structural whole. Permanent dispositions and consistent habits are built up, the spiritual life is organised in contrast with the life of animal instinct, and in devotion to high tasks and lofty ideals the individual is set free from the 'iron band' of natural causality; yet never wholly free, and never so free that corruption ceases to be possible.

The study of this formative process and the laws controlling it is the only key to knowledge of the individual. For knowledge can only work with universals; even the historian cannot depict the individual except by describing him in relation to various systems of facts or values, and it is the object of the historian, as of the poet, to select for portrayal the individual who is *representative* of a given race, period, or character. Throughout the human studies the individual is understood only in his relation to the universal. Therefore, Dilthey concludes, the human studies have nothing to gain from idealist metaphysics, which has 'set the universal and the individual side by side with no connection, or only an aesthetic mediation, between them'; the true security of the human studies lies in an empirical psychology which shall make known the laws in accordance with which the universal becomes individuated (*G.S.*, V, 226–37).

The appearance of Dilthey's *Ideen* was the signal for a chorus of criticism, and a debate began which lasted to the end of Dilthey's life and went on long afterwards. Objections were raised from two sides, by the psychologists and by the philosophers. Neither party could believe in the picture of descriptive pyschology as Dilthey painted it.

On the philosophical side the Kantians took the lead. Their criticisms of Dilthey may be found in numerous passages in the writings of Windelband and Rickert and their followers. They say that psychology cannot be the foundation for the human studies (historical and cultural studies, as the Baden school prefers to call them), because it is not even one of them, and differs from them alike in aims and in method. (1) The historical and cultural studies deal with ideal contents (meaning-complexes, values) and the *a priori* principles which are manifested in them, whereas psychology concerns itself solely with psychical facts and with the causal connections between them. (2) The historical and cultural studies are chiefly concerned with the study of individuals and general types, whereas psychology concerns itself chiefly, so the Kantians say, with general laws, as do the natural sciences. (3) Inner experience does not exhibit in itself a coherent system as Dilthey alleges, but only fragmentary data which have to be brought into an intelligible order, in the same way as the data of external perception, by the application of the categories; and the self whose life we thus construct for knowledge is a phenomenon, like the physical world, not a reality in the sense that Dilthey says it is. In short, Dilthey's attempt to set psychology in antithesis to the natural sciences is a failure. Psychology is itself a natural science, and quite different in all important respects from the historical and cultural studies with which he wrongly classes it. In particular, the method of 'understanding', which is the keystone of the argument of the *Ideen*, cannot produce the results in psychology which Dilthey hopes from it.

Much of this criticism depends on the peculiar doctrines of Kantianism, and will be considered at greater length in the following chapter, where the confrontation between Dilthey and the Kantians in questions relating to the human studies will be brought to a head. The last point, however, viz. that the method of 'understanding' cannot lead us to the discovery of a coherent order in lived experience with the certitude which Dilthey ascribes to it, brings the Kantians on to common ground with his critics from the psychological side.

The psychological attack was opened by Ebbinghaus with an article[1] in the *Zeitschrift für Psychologie* in October 1895. This article remains the classic statement of the case against Dilthey as seen from the psychologist's point of view. In brief, it says that Dilthey has overestimated both his own powers and the shortcomings of others. His criticisms of 'explanatory psychology' are ill-informed. Psychological methods and principles were never so dogmatic as he pretends. Psychologists have always been ready to alter their ideas to bring them into accord with growing experience, and experience has led them by now to abandon most of the views which Dilthey criticises (so far as they ever held them) and to adopt most of the views which Dilthey propounds (so far as these are true). Dilthey's polemic, in fact, is out of date, and he is hammering at an open door— except for one thing. He is wrong in saying that the structural system of mental life is directly experienced (*erlebt*). Introspection does indeed reveal unities of various kinds in consciousness, but it does not reveal the deep-seated unity of the whole. Dilthey's account of that unity is a hypothetical construction, put together out of fragmentary data. There is nothing wrong in

[1] 'Über erklärende u. beschreibende Psychologie', in *Zeitschrift für Psychologie*, Bd. IX, pp. 161–205.

making hypothetical constructions; Dilthey himself is wrong in thinking that there is, and wrong in thinking that he himself does not do it. But it means that the certitude which Dilthey demands of psychology for the sake of the human studies which are based on it is unattainable, even by his own psychology.

Dilthey's reply to Ebbinghaus may be read in *G.S.*, V, 237–40, and in various letters to von Wartenburg. The essential point of it is that Ebbinghaus has misunderstood him about the structural system. It is true that our perception of our own minds is fragmentary; but each fragment is itself an organised whole, with the principle of unity recognisable in it. The kind of unity which we attribute to the whole is the same which we find in every part. And this, says Dilthey, is really undeniable, for this is the source from which all our ideas of systematic connection are derived.

Is this a sufficient reply to the objection raised in common by psychologists and Kantians? Dilthey himself was satisfied with it for ten years or so, but in the end he began to change his ground. Without adopting the criticisms brought by others against the *Ideen*, he began to bring serious criticisms of his own. These appear in various writings of the period between 1907 and 1911, and they characterise the third and final period in the development of his views.

His *first* difficulty is that, although lived experience can give us the structural system, or formal unity in the process of mental life, it cannot reveal the actual movement of the process, just because our experience is itself involved in the process. 'Lived experience is a process in time, in which every state changes before it becomes a definite object, . . . and in which every moment, before it is grasped, becomes past.' And yet, in order to attend to anything, we must needs dwell upon it and hold it steadily before us for a time. Therefore, in order to attend to a mental event, we have to keep it before us even after it has ceased to be a present event; we fix it in memory, and thus in a manner bring the flow of time and change to a standstill. 'The presentness (*Präsenz*) of the past does duty for us instead of an immediate enjoyment (*Erleben*). When we wish to observe time, our observation distorts it, for it fixes it by virtue of attention; it brings the flow to a standstill, it makes the changing stable.' We can observe that our experience in the present is the same as in the immediate past, i.e. we can observe permanence; or that present experience is different from that of the immediate past, i.e. we can observe change. But in either case all we do is to notice that something has changed, or that something has endured, in the stream of time. 'The stream itself we do not enjoy.' 'However we may strengthen in ourselves the consciousness of the flow, every moment of life itself which is observed is the remembered moment, no longer a flow; for *it is fixed by attention, which holds fast what in itself is fleeting.* And so we cannot grasp the actual nature of this life. What the youth of Sais unveils[1] is form *(Gestalt)* and not life' *(G.S.,* VII, 194–5).

In the *second* place, the range of mental life which is open, even to such faulty observation as this, is limited. Some mental processes are as good as unobservable. Dilthey never pretended to know the nature of the processes which make possible our acts of conception, judgment, and inference. And now he gives judgment as an example of a process which even experimental methods fail to bring under clear observation. 'What do we know of the process of judgment, whether by observation, memory, or even experiment?' *(G.S.,* VII, 321). Furthermore, even where we can observe a process fairly well by introspection, there is always an immense amount of mental life, structurally connected with it, which introspection will not reveal, though a vital expression may. 'If we had only the testimonies of the poets about their creative activity, but all their works had been lost, how little the testimonies would tell us!' *(ibid.)*

Again, the very terms in which we set the problem for introspection and interpret its results 'belong to a linguistic usage conditioned by many factors', and inevitably beg questions. We find what we look for, or import into our experience the very factors whose presence we are trying to test. 'If I ask myself or others whether the aesthetic impression of a mountain range includes empathy, then empathy immediately appears' *(G.S.,* VI, 318). Even apart from this, the mere effort to observe mental facts has the effect of altering the facts which are to be observed. 'Deliberate attention to these processes alters and

[1] The reference is to the *Lehrlinge von Sais* of Novalis, especially to the couplet:

> Einem gelang es,—er hob den Schleier der Göttin von Sais—
> Aber was sah er?—er sah—Wunder des Wunders, sich selbst.

214

destroys the energy, or even the existence, of the processes themselves' (*G.S.*, VII, 319).

Finally, Dilthey begins to doubt whether even the structural system itself is discoverable by direct introspection; for it is impossible on grounds of mere observation to draw a rigid distinction between different classes of mental facts, e.g. between sensations and feelings. 'The boundaries between immediately experienced states are insecure. Are there feelings unrelated to a content? Is hatred a feeling, or does it also include an impulse? etc.' (*G.S.*, VI, 318).

Guided by these considerations, Dilthey revises his old appeal to lived experience as the basis of psychological knowledge, and even speaks with a new-found respect of Comte as 'the great critic of the introspective method'. True knowledge of mental life is not, after all, to be sought by a direct approach. We must take a roundabout route, and come at the lived experience by way of the vital expression. For every experience, as we saw long ago, tends to find an outlet in a physical expression, whether in look or gesture, or through the more subtle medium of language. Such expressions are free from the distortions which attend upon deliberate self-observation; for they 'take place without the formation of psychological concepts, and do not require it' (*G.S.*, VI, 317). On the other hand, they are a great aid to observation and memory in holding the experience before our attention, because they actually impart to the experience a degree of permanence. The expression 'stands external, independent and enduring over against the experience itself', and 'in the expression the fixity of the experience increases' (*G.S.*, VII, 329). Moreover, the expression brings to light a wide range of mental facts, structurally involved in a lived experience, of which the experience itself, unexpressed, gives no evidence, and which sheer introspection would certainly miss. 'What appears in lived experience without being noticed is, in the expression of the experience, as it were hauled up out of the depths of mental life. For the expression wells up out of the soul immediately, without reflection, and then, by virtue of its fixity, stands up to be understood; thus it contains (*enthält*) more of the experience actually lived than self-observation can find out' (*G.S.*, VII, 328–9).

These facts give Dilthey the basis for his new method. If vital expressions are a revealing utterance of the experiences lived through, and if there really are systematic structural relations between these experiences, then, however obscure these relations may be in introspection, they will appear more clearly in the expression. The psychological analysis of mental structure can therefore be based with confidence upon a study of the most explicit vital expressions, by which, of course, literature is meant.

From this time forward, therefore, Dilthey's fundamental classification of mental acts into cognitive, affective, and volitional, instead of being based on a direct appeal to experience, is read off from the forms of language. It is evident that one important function of language is to express the mental attitudes which we adopt towards objects of our experience. 'I perceive something, I judge about it, I have pleasure in it, I will something—in these and a hundred similar combinations of words we give utterance to lived experiences, without reflecting upon the inner relation which finds expression therein' (*G.S.*, VII, 326). Now, examination of these expressions will show that the attitudes expressed fall into three great classes, each of which may be represented by a special preposition. I have an intuition, or I form a conception, *of* (*von*) an object. I feel pleasure or pain *over* (*über*) it. I am intent, or I set my heart, *upon* (*auf*) it. All mental attitudes can be expressed in the last resort by one of these three prepositions, *von*, *über*, or *auf*,[1] and these three are

[1] Dilthey is not quite consistent. Thus, in the passage quoted immediately above, he writes, *ich urteile über es, ich habe Lust an ihm*, and elsewhere in one passage he gives as an expression of a volitional attitude the phrase 'longing after something' (*Verlangen nach etwas: G.S.*, VII, 322). It is clear that more than three propositions are used, even in German, to express mental attitudes, and the usages in other languages are of course different and yet equally various. But Dilthey could urge that, e.g. in the expression of volitional attitudes, *auf* and *nach* are really synonymous, since they express the same relation of the subject to the object; and thus, while not pretending that the prepositions expressing mental attitudes are in any one language just three in number, he could yet maintain that the relations expressed by them all reduce to three. That he really did mean the investigation to be carried thus below the surface is shown by a brief unexplained reference to 'Husserl's conception of pure grammar' (*loc. cit.*). An obvious difficulty is that some prepositions apply indifferently to more than one of his three mental attitudes, e.g. *über* to cognition or feeling, corresponding precisely to *over* in English (think *over* it, grieve *over* it), or again *upon* in English (think *upon* it, be set *upon* it). Alternative usages like these can only be distinguished by *understanding* them; i.e. the real appeal is still to experience, but to an experience steadied and clarified by the expression which reflects it.

not further reducible. This fact points clearly to the existence in mental life of three distinct and fundamental attitudes of consciousness, which find spontaneous expression in the three prepositions. Confirmation is found in the fact that words combined in the sentence-form may bear any one of three senses; they may be a statement, an exclamation, or a command. 'All three attitudes have their direct expression in speech. Thus the affective attitude finds expression in the exclamation, and the volitional attitude in the imperative' (*G.S.*, VII, 296). From these three fundamental attitudes we pass to their dynamic interactions, and here the grammatical analysis of language fails us; but the more complex linguistic expressions, e.g. poetry and autobiography, come in, and portray with fidelity the structural type of all mental processes. 'The poet's verses, the narratives of historians from the earliest accessible times, and therefore before all psychological reflection, depict, sing, and reveal lived experiences in their proper character. They let us see an objective content, then they pass to our attitude towards it, they unfold the relations and teach us to distinguish them. Springing as they do from a strong inner life (*Erleben*), they give it expression' (*G.S.*, VII, 326).

This new position has an interesting effect upon Dilthey's view of the structural system. It should be remembered that the approach to this system through its expressions is not introduced by him merely as an additional resource, his original views about the givenness of the system 'in lived experience' being left unchanged. On the contrary, it is introduced because he has come to think that lived experience alone cannot reveal the system adequately. What was previously to be perceived in experience *sans phrase* is now to be perceived in expressed experience, and our interpretative concepts are to be formed not directly from the experience itself, but under the guidance of the expression. But an experience which only speaks when made articulate by an expression can hardly be given the same credit, when it does speak, as an experience which tells its own tale uncommented. Dilthey must reconsider what manner of experience it is, and how deeply the reality of mental life is revealed in it.

His conception of lived experience as the undifferentiated unity, in which subject and object, appearance and reality, substance and attribute are not yet distinguished, an experience prior to all thought, and lit up by a certitude of its own reality which is peculiar to itself—this conception remains unchanged. In my account of it in Chapter Two I have drawn freely on MSS. of Dilthey's very latest years, and their doctrine differs from that of the *Ideen* only in being more circumstantial and detailed. Nor does Dilthey deny that this experience includes an awareness (indeed, our primary awareness) of causal or 'structural' connection. We experience mental events as producing (*erwirkend*) one another. But Dilthey's analysis of the mental process into acts, or attitudes, and contents is subtly changed. Hitherto he has spoken as if the three kinds of act or attitude were clearly distinct in character, and irreducible to one another or to anything more primitive, and he has defined the structural system in terms of the relations between these three types of attitude. After the change in his views about introspection, the perspective changes, and the unity of the mind is made more prominent than before. A concept is sought which shall express this unity without any trace of abstraction or division. Even the concept of the structural system is now found to be inadequate; for this concept is based on the separation of the three attitude-types, it combines only what has already been separated. Only the concept of meaning (*Bedeutung*) can express 'the unanalysed life-system'. Dilthey now sees the mind as a whole which is present as a totality in each of its manifestations; it is differentiated simply by the fact that this totality can enter into different relations (*Bezüge*) with different elements in its environment. 'Life a whole. Structure: the system of this whole, conditioned by its real relations to the external world. Attitude (*Verhaltungsweise*) merely such a relation' (*G.S.*, VII, 237–8).

The inevitable result is that Dilthey's description of mental life can no longer claim the precision and universal validity which he claimed for it in the *Ideen*. Since he no longer hopes to find ultimate simple components of mind, but merely a classification of the infinitely numerous ways in which the human being can set himself in relation to his world, there is no reason to suppose that there is one classification which is definitive and final. It may be that there are several, and that the choice may be left to the personal outlook, purpose, and 'psychological tact' of the investigator. If he is a student of social and historical phenomena, he will naturally prefer an analysis, if one is available, which corresponds with some far-reaching distinction that he has to draw between modes or aspects of human activity in that field; he will let his reading of history be reflected back into his psychology. Dilthey himself now does something of the kind. He seeks to confirm the evidence of language as to his structural trichotomy by treating it as a reflection of another distinction which plays a large part in his latest writings—the distinction between the backward-looking attitude of mind in which we apprehend the meaning of past facts, the forward-looking attitude in which we set ourselves a task for the future, and the attitude in which we sink ourselves in the appreciation of a present value. These three attitudes determine our outlook upon history in ways which are irreducible to one another; the forms under which they respectively view the life-process are represented by the three ultimate categories of life, viz. *meaning, end,* and *value*; and it is natural that so far-reaching a triplicity should have its roots in the structure of the mind itself.

This new position is well summed up in a passage which seems to have been intended for inclusion in the *Aufbau der geschichtlichen Welt in den Geisteswissenschaften,* and whose date is therefore probably 1909. In this passage he says that the distinctions he draws between types of mental attitude are not meant to tell us the inner nature or underlying causes of what they describe. It is not a question of parcelling out the mind into 'faculties', nor of explaining the wealth of mental activities in terms of a few simple elements or processes. He is not concerned to say whether such an explanation is or is not possible. What he says is· that, in the complex life of the mind as we actually find it, there are infinitely various attitudes taken up by the mind towards its surroundings. On the basis of lived experience and understanding we can roughly group these into a few main types, representing a few 'basic attitudes' (*Grundstellungen*). Philosophers have always made such groupings, but have never agreed about them in detail, and never will. Dilthey offers reasons from common experience in defence of his own distinction between the three types of attitude. Then he goes on: 'If it is a matter of providing a basis for the human studies—our present task—one ground here for separating between the types of objective apprehension, feeling, and volition, lies in the fact that the division into reality, values,[1] and ends runs through the whole domain of mind. Perhaps representation and expression here reveal a distinction in the experiences actually lived through, which however has not the same clarity in introspection' (*G.S.*, VII, 326–8). That 'perhaps' is a far cry from the confidence of the *Ideen*.

We may add another passage of similar date to the above, where Dilthey disclaims for his terminology scientific precision, but claims for it the status of adequate expression. 'Feeling or will are only concepts which are a hint to relive (*nachbilden*) the corresponding part of life' (*G.S.*, VII, 238).

A 'descriptive and analytical psychology' constructed under these conditions may claim to apply the method of understanding the part in terms of the whole, and it may quite conceivably develop into an account of human nature and even a typology of character and outlook, such as Dilthey desires. But it seems quite impossible that it should be identical with the experimental science of psychology. Dilthey finally recognises this, and abandons his hope of making one study cover all our knowledge of mental life. The mind, he says, has been studied and analysed from different angles and by different methods. One approach is represented by 'the science of psychology in the proper sense' (*die eigentliche Wissenschaft der Psychologie*) or 'the science of psychology as it has taken shape today'. A different approach leads to what may be called 'content-psychology' (*inhaltliche Psychologie*), or 'concrete psychology', or 'anthropology'. Its method, the 'anthropological method', is that which 'describes and analyses the succession and coexistence of concrete mental states'; it finds them to be conditioned partly by external circumstances, and partly from within by a 'forward-striving energy' whose operation, when more closely analysed, reveals in itself the structural system. This is the method which 'stands nearest to life itself', and between it and the 'science of psychology' in the proper sense there is 'the greatest opposition existing in this field'; it 'stands near to questions about the meaning of life and its value, because it stands so near to the concrete life itself'. By its analyses 'the lived experience is imaginatively elaborated according to its inherent meaning, and thus the relation of the mental process to the surrounding life is

[1] Read *Werten* for *Worten*: *G.S.*, VII, 327, line 2 fr. ft.

portrayed in its concrete reality'; and the method ends by enabling us to construct a typology. Dilthey remarks that this kind of psychology is, both in method and in subject-matter, closely allied to poetry (*G.S.*, VI, 305, VII, 239–40).

It is clear that 'the science of psychology in the proper sense', or 'the science of psychology as it has taken shape today', which stands at the opposite extreme to 'anthropology', has no claim to a fundamental place among the human studies. Dilthey never raises the question whether it is one of the human studies at all; and, since he says that *all* the approaches to the study of mind depend on the twin processes of lived experience and understanding, and since in his final theory dependence on these processes is made the distinguishing mark of the human studies, we are left to infer that experimental psychology is one of these studies. It receives, however, no further mention, and of course the 'descriptive and analytical psychology' of the *Ideen*, which is to support the edifice of the human studies as well as of philosophy, is now represented not by this 'psychology in the proper sense', but by 'anthropology'.

The only doubt remaining is whether anthropology, after the admissions which Dilthey has now made about it, can be trusted with the burden. So long as anthropology was held to draw its concepts direct from experience, while all the other human studies were held to depend on expressions whose interpretation may be uncertain, anthropology could properly figure as the basis of the other human studies and the guarantor of their concepts; but, if it appears that anthropology too obtains its concepts from expressions, it can claim no privileges over the other studies, but must stand side by side with them in a common dependence upon understanding. There is no one discipline among the human studies which can guarantee the fundamental concepts of the rest; they check and confirm one another in a relation of 'reciprocal dependence'. At the same time the epistemological *Grundlegung* of the human studies must shift its emphasis, laying less stress in future upon the descriptive analysis of lived experience, and much more upon hermeneutics.

Bernhard Groethuysen, who was in close touch with Dilthey from 1907 until the end, tells us how these considerations were present in Dilthey's mind during these last years (*G.S.*, VII, vi–viii). Nevertheless, in spite of the positive statements of at least one writer to the contrary (see A. Stein, *Der Begriff des Verstehens bei Dilthey*, p. 79), there is strong evidence that Dilthey never did finally renounce the belief in descriptive psychology as the basis both of the human studies and of the theory of knowledge. (1) In a footnote in the *Aufbau der geschichtlichen Welt in den Geisteswissenschaften* (1910), where Dilthey declares his adherence *im ganzen* to the doctrine of the *Einleitung*, the *Ideen*, and the first *Studie zur Grundlegung der Geisteswissenschaften* on this point, he specifies one passage in which the function of psychology as the basis for epistemology is set forth (*G.S.*, VII, 160 n., referring *inter alia* to *G.S.*, VII, 12). (2) In a MS. of roughly the same date, whose contents relate to the final revision of the *Kritik der historischen Vernunft*, and comprise a well-drawn-out architectonic for one section of the *Kritik*, is added a note: 'System in the human studies. As basis: "anthropology"' (*G.S.*, VII, 369, n. 39). (3) When Dilthey prepared to rewrite *Die Einbildungskraft des Dichters* (1907–8), he drew up a plan in which 'structure-psychology' formed the basis, and worked out this 'structure-psychology' in considerable detail for the purpose (*G.S.*, VI, 310–20). (4) In a fragment entitled *Das Problem der Religion* (1911), he says that the historical and comparative study of religion 'needs an answer to the question: how are higher psychological ground-concepts for the analysis of historical data possible?' The context shows that these 'higher psychological ground-concepts' are the 'concepts of the second order' of which Dilthey speaks in the *Einleitung* (above, p. 183), and which presuppose a psychology from which they are derived; the fragment, moreover, ends with remarks about 'anthropology' and the method of description and analysis (*G.S.*, VI, 302–5). This fragment is one of the very last things that Dilthey wrote.

It seems, then, that in the last period of Dilthey's life the two sides of his thought proved to be incapable of unification by the simple formula which he had so long striven to apply. The 'anthropology' or 'content-psychology' or 'structure-psychology', which represents the legacy of the romantics and the post-Kantians to him, remained central in his thinking to the end. But the attempt to identify this with the experimental science of psychology broke down. He decided that the kind of psychology which the human studies require, a psychology based on the understanding of the structural system of mental life, cannot be incorporated in, or developed out of, psychology as commonly conceived and practised; and he dissociated his structure-psychology so far from science. and brought it so close to literature, that he was forced to reconsider its position in the scheme of the human studies, though he never formally adopted a new position on that point. All this represents a final victory for Schleiermacher and Novalis over Wundt and Mill. It means that Hume's programme can be carried out only if the study of human nature, of which he speaks so highly in his Preface, is carefully distinguished from experimental psychology, not identified with it as he proposes.

Dilthey had insisted from the beginning that one function of 'anthropology' was to deal systematically with the same body of experience with which poets and religious writers have dealt unsystematically. The *Realpsycholog* is to have the human interest and the penetrating insight of the artist, together with a power of precise definition and a sense of method and system, which are to be his own. In Dilthey's latest writings, the precision of the structure-psychologist's descriptions and definitions is less emphasised. It is no longer claimed that his results can command universal acceptance; it is enough if they are suggestive and illuminating. At the same time his dependence on the understanding of expressions is brought into the open. In short, he is increasingly assimilated to the artist.

'No man was ever yet a great poet, without being at the same time a profound philosopher', wrote Coleridge; and the context shows that what he means here by 'philosophy' is insight into human nature. We might fairly express Dilthey's view by reversing Coleridge's sentence, and saying 'no man was ever yet a profound student of philosophy or the human studies, without being at the same time something of a poet'. Dilthey does in fact speak in one passage of 'the poet in me'. It was the poet, the student of literature and music, as well as the historian in Dilthey, who found voice in his philosophy of the human studies. We have seen in Chapter Four how he believes that psychology has much to tell us about the poet's mind; but we need not be surprised if, on looking more closely at his psychology, we find it to be very much a poet's psychology.

This discovery ends the argument of the present chapter, and points us forward to the next. One of Dilthey's most constantly repeated contentions about the human studies is his contention that 'psychology' must stand at their basis. He spoiled his case by trying to make the 'psychology' in this proposition mean experimental psychology. By so doing he earned the suspicion, or worse, of philosophers who should have been his allies; and in the end he had to see that the equation could not be sustained, and that the 'psychology' really referred to in his proposition was something more nearly akin to art than to experimental science. But this opens up a new set of questions. Dilthey had many other things to say about the human studies besides this contention about 'psychology', and so had his rivals and critics, the Kantians of the Baden school. His long-lasting controversy with them centred on a quite different set of issues. In the next chapter we shall examine these issues and this controversy; and in so doing we shall have occasion to note, in passing, from a fresh point of view, the contribution which poetry and the other arts can make to the understanding of human life.

CHAPTER EIGHT

O N the question of psychology Dilthey spent much labour for a largely negative result. There is another controversial issue in dealing with which he was more fortunate. This is the issue of the distinctive character of the human studies and the delimitation of the frontier between them and the natural sciences. On this question he became involved in a controversy with Windelband and Rickert which has gone on long after his death, but in which he certainly gave as good as he got.

The first blow was struck by Windelband, who in 1894 delivered at Strassburg a Rectorial address entitled *Geschichte u. Naturwissenschaft*. In this address, while recognising and even stressing the importance of Dilthey's problem, he contested on fundamental points the solution adumbrated in the *Einleitung*.

The general lines of Windelband's philosophy have been described in Chapter Three. The business of philosophy, he thinks, is to find the meaning (*Bedeutung, Sinn*) of human life, and he finds it in the universally valid value-norms of pure reason. These norms or values find embodiment in actual life through the activities of men in science, morality, and art. The process of their actualisation is history, and it is studied in a group of enquiries which may be called the historical sciences (*Geschichtswissenschaften*). For various reasons the study of the logical presuppositions of knowledge, which Kant inaugurated by his analysis of the presuppositions of natural science, has never been extended to include those of the historical sciences, but, according to Windelband, it is now time that this step should be taken.

So far he agrees with Dilthey; but the thesis of *Geschichte u. Naturwissenschaft* is that the fundamental distinction in terms of which the problem is usually seen, viz. that between *Natur-wissenschaften* and *Geisteswissenschaften*, is wrongly drawn. The basis of this distinction is material, i.e. the two groups of studies are defined in terms of the subject-matter dealt with; the *Naturwissenschaften* study the world of matter, revealed in outer perception, while the *Geisteswissenschaften* study the world of mind, which is known to us by inner perception and through psychology. Now *first* of all, as a dutiful Kantian, Windelband doubts the existence or at any rate the objectivity of inner perception; but he does not stay to argue this point. *Next*, he urges that the historical studies do not deal exclusively with mental facts, but also and to a large extent with the physical conditions under which human action takes place, and the physical medium in which it is carried out; thus, a battle is certainly material for history, but it is also a very complicated physical and chemical process. Now, if the historical studies share their subject-matter in part with the natural sciences, the distinction between them cannot be based on a difference of subject-matter. *Thirdly*, the position of psychology under the usual arrangement is unnatural; for although it is called a *Geisteswissenschaft* because its subject-matter is mind, yet its method is that of the natural sciences, and alien to the historical studies.

Accordingly, Windelband proposes a new division which is formal, i.e. based on differences of method. There are two ways, he says, in which the mind can deal with any subject-matter, viz. by generalising and laying down laws, or by describing individual facts; the first Windelband calls the *nomothetic* method, and the second he calls *idiographic*, and he defines natural science as enquiry on nomothetic lines, historical science as enquiry on idiographic lines. The resulting line of division cuts across any line that could possibly be drawn according to subject-matter, because, as Windelband says, the same object can be regarded from either of the two methodological standpoints. Thus, a language is studied nomothetically when we examine its principles and lay down laws which govern its behaviour and development; but it is studied idiographically when we compare and contrast it with other languages, and take it as one of the various individual forms in which the linguistic capacity of mankind has fulfilled itself. Similarly facts in astronomy, or physiology, or geology can be studied from either point of view. Windelband is not at all perturbed by this. He simply redefines nature and history so as to make the distinction between them accord with

226

that between the natural and the historical sciences. 'Nature' is defined as whatever can be studied nomothetically, and 'history' as whatever can be studied idiographically; and so we find that nature and history are coextensive, and that every fact is in one aspect material for natural science, and in another aspect material for history. But the historical studies as defined by this criterion are less extensive than the old *Geisteswissenschaften*, for it turns out that the method of psychology is altogether nomothetic, and so, by the new test, psychology is altogether a natural science.

The aim of history, then, is not to explain, but to portray, and here it is allied with art and literature in opposition to natural science. (1) The natural scientist has no interest in individual things. The units of his world, the atoms, are mere shadows of individuals; they have to be there in order to be the terms of the relations which he formulates, but they are the most abstract kind of units that can be conceived, homogeneous and without individual character, 'colourless and soundless, without any smack of the sensible qualities'. Movement and development as such do not interest the scientist either, but only the laws which he can abstract from them. 'Science seeks not the changeful as such, but the changeless form of change.' History, on the other hand, lays all its emphasis on the individual, the unique. (2) But this difference is reinforced by another. Science seeks the unchanging law because its real interest is in necessary existence, and law is the form of necessity; whereas history is interested in things from the standpoint of their value, and all value resides in individuality. What is it that is so eerie about the idea of the *Doppelgänger*? It is the chill of finding that I am not unique; for, in losing that uniqueness, I seem also to be robbed of moral worth and of my very personality. Hence too the insidious cynicism of Mephistopheles' simple remark: *sie ist die erste nicht*. The Christian philosophy of history has well embodied this truth, by making the two factors on which the whole meaning of human life depends, viz. the Fall and the Redemption, into events which have occurred once and cannot recur. (3) It is true, Windelband admits in conclusion, that history cannot in practice reduce itself to a gallery of disconnected portraits; connections have to be traced, causes assigned, the working of laws made visible. But even here, for such general

227

knowledge as history requires, there is no need to appeal to psychology. History got on very well in all the centuries before psychology began, and will make its way hereafter as before, 'by the natural knowledge of man, by tact and the intuition of genius' (*op. cit.*).

Though Dilthey is not named in Windelband's lecture, it is essentially his position which is there attacked. His reply followed at once, in 1895, in an essay which was at first entitled *Über vergleichende Psychologie*. The essay begins by reasserting Dilthey's position against Windelband, and goes on to discuss in detail the characteristic aims and methods of the human studies. The original title, *Über vergleichende Psychologie*, is misleading. It is meant to link the essay with the *Ideen*, which had appeared in the preceding year, and which ended with a call for a comparative psychology, or study of psychological types; but in fact the essay deals with the comparative method and typology as they appear over the whole field of the human studies, besides including a section on the value of the arts as a vehicle of understanding. Dilthey later changed the title to *Beiträge zum Studium der Individualität*, but what he published under that title was not the whole of the essay. In the *Gesammelte Schriften* the complete text is printed with both titles.

Dilthey makes clear at the outset that what interests him is not history in particular, but the human studies, including psychology; and that psychology deals with its subject-matter both nomothetically and idiographically (*G.S.*, V, 241–2). Then he launches out at once into his counter-attack on Windelband.

First of all he repeats that we *do* obtain a real knowledge of the self from inner experience. He describes at length how the consciousness of self and not-self arises, and how the life of the self comes to be explored by poets, autobiographers, and philosophers (*G.S.*, V, 242–8). Having thus shown that we have a workable knowledge of our own minds, he appeals to a simple inspection of the human studies to show that the study of mind is the distinguishing characteristic of this group of disciplines. Wherever there is cognitive activity, wherever values are appreciated or ends pursued, wherever in the midst of the process of nature a free agent appears, there is matter for the *Geisteswissenschaften*; and they not only study the processes and products of mental life, but subserve it too in all its branches, by laying

228

down precepts as well as describing and explaining facts. It is true, of course, as Windelband says, that they also deal with many physical facts; but they deal with them only in so far as they are related to an inner life, having value for a subject or conditioning the execution of his purposes (*G.S.*, V, 250–3).

The formal or methodological differentia of the human studies is correlative with this. It lies partly in the cultivation of inner experience and the art of reflection on it, and partly in the understanding of other minds. These other minds belong to the same external world with which the natural sciences also are concerned. They are known to us through their expressions, which are objects of sense-perception. But the fact is that some objects of sense can be made intelligible in terms of physical laws alone, i.e. laws which correlate sense-data with other sense-data, while others, viz. organisms, have characteristics which we can only make intelligible by a 'transference' into them of an inner life and a structural system more or less like our own. Where the inner life imputed to the object is altogether like our own, we enter the sphere of history and the human studies. Thus the natural sciences and the human studies both deal with aspects of the external world, but they deal with different aspects of it. The human studies deal with that in the external world which demands to be understood in terms of an inner life (*G.S.*, V, 248–51, 253–5).

This distinction between *Naturwissenschaften* and *Geisteswissenschaften* cannot be correlated with that between nomothetic and idiographic methods, because both methods are used in both groups of studies. There is an idiographic element in geography and astronomy, natural history, and comparative psychology, as well as a search for laws; on the other hand, economics, aesthetics, philology, and the other *Geisteswissenschaften* have all a nomothetic aspect. Even historiography, in the hands of a Polybius or a Machiavelli, is in a degree nomothetic,[1] since it

[1] Windelband admitted, years afterwards, that it would be wrong to say that the natural sciences are exclusively nomothetic or the historical studies exclusively idiographic. Each group has elements of both methods. But in natural science the discovery of timelessly valid laws is the final aim, and all description of particulars is a mere stage on the road to it; while for the historical studies the significance of a thing lies in its uniqueness, and general ideas, or the laws revealed by comparative study, are used only as an aid to analysis and description (*The Principles of Logic*, in the *Encyclopædia*

reveals in its facts the working of general laws (*G.S.*, V, 255–8). Therefore, again, there would be no reason to rank psychology as a natural science, even if it were wholly nomothetic, as Windelband alleges; but in fact it is not, for there is a comparative psychology, whose object of study is human individuality and the relative values of different human types (*G.S.*, V, 255–6).

Dilthey goes on to describe the methodological differences between the natural sciences and the human studies as they really are. The two groups of studies have many points of agreement as well as of difference. (*a*) Both depend on experience illuminated by the operations of 'silent thought', and these operations are the same in all spheres of experience. (*b*) The logical processes of judgment and inference are always the same. So are the 'formal categories', though, as we have seen in earlier chapters, the 'real categories' are different in the two spheres. (*c*) Experimental and comparative methods are used in both, though the scope for experiment in the human studies is narrower, and that for the comparative method correspondingly wider. (*d*) Peculiar to the human studies, and common to them all, is the technique of hermeneutics and source-criticism. (*e*) But the greatest difference of all is due to the fact that we do not know the inner nature of physical things and processes, and have to read causal order into them by hypothesis, whereas in the world of mind we know directly what we are dealing with. (*f*) The natural sciences and the human studies also have different ways of systematising their data. Natural science systematises by moving towards the abstract; it seeks the kind of relation which can be put into equational form. The human studies systematise by seeing the particular fact more and more fully in its context among other facts structurally related to it. We do analyse and abstract, of course, when we distinguish the cultural systems and the social organisations as recurrent features

---

of the Philosophical Sciences, Engl. v, vol. i, p. 48). Dilthey would reply that, in natural science, the idiographic and the nomothetic interest are coordinate and inseparable. 'The natural task of the scientist is not the apprehension of laws, but rather (1) he must express a fact of a certain limited character, e.g. the path of Mars, (2) this task leads him on to fulfil it through analysis, by grasping the regularity of the homogeneous, (3) finally he must obtain a synthesis' (*G.S.*, VII, 275). The human studies share this point of view, but have also a peculiar interest in the individual for his own sake, on account of his intrinsic value, as will appear shortly.

of the historical and social world. But then we try to account for these by showing how they arise from the structural system of the mind, in response to various sets of circumstances (*G.S.*, V, 259–66, and cf. 273).

A further peculiarity of the human studies is that we take an interest in the individual for his own sake, just as he is, apart from all thought of his relation to laws and determining conditions, and without any attempt to explain him at all. There is in the human studies an element of pure description and appreciation, a 'loving understanding (*Verständnis*) of the personal, a reliving of the inexhaustible totalities', which is seen at its simplest in biography (*G.S.*, V, 266–7). It is only the *human* individual who has this inherent value, because he alone has a structural system which we can relive. 'If I notice how heated, liquid lead, dropping into cold water, takes on various marvellous forms, I can have in these forms as such only a passing interest: the scientist's attention fastens exclusively upon the laws determining these forms. And if, for the Arab, in a living relation, his horse achieves an independent value as an individuality, or for the hunter his hound, yet from the standpoint of natural science every individual animal is interesting only in respect of its relation to the species' (*G.S.*, V, 272).

Because the value of the individual thus depends on his possession of an inner life and a structural system like our own, the understanding of what he is carries with it an appreciation of his worth. 'That which is shows itself to be inseparable from what it is worth and what it ought to be. So to the facts of life its norms are attached' (*G.S.*, V, 267). The essential characteristics, in fact, which constitute the type, are also its norm of value; and in the concept of the *normal* the human studies possess a concept whose use is both descriptive and evaluative. From this relation between fact and value in the normal we can conclude to a further characteristic of the human studies. 'The truths must not be separated from the ideal concepts and the norms. For this division into two classes of statements, the one containing what is and the other saying what ought to be, robs knowledge of its fruitfulness, and the ideals and norms of their coherence and their firm basis. Therefore we have to discover the regular process whereby, from the essential features of the great activities of human life, their norms emerge.' This holds good over the whole field of the human studies. 'Even history will always combine description, causal knowledge, and judgment: only not exclusively moral judgment, but that which proceeds from the value-determinations and norms of all the activities of human life. . . . Judgment upon what has happened is, in and for itself, inseparable from the description of it' (*G.S.*, V, 267–8).

From this peculiar relation between the general type and the individual form, coinciding with the relation between the general norm and its individual embodiment, arise many of the keenest controversies in the human studies. 'Throughout these studies men quarrel over the extent to which homogeneity, uniformity, laws determine the particular, and at what points the positive, the historical, the singular appears. In particular political economy, jurisprudence, and political theory are filled with passionate strife on this point.' The solution of the problem lies in systematic study of the individual, to be pursued according to the comparative method, reinforced by analogy and generalisation. This method is already in use in the human studies. 'It took shape in philology, was then transferred to mythology, and it follows from what has been said that every systematic human study, in the course of its development, must arrive at comparative methods' (*G.S.*, V, 268–9).

Dilthey proceeds to lay down three principles which govern all understanding of the individual. (1) There are uniformities of *type*. Certain combinations of parts or functions constantly recur. They are so related that from the presence of one element in such a combination we can infer the presence of all the rest. In the higher organic world and in the world of mind the type becomes rich and complex, and the inferences drawn from it can be far-reaching, as e.g. when Cuvier restores an extinct species from fossil fragments, or Wolf and Niebuhr 'restore' ancient historical processes from a fragmentary and tendentious tradition. (2) In the organic and historical worlds, the various forms of life can be graded according to the complexity of their parts and functions; and since complexity of structure goes hand in hand with inherent value (*Lebenswert*), the scale of increasingly complex articulation is also a scale of increasingly 'high' or valuable *development*. (3) All differences of type or of development correspond to and depend upon differences of *environment*;

physical environment for organisms, physical and social or historical environment for human beings and institutions. All biography and all historiography have to take account of this (*G.S.*, V, 269–71).

Turning now to consider the ways in which an understanding of individuals is reached, we find at once a notable peculiarity of the human studies. Natural science forms its concepts directly by abstraction from 'the sensuous appearance of vulgar experience'; but the passage from our common experience of mind to the concepts of the human studies is mediated by a third factor, the expression of mind in the arts. The artist's work is a help towards knowledge in two ways. First, by virtue of the breadth of insight and the power of creative imagination which the artist possesses, he widens our horizon, and carries us with him into a world apart from, and richer and fuller than, our everyday experience. He sets us free from our limitations. But he does more than this. He sharpens our eye for types. We saw in Chapter Four, and again a few paragraphs back, how in our knowledge of human beings and their activities we cannot apprehend fact and process without also discerning the type and the norm. The eye for types (*das typische Sehen*) is present in some degree in all of us; as Dilthey says, 'we may pronounce that the apprehension of human life by a developed consciousness always was and could not but be typical'. But the artist strengthens this capacity in us. Himself highly gifted with the power of seeing the type in the individual, he gives expression to it in images so clear that they are to ordinary man an actual invitation to vision (*Anleitung zu sehen*), and familiarity with his work heightens this power in us (*G.S.*, V, 276–80).

Without this influence, even our common experience of life would be poorer than it is. 'None of us would possess more than a meagre part of our present understanding of human conditions, if we had not become used to seeing through the poet's eyes, and beholding Hamlets and Gretchens, Richards and Cordelias, Marquis Posas and Philips in the men around us.' Art thus reacts upon that very experience which is its only source and material. But it also affects the human studies, because the formation of concepts in them depends on the power of imaginative reconstruction and the eye for types, and the convincing exposition of these concepts also requires literary

233

skill. Dilthey finds this especially true of history. 'Peaks of historiographical achievement are always in fact conditioned by similar peaks in poetry. Great historians not seldom began with poetic attempts, and outstanding poets have often given the historical art a powerful impetus.' On the other hand, it is no less true that the artist, especially the poet, is intimately affected by the ideas and the prevailing controversies of his time.

Art and the human studies, in fact, are reciprocally dependent, and both together constitute a world of cultural achievement into which we are born, and by which all our own experience of life is unconsciously governed. 'Painters taught us to read in the countenances of men and to interpret attitude and demeanour. Poets are our organs for the understanding of men, and they influence the way in which we lead our lives in love, in marriage, and with friends. Historians give us an understanding of the historical world, in which everyone by his activities must intervene with some degree of understanding.' But art is earlier in time than the human studies, and 'the whole individuation of the world of man and history comes first of all to be understood in poetry, long before science seeks to know it'. And when science does begin, it can never transform into knowledge the whole of what poetic understanding reveals. Therefore, though art has the function of preparing the way for the human studies, it has also an independent and intrinsic value. The human studies give us knowledge about life, but art is our organ for the understanding of it; and we understand more than we know (*G.S.*, V, 273–6, 280).

Dilthey then shows how the history of poetry reveals a gradual advance in the understanding and portrayal of individuality. The first stage is represented by Homer, who already makes it his business to understand life in terms of itself rather than in theological terms. He sees how men's actions and destinies are determined in the last resort not by the gods, but by their own passions and characters; and he portrays various outstanding *types*. Homer's characters, however, are all of one piece, and do not grow The next stage comes with Shakespeare, who understands the impulse of the human mind towards the full *development* of its powers, and sees how this can sometimes lead to inner conflict and disruption. His types are active and dynamic. The third stage is represented by Schiller, who grasps the influence

234

upon this inner development of the *outer circumstances* in which the hero stands, and sees him as fundamentally a historical phenomenon. His *Wallenstein* interprets its hero with an insight so profound that history can only accept and confirm it. The same outlook is now universally prevalent in poetry and the novel (*G.S.*, V, 283–302).

Dilthey seems to have chosen these three stages to correspond with his three principles for the understanding of individuality, viz. type, development, and environment. But his third stage has this further characteristic, that it shows poetry now making a direct contribution to history, and so forms an easy transition to a discussion of the study of individuality as it is conducted in the human studies. He points out, in fact, that Schiller's contemporary, Goethe, who shared his understanding of individuality from the poetic side, was also deeply involved in those biological, anthropological, and historical enquiries which ultimately led to the triumph of the comparative method in the human studies (*G.S.*, V, 302–3).

By the 'comparative method', says Dilthey, is meant that mode of enquiry which tries, not to find regularities and homogeneities in its material, or to formulate laws, but to observe individual variations, to distinguish classes and types, and to find the causes of differentiation. This method is applied in geography, botany, biology, and all the studies concerned with man. The Greek mind, with its aesthetic attitude to the world and its keen sense of form, was peculiarly adapted to make progress here, and the best services rendered by Greek science come mostly under this head. An outstanding instance of it can be seen in the biological work of Aristotle, and the same procedure, transferred to the study of mind, gave rise also to his brilliant comparative psychology and to his comparative study of political institutions (*G.S.*, V, 303–7).

Modern science, on the other hand, set itself from the first to discover universal laws, and so built up a great system of knowledge in mechanics and astronomy, physics, and chemistry. The transference of this method to the human studies led to a search for homogeneous elements, universal laws, and absolute norms or 'natural principles' in every sphere of human life, in abstraction from and to the neglect of the individual character of men and peoples, and the circumstances by which their activity is informed. Thus arose what Dilthey calls the 'natural system of the human studies'. This 'natural system' may be seen at its best, fortified by kindred doctrines derived from the ancient Stoics, and lit up by a deep understanding of the poetic and symbolic cast of the primitive mind, in Vico's *Scienza Nuova* (*G.S.*, V, 307–8).

Interest in individuality began to return in the eighteenth century, first of all in botany, biology, and physiology. Dilthey traces the development of these sciences from Linnaeus, who set them on the right road by discovering a truly scientific principle of classification, through the work of Buffon and Cuvier, to Darwin. He ends by saying that the comparative method in the human studies has hitherto consisted very largely of a transference to them of concepts originally worked out in biology; and thus the human studies, since the eighteenth century, have passed through the same stages of development as the sciences of organic nature. But ideas so transferred may have disadvantageous as well as useful consequences; and, in any case, they need to be amplified by ideas and methods adapted to the specific nature of mental life and developed in the actual study of it (*G.S.*, V, 309–16).

At this point, when Dilthey should obviously proceed to specify these new ideas and methods, the essay provokingly breaks off short; but the theme is taken up five years later in *Die Entstehung der Hermeneutik* (1900). Dilthey points out first of all that the character of the individual can be apprehended only by comparison and contrast with others; and this, again, implies acquaintance with a number of people, which can only be obtained through the understanding of the expressions in which they reveal themselves. Such understanding attains the highest degree of objectivity where its data are literary monuments, and the art of interpreting literary sources, which is embodied in the science of philology, has grown up through a long history, no less gradually and painfully than the art of interrogating nature by experiment. Out of the genius of great interpreters came rules of procedure; the conflict of such rules gave rise to a hermeneutic science, which is 'the technology of the exposition of written records'; and this in turn has led back to an analysis of the process of understanding in general, which has finally merged with the theory of knowledge as a whole (*G.S.*, V, 317–20).

Dilthey shows how the process began in Greece with the development of rhetoric, which laid down the fundamental rules of literary composition. The first systematic treatment of the subject was given by Aristotle, who in the *Rhetorica ad Alexandrum* analyses a literary whole very thoroughly into its parts, and in the *Poetics* deduces the outer form of the work from its inner form, and this in turn from the essence and final aim of poetry as such. Then came the Alexandrian scholars, partly influenced by Aristotle, and by them all the essential methods of textual criticism, higher criticism, and source-criticism were discovered and practised. The Pergamene school, after the Stoic Crates, introduced the practice of allegorical interpretation as a means of making crude or antiquated religious ideas and writings palatable to a later generation. The conflict between the Alexandrian and Pergamene schools on this point was continued among the Christian scholars, to whom some use of allegory was necessary as a weapon against the Jews, while too much of it was dangerous as leading to Gnosticism; so we find Justin, Irenaeus, Tertullian, and the Alexandrian Fathers appealing to allegory and laying down rules for its use, while the Antiochene school clung to the rigour of grammatical and historical interpretation (*G.S.*, V, 321–3).

The rebirth of classical scholarship at the Renaissance confronted students with the unprecedented task of reconstructing a vanished civilisation with the sole aid of a few ruins and the written sources, and the result was the appearance of a number of essays *de interpretatione*. But still the most important developments were in the religious-field. Protestantism, which made Scripture its one court of appeal in religious matters, necessarily held that Scripture is intrinsically intelligible; and this position had to be defended against the traditionalism of the Catholic Church, dogmatically formulated in the Council of Trent, as well as against the prophetic illuminism of the Anabaptists. This work was done by Flacius, the chief of the Magdeburg Centuriators (1567), who laid down the principle that every passage must and can be adequately interpreted by its context, with reference to the style, sense, and general intention of the whole work in which it occurs. The next step was to determine the intention of the work by reference to the historical circumstances in which it was written; the interpretation of the New

Testament on these lines, in the light of the internal history of the primitive Church, was begun by the English Deists and made known to German theologians by Baumgarten. Through the *Institutio Interpretis* of Ernesti, it influenced Schleiermacher (*G.S.*, V, 323–6).

But Schleiermacher was the maker of a revolution in hermeneutics. He began by showing that the interpretation of literary sources is only one instance of a phenomenon which is as widespread as life itself, viz. the phenomenon of understanding. The first task, then, must be to analyse the process of understanding. Then, drawing upon the teachings of the transcendental philosophy, he urged that understanding is itself inexplicable except in the light of the originative or creative process of which it is, indeed, a reproduction (*Nachbildung*). This is not a deliberate process, in which an idea is first conceived, then worked into a logical form, then clothed in language and imagery according to the established rules of composition. It is an unconscious creative activity, in which our receptivity to stimulus and suggestion is inseparable from our spontaneous transmutation of the suggestion received into an original form. The whole outlook and personality of the author is reflected in every part of his work; and the business of interpretation, after settling the grammatical sense of the text, is to go back through that to the outer form of the work, then to the inner form or animating idea of it, then to the mind of the author, and finally to the whole literary and historical process, in which the production of this particular work is but one incident. The hermeneutic of Schleiermacher, worked out in detail on these lines, was made known to the general public by Böckh, and has never yet been surpassed (*G.S.*, V, 326–31).

The essay on individuality and that on hermeneutics together contain Dilthey's account of the methodology of the human studies as he worked it out in pursuance of his own plan, and incidentally also in answer to Windelband. But meanwhile the view originally put forward by Windelband had been taken up and developed far more ably and systematically by Rickert. In his large book, *Die Grenzen der naturwissenschaftlichen Begriffsbildung* (1896–1902), and in smaller essays such as *Kulturwissenschaft u. Naturwissenschaft* (1898) and *Die Probleme der Geschichtsphilosophie: eine Einführung* (1904), Rickert made known the chief points of a striking philosophy, constructed on Kantian lines, which he continued to enrich and develop in subsequent years, both in Dilthey's lifetime and after his death.

The years 1896–1904, during which Rickert's theory was given to the world, were for Dilthey a period of philosophical incubation. He had published the *Ideen* in 1894 and written the essay on individuality in 1895, and in the winter of 1895–6 he made an attempt to fulfil his long-standing plan for the completion of the *Einleitung in die Geisteswissenschaften*. The attempt did not succeed, and a number of factors, coming together about this time, seem to have led to a break in the sequence of his thought. There was Windelband's lecture in 1894, and Ebbinghaus' strong attack on the *Ideen* in 1895. The latter reduced Dilthey to a state of excitement and anger which can be clearly seen in his correspondence with the Graf von Wartenburg. Rickert's *Grenzen* first appeared in 1896, and in 1897 von Wartenburg died. This was a heavy loss to Dilthey, who at the same time began to feel in himself the effects of advancing age. These factors probably explain why, between 1895 and 1905, no original contribution to philosophy came from him. The essay on hermeneutics (1900) is no real exception; it is little more than a historical retrospect, a survey of the past growth of the hermeneutic discipline, not an independent contribution to it by Dilthey himself.

Yet he was not inactive. He had merely transferred his activity to other fields. To this period belongs the conception of a great work, to be called *Studien zur Geschichte des deutschen Geistes*, which was to contain a history of the German mind and spirit from the earliest times. This work was never completed, but large masses of material intended for inclusion in it may now be found in *G.S.* II, III, and IV, as well as in *Von deutscher Dichtung u. Musik*. At the same time Dilthey undertook a course of research among Hegel's early MSS., which led to the publication of his *Jugendgeschichte Hegels* in 1904. This is an important work in itself, revealing Hegel in what will be to many an unexpected light, and it was important in Dilthey's own development; for it revealed to him a new philosophical star of the first magnitude, whose influence upon him henceforward rivalled that of Schleiermacher, and gave him ideas which were useful against Rickert. And in 1906 he collected, revised, and published

239

a group of forty-year-old essays on the German romantic poets under the title *Das Erlebnis u. die Dichtung*.

In all this work Dilthey was renewing his strength by a return to the original sources of his inspiration, in history, in poetry, and in the post-Kantian philosophy. At last, in 1905, he gathered together the threads of his ideas and embarked upon a final effort to write his *Kritik der historischen Vernunft*. From then until his death he was continually at work, and much that is of great value belongs to this period. To it belongs the change in his attitude to psychology, which was described in the preceding chapter. To it belongs also a bold restatement of his position with regard to the human studies generally, through which there runs a vigorous polemic against Rickert. Though Rickert's name is hardly mentioned in Dilthey's latest writings, his doctrines are everywhere chosen for attack; and we may say that Dilthey's philosophical career ended, as it had begun, with a polemic against transcendental idealism.

The essential points of Rickert's philosophy have been summarised above, in Chapters Three and Five. I need not go over that ground again, but will proceed to show how, within that framework, Rickert analyses in detail the methods, categories, and presuppositions of the historical and cultural studies.

Windelband in his Rectorial address distinguished the historical studies from the natural sciences by two criteria. One was the methodological criterion: natural science is nomothetic, and historical study is idiographic. The other was the criterion of subject-matter: natural science studies facts without reference to value, and historical study deals with what has value and meaning. Rickert uses the same two criteria, and works out the details of their application far more fully than Windelband; but in his handling of them he gives greater weight to the criterion of value and meaning.

Not every fact, he says, is material for historical study, but only such facts as are important (*wichtig*) or interesting (*interessant*) or significant (*bedeutsam*); and importance, interest, significance attaches only to those facts which embody, or somehow causally affect the embodiment of, cultural values.[1] The his-

[1] Eduard Meyer (*Zur Theorie u. Methodik der Geschichte*, 1902) contends that the historian's criterion of the importance of events is not their value, but their influence (*Wirksamkeit*), the extensiveness of their effects. But an

torical enquirer is thus always concerned, in the long run, with the study of events from the standpoint of value; and this truth, interpreted in the sense that the historian passes judgment on the value of the events which he records, has sometimes led to serious errors in respect of the claim of scientific objectivity which history makes. All value-judgment, it is sometimes said, represents a personal view, a subjective interpretation; and the historian is either told that he must not hope to claim the prestige of an objective investigator, or else is exhorted (e.g. by Lamprecht) to acquire this prestige by a radical alteration of his method, abandoning his axiological criteria and concepts, and adopting the methods and ideas of natural science instead.

According to Rickert, this is a misrepresentation of the interest which the historical student takes in values. He may indeed make and express a personal judgment upon the value of events; no one can prevent him from doing so. But, if he does, he is going beyond what is essential to his historical work, and taking a responsibility which he need not take. For there is a way of *referring* an event *to a value* (*Wertbeziehung*) which is not, and does not involve, an actual *valuation* (*Wertung*) of it. It is a fact that, at all times, value-standards have been recognised by human beings, and events judged good or bad by them according to these standards. The standards may have been right or wrong, and it is not primarily the historian's business to decide that point; but he takes up the standards which have been recognised, and selects for study those events which are important according to these standards. Thus the actions and sufferings of historical agents are judged important by the criteria which the historical agents have themselves entertained; the selection is not made from without by the historian's private judgment, but history itself furnishes an immanent criterion by which it is made.

Of course, there is a multiplicity of such criteria, springing from the multiplicity of human interests. The refusal of the German Imperial crown by Frederick William IV of Prussia is

---

event can only become important by virtue of its effects if they themselves are intrinsically important; and it is this intrinsic importance that Rickert finds in cultural value. An event is historically important if it *either* is itself the embodiment of cultural value, *or* has considerable influence upon the realisation of such value. Cf. *Kulturwissenschaft u. Naturwissenschaft*, 7th ed., 1926, pp. 93–4, and *Die Probleme der Geschichtsphilosophie*, 3rd ed., 1924, p. 59.

more important from one point of view, viz. that of political history, than the identity of the tailor who made his coat; but there is also a point of view, capable of embodiment in a history, e.g. of fashions, or of the tailoring industry, or of commodity prices, from which the tailor is more important than the political incident (cf. *Kulturwissenschaft u. Naturwissenschaft*, p. 89). More, the same event may be important in opposite ways according to the point of view, as e.g. it may be argued that the French Revolution was a good thing for France and Europe, and again that it was a bad thing. Here it is evident, says Rickert, that the historian cannot, as historian, decide whether the Revolution was good or bad, and yet he must recognise that, whether it was good or bad, whichever value-system is applied, it is in any case important; in other words, he must judge it by reference to value, but must not judge its value (*op. cit.*, p. 88).

If the individual facts which historical science examines are selected by reference to value, the complex wholes into which they fall, such as the individual life, the social group, the nation or State, the period, will also be delimited by reference to value, and the fundamental concepts in which historical generalisation expresses their nature will be not merely general, but also normative. The idea e.g. of a nation will express not primarily what is in fact common to all nations, but rather what is axiologically essential to a nation, i.e. essential to that manifestation of value which a nation, or this or that nation, is or embodies. The axiologically essential elements may and do, of course, often coincide with the elements which a purely factual morphological study of social phenomena would recognise as essential from its own point of view, and thus it is that biological and psychological science can occasionally be useful to the cultural studies; but the axiological element in the concepts of the cultural studies is always the fundamental element.[1] Like-

[1] This is the reason why Rickert speaks of the historical studies as *Geschichtswissenschaften* and as *Kulturwissenschaften*, but never as *Geisteswissenschaften*. He admits that a distinction used to be drawn between soul (*Seele*) and spirit (*Geist*), which determined *Geist* to a non-psychological or cultural meaning, and it was thus that e.g. Hegel used the word. Since then, however, *Geist* has often come to be used as equivalent to *Seele*, and the distinction between *Geisteswissenschaften* and *Naturwissenschaften* is commonly understood, like Mill's distinction between 'moral sciences' and 'natural sciences', as a distinction between two groups of sciences of fact, differing only in that

wise when, from the tangled web of historical change, we single out a particular process for study, it is as a development (*Entwicklung*) towards some specific result that we single it out; and the result itself, whose intrinsic importance sheds an interest upon the process leading up to it, is important simply as a realisation of cultural value.

If the values, by reference to which the historian selects his facts, were such as no one but himself and a few eccentrics, either in his own day or at the time of the events which he studies, could appreciate, then his history would itself be eccentric or subjective, and could neither reach a wide public, nor claim the right to do so. The aim of the scientific historian is to avoid this subjectivity, and it can only be achieved if the value-standards which he employs are generally recognised throughout his own society, and over considerable periods of time, not necessarily to be obvious and ineluctable, but at least to be such as a reasonable man may fairly entertain. Such standards are to be found in the general cultural tradition of a civilisation. 'In Europe, wherever historical works are read, the cultural values attaching to religion, the Church, law, the State, science, language, literature, art, economic organisation etc., will certainly

---

the one group studies physical fact and the other psychical fact. During the present century there has been a partial return to the older meaning of *Geist*, and it is now used again, especially in the phrase *objektiver Geist*, in a sense corresponding to Rickert's *Kultur*. Rickert himself admits this in respect of some modern writers, but still thinks that Dilthey meant by *Geisteswissenschaften* no more than 'moral sciences' in Mill's sense (*Kulturwissenschaft u. Naturwissenschaft*, intro. to 7th ed., 1926). The present and the following chapter will suffice to show how unjust this is to Dilthey. Dilthey, on the other hand, objects to the term *Kulturwissenschaften*, as not doing justice to the complexity of the subject-matter of historical science, viz. human nature, which, besides being a vehicle of value, has other less pleasing but not less interesting or important capacities. 'It embodies an undemonstrable, indeed a one-sided determination of a meaning (*Sinn*) and an aim (*Ziel*) in history. This is too friendly and benevolent a view of human nature, in which the dark instincts of mutual oppression and destruction play a very notable part' (*G.S.*, VII, 323). Here Dilthey, in turn, is unjust to Rickert, who makes room in his theory for the phenomena which Dilthey cites. 'It will be evident that historical importance and meaning do not attach only to that which *furthers* the realisation of cultural goods, but also to that which *hinders* it. That which is hostile to value has also a meaning (*Sinn*) which we understand (*verstehen*)' (*Kulturwissenschaft u. Naturwissenschaft*, p. 88).

be understood as values, and therefore it will not be regarded as arbitrary that these values should guide the selection of what is essential, and so limit the historical narrative to that which is important or significant with respect to them' (*Kulturwissenschaft u. Naturwissenschaft*, pp. 132–3).

This is enough for the specialist. It is not, however, enough when we take a comprehensive or 'philosophical' view of the problem. For then we see that even Europe is only one of many cultural units, limited both in extent and in duration; and standards which are valid only for the European mind are not really objective, and the historical narrative and interpretative concepts derived from them are not really worthy of the name of science. If this is all that can be said, then the position of relativism or historicism is the only one left to us, and that is the death of the historical and cultural studies. How can we claim real truth for our version of any historical process or incident? How can we put together all our knowledge of particular processes into a whole, a system of world history (*Universalgeschichte*), and make within this whole a real distinction between the more important and the less important elements, and perhaps detect a thread of progress? How can we combine the various cultural traditions, the religious, artistic, scientific, political, economic aspects of life, in a comprehensive view where each has its proper place and value in relation to the rest, and all of them together build up the system of culture (*Kultur*) according to an objectively intelligible plan? We can only claim the right to do this if we believe that the values recognised by us, in spite of their historical relativity, represent real approximations to a system of absolute values, in the same way as the laws formulated by natural science, though continually undergoing modification, are always an approximation to a real system of laws prevailing in nature. We may not know to the full what these absolute values are; but we can know that they really hold good (*gelten*), and can seem to detect in all our actual value-standards some trace of their lineaments, and in the historical changes of our standards a slow progress towards a clearer and fuller understanding of the absolute norms. 'Like the stars in the sky, with the progress of culture they gradually come within the range of human vision. They are not *old* values, not *new* values, they are *the* values' (Riehl, quoted by Rickert, *op. cit.*, p. 143).

If this be true, there is a clear place for a philosophy of history over and above the work of the empirical historian. We must not, however, misconceive its scope. It cannot be a sociology, and lay down causal laws for historical processes. Such laws are only discoverable in the psychical life which is the vehicle of culture, not in the cultural order itself. Nay, the very form of a law contradicts the nature of historical reality, since a law formulates regularities in a world where processes can recur, whereas nothing in history recurs, everything is unique, and even the whole complex of world history is not a world of processes, but itself one individual process. There cannot even be a 'law of progress'; for the necessity, biological (Darwin) or sociological (Marx), which would constitute the *law* would be causal and factual, and therefore outside the scope of history, while the standard of value, which would enable us to judge that the evolutionary or dialectical process was a *progress*, would not assure us of its necessity. The real business of the philosophy of history is threefold. (1) It must make an epistemological and logical analysis of the historical studies. (2) It must set forth their general principles, i.e. not laws, but the most general values which determine the meaning (*Sinn*) of history, and from which the concepts of historical interpretation are derived. And (3) it must go over the historical process as the specialists, each in his own sphere or period, have reconstructed it, grasp it as a whole in the light of the highest values, single out the most important elements of progress or retrogression which appear in it, and divide the whole into broad periods whose limits are determined not now by the interest of a particular investigator, the extent or limitation of his knowledge or understanding, but by objective philosophical principles; and this is the true world history (*Die Probleme der Geschichtsphilosophie*).

It will be seen that, if we abstract from the actual details of Rickert's theory of knowledge, the first two of the tasks which he assigns to the philosophy of history answer to the epistemological, logical, and methodological task of Dilthey's *Kritik der historischen Vernunft*; while the third would find a place in the 'encyclopaedia of the sciences' which also, according to Dilthey, is a part of philosophy, though a part in which he himself never showed any interest. If, however, we examine the way in which Rickert actually carries out the philosophical critique, we see at

245

once that it was bound to antagonise Dilthey. For Dilthey's first principle in his philosophical enquiries was 'to try to understand life in terms of itself'. This meant, in particular, that life is not to be understood in terms of the transcendental self and *a priori* norms. The Kantian formalism is no more acceptable to him when applied by Rickert to historical knowledge than it was when applied by Cohen and Natorp to perception and natural science. He counts it as metaphysics, and rejects it as, in the second book of the *Einleitung*, he rejected every possible metaphysical *Grundlegung der Geisteswissenschaften*.

This rejection of contemporary Kantianism is a recurrent theme in the writings of Dilthey's last years, and is worked out at some length in the notes which he made at that time in preparation for a fresh edition of the *Einleitung*. Here he takes the offensive by suggesting that the procedure of the 'Kantians' is not really Kantian at all, and that the real Kant is on his own side. It was Fichte, not Kant, he says, who first pretended to deduce the forms of all possible experience and knowledge from the conditions of the possibility of consciousness. It is Fichte's spirit that is at work when the 'Kantians' divide the sciences into two groups by an *a priori* methodological division, instead of asking how the sciences group themselves in real life. Kant himself was a more modest thinker, who was content to take the sciences as he found them, and set his epistemology the humble task of analysing them without explaining them away. This is what we also must do. 'Epistemology is never anything definitive. It will never have any validity except in so far as it does justice from the outset to the results attained in the empirical sciences' (*G.S.*, I, 418–20, cf. 415, 417). This is the real way to deal with Rickert's questions. Is psychology to be counted among the human studies? Let us see how it stands in relation to the tasks which the human studies in fact pursue. Is the nomothetic standpoint alien to the human studies? Let us see whether they in fact make successful use of it. Is there a sense or meaning in history? Let us consult the human studies, and see whether they can find one (*G.S.*, I, 417–18). Thus at every point Dilthey appeals to the facts of experience, as the empirical human studies bring them before us, and rejects the idea of philosophy as a source of some higher or profounder insight.

Dilthey does not stop at denying the absolute values; he also objects to defining the human studies exclusively in terms of the study of values at all. Not that he thinks there is anything in the subject-matter of the human studies which bears no value-predicate; but he holds that the concept of value, properly understood, is not only not the fundamental concept of these studies, but actually represents a partial and fragmentary view of their subject-matter. Perhaps it is not only the philosopher in Dilthey who speaks here; the historian may also have a word to say. If we interpret history in terms of values or norms, we shall be led to relate the individual event to the value which it embodies or fails to embody—i.e. to something non-temporal and non-historical—rather than to the earlier and later events with which it is causally or 'structurally' connected. But in real life the historian is concerned with the process, with the follow-on of one event from another, much more than with the value of the event taken by itself. Dilthey is in search of a fundamental category which will describe what the historian does, rather than what the neo-Fichtean philosopher thinks he ought to do.

Dilthey is thus at odds with Rickert on all the main points of Rickert's system. And yet it is fair to say that he is greatly indebted to Rickert. That philosopher had, after all, raised a number of questions of fundamental importance, and answered them in his own way, and to some of them Dilthey himself had not yet given a precise and definite answer. He was now compelled to do so. If he was to reject Rickert's answers, he could no longer avoid coming forward with his own. This necessity acted upon him as a stimulus, and helped him to bring his ideas to a focus. Without it, his latest writings would have been less fruitful and suggestive than they actually are.

Let us enumerate briefly the issues involved.

(1) If the differentia of the human studies is not found in their concern with cultural values, nor yet in their idiographic method, where is it to be found? Dilthey's original view was that it lies in their concern with the human mind; but this needs further analysis and elucidation. This is the problem of the delimitation of the human studies (*Abgrenzung der Geisteswissenschaften*), to which Dilthey gave much attention in his later years.

(2) If the subject-matter of the human studies consists of values, their categories or ruling concepts will of course all be

derived from the concept of value. But if not, what are their categories, and whence are they derived?

(3) The human studies analyse their subject-matter for purposes of study into parts which are relatively self-contained, such as the individual man, the cultural system, the nation, the historical movement or period. According to Rickert, each of these subordinate wholes is a centre of the realisation of values, and it is by this test that they are recognised and discriminated. If value is not the ground of these distinctions, what is?[r]

(4) The doctrine of absolute values enables Rickert to avoid historicism and to find a meaning in history. Dilthey denies absolute values, and will not interpret history exclusively in terms of value at all. In what sense, if at all, can he still find a meaning in history?

We shall see in the next chapter how Dilthey finally answered these questions. His work in search of the answer occupies the whole period from 1904 until his death in 1911. It was a period of intense and many-sided activity. In addition to working towards his *Kritik der historischen Vernunft*, Dilthey was writing *Das Wesen der Philosophie*, *Das geschichtliche Bewusstsein u. die Weltanschauungen*, and *Die Typen der Weltanschauung u. ihre Ausbildung in den metaphysischen Systemen*. He was preparing fresh editions—which never came out—of the *Einleitung* and *Die Einbildungskraft des Dichters*. To this period belong his fullest and clearest statements about the nature of lived experience, about expression and understanding, and to it belongs his final change of view in respect of psychology. Important as these various developments are in themselves, they all find their focus in Dilthey's central task, which was that of completing his *Kritik der historischen Vernunft*, and it was impossible to do this without taking account of Rickert.

If we look at dates and themes, we can find a development in Dilthey's ideas and way of approach to the problem.

[1] A particular case of this question is the question, how philosophy is distinguished from other systems of cultural activity, and on what principle it falls into subordinate divisions. Dilthey's interest in this question during his later years is vouched for by *Das Wesen der Philosophie* (1907) and by the many attempts at a *Weltanschauungslehre*, all belonging to this period, which appear in *G.S.*, VIII. Here too he came into conflict with Windelband's architectonic. Cf. also *Das Problem der Religion* (1911), an unfinished fragment which is one of the latest products of his pen (*G.S.*, VI, 288–305).

At first he thought of going at some length into the general questions of epistemology, and working from there towards his special problem. The epistemological problem for the human studies is in one respect a wider problem than for the natural sciences; for the natural sciences include only statements of fact and generalisations from these, whereas in the human studies we also meet value-judgments, ends, norms, and imperatives (*G.S.*, VII, 5–6). All these forms of expression must be examined; we must see how they are related to lived experience, what is their meaning and function, and in what sense they can be said to be 'objective' or 'true'. To do this requires a descriptive analysis of the structural system of the mind. We have gone into all this in Chapters Two and Three. The exposition given there was based very largely on the first two *Studien zur Grundlegung der Geisteswissenschaften*, which Dilthey wrote in 1905.

Very soon, however, he gave up this line of approach in favour of one which was more direct. The new way was to begin by pointing to the human studies as a body of knowledge which exists and must be accounted for. From this point of view the first question to come into view was that of the delimitation of the human studies. Is experimental psychology one of them? What is their defining characteristic? In the years 1906–9 Dilthey wrote four successive essays (or sketches for an essay) with the same title, *Die Abgrenzung der Geisteswissenschaften*. In these we can see him moving gradually away from his pre-occupation with structure-psychology, and giving ever greater prominence to the study of the relations between lived experience, expression, and understanding, until in the fourth and final version of the *Abgrenzung* this relation becomes the defining characteristic of the human studies. 'A science belongs to the human studies only if its object becomes accessible to us through the attitude based on the systematic relation between life, expression, and understanding' (*G.S.*, VII, 86–8).

The essay begins with a rough list of the human studies, including among others history, political economy, jurisprudence, art history and criticism, and ending with psychology (*die Psychologie*). These studies, he says, have grown up together and form a natural unity. They are united by a common interest in man, individual and collective, and in his activities. But they are not interested equally in all aspects of man's life. His physical organism is of importance to them only as the vehicle of his mind. Indeed, it is characteristic of the human studies that they are not interested in physical objects and processes as such, but only as expressions of an inner life. This applies to the works of men's hands, and to social institutions, as well as to human bodies. 'Whether it is a question of States, Churches, institutions, customs, books, works of art—such objects, like man himself, always involve the relation of a sensible exterior to another side which is inaccessible to the senses, and therefore interior' (*G.S.*, VII, 84).

This interior reality, the true object of the human studies, is *der Geist*; and Dilthey goes on to explain what he means by this word. The object of the human studies is not the process of mental life (*der psychische Lebensverlauf*) which is studied in psychology. In jurisprudence, for example, what we study is the law, and this is something distinct from the particular persons through whom, and circumstances in which, it works itself out in action. Particular judges and particular litigants, the motives of this criminal, the illness of that witness—these have nothing to do with jurisprudence. That study is concerned with the principles of the law and the structure of the system to which all legal activities belong: it was of this that Montesquieu wrote in *L'esprit des lois*, and Jhering in *Der Geist des römischen Rechts*. Similarly the literary historian, the critic, the aesthetician have not to do with the inner processes of the poet's mind, but with the poem which he writes, and this is a *geistiger Zusammenhang* which can be separated from the psychology of its author. Both the poem and the legal system are instances of what Hegel meant when he spoke of *objektiver Geist* (*G.S.*, VII, 84–6).

This passage, read in isolation, gives the impression of a close approximation to Rickert. That philosopher himself used it as evidence that Dilthey's underlying intention was the same as his own (*Die Grenzen der naturwissenschaftlichen Begriffsbildung*, Pref. to 2nd ed., 1913).[1] The distinction between the *geistiger Zusammenhang* or *geistiges Gebilde* and the *psychischer Lebensverlauf* looks suspiciously like Rickert's distinction between the *irrealer Sinn* or *Sinngebilde* and the psychological process. Yet, in fact, there is little here that Dilthey has not said often enough before. He has often said that we do not understand people—or even ourselves—by look-

[1] Thirteen years later his judgment was less favourable: see above, p. 243 n.

ing at the inner movements of the mind, but at its objective expressions. The conception of 'objective mind' is used in the *Einleitung* and in the *Ideen*. A year after this *Abgrenzung* essay it was given a new amplitude, and the form which it then took, as we shall shortly see, was characteristically Diltheian and not Rickertian. Dilthey was thinking of expressions and what they express, not of absolute principles and 'unreal' values in the Rickertian manner.

There is a real incoherence in the essay, however, and it lies in Dilthey's treatment of psychology. He gives jurisprudence and literary study as examples—his only detailed examples—of the human studies, and to each of them he says that psychological knowledge is irrelevant. He says that it is a mistake to equate psychology with the knowledge of the object of the human studies. That object is *Geist*, not the psychological process. This reads like a surrender to Rickert and an exclusion of psychology from the human studies. But that is certainly not what he means; for in this very essay *die Psychologie* is expressly listed among the *Geisteswissenschaften*, and, as we have seen in Chapter Seven, he never unmistakably declared that psychology, even experimental psychology, was not one of them. There is, however, an undeniable obscurity in his utterances on the subject. He gives the impression of avoiding it because his mind was not clear. It is hard to see, on the one hand, how he could have expelled experimental psychology altogether from the society of the human studies, and on the other hand how he could have avoided assigning to it a peculiar and in some respects a subordinate status among them. But these are questions which he never finally answered.

This *Abgrenzung* essay was completed by the beginning of 1909. At the same time Dilthey also completed an essay entitled *Das Erlebnis u. die Selbstbiographie*; and a year later came *Das Verstehen anderer Personen u. ihrer Lebensäusserungen*. With these materials taking shape in his hands, and his ideas beginning to crystallise into a reasoned reply to Rickert over the whole field of the subject, Dilthey now felt that the time had come for a final effort to write his *Kritik der historischen Vernunft*. In the next chapter we shall see how far he got in this attempt.

The work was not, in fact, fully carried out. A promising beginning was made in *Der Aufbau der geschichtlichen Welt in den*

Geisteswissenschaften, which was given to the press in March 1910, and appeared in the following December. This is Dilthey's last important work, and includes a great deal of new material, some of which is of considerable interest, as we shall see. A continuation was promised, and Dilthey had made some progress in preparing this when he was compelled by ill health to lay it aside and take up easier work for a time. Accordingly, he began at first to prepare a new edition of the *Leben Schleiermachers*; then he set himself to make a collection of his earlier essays from 1864 onward, under the title of *Die geistige Welt*. This collection appears substantially as he planned it in *G.S.* V and VI (see V, vii–xii), but Dilthey did not live to finish it himself. He died on the 1st of October 1911. The *Kritik der historischen Vernunft*, therefore, did not receive the last touches from his hand. Yet he had brought the preparation of his material to such a point that the plan of the whole is not in doubt, and the editor of *G.S.* VII has been able, by fitting the most explicit of the innumerable MSS. available into this framework, to reconstruct the *Kritik* in a form very like that which Dilthey himself must have given it, if he had lived.

In the following chapter I shall expound, mostly without comment, the contents of this, Dilthey's *opus magnum*.

CHAPTER NINE

THE *Kritik der historischen Vernunft* is the result of Dilthey's patient efforts to finish his *Einleitung in die Geisteswissenschaften*, and in a sense it really is the completion of that work. There is, it is true, another sense in which the *Einleitung* was not and could not be completed. The original conception of a work in five books, summarised above on p. 168, had at last to be given up. For the existing first book, whose ostensible purpose was to open the discussion by describing the actual state of the human studies, their aims and methods, their distinctive character as against the natural sciences, and to show their need of a philosophical *Grundlegung*, does in fact much more than this. It describes an ideal, not a real state of affairs, notably in respect of psychology, and again in respect of moral theory; in discussing sociology, it does not merely point to the actual sterility of that science, but goes on to argue in principle the question of its possibility; and it similarly discusses the possibility of a philosophy of history. In all these respects, the *Einleitung* anticipates the promised epistemological *Grundlegung*. Again, the existing second book, which begins the historical demonstration of the impossibility of a metaphysical foundation for the human studies, covers the ground in such detail that the history could not have been completed on the same scale without occupying far too large a proportion of the finished work. The materials which Dilthey actually collected for that purpose were, in fact, ultimately given a different setting, and brought into relation with his *Studien zur Geschichte des deutschen Geistes*.

Accordingly, in writing the final *Kritik*, Dilthey does not presuppose the *Einleitung* and go on from where it ended, he makes a new beginning. The *Abgrenzung* essay (see above, pp. 249–51) is brought in as an introduction; describing as it does the aims, methods, and distinctive character of the human studies, it fulfils the essential purpose of the first book of the *Einleitung*, and

253

is in fact a highly abbreviated substitute for it. Then comes a historical section which roughly answers to the second book of the *Einleitung* and the projected third book; but all the earlier part of the history of philosophy and the human studies is left out, the story begins with the *Aufklärung*, and resolves itself into an account of the development of the historical movement in the nineteenth century and the contemporary efforts towards a philosophy of history. Thus all the unwieldy mass of introductory matter is cut away, and Dilthey can proceed at once to the real business of the *Grundlegung*. The *Kritik der historischen Vernunft*, so constituted, is a work complete in itself.

In the present chapter I shall summarise the contents of this *Kritik*, for the first part as they were completed and published by Dilthey in the *Aufbau der geschichtlichen Welt in den Geisteswissenschaften* (1910), and for the rest as his editor has made it possible to recapture them from the fragments.

At its head, by way of introduction, Dilthey sets his essay on the *Abgrenzung der Geisteswissenschaften*. The contents of this essay were dealt with in our previous chapter, and need only be briefly summarised here. The human studies are singled out as the object of enquiry. On a preliminary view, they are found to be a group of studies having a common interest in man. This, however, cannot be their essence, because in itself it is not enough to distinguish them from some of the natural sciences. They are distinguished from natural science not by their subject-matter, but by their manner of dealing with it; for, whereas natural science abstracts from the perceived world those aspects which can be built up into a regular quantitative system, the human studies treat the world, or rather certain objects in it, as matter for understanding. Although psychology is a human study, yet the human studies as a whole are not primarily concerned with the processes which it studies, but rather with mental complexes (*geistige Gebilde*) which are the contents of the cultural consciousness.

The next section is entitled *Die Verschiedenheit des Aufbaus in den Naturwissenschaften u. den Geisteswissenschaften: historische Orientierung*, and its purpose is to furnish a historical background against which the problem of the *Kritik* may be seen. Dilthey describes the logical form of the natural sciences, how they stand pyramid-wise upon one another's shoulders, and how their whole structure is dominated by mathematics and the principle of causal necessity. He shows how philosophy, reflecting upon their principles and methods, has failed to reach an agreed conclusion, but has produced two types of theory; the one type fastens upon the mathematical element in natural-scientific reasoning, and traces it back to *a priori* principles, while the other appeals to the power of prediction and the control over nature which we obtain through the discovery of laws, and develops on that basis the various forms of positivism and pragmatism (*G.S.*, VII, 88–93). With this as a rough background, Dilthey goes on to sketch first of all the great advance of historical enquiry in the early nineteenth century, and then the attempts of the philosophers to deal with the problems which it raised.

A foundation had been laid in the seventeenth and eighteenth centuries by the 'natural system' of the human studies. The several branches of cultural and social life had been distinguished and studied separately. Each was supposed to be governed by rational principles; their history was seen as a gradual approximation to an adequate embodiment of these principles; and, under this general conception of progress, it was possible to see the course of history as an intelligible whole.

The first breach in the citadel of rationalism was made by Herder, who saw that the individual nation or period cannot be understood merely as a stage in a progress to an end which lies beyond itself, but has a value and significance of its own. Then came (1) a great movement in philology, initiated by F. A. Wolf. He conceived philology as a science which, beginning with the study of language and literature, should progressively widen its range until at last it should take in the whole cultural and spiritual life of a nation. For this purpose it could draw upon two great aids: source-criticism, of which Wolf's own Homeric researches gave the example, and the hermeneutic which was evolved by Schleiermacher and made current by Böckh (cf. above, p. 238). Through the application of these, by the efforts of J. Grimm, Niebuhr, Mommsen, and others, it was found possible to see the life of a people as a living whole, where the different elements of language, literature, religion, morality, law, are all parallel manifestations of a single communal mind (*Gemeingeist*). This conception was formulated as a principle by Savigny: the branches of cultural and social life are not independent systems of phenomena, the nation is the one reality behind them all, and their apparent distinctness from one another in a sophisticated society represents only a differentiation of function within the overriding whole. (2) In the eighteenth century the comparative method had been exploited for the purposes of natural history, and the study of organic types had gone so far that Cuvier, from a few fragments of a skeleton, could confidently reconstruct the whole. This method was now taken over by the philologists and historians; Franz Bopp and J. Grimm divined the structure of vanished language-groups, and de Tocqueville analysed the anatomy of the body politic. (3) These various separate enquiries and discoveries were welded into a whole through the work of Hegel, who formulated the law of dialectical development to which all historical events are alike subject; it was thus made possible to see the past life of mankind as a single process, a world history (*Weltgeschichte*), in which every event has its necessary place as a stage in the evolution of consciousness (*G.S.*, VII, 93–101).

From these discoveries and experiments there came at last the exemplary embodiment of the historical consciousness in Ranke. Endowed with 'Goethe's contemplative attitude to life and his artistic approach to the world', having the poet's power of understanding and description, and equipped with all Niebuhr's critical skill, Ranke had this limitation, that he feared general ideas, and shrank from any attempt to analyse behind the facts. Yet this limitation was also an advantage to him; for it led him to formulate decisively what must always be a chief aim, though not the sole aim, of historical enquiry, viz. the portrayal of the overt fact, of the historical process in its detailed individuality. And so, from a penetrating study of archives, he spun again in imagination that web of political and military intrigue and conflict which has shaped the outward and inward history of the States of modern Europe, and set it forth with 'a will to historical objectivity and a power to achieve it which have no parallel'.

Dilthey places two other historians beside Ranke. The first is Carlyle, through whose 'one-sided and quite singular genius' the heroic philosophy of Fichte found its reflection in history. 'If Ranke is all eye, and lives in the objective world, Carlyle's historical writing rests on the struggle with the problem of the inner life; thus these two supplement one another, like the two tendencies in poetry, the one of which takes its start from objective fact and the other from the development of the poet's own being.' The second is de Tocqueville, 'the greatest analyst of the political world since Aristotle and Machiavelli', who, without either praise or condemnation, laid bare the structure of the modern State, the forces at work in it, the long-run tendencies resulting from them, and made historical generalisations which proved capable of exerting practical influence in his own time (*G.S.*, VII, 101–5).

Parallel with this development in the historical studies went the growth of a philosophy of history, and here at first the influence of the transcendental philosophy was altogether dominant. Kant himself set the fashion. Neglecting entirely the epistemological question, how knowledge of historical reality is possible, he undertook to show *a priori* the rational principles which must govern all interpretation of the historical process. Empirical or 'anthropological' research can, of course, discover causal laws by which the social order will seem to be governed; but, Kant continues, since man is really a free agent, not subject to natural causality, this system of laws cannot be the truth about him and his history. The truth about man lies in the moral law, and history is to be understood as a teleological process in which, through conflict and opposition, the moral law comes gradually to be realised in action. There is a slow advance of those forces in human nature which subserve the moral end, and their victory will finally be secured in a world-wide free, and wholly just, social order.

In a like spirit Fichte distinguished between empirical history, which takes the present state of the world as its starting-point and proceeds to find its causes in the past, and the philosophy of history, which singles out the rational aspects of the historical process and interprets the whole in terms of these. History as he sees it is the manifestation of the free power of the self in conflict with dead nature. Every human act is the fulfilment of a task freely willed by a moral agent, and every such fulfilment gives rise to further tasks for the future. But Fichte, unlike Kant, sees in each stage of this endless process a unique form of life, with a value of its own which lies in its individual character; and he also gives a peculiar significance to the great individuals or

257

'heroes' of history, as men who have enriched our conception of the rational end of life. Thus he overcomes the abstractness of Kant's theory.

It was this same transcendental philosophy, enriched but not essentially changed by the work of Schleiermacher and Hegel, which inspired Humboldt's theory of the problem and method of history. Over and above the causal influences of temperament and capacity, of physical and social environment, which work upon the historical agent, Humboldt summons us to recognise certain 'ideas' or value-norms, which define the purpose of human life and history. Not only are human beings in their actions consciously guided by these values, but the accidental circumstances of life and the impersonal trend of events are providentially controlled with the same end in view. This general conception persists in the works of Gervinus, Ranke, and Droysen. Their philosophy of history is an *a priori* construction, which appeals to a providential plan imposed upon the temporal sequence from above, and divides the past into periods, more or less arbitrarily, by means of this clue (*G.S.*, VII, 106–15).

In the last decades of the nineteenth century, a more critical outlook developed. The attempt to construct the course of history *a priori* was pushed into the background, and the epistemological and logical question, how historical knowledge is possible, became the centre of interest. Dilthey divides those who have dealt with this problem into two groups. (1) One powerful group has continued the tradition of transcendental idealism, usually along the lines laid down by Fichte; they still appeal to the *a priori* norms, both as a principle of selection to guide the empirical historian, and as the basis of a philosophical construction of world history. Hegel has had less influence upon philosophy proper than Fichte; but the 'systematic human studies' have learned increasingly from him, and 'the time is coming when his attempt to form a system of concepts which can master the ceaseless stream of history will also be valued and turned to account'. On the other hand, (2) another movement has arisen which repudiates the belief in absolute values or principles, and undertakes to understand history without any transcendental or metaphysical aids, purely in terms of itself, i.e. in terms of the principles which have actually found expression in the empirical

258

human studies. There are differences of opinion in this movement, especially on the rival merits of the psychological and the
sociological approach (*G.S.*, VII, 115–17).

Dilthey defines his own position by reference to the *Einleitung*,
emphasising his opposition to intellectualism and the transcendental philosophy, and his belief in the totality of human
nature as the proper basis for epistemology. At least it is the
right basis for an epistemology of the human studies, which
differ from natural science precisely in this, that they do not
interpret their data in terms of abstract and hypothetical entities, but in terms of a concrete system of life, which the enquirer
relives in his own experience, and so understands (*G.S.*, VII,
117–20).

And so Dilthey proceeds to the real business of his *Kritik*, the
epistemological and logical analysis of the human studies. Starting with the general principles of epistemology and logic, he
gradually narrows the sphere of enquiry until we are brought
face to face with the distinctive characteristics of the human
studies, and can study their methods in detail. His views on the
more general questions of epistemology and logic have already
been considered at length in Chapters Two, Three, and Five,
and need not be repeated here; I shall summarise this part of
the *Kritik* as briefly as possible, enlarging only on those points
which represent a new development in Dilthey's thought.

He begins with a revised and amplified version of that part
of the second *Studie zur Grundlegung der Geisteswissenschaften* which
deals with the processes of thought. The contents of this section
were summarised in Chapter Two. It describes the function of
silent thought, the formation of the *Totalvorstellung*, the processes
of judging and inferring; and it shows how every process of
thought is in the long run based on experience. In short, it reaffirms Dilthey's empiricist and non-Kantian view with regard
to the functions of thought. Thought is not the source of form
and meaning in experience; it merely elicits the form and meaning which are there already, and, by following up beyond lived
experience the relations which are found in lived experience,
pursues its endless task of exploring the world order (*G.S.*, VII,
120–9).

Of course, in each particular branch of enquiry, the specific
nature of the subject-matter affects the process of thought. Not

only does each separate study come to have concepts and methods peculiar to itself, as we shall see; but even the process by which concepts are formed from experience may differ, and the relation between the whole intellectual superstructure and its experiential foundations may be different, in one sphere from what it is in another. Dilthey proceeds to draw a contrast in this respect between the human studies and natural science.

He describes first of all how our knowledge of the world arises, not in an intellectual vacuum, but in the course of our active life and intercourse with the world. Our relation to the object is not merely a cognitive relation, but a vital one (*Lebensbezug*). He goes on to show how not only individual human beings, but also social groups can enter into this active relation with their environment, and out of it build up a body of experience and a set of ideas. The individual is deeply influenced by the ideas and attitudes prevalent in the groups to which he belongs (*G.S.*, VII, 131–5).

Now, the natural sciences do not rest directly upon this body of common experience and ideas. They have a special standpoint and method, which is 'esoteric'. But there is nothing esoteric about the human studies. They stand nearer to common experience. They use concepts and methods which have been worked out and applied already in ordinary life and reflection, and are often used there with more profitable results than in the human studies themselves. 'A man of action like Bismarck, whose nature it is to keep his aims in view in every letter he writes and every conversation he holds, will never be equalled in the art of reading behind expressions to purposes by any exponent of political actions or any critic of historical records. Between the comprehension of a play by a listener of strong poetic sensibility and the finest literary-historical analysis there is often no difference' (*G.S.*, VII, 136).

One result of this is that the general experience of life possessed by a given society must determine the form which the human studies take in that society. Thus French society in the *grand siècle*, centred upon the Court, and interested more in men than in principles, threw up an unequalled crop of memoirs and empirical treatises on the characters and passions of men; these treatises affected the poetry of the time, and through that, in turn, the philosophers and the historians. The extent to which theory depends on antecedent fact is evident in the Greek political theorists, as well as in the history of both Roman and Germanic law.

It follows that every theory propounded in the human studies includes assumptions, conscious or unconscious, as to matters of fact or value, which are simply due to its date and place of origin; not to mention that many such theories are designed in part with a view to exerting practical influence. And yet, if the human studies are to merit their name, they must surely be impartial and give universally valid results. Here is a problem of long standing, but it is not insoluble. The human studies must not give up the attempt to influence life; it is here that their social significance lies, and this fact is coming to be more and more appreciated. Only, the way to fulfil this function is precisely by gaining the prestige of scientific objectivity. How we can resist the distortion of our outlook by contemporary conditions is a question which we shall be able to answer at a later stage, when we have defined the concept of a *dynamic system* (*Wirkungs-zusammenhang*) and applied it to the problem of method (*G.S.*, VII, 136–8).

A further peculiarity of the human studies emerges from a consideration of the conditions under which we understand other persons. Mutual understanding would be impossible if it were not for the fundamental identity of human nature and the presence of common interests in the persons concerned. The very fact that understanding takes place proves the existence of such a fundamental identity and of such common interests; and that further carries with it the possibility of generalisation and the discovery of general truths in the human studies. Now, it might seem obvious that generalisation must depend on the prior understanding of particular instances. Yet in fact it is equally true that the understanding of particular instances depends on a prior knowledge of general truths. Suppose, for example, that we are trying to understand Bismarck. It is obvious that our understanding of this individual person will be affected by what we already know, or believe, about the general characteristics of men of action; about the Prussian landed aristocracy; about cultural systems such as religion, by which Bismarck was in some degree influenced. This is a different situation from what we find in the natural sciences.

261

'Knowledge of inorganic nature is achieved in an edifice of sciences wherein the lower layer is always independent of that which is based upon it: in the human studies, from the process of understanding upwards, everything is determined by the relation of *mutual dependence*.' Indeed, the relation extends below the process of understanding, and embraces lived experience itself. Understanding presupposes lived experience, but lived experience in turn can only develop into experience of life by means of understanding. Again, the understanding of individuals presupposes systematic knowledge, while systematic knowledge rests upon the understanding of individuals (*G.S.*, VII, 141–3).

Dilthey enforces this conclusion by showing how historiography in Thucydides and Polybius, in Machiavelli and Guicciardini, in Ranke and his contemporaries, has always depended on the progress achieved up to their time by the systematic human studies, whether the historians themselves and their public were aware of this or not. 'Ranke may seem to approach things with a naïve delight in story-telling, but his historical writing can only be understood if we follow up the manifold sources of systematic thought which mingled in his education.' The same is true of historical criticism, e.g. the new Homeric criticism in Wolf and his predecessors arose from a new theory of poetry, and Schleiermacher's work on Plato was made possible by the partial return of philosophy to the Platonic standpoint in the post-Kantians. On the other hand, progress in the systematic human studies depends on the discovery of new historical sources, new discoveries which widen the range of human experience, spiritual movements which deepen it, or times of crisis which disturb old certitudes; cf. the origin of political theory, rhetoric, and poetics in the late fifth century B.C. The whole history of the human studies is dominated by this relation of mutual dependence between lived experience and historical understanding, and again between historical understanding and systematic enquiry into general laws. Every advance in any one of these three factors brings a corresponding advance in the others, and the progress of knowledge is wrought out by their continual co-operation. 'From the basic function of understanding upward, lived experience, experience relived, and universal truths are bound up together. The formation of concepts is not based on norms or values appearing beyond the world of objective knowledge, but arises from the tendency, dominant in all conceptual thought, to show up what is firm and enduring in the flow of events' (*G.S.*, VII, 143–6).

From the relation between the general and the particular in the human studies Dilthey passes on to consider the dependence of these studies on the physical expressions of mental life. We saw in Chapter Five what he has to say in general about expressions and the interpretation of them. Here in the *Aufbau*, however, he presents the matter in a somewhat new light.

The expressions of life, he says, are of course physical facts; but they are unlike other physical facts, precisely because they are expressions, because they 'contain' (*enthalten*) and disclose a mental activity from which they are sprung, and which they bring, over the gap of years and centuries, in living freshness to our doors. They are not merely things which exist, or events which occur, at a determinate place and date. They proceed from life and are themselves an incident in its development; their structural affinities reach out beyond them into the past and the future, and their whole essence as data for historical knowledge lies just in this their reference beyond themselves. An ordinary physical event is causally connected with past and future, but the connections are no part of the fact as observed; historical data, on the other hand, are instinct from the beginning with the moving life which produced them. We cannot observe a historical fact at all without observing it as dynamic, and this is the very thing that is meant by calling it 'historical'. 'It is through the idea of the objectification of life that we first obtain a glimpse into the essence of the historical. Everything here has arisen by mental agency, and therefore bears the character of historicity. It is woven into the sensible world itself as a product of history. From the distribution of the trees in a park, the arrangement of the houses in a street, or the purposive tool of a handicraftsman to the sentence pronounced in the law courts, we are surrounded every hour by things which have come to be in the course of history. That which the mind today imparts of its own character to its manifestations, tomorrow, if it exists, is history. As time moves on we are surrounded by Roman ruins, cathedrals, pleasure-castles of the independent princes. History is not something separate from life, severed from the present by its distance in time. . . . Everything fixed, everything alien, such as is proper to the sense-images of the physical world, must be thought away from the concept of the given in this realm. All that is given is here a product, and so historical. . . . Mind understands only what it has created. Nature, the object of natural science, embraces that reality which is produced independently of the activity (*vom Wirken*) of mind. Everything upon which man by acting (*wirkend*) has set his stamp forms the object of the human studies' (*G.S.*, VII, 147–8).

To characterise this world of expressions or objectifications of mind, Dilthey borrows Hegel's phrase, *objective mind* (*objektiver Geist*); but he is careful to add that he does not mean it in Hegel's sense. Hegel's conception, he says, in so far as it is true, has three sources. In the first place, the thinkers of the *Aufklärung*, with the Prussia of Frederick the Great before their eyes, had come to recognise that law and the state can be a moral and intellectual influence. In the second place, Hegel himself had learned the same lesson from his study of the Greeks. Thirdly, the same thing was to be learned from the new school of historical research which was growing up in his time. From one point of view, Hegel's conception of objective mind is simply his way of formulating this widely recognised truth. On the other hand, it is also given a place in his metaphysical system, where it comes to denote one stage in the dialectical process through which the Idea, as free rational will, realises itself in history and society.

With this version of it Dilthey has of course no sympathy, and he states his quarrel with Hegel under four heads.

(1) Hegel makes a metaphysical construction, Dilthey an empirical analysis.

(2) Hegel accounts for history and society in terms of a rational will. Dilthey, conscious of the evil as well as the good innate in man, 'the power of dark instinct, the suffering from darkness and illusion', replaces this rational will by the structural system and its underlying 'bundle' of instincts.

(3) Hegel, for reasons of architectonic, confines the phrase 'objective mind' to the phenomena of law, morality, and social life, and places art, religion, and philosophy under the concept of 'absolute mind'. Dilthey classes religion, art, and philosophy

under the same heading with language, custom, morality, the family, civil society, law and the state. For all these are equally products of mind, living traditions, in which the mind of man is expressed and made accessible to knowledge. 'It is just in their mighty forms that the mind objectifies itself, and is known in them.' 'In this objective mind the past, in which the great massed forces of history have taken shape, is present. The individual, as bearer and representative of the common traditions woven together in him, enjoys and comprehends the history in which they arose.'

(4) Hegel embodies his conception of objective mind in an intellectualist metaphysic which asserts that mind and nature, subject and object, are ultimately one in the universal Spirit; and in this way he circumvents the whole problem of epistemology. Dilthey, recognising in the expressions of mind the true data and basis of historical enquiry, but seeing behind them not pure reason, but the totality of life and 'the power of the irrational in it', has to face the question how these expressions' can be interpreted, and 'how historical knowledge is possible' (*G.S.*, VII, 148–52, cf. 258). That is why, instead of making a dialectical construction like Hegel's *Philosophie des Geistes*, Dilthey returns to the Kantian form and writes a *Kritik der historischen Vernunft*.

In speaking of the objectifications of mind, Dilthey has emphasised their dynamic character. They are, he says, instinct with the life from which they spring. The reality expressed in them is an active reality, a living, changing process; and that fact raises a problem which we must now face. In formulating it, and Dilthey's answer to it, we are able to amplify the published *Aufbau* by reference to fragments which were written to form part of its sequel; and the account to be gathered from the *Aufbau* and these fragments together runs as follows.

Life is activity, energy, process in time, and all its moments are fluid and transient; yet it is to be expressed in the human studies by concepts, which must be clearly defined, and self-identical irrespective of the time or context of their use. Here is a seeming incompatibility between the intellect (*Verstand*) and real life, which has been vigorously though misleadingly expressed by Hegel. To him it seemed that process cannot be conceptually expressed without violence to the principle of contradiction, and he therefore worked out, in his dialectic, a mode of thought which defies that principle.[1] Others (by whom Dilthey means Bergson) have concluded that life cannot be conceptually expressed at all, and have appealed from thought to a profound 'intuition'. Both Hegel and Bergson, however, are in error here. For, although there is contradiction in the attempt to explain (*erklären*) life, there is none in trying to conceive it. The definiteness and the timeless self-identity of the concept concern only its logical form, or *its nature and function as a concept*, and have nothing to do with its content, or *that of which it is* the concept. No concept can be suffered to *change its content* from time to time as we use it; but that does not mean that there can be no *concept of change*. And yet both Hegel and Bergson are on the track of a genuine problem. There is a real danger that, in avoiding changefulness or fluidity in our concepts, we may neglect to ensure that they are indeed concepts of change. Many of the concepts now in use in the human studies represent their objects as if they were static, and these must be remodelled if they are to do their work properly. 'At bottom, the problem is like that of the higher mathematics, which seeks to master changes in nature.' It is the business of the human studies, since their object is a ceaseless process, to develop concepts of process and activity, and no concept which does not express this should be allowed in the human studies at all (*G.S.*, VII, 280–1, 156–7).

Dilthey singles out Fichte as the first philosopher to see this, and finds here the real kernel of his system. 'When the self penetrates earnestly into itself, it finds itself not as substance, being, fact, but as life, activity, energy. And he already elaborated the dynamic concepts of the historical world' (*G.S.*, VII, 157). His work, with that of Hegel and Herbart, in combination with the romantic movement in literature, began the

---

[1] This is not fair to Hegel. Hegel's dialectic does not defy the principle of contradiction. His charge against the concepts of the abstract understanding (*Verstand*) is that they involve defying it, and that is why he seeks to transcend them. (The nature of the 'contradiction' involved in abstract concepts is not made clear, and therefore the nature of the dialectical movement of thought is not made clear either, and Hegel can make very ill-considered statements at times; but that is another story.) And he never thinks that mind is inconceivable, but only that it cannot be truly conceived in abstract or static terms.

process which has since revolutionised historical studies. But it was only a beginning. Fichte, in carrying out his intention, was overborne by the *force majeure* of Kant's theory of knowledge, and 'clung to Kant's ideas instead of to reality' (*G.S.*, VII, 280). Dilthey does not say it here, but we are not in doubt as to his opinion that the same is true of the Neo-Fichteans of the Baden school. At the same time we have seen some of the reasons why Dilthey cannot follow Hegel. He must find his own way to a solution of the problem, and the next few sections of the *Kritik* are all concerned in one fashion or another with doing this.

Dilthey goes straight to the heart of the matter. He introduces us to the concept of a *dynamic system* (*Wirkungszusammenhang*) as that which most adequately expresses the nature of historical reality. From the unit of historical life, the smallest whole which can be studied as a unity in itself, through the larger wholes which we meet as our horizon widens, up to the comprehensive whole of world history, everything that we meet is a dynamic system. This is a new term, introduced here in the *Aufbau* for the first time, and it calls for closer definition.

What is a *Wirkungszusammenhang*? Evidently, a system or complex of *Wirkungen*. What then does Dilthey mean by a *Wirkung*? Normally, he means by it the process whereby any fact or event exerts influence, or effects (*erwirkt*) results, within the structural system of life. Thus, the perception of something may lead to (*erwirken*) pleasure in it, and so to desire and action; a motive, hidden in the recesses of someone's character, may affect the whole course of his dealings with some practical problem; a doctrine preached in one country may have influence ages afterwards in another; the deposit of experience in a poet's mind may crystallise and express itself in a work which makes it the permanent possession of thousands. These, and all the other numberless processes, simple or complex, wherein one fact or event leads to (*erwirkt*) another in the structural system, are *Wirkungen*. Sometimes also Dilthey applies the term to an objective expression of mind which is produced (*erwirkt*) in such a process; thus a poem might be called a *Wirkung* because it is produced by a process in the poet's mind, or a system of laws might be called a *Wirkung* of the legislator. As a matter of fact, we have seen that whatever happens in the mind tends to find objective expression somehow; hence it follows that, wherever there is a *Wirkung* in the sense of a structural process, there is likely to be a *Wirkung* in the sense of an objective expression of mind, brought about through that process. Dilthey himself, in introducing us to the concept of a *Wirkungszusammenhang*, refers to it as 'a system which is contained (*enthalten*) in its enduring products (*Produkten*)' (*G.S.*, VII, 153).

It is thus clear that a *Wirkung*, in Dilthey's sense, is either a causal process or the effect of such a process, and to call the historical object a *Wirkungszusammenhang* is to call it a causal system. Why then *Wirkungszusammenhang*, and not simply *Kausalzusammenhang*? Because Dilthey wishes to remind us that historical causality differs specifically from the mechanical causality which rules in nature. Its distinctive character lies first and foremost in its immanent teleology, by virtue of which it generates values and fulfils ends. 'This it does not casually, not here and there, but it is the very structure of mind, in its dynamic system, on the basis of cognition, to generate values and to realise ends. . . . Historical life creates. It is continually active in the generation of goods and values.' This process goes on in every individual; every individual is a dynamic system on a small scale, and, by virtue of the structure which binds together the cognitive, affective, and volitional elements in his life, he is a mental unity (*geistige Einheit*) whose unifying principle or centre is in himself. But individuals are not the only channels through which the creative process works. The individual is the point of intersection of various cultural systems, and a member of various societies, each of which is a 'permanent vehicle of activity', and has within itself 'communal goods, and rules to regulate their realisation'. And in these too we find a structural unity, comparable with that which we find in an individual. 'Like the individual, every cultural system and every society has a centre in itself. The apprehension of reality, in them, is bound up into a whole with valuation and the generation of goods' (*G.S.*, VII, 153–4).

Individuals, cultural systems, and societies live in constant interaction, and draw life and inspiration from one another. But there are wider and more complex dynamic systems, built up out of these, which are more self-contained. One such dynamic system is the nation; for a nation, unlike an individual or a cultural system, can live secluded from the outer world, 'self-centred' in a different sense of the word, shut up within its own limited horizon. Still greater is the self-centredness of historical periods (*Zeitalter, historische Perioden*) which occur in the life of a whole group of nations, e.g. the period in European history which is known as the Middle Age. Such a period is marked out by common characteristics, which pervade all the branches of social and individual life at the time.

They come out at once in the art of the period, in its religion, its philosophy, its economic and political system. Even the relics of earlier times which survive in it, as e.g. ancient philosophy lives on into the Middle Age, are assimilated to and bear the impress of the period (*G.S.*, VII, 154-5).

'The historical world as a whole, this whole as a dynamic system, this dynamic system as value-giving, end-proposing, in short, creating, and then the understanding of this whole in terms of itself, and finally the centring of values and ends in periods, epochs, and in world history—these are the points of view from which we must conceive the systematic unity of the human studies, towards which we must strive' (*G.S.*, VII, 155).

This, then, is the concept which is to dominate the human studies. The historical world is a whole composed of lesser wholes, a dynamic system whose parts are also dynamic systems, and the human studies are all to be conceived as singling out particular dynamic systems within the all-embracing whole for closer study. We can thus single out individuals, ourselves or others; or we can fix upon some historical process, e.g. the change in German literature from the *Aufklärung* period to what followed, and analyse the factors contributing to it; or we can start with one of the objectifications of mind, 'works which, set loose from their creator, bear their own life and law in themselves', and proceed to understand it and the sources from which it came (*G.S.*, VII, 156-8).

In all cases the human studies have the advantage over the natural sciences that they know the nature of the dynamic system they are dealing with. On the other hand, Dilthey shows, by the same reasons as in the essay of 1875 and in the *Einleitung*, that the limits within which we can discover universal laws must be very narrow, and the importance of the comparative method correspondingly wider than in natural science. We cannot measure accurately as we can there; nor can we separate out from the historical complex units which are really simple and homogeneous. In the human studies the description of individuals takes the place held in natural science by the discovery of laws of nature; the human studies 'have a predominantly descriptive and analytical character'. This clearly applies no less to psychology than to the special human studies; here Dilthey reaffirms what he said in the *Ideen* of 1894 (*G.S.*, VII, 159–60).

Up to this point in the *Aufbau*, Dilthey has discussed the methods and categories of the human studies only in general terms, not distinguishing or trying to mark off one human study from another. From this point to the end of the *Aufbau*, he proceeds to a particular examination of those among the human studies which analyse the dynamic system of history, leaving out those which concern the individual. I shall not here follow this discussion, because it anticipates matters which properly belong not to the *Aufbau* at all, but to its sequel; I shall pass, instead, to a consideration of the sequel itself. Although this was never completed for publication, the materials collected by Dilthey for the purpose are very copious, and enable us to restore the argument with considerable confidence, even in detail. It was to be in two parts, of which the first was to analyse in detail the methods and categories employed in our knowledge of individual minds and their expressions, while the second was to show what further elements enter in when from the individual we pass to a study of the group and of the historical process. The first part incorporates the two essays, *Das Erlebnis u. die Selbstbiographie* and *Das Verstehen anderer Personen u. ihrer Lebensäusserungen*, mentioned in the previous chapter, and it is to *Das Erlebnis u. die Selbstbiographie* that we now turn.

The essay opens by describing the 'stream' of life in its 'restless' movement from past to future, one experience following another in unbroken continuity, each experience no sooner come than gone. This form of continuous change Dilthey calls *temporality* (*Zeitlichkeit*), the first category of life, upon which all the rest depend (*G.S.*, VII, 192–3).

Within the temporal process, the form of consciousness is the same at every moment. In its centre is the conscious present, the *Lebensfülle*, or *Erfüllung mit Realität*, of immediate experience, and behind it stretches memory, its images dimming slowly as we go further back, until they are lost in darkness; if we turn to the future, we have a prospect of probable future feelings, external happenings, ends to be pursued and means to be taken, which becomes richer in its possibilities, so making it harder to predict, the further on we go. 'When we look back at the past, we are in a passive attitude; the past is the unalterable; man, determined by it, batters against it in vain by dreams of how it might have been otherwise. When we face the future, we find ourselves active, free. Here, beside the category of *reality* (*Wirklichkeit*) which the present reveals to us, arises that of *possibility* (*Möglichkeit*). We feel ourselves in possession of endless possibilities. So this experience of time determines in all directions the content (*Gehalt*) of our life' (*G.S.*, VII, 193–4).

Again, the process of life consists of experiences which are related to one another in various ways. 'Each particular experience is referred to a self of which it is a part; by virtue of structure it is bound up with other parts into a system. In all that is mental we find system; thus *system* (*Zusammenhang*) is a category which arises out of life.' And this is only a special case of a wider category, viz. *whole and part* (*G.S.*, VII, 195). Here, of course, is an ambiguity. *Whole and part* in the strict sense is reckoned by Dilthey among the 'formal categories' which are common to all objects of thought, because they represent that in the object which makes apprehension of it possible at all; we cannot apprehend without dividing and combining, and any object of apprehension must give scope for division and combination, i.e. must be a whole consisting of parts. But the actual relation between the whole and its parts, the way in which they combine to form the whole, is different in inorganic nature, in organic nature, and in the world of mind, and *whole and part* becomes a category for the human studies by coming to mean that relation, between parts within a whole, which is peculiar to the mental system, viz. structurality (*G.S.*, VII, 197).

In a similar way Dilthey takes the category of *force* (*Kraft*), and shows how it means something different in the human studies from what it means in natural science. In the human studies, force means the influence which any experience has in determining what other experiences shall succeed it. A memory is a force in so far as it affects our present experiences and actions. All the factors which together lead up to a practical decision are forces, and the decision itself is a force in so far as it leads to action. This category, so conceived, is an expression of something which we know in our own lives. In natural science it is different. There it is not drawn from experience of the physical world, but projected into it from our inner life; and it is bound up with the idea of laws of nature and physical necessity, to which the human studies offer no parallel (*G.S.*, VII, 202–3).

If a human being looks back upon his previous life, he finds it to be a structural unity to whose total character every past experience has contributed something. If he goes further and seeks to understand (*verstehen*) or interpret (*deuten*) it, to explore in detail the character of the whole and the contributions made by its various parts, he will find himself using fresh categories; the contribution to the whole made by any part is the *meaning*[1] (*Bedeutung*) of that part, and the resultant character of the whole is its *meaning* (*Bedeutung*) or *sense* (*Sinn*). To show how these categories apply, Dilthey appeals to three notable autobiographies, viz. those of St. Augustine, of Rousseau, and of Goethe, and finds that in each instance the categories of *value* (*Wert*) and *end* (*Zweck*) or *good* (*Gut*) also enter in, but that the relations between these categories and that of meaning may vary. (1) For St. Augustine, the meaning of life lies in the relation between the soul and God. The centre of his own life is his conversion; all previous events lead up to that as their end, and nothing has value except in relation to it. (2) Rousseau was a man out of harmony with his social surroundings, who wrote in order to vindicate his right to be himself. He did so by showing that the meaning of his life lay in the embodiment of a certain value or ideal (that of the sensitive, sympathetic soul) which was in fact the ideal recognized by his contemporaries. (3) Goethe sees his own life as a historical *development* (*Entwicklung*) or *crystallisation* (*Gestaltung*), and every event in it has a twofold meaning: as a value in itself for the experience of the moment, and also as a force in the development of the future (*G.S.*, VII, 198–9).

Dilthey goes on to correlate meaning, value, and end with the three structural attitudes of consciousness and the three determinations of time. The category of meaning arises in memory,

[1] Or *significance* (*Bedeutsamkeit*): see above, p. 143 n.

272

i.e. in cognition of the past; that of value arises from feeling, i.e. the affective enjoyment of the present; that of end arises from volition, which refers to the future. Therefore the three categories, like the three structural attitudes, are irreducible, and cannot be subordinated to one another. But they are not all equally useful as principles of understanding and interpretation. (1) Value, properly speaking, can only belong to an experience in a conscious present. Now, the conscious presents of which life consists have, purely as present moments, no inner connection; they stand one behind another in temporal sequence, comparable indeed as values with one another, but forming, as momentary values, no coherent whole. 'From the standpoint of value, life appears as an infinite assortment of positive and negative existence-values. It is like a chaos of harmonies and discords. Each of these is a tone-structure which fills a present; but they have no musical relation to one another.' (2) The category of end or good depends upon that of value, and shares its limitations; it can show life as a series of choices between ends, but finds no unity in this sequence of choices. (3) Only the category of meaning enables us to conceive an intrinsic affinity between the successive events in life, and all that the categories of value and end can tell us is caught up into this synthesis. Moreover, since meaning is specifically based on the cognitive attitude of memory, and 'history is memory', meaning is naturally 'the category most proper to historical thought' (*G.S.*, VII, 201–2, 236).

But meaning is not merely the principal category under which historical knowledge apprehends its object; the structural relations which constitute the meaning of our lives are also the psychological conditions which make it possible for us to know that meaning. Every experience has structural connections with past experiences which have led up to it, and with future possibilities which it tends to bring about, and it is these connections which constitute its meaning. But the structural relations which constitute the meaning of the experience also condition the reflective process (*sc. das Fortgezogenwerden*) whereby this meaning is revealed.

In the first place, they guide the operations of silent thought, which clarify the present experience and bring into apperception the relations between its elements. 'Of what is embraced in my intuition (this word being taken in the widest sense) a part is raised by virtue of significance into the centre of attention, is apperceived' (*G.S.*, VII, 230).

Then, when memory comes into play, the events which I shall remember are selected, and their meaning for my reflective consciousness assigned, in the last resort by the interpretation (*Deutung*) which I now put upon my life. 'It is through my present view of life that every part of it which is significant receives, in the light of this view, the form in which it is today apprehended by me. It receives from it its relation to other significant parts; it belongs to a system determined by the relations between the significant moments of life and my present interpretation (*Deutung*) of it.' This interpretation in turn is determined by the same past experiences whose significance it reveals, indeed they are significant just because they have affected my present interpretation of life. 'These meaning-relations constitute the present experience and pervade it' (*G.S.*, VII, 74). Thus in memory too the meaning of life informs the apprehension of itself; the object to be apprehended enters into and determines the apprehending subject, and memory-representations derive hence a security which makes them the basis of all historical understanding.

From memory and retrospect we advance to deliberate reflection (*Besinnung*) on the meaning of our own lives. 'Both our fortunes and our own nature cause us pain, and so they force us to come to terms with them through understanding. The past mysteriously invites us to know the closely-woven meaning of its moments' (*loc. cit.*). This kind of reflection clothes itself in various forms, 'it is present in the verses of Solon as well as in the self-examinations of the Stoic philosophers, in the meditations of the saints, in the philosophy of life (*Lebensphilosophie*) of modern times', but it finds its highest development in autobiography. Here again the same dual relation holds good; the object is identical with the subject and conditions the apprehension of itself. For the autobiographer has himself already lived the life which he now portrays, and in living it he has reflected upon its meaning. He has singled out its significant moments; what was erroneous in his judgment upon it has been corrected by experience; and there is now stored up in his memory a system of ideas through which his life has already interpreted itself.

His autobiography is merely a detailed literary presentment of this system, and the system itself, through the relation of 'presentness', determines the form in which he presents it. Therefore 'autobiography is the highest and most instructive form in which the understanding of life comes before us' (*G.S.*, VII, 199–200).

From autobiography to history is a short step. For, in the first place, that reflective self-analysis which finds expression in autobiography is also our road to the understanding of other persons. 'The power and breadth of our own life, and the energy of reflection upon it, is the foundation of historical vision. It alone enables us to give a second life to the bloodless shades of the past' (*G.S.*, VII, 201). Moreover, the expression of this reflection in autobiography may pass insensibly into 'a historical picture'; for in it the self is apprehended in relation to the society in which he has moved, and the story of his life may broaden out into the story of that society as seen from his point of view. The historical account so given has the privilege of being based upon the writer's own experience, and 'draws its understanding of the self and its relations with the world from that depth' (*G.S.*, VII, 204). On the other hand, of course, it is subject to a danger of one-sidedness, which is only to be overcome if the author amplifies his own experience by that of other persons.

This points naturally to our next task, viz. an analysis of the processes and methods involved in the understanding of other persons; and such an analysis will serve to confirm the conclusions to which our account of lived experience and autobiography has already led. The categories gained by reflection upon our own individual lives will be seen to be of universal application when they are rediscovered in the understanding of other lives; their claim to be categories generally valid throughout the human studies rests upon the fact that they have 'objective mind for their background and the apprehension of other persons as their constant correlate' (*G.S.*, VII, 203–4).

So we pass to the essay on *Das Verstehen anderer Personen u. ihrer Lebensäusserungen*. The description of the process of understanding and the sketch of a hermeneutic theory, which form the main contents of this essay, were set forth and discussed in Chapter Five above. Our present object must rather be to see the essay in terms of its position in the *Kritik der historischen Vernunft*.

It is meant as a contribution to epistemology which shall avoid the formalism of Neo-Kantian logic, yet without ceasing to face the epistemological problem or falling back upon bare psychology. 'It is a question not of logical construction or psychological analysis, but of analysis with an eye to the theory of knowledge. The contribution made by the understanding of others to historical knowledge is to be assessed' (*G.S.*, VII, 205).

The obvious and native function of understanding is that it opens to us the world of individual persons and their creations. 'Understanding has always an individual for its object.' And, since the individual is a value in himself (*Selbstwert*), we have an interest in him for his own sake, independently of all practical concerns. 'The secret of the person entices us for its own sake to ever new and deeper attempts to understand.' Further, since all understanding of men moves from the common elements in them to their individual peculiarities, we may be said in understanding to relive (*durchleben*) the very process whereby the common nature of man develops its individuality. In the understanding of men and of works of literature we apprehend together the two determining factors which give the individual his peculiar character: the inner balance and proportion between his various abilities and tendencies, which constitute his temperamental endowment, and the force of outer circumstances to which he, being inwardly what he is, can only respond in the way he actually does. Such understanding Dilthey calls an 'access to the greatest mystery of life' (*G.S.*, VII, 212–13).

The second function of understanding is that it opens to us possibilities in our own nature, of which we could otherwise never become aware. Every man knows that the crystallisation (*Gestaltung*) of his character and outlook, under the combined pressure of outer circumstances and of his own acquired system, gradually restricts his development (*Entwicklung*) to fewer and fewer possibilities; but 'understanding opens to him a wide realm of possibilities which are not forthcoming in the determination of his actual life'. This is commonly recognised as one of the virtues of art, but Dilthey insists that it constitutes a great part of the value of history too. He instances himself. 'The possibility of experiencing (*zu erleben*) religious states in my own existence is for me, as for most men to-day, strictly limited. But when I run through the letters and writings of Luther, the

reports of his contemporaries, the records of the religious con-
ferences and councils and of his official activities, I experience
a religious process of such eruptive power, of such energy, in
which life and death are at stake, that it lies beyond all possibility of being actually lived through by a man of our day. But
I can re-live it. . . . And so this process opens to us a religious
world in him and in his contemporaries of early Reformation
times, which broadens our horizon to include possibilities of
human life which only so become accessible to us. . . . Man,
bound and determined by the reality of life, is set free not only
through art—as has often been set forth—but also through the
understanding of history. And this effect of history, which its
most modern detractors have not seen, is broadened and
deepened in the further stages of the historical consciousness'
(*G.S.*, VII, 215–16, cf. 252, 259).

After the essay on *Das Verstehen anderer Personen u. ihrer Lebensäusserungen* was to come a section entitled *Die Kategorien des
Lebens*, in which the categories already discovered through autobiography were to be further characterised, analysed, and amplified. Dilthey left plenty of material for this section, but in such
disorder as even his editor has not been able wholly to overcome. On the other hand, it is of considerable interest as a
detailed account of the kind of system which he supposes human
minds in history and society to constitute. Throughout the
greater part of his life, his analysis hardly went beyond the
conception of the structural system, which was derived from an
analysis of the individual mind, and was meant to embrace
what is regular in and common to all such minds. This was
hardly enough even for a psychology, and was quite inadequate
as an account of the fundamental conceptions of historical and
social study. To begin with, it is itself a complex conception,
and should be analysed into its various aspects. On the other
hand, when several individuals act upon one another, singly or
in a group, accidentally or deliberately, a more complex type
of relation must be set up than is found in the individual mind
by itself, and for this the concept of the structural system will be
too narrow. For these reasons, a fuller treatment of the problem
of categories was obviously called for, and in this section of his
work Dilthey tries to give it. We must, however, remember
that his discussion is unsystematic, not merely because his

material was never finally worked up for publication, but because of the very nature of the subject. If Dilthey derived his categories from pure reason, like many philosophers who have dealt with historical questions, they would of course fall into a clear-cut and logically coherent group. But he derives them empirically, from actual experience, and therefore they can neither be rigidly defined, nor do they form a closed logical system. 'We can neither delimit a precise number of categories, nor bring their mutual relations into a definitive order' (*G.S.*, VII, 302, cf. 232).

We need not dwell on all the categories in his list. As in the previous discussion, he takes occasion to point to the difference between certain historical categories and their homonyms in the natural sciences; he treats *whole and part* from this point of view, and also *interaction*. He also re-emphasises the fluid, changing, active character of lived experience, and says that, to understand it fully, we must see it through an expression which itself is a process in time, such as instrumental music. 'There is a direction (*Richtung*), an action reaching out to a realisation, an onward movement of mental activity itself, a being conditioned by the past while yet containing various possibilities, an explication which is also creation' (*G.S.*, VII, 231–2). This conception of life as a free creative development is worked out further in a fairly long fragment entitled *Das musikalische Verstehen* (*G.S.*, VII, 220–4).

The only category on which we need dwell at length is that of *meaning*, and even here we shall not consider all that Dilthey says in this section of the *Kritik*. This section is, in fact, one of the chief sources for his use of the word, and was heavily drawn upon in our examination of the idea of meaning in Chapter Five. Here we shall consider only those points in his discussion of it which fit into the scheme of the *Kritik*, and help to carry on the argument from the analysis of understanding to the aims and methods of biographical and historical study.

The category of meaning is, says Dilthey, all-pervading in history, and is used in the most various applications. 'The story-teller gains his effect by bringing out the significant moments in a process. The historian characterises men as significant, turning-points in life (*Lebenswendungen*) as full of meaning; in a definite effect of a work or a human being upon the general

278

destiny he recognises the meaning of such a work or such a human being' (*G.S.*, VII, 234). Meaning is the only category which grasps the full relation of the part to the whole in life. In the category of value, or again in that of good or end, some aspect of this relation is of course made visible; but these categories are, as we saw above, always abstract and one-sided, and we cannot think in terms of them without finally meeting some brute fact, some empirical coexistence of experiences, which these categories do not help us to resolve into a living whole. Then we must call in the comprehensive category of meaning, and the whole becomes intelligible, of which value and end were but aspects (*G.S.*, VII, 236).

Our awareness of meaning we owe primarily to memory, in which the individual can overlook the whole course of his past life and so apprehend the elements in their relation to the whole (*G.S.*, VII, 233). After this comes history, which performs the same function for the race as memory does for the individual. In either case we apprehend meaning by looking back over a process in time, and assess the meaning of every part of the process by its contribution to the total result. It follows, as Dilthey points out, that the meaning of the actions of an individual human being can be assessed from at least two points of view, viz. as contributing to the inner worth of his own life, regarded as a value in itself, or as affecting the wider issues of social history. Thus Luther's life may be taken as a self-enclosed whole with a meaning inherent in itself. That is how it would appear to Luther himself, by virtue of his subjective 'feeling of life'. Or it may be given its meaning as a stage in the process which led to a revolution in the religious life of Europe, which in turn has its meaning in reference to the wider system of history in general (*G.S.*, VII, 237). In neither case, however, can the meaning of any factor in a process be assessed until the whole process is past. Thus the meaning of a man's life, and of each moment in it, becomes visible to others only when his life is ended, and to himself only in the very hour of death. Likewise the meaning of processes in world history is not and will not be known until the end of history itself (*G.S.*, VII, 233, 237). We do, of course, in the meantime often make judgments about the meaning of events, but every such judgment is provisional, and relative to the moment at which it is made. At every moment the meaning of the past is judged by reference to the present; this judgment upon the past determines our plans for the future, and these in turn react upon our view of the meaning of the past. In this way our apprehension of the meaning of life is always relative, and involved in perpetual change (*G.S.*, VII, 233).

Of the subordinate categories derived from that of meaning, Dilthey says little, but that little is interesting. He begins with the category of *crystallisation* (*Gestaltung*), which refers to the process whereby, within the structural system of the individual life, a deposit of acquired experience is gradually built up, which constitutes the determinate individuality or *nature* (*Wesen*) of that life. The individual is at first in possession of innumerable possibilities between which he is free to choose; but as his acquired experience grows, and his nature assumes a more definite shape (*Gestalt*), he finds the range of possibilities slowly narrowing. A complex of acquired ideas determines what further ideas he can take in, acquired attitudes affect his power of responding to new situations. It is this circumstance which gives to his life its continuity and personal identity; but it shows itself also as a limitation upon him, which he constantly struggles to overcome, and in this reaction against his limitations arises his will to inner freedom. Usually this struggle is so far successful that, as circumstances change, the individual can adjust himself to them in part, and in part ignore them; and this very fact, that circumstances change and his own responses change with them, strengthens his will to inner freedom, by which he may stand independent over against what is transient in the world and in himself. Sometimes the pressure of new circumstances is too hard, the subject cannot readjust itself, and his life comes to a standstill. This struggle with inner limitations is what Dilthey calls the 'tragedy of finitude', and when circumstances grow so hard that the subject cannot face them, but by virtue of his inner limitation is overcome and suffers catastrophe, there we have the tragic fate. On the other hand, the readjustment to new circumstances, the free choice and realisation of possibilities not prescribed by the determined nature of the subject, is represented by the category of *development* (*Entwicklung*). This is the only sense in which we can speak of development in the human studies. We cannot accept any theory of a progress, whether in individual lives or in history at large, which marches

280

forward from stage to stage in pursuit of some definite end. Such an end would transcend experience, and the appeal to it would therefore be open to challenge. But we can say that life tends, on the whole, to an increasing clarification of issues and differentiation of character and achievement in the very various spheres of human endeavour. Yet there are some who are content to vegetate through life, and others who actually degenerate (*G.S.*, VII, 232–3, 244–5, cf. 253).

Dilthey adds some remarks on the category of *value*, but they include nothing which has not already been dealt with above.

The next section of the *Kritik* is entitled *Die Biographie*, and contains a discussion of the question 'whether biography, as a universally valid solution of a scientific problem, is possible'. Dilthey conceives biography as an indispensable element in historical research. For the business of the historian is to trace the dynamic system of history and society, and this he does by breaking it up into particular systems and studying these separately. Now, the fundamental particular system is that constituted by the individual life, with the influences which it receives from its environment and those which it in turn exerts upon the surrounding world. It is in the individual life, as we have seen, that memory discovers and autobiography expresses the categories of human life, and the passage from autobiography to the biography of others is easy and natural. Various interests may determine our choice of a subject for biography. 'The family preserves its reminiscences. Criminal justice and its theories may preserve the life of an offender, psychopathology that of an abnormal man.' But the men who most invite biographical study are those who have had a lasting influence, and among these, again, we are most interested in those whose influence springs from some apparently unfathomable depth of character and spiritual endowment. For here the depths of human nature and the broad range of historical interactions are seen together in a comprehensive glance. Dilthey asks whether biography, dealing with such a subject, can lead to universally valid results (*G.S.*, VII, 246–7).

Biography may be regarded both as a contribution to knowledge and as a work of art. As a contribution to knowledge, it is only possible because the innumerable influences to which the individual is subject, the innumerable historical and social forces with which he has to reckon, are not in their nature infinitely various. They fall easily under a few headings, corresponding to the cultural systems and the social organisations of which the individual is a member. Is he notable for his influence in religion? Then his outlook will be found to be affected, and his chances of exerting influence determined, by the situation within that particular cultural system in his day. So too with the man who is influential in some other department of life. But there are men, such as Schleiermacher, whose influence is felt in so many spheres that their biography seems to fall apart into fragments. How are we to deal with them? We shall find, on a closer approach, that there is really one fundamental element in their outlook and character, which has shown itself in diverse ways, and the recognition of this will reveal the inner unity of their life. Thus the unity in Schleiermacher's case lies in the combination of an intense inner life and great clarity of understanding with an equally great capacity for practical affairs, a combination made possible in the last resort by his peculiar religious outlook. By this single thread all his scattered activities 'in religion, philosophy, criticism, reinterpretation of Plato and of the Apostle Paul, in Church and State', are held together (*G.S.*, VII, 248).

For biography, regarded as a work of art, the problem is less simple. The writer has to make visible the meaning of the life which he records. He has the advantage of dealing with a life which is already ended, and in so far he is better off than the autobiographer. He can obtain from letters and other documents the view which his subject took from moment to moment of the meaning of his own past life, together with the values which he enjoyed and the plans which he formed; while he also knows what came of all this, how his hero was misled as to his own powers or the circumstances with which he had to deal, where his limitations lay, and where he was influential. But this is just the difficulty. The biographer has to regard his subject from two points of view, viz. from within, in so far as he tries to interpret the inner consciousness of the agent, and from without, in so far as he sees the agent in relation to his social and historical environment. The first standpoint is akin to that of autobiography, in that the individual subject is the standard by reference to which all meaning is to be assessed; the second is

282

akin to that of history, in that the individual is to be seen and judged as a factor in a wider system, the history of his own time. The literary unity of the biography, therefore, can only be saved if a point of view can be found which embraces a wide social and historical dynamic system, and yet leaves the individual in a central position. This, again, can only be done if the subject of the biography is a person of real historical importance, who really does stand near the centre of a particular dynamic system; and even then he is never quite at the centre, and the literary problem is never wholly solved.

The truth is that biography tries to combine two different kinds of knowledge, viz. knowledge of the individual, and knowledge of the universal movements which affect and are affected by him. These latter cannot really be understood by the same methods or in the same categories as the individual life, and the study of them belongs to a different group among the human studies. Biography, therefore, in combining both kinds of procedure in one enquiry, straddles across a methodological division and is a logical hybrid. 'Biography by itself has not the possibility of taking shape as a scientific work of art. There are new categories, types, and forms of life, to which we must turn, and which cannot be found in the individual life itself. The individual is only the point of intersection for cultural systems, organisations, in which his existence is embedded: how could they be understood in terms of him?' (*G.S.*, VII, 248–51).

Thus the portrayal of the individual life, both in autobiography and in biography, has been found to lead beyond itself to the portrayal of social groups and institutions. We shall have very soon to turn and examine how our 'knowledge of the system of world history' is built up. Before we do this, however, we must round off our account of the studies which deal with the individual, by considering 'the theory of the individual life' (*die Theorie der Einzelexistenz*). This consists of two closely related parts viz. 'I. The doctrine of structure and descriptive psychology. II. Anthropological reflection' (*G.S.*, VII, 365–6).

The 'doctrine of structure and descriptive psychology' is the same as the 'anthropology' or 'content-psychology' or 'concrete psychology' which, as we have seen in Chapter Seven, Dilthey distinguishes sharply from experimental psychology, or 'the science of psychology in the proper sense', and regards as the heir of his projects in the *Ideen*. All that need be said about this was said in Chapter Seven. 'Anthropological reflection', on the other hand, presents an old feature of his teaching in a new way. He means by it that extensive literature of introspection and observation of life, which Dilthey always recognised as providing much of the material for 'anthropology' or 'descriptive psychology' to systematise (above, pp. 201–2). In it we find empirical studies of human nature, especially of 'the passions', together with generalisations about values, advice about ends to be pursued, and pronouncements on the meaning of life. All this material, finding expression in various literary forms, comes ultimately to constitute a great body of traditional floating wisdom, which may be regarded as the primary utterance of life about itself, and the source from which all the more elaborate forms of expression in art, history, or philosophy draw their material. The truths of anthropological reflection 'form a peculiar stratum lying between life itself, on the one side, and art and the record of world history on the other. It is a literature of almost boundless extent' (*G.S.*, VII, 239–40).[1]

It will be remembered that, in the essay of 1894, descriptive psychology was exalted above art as a higher mode of portrayal, in which the scattered wisdom of the poets and sages was systematised and made scientific. The changes in Dilthey's view of psychology since then have obviously had their effect, and in the *Kritik* this relation is reversed. Thus, in another passage on the same theme, Dilthey speaks first of anthropological reflection, and then goes on to speak of poetry as a vehicle by which the meaning of life comes to yet more vivid and adequate expression. The poet perceives events not abstractly, but in their full rich relation to life, and in this relation he sees their significance. What he thus learns from experience, he expresses in imaginative constructions which symbolise the meaning (*Sinn*) of life. His work is always based upon some actual experience; but it 'gives shape to the event by raising its parts in imagination to signifi-

[1] We may ask, what about 'the science of psychology in the proper sense'? Ought it not also to come in here? The fact is that Dilthey says nothing about it, except to distinguish it from 'anthropology'. Dilthey never adopts the Neo-Kantian view that it belongs with the natural sciences. When he mentions it at all, he always treats it as one of the human studies. But in his latest writings he loses interest in it, and in the final plans for his *Kritik* he simply passes it by.

cance according to its [i e. poetry's] distinctive character of free formation'. He can give new life to the dim past, and freshness to the forgotten or the commonplace. 'By his power of reliving experience, the poet restores the relation to life, which has retired into the background in the course of intellectual development and practical interest.' The weakness of poetry lies, however, in its lack of *methodical* understanding, its dependence upon inspiration, and the fragmentary character of its revelations. So we are led on to historiography, where we find ample material, a systematic method, and a claim of factual as well as symbolic truth (*G.S.*, VII, 240–1).

This brings us to the second part of the sequel to the *Aufbau*. The same procedure of methodological and categorial analysis, applied above to our knowledge of the individual life, is now to be turned upon those branches of enquiry whose object is history and society at large. Our materials for this part of the work are scantier and more fragmentary than for the preceding part. There are two plans, both drawn up by Dilthey, and both late, though it is not known which is the later. One, which I shall call Plan A, is a list of seventeen section-headings, with here and there a short paragraph sketching the theme of a section; into this cadre the editor of *G.S.* VII has inserted a large number of MS. fragments which seem to have some bearing upon the headings, but the reader of *G.S.* VII must remember that hardly any of these MSS. were so placed by Dilthey himself. The other plan, which I shall call Plan B, has fewer headings, but much more matter in it, and is very useful on the wider issues of the *Grundlegung*. Different as these two plans are, they are easily combined. Moreover, the published *Aufbau* contains much matter which deals with methodology, and which, in a final revision, would certainly have been brought down to fill the empty cadres of Plan A. The exposition here following is therefore based upon the two plans A and B, together with the unattached fragments which seem relevant, and with such parts of the *Aufbau* as would finally have been woven into these later sections of the *Grundlegung*.

It will be convenient to begin with a number of passages in which Dilthey examines the procedure of the historian, not asking what the historian ought to do, but rather what, on an empirical examination, he is actually found to do.

His first point is that historical enquiry is impossible without some deliberate selection of materials. The historian does not try to describe everything which has happened since the beginning of recorded time; he picks up the stream of events at a certain point, and proceeds from there to deal with a limited range of facts. But his choice of starting-point and the limits of his enquiry are not arbitrary. The object itself includes 'a principle of selection', which the historian must detect and apply; he must learn to regard things from the appropriate standpoint, and acquire 'a definite way of seeing'. What is this principle of selection? The events of history fall naturally apart into groups, forming relatively self-contained processes, or dynamic systems; the essence of such a dynamic system is that, in it, many forces of various sorts combine, strengthen, and modify each other's influence, and produce as their common effect some notable historical change, such as the Reformation, the French Revolution, the decline and fall of Rome, or, on a small scale, e.g. the liberation of the Netherlands. The historian singles out such a dynamic system, and so describes it as to make visible all the forces contributing to the total effect (*G.S.*, VII, 165).

Now, it is clear that the wholeness of such a dynamic system depends primarily upon the unity of the result effected in it; a certain number of events are regarded as constituting a total effect, and then they and their causes are taken together as forming a particular dynamic system. But why, we may ask, in any given case, do we select just the events we do select? What inner unity have they that they, and no more or less, should count as a total effect? Dilthey's answer is simple. Their unity lies in some single social end which is striven after, and perhaps attained, in some single social value which is in a degree realised, or it may be destroyed, in them. And as, in the individual life, the relations between ends and values, and the way in which particular events are subordinated to their realisation, constitute the meaning of that life and of events in it, so too in the historical process. Every dynamic system is a meaning-system (*Bedeutungszusammenhang*), and it is so that the historian must regard it.

But, further, the pursuit of values and ends by society is really the pursuit of them by individuals acting in concert. Every meaning-system is built up of individuals, the same individuals who are the object of biographical study. But history sets them in a new light. For biography, the individual is the centre of his world, a value in himself, and all meaning-relations are determined by reference to this value. But such a view is one-sided; the individual can no more live by and for himself than the atom can function in isolation from its molecule and the body of which it is a part. From the standpoint of history, this one-sidedness falls away. It is the community which is the vehicle of value, it is in historical processes that ends are realised, and the individual, instead of being a centre of meaning, is seen to derive his own meaning from his place in the historical and social process into which he is caught up (*G.S.*, VII, 257–8).

Dilthey defines, in two short passages, the point of view from which the historian is interested in such meaning-systems. The historian's fundamental interest is the same as that of the psychologist or anthropologist, viz. an interest in human nature; but his peculiar method is to study it in its various concrete manifestations, of which historiography is the record and interpretation. His data, however, are always too few to be a complete manifestation of human nature. Infinite possibilities are implicit in the structural system, but all that history presents to us are those possibilities which the outward circumstances of men's lives permit or compel them to work out. 'The individual man never realises more than a possibility of his development, which from the stations of his will could always have taken a different direction. Man in general exists for us only under the condition of realised possibilities.' But our object in historical enquiry is to discover man himself, the whole of his nature, the fullness of his capabilities; and if he never realises more than one of several possibilities, we wish at least to see in the background the possibilities which were not realised, and the circumstances which forbade their realisation. 'The point at issue is to seek out the mind itself, how it is always, under the conditions of a present and a space, tied to definite possibilities—one case, as it were, among the limitless possibilities which the historical process brings forth' (*G.S.*, VII, 279, 254).

It is at this point that Dilthey raises the issue of historical scepticism. I have summarised his treatment of the question in Chapter Five (pp. 155–8), and need not here do more than remind the reader of the points which were found to be at issue.

287

The kind of scepticism which alleges that we cannot recover even the outwardly visible course of past events, on the ground that the sources are radically untrustworthy, needs no serious answer, and Dilthey does not linger over it. The really dangerous kind of scepticism is that which admits our knowledge of the external events, but denies that we can know what was in the minds of the agents. As I have shown, Dilthey's reply to this depends upon a distinction between two senses in which we might be said to know what was in their minds. In the one sense, which is that of the 'pragmatic' method in historiography, the sceptic is right; we cannot know, in most instances, the personal motives, the prejudices and caprices, which affected the decisions of the historical agents. But Dilthey finds another sense in which the sceptic is wrong. All historical action falls within the ambit of one or more of the various cultural systems and organised institutions of society, and the ultimately decisive factors in shaping it are to be sought, according to Dilthey, in the relation of the agent to these systems and the condition in which he finds them. Traditional ideals and methods determine his volition, the existing state of the social and cultural order dictates what he cannot, or can, or must do; and in the last analysis we shall find in his action not merely the response of an individual to stimuli affecting him personally, but also and chiefly the activity of one who is a conscious member of a social and cultural complex far greater than himself, and allows, because he must allow, that great system to work out its own ends in and through him. And thus his mind is open to our investigation, sc. the possibilities which the historical situation offers and even presses upon him, and those which it closes to him; they are clearly visible, from the moment that we consider him not as a mere individual, but in relation to the cultural systems and social organisations.

Historical knowledge, therefore, as Dilthey conceives it, is a description of the way in which the human mind realises its inherent possibilities, in time, through a process whose vehicle is society. Such knowledge is attainable, but only because, in our study of the narratives and other evidence, we can also draw upon those more abstract studies which analyse the specific character of the cultural systems and social organisations; for it is in these systems and organisations that those laws operate, by which the realisation of human possibilities is conditioned. We are dealing all the time with dynamic systems which transcend the individual, and at the same time condition all his activities; and these 'transpersonal' systems persist and develop through time and change, they work for the fulfilment of purposes, and are the real vehicles of cultural values. The historian is forced to speak of them as if they were personal agents, and ascribe to them many of the effects which he studies. He applies to them the categories which we have found applicable to the individual mind, treating them as forces, finding in them a meaning, and so on. And so the critical question arises: what right have we to transfer our categories to these transpersonal subjects? Must they not undergo modification when so applied? Is meaning, for instance, in the history of a nation quite the same as meaning in the individual life? And in what sense can the nation be regarded as a single agent at all? 'The question now arises, how can a system which is not produced as such in one mind, and which therefore is neither directly enjoyed (*erlebt*) nor can be reduced to the lived experience of one person, take shape as a system in the historian's mind from the expressions of persons and statements about them? This presupposes that logical subjects can be formed which are not psychological subjects. There must be means of delimiting them, there must be a justification for conceiving them as units or as a system. We are in search of mind; this is the final result to which a long development of historiography has led us. And here arises the great problem: certainly all is interaction of mental units, but along what road do we find mind, where individual mind is not?' (*G.S.*, VII, 282, cf. 262, 264, 286).

We must first recognise (1) that no transpersonal system ever includes the whole of any individual; he belongs to it by virtue of one aspect of himself, and there are other aspects of him which the system does not absorb. (2) Secondly, these systems all differ from individuals in that they can expand through *space*; they can take in new members almost without limit, and their members may be far apart without the bond between them being weakened. Also, these systems can endure through a long *time*, and undergo slow change. (3) Each system is a *whole of parts*, and the whole is enjoyed (*erlebt*) by the parts, i.e. the persons comprising it, in the form of a consciousness of community;

they may be conscious, e.g. of sharing the same feelings about some matter, or of having a common end in view, or of being under a common leadership. Some such consciousness of community is always present. (4) Further, the relation between such a whole and its parts comes under the category of *structure*, and the members of the system, by virtue of that which they have in common, operate as a single force. For because each individual is in himself a structural whole, this experience which he shares with other members of his system will, in obedience to the law of mental structure, either be, or give rise to, a movement of his will towards the future; and as this movement arises in every member of the system, it must appear in the system as a whole, which may therefore be said, in a certain sense, to entertain purposes and realise *ends*. In a parallel sense, the system will generate and embody *values*. Thus the system possesses a kind of feeling and a kind of will, consisting in the homogeneous elements of feeling and will which are found in all its members. To complete the structural system, it should also have a kind of cognition; and so it has. Whatever is of interest to the system, i.e. to its members in so far as they have common feelings and purposes, is stored up in their memory, and, being handed down from generation to generation of them in the form of history, may be said to constitute the system's memory. (5) Here, too, as in the memory of an individual, that is retained which has *meaning* for the system; and this, being retained in memory, influences the behaviour of the system in the present, and its designs for the future. The possession of a common history is a strong bond of union among members of a system; on the other hand, the consciousness of present unity is sometimes reflected back into the past in the form of legends about national heroes, religious founders, and the like. Such is the structure of a transpersonal system (*G.S.*, VII, 262–4, and cf. 135).

The foregoing analysis is taken from the fragment which I have called Plan A; there it is followed by twelve headings, mostly with nothing under them, which mark the course of Dilthey's projected argument from this point. He meant to take all the transpersonal systems one by one, and infer from the structure of each the method most appropriate to the study of it. The first heading runs: 'The concrete-historical subjects of race, people, etc.', and not only has it nothing under it, but there is nothing elsewhere which can be brought in to fill the gap except two sentences from the *Aufbau*, which run as follows. 'The study of society rests on the analysis of the dynamic systems contained in history. This analysis advances from the concrete to the abstract, from the scientific study of the natural articulation of mankind and the peoples to the severance of the particular science of culture and the separation of spheres in the outer organisation of society' (*G.S.*, VII, 187). The reader will be reminded how, in the *Einleitung in die Geisteswissenschaften*, the analysis of cultural systems and social organisations is preceded by a reference to ethnology; it is clear that, on this point, Dilthey in later years had neither changed his mind nor yet found anything new to say.

We pass to the cultural systems and the organisations of society.

Dilthey takes the *cultural systems* first, giving as a list of the simplest among them 'education, economic life, law, political functions, religions, sociality (*Geselligkeit*),[1] art, philosophy, science'. Each of these is based on the discharge of a single function. It may fulfil its function in such different ways at different times that the unity is hard to find; e.g. it is not easy to see, amid all the forms that philosophy has taken, what ultimate unity it can have. But the unity is there, and the fact that it manifests itself differently in response to different circumstances constitutes the structure of that particular cultural system. The fulfilment of the function is a complicated process, to which many persons contribute in various ways. Thus, (1) each cultural system has those who are devoted to it and make it their main business in life, whether from sheer liking or professionally; (2) among these will be a few talented individuals, so penetrated with the spirit of the system that it is as it were incarnate in them, and they become its representatives; (3) still rarer are the creative minds, discoverers of new truths or founders of schools. Through the activities of these its members, the system becomes continually richer in detail and wider in range. A want is felt; much effort is directed by adherents of the system to removing this dissatisfaction; a creative mind discovers the key to the problem; men of talent accept his idea, and work it out further, the professional and amateur adherents of the

[1] A similar list in Plan A gives two headings as corresponding to this, viz. *die Gliederung der Gesellschaft* and *Sitte, Ethos und Lebensideal*.

system receive it and spread it among the general public. New wants arise, a new cycle begins, and so on for ever. And in this endless process arises an order of values in which the function of this cultural system is expressed; treatises, works of art, and the like, give these values objective embodiment; organisations are set up, and all material means are applied, to assist communication between the co-workers in the system, and to perpetuate their achievements (*G.S.*, VII, 166–9).

In the study of cultural systems, Dilthey begins by warning us off the question of origins. How is religion to be explained, or morality, or art? Are we to offer a rational explanation, or a psychological one, or a historical one? We shall do best if we offer no explanation at all, and concentrate, here as in psychology, on descriptive analysis. Our aim should be to make clear the different factors which are now at work in a cultural system, the different types of function performed with it—in a word, the kind of relations which have been briefly sketched in the previous paragraph. Our evidence for these will be the objective expressions of the cultural system in question, e.g. the books in which philosophy is given to the world, or the system of institutions and conventions which is the outward and visible form of law. We must take these visible facts and read behind them to this meaning or function in the cultural system to which they belong (*G.S.*, VII, 265–8).

Even this modest task presupposes that we know what phenomena we are to interpret; but here too is a problem. We cannot analyse for example religion and form a well-grounded concept of it, until we know what facts are to be taken as religious; yet this is a matter of dispute, and the dispute can only be settled by forming and applying a concept of religion. We have to draw our concept from the facts, and yet select the facts by means of our concept. The trouble is that every cultural system contains extraneous elements. A man is a member of such a system by virtue of one element in himself; but this element cannot fail to be affected in its functioning by the rest of his nature. The cultural system will therefore always contain factors irrelevant to its proper function; these will change with historical conditions, and greatly complicate the history of the system. Dilthey calls this the 'fundamental logical problem in the science of the cultural systems' (*G.S.*, VII, 188).

He notes a further limitation in our power of concept-forming. Because the cultural systems are teleological wholes, the concept of such a system cannot be a mere general idea abstracted from a comparison of all the cases, but must express the *type* to which the system should conform. Now, in every cultural system there are facts which contradict its real intention, cases where the attempt to fulfil the function of the system has failed. In forming the concept, we must ignore these cases, and concentrate on those which show the function realised. 'The manifold of phenomena in such a sphere groups itself about a centre constituted by the ideal case in which the function is completely realised.' Once again we have to select among the facts in order to form our concept. The dangers attendant on this procedure will be evident (*G.S.*, VII, 188).

We turn to the *social organisations*; here Dilthey confines his analysis to the State, and that in a particular form, viz. the nation-State. This is a frequent subject of historical predication, and we must ask where the unity of this subject lies. The question may be asked, and must be answered, in two senses. By what outward marks does the historian distinguish the nation from other historical and social phenomena, so as to treat it as an individual unit? And what is its inner unity, in what sense does it live with a life of its own?

(1) The outward unity of a nation is not easily determined; the criteria, e.g. of language or of common culture, on which it rests, are only relative, and vary from time to time. In his actual analysis, however, Dilthey takes as the mark of national unity the self-contained political organisation with supreme power, the sovereign State. Comprehended in and subordinate to this supreme organisation are a multitude of smaller organisations, the family, the city or province, and the differentiation of function within the State gives rise also to class distinctions based on occupational interests. All these social groups and organisations, existing within the State, are assigned their functions and kept in due subordination to one another by it; the cultural organisations also, though not of the same nature as these, exist under the shadow of the State and are influenced by it. Sometimes it deliberately sets out to influence them.

(2) The inner unity of the nation lies in the 'national consciousness', i.e. a common spirit and outlook, present in all the

members of the nation, which colours all their cultural and social activities and even their private life. This 'national consciousness' has nothing to do with the theory of a group mind or corporate personality in the nation, as we find it in some sociologists and in philosophers such as Hegel. That is a metaphysical construction, as baseless as all such constructions. What Dilthey means by 'national consciousness' is simply that the individual feels the nation's fortunes as his own. 'Common experiences of a nation, common ends and memories are the reality. . . . An individual wills national ends as his own, experiences (*erfährt*) the nation's experiences (*Erlebnisse*) as his own, has memories of such experiences as belonging to himself, is filled with them and carried along by them' (*G.S.*, VII, 284–5).

In actual fact the inner unity of the nation and its outer unity coincide; for the common spirit finds a vehicle in the State, which is itself affected by the national outlook and temper, and sets out to foster it in all subordinate associations and in the cultural life. So there grows up a complex of social and cultural institutions in which the spirit of the people is expressed and made self-conscious. They feel for these their institutions a common concern, they set the interest of the State above all private aims, and judge all that they do and suffer not from a personal standpoint, but by reference to the national good.

The 'national good', again, is not to be conceived as something abstract and unchanging, lifted above the day-to-day circumstances and vicissitudes of the national life. On the contrary, the national good is simply the form in which the nation seeks its welfare and satisfaction, and this is always liable to change. For, says Dilthey, a nation has a far longer time-perspective than an individual. It never reckons with the possibility of its own death; 'therefore plans and purposes have here a quite different place from that which they hold in the life of the individual. They have never more than a temporal, relative connection with the inwardness of the nation. This inwardness is capable of boundless possibilities.' The State, in obedience to the national will, pursues different ends and functions. 'The machine, as it were, is applied to the fulfilment of a different task, quite heterogeneous problems are solved side by side, and values of quite different classes are realised.' Every form it assumes is transitory, every development is liable to a reaction.

The State has no definite essence, and therefore we cannot find in its history any development according to an inner law, as we can in the individual life or in a cultural system. It has not even the continuity due to the slow accumulation of experience; for in political matters 'every generation forgets the experiences of its predecessors' (*G.S.*, VII, 169–77, 282–4).

About the method of studying political systems, Dilthey says very little, and that in passing. It corresponds closely with his teaching about the study of cultural systems. We are not to make our primary object an enquiry into origins, but rather a descriptive analysis of what constitutes a nation or a State, such an analysis, in fact, as we have just made in the preceding paragraph. Here too, as in the study of cultural systems, there will be difficulty in defining our concepts precisely, because the criteria of definition are vague and change from time to time. Dilthey gives an example of this method at work, in the shape of an analysis of the German nation as it was in the time of Tacitus (*G.S.*, VII, 174–6).

The discussion of cultural systems and social organisations has given us a cross-section of history; we know now what factors will be found, at any time, working together in society, and have therefore a principle of analysis and selection. True, though we now see how to select the subject for our historical enquiries, we do not yet see how to determine the temporal limits of our survey; but here too the historical process helps us by falling easily into periods (*Zeitalter, Epochen, Perioden*), which are the natural time-limits for analysis. The mark of a historical period is that, between certain dates, the minds of men and nations are filled with common ideas, common values, and ends which they all pursue. A common spirit and outlook takes possession of all the branches of individual and social activity. 'It is expressed in stone, on canvas, in deeds or words. It is objectified in the constitution and legislation of nations. It fills the historian in his comprehension of earlier times, and the philosopher starts from it in his attempt to interpret the meaning (*Sinn*) of the world.'

This comes about when the development of the various dynamic systems in society, each fulfilling its own peculiar function, happens to produce in all of them at one time tendencies which partly coincide, foster and amplify one another, and work together to effect a single complex result: Dilthey gives as an example the *Aufklärung* period in Germany, when intellectual, moral and social, and political developments all worked together to foster the ideal of a life guided by reason. We must not try to explain the *Aufklärung* period merely in terms of a ruling *idea*, a common *belief* which is alleged to have dominated all the minds of men at that time. The *Aufklärung* springs not merely from a movement of thought, but from the tendencies of human life as a whole; it includes not only common beliefs and ways of thinking, but common ways of feeling too, common values and common ends. These common ideas, feelings, ends together constitute the spirit of the age (*Zeitgeist*), which determines the attitude of all men and all societies to all the issues of life. It is always one-sided, of course, and there will be some who see this and protest; but even their protest will be made in the language of the period, and conceived in the same terms as what it denounces. Thus even the opponents of the *Zeitgeist* are determined by it in their very opposition. The horizon of the period is closed, its conceptions and its values are regarded as absolute, and are formulated as such, with great parade of logic, by the metaphysicians. The dominant outlook gives to every individual, society, or movement in the period a meaning (*Bedeutung*) which is regarded as absolute; those who make a notable contribution to the realisation of the ideals of the period become its leaders and representative figures. It should be added that the homogeneity of a historical period is never quite complete. It always includes some whose outlook is that of the preceding period, though they often try to express their views in up-to-date language and bring them into accord with their own time. And it includes some who already think, feel, or will in a way prophetic of the period next to come (*G.S.*, VII, 177–86).

The study of a historical period must follow the same lines as that of a cultural system or a nation. The period is a structural system, a whole whose parts have meaning. Our business is to analyse this structural system into its parts, viz. the various *tendencies* (*Richtungen, Strömungen, Bewegungen*), in different spheres of activity, which contribute to the total result; we shall thus discover how the various factors in the life of the period affect one another, and what they have in common which enables them to combine (*G.S.*, VII, 178, 185, 286). This common element will constitute the *peculiar essence* (*Eigenwesen*) of the period; the concepts which express it will apply universally within the period, as the general categories of life apply universally throughout the world of life, and they may be called *historical categories* (*G.S.*, VII, 286). Dilthey promises in the *Aufbau* to show later (*sc.* in the *Kritik der historischen Vernunft*) how the comparative method can be used to reveal the common structure of all historical periods as such (*G.S.*, VII, 185). This promise he does not literally fulfil. But he gives brilliant examples of how to analyse a particular period, in the shape of an analysis of the *Aufklärung* twice repeated (*G.S.*, VII, 178–85, 335–45).

The study of historical periods is inseparable from that of great changes in history. Indeed, the former may be regarded as a part of the latter. For, although we speak of periods as if each of them had a fixed character which endured without change between certain dates, and then gave place to another, we know that this is far from the truth. If it were true, we should have little difficulty, in each case, in fixing the limits of our study; that it is not true, but that everything is involved in ceaseless change, is the most troublesome fact we have to face. 'No part of history, such as a period, can be grasped through concepts bringing to expression something fixed in it, i.e. a system of relations between fixed qualities. . . . Rather we have to do with a system of relations whose parts are dynamic, i.e. show continual qualitative changes in their interaction. Even the relations themselves, because they rest on interaction between forces, are changeable' (*G.S.*, VII, 281). A historical period, in fact, is to be regarded not as a fixed state of things, but as a process—a stage, indeed, in a wider process from which it is marked off by no clear limits. 'It is as if, in a constantly flowing river, lines had to be drawn or figures traced which should stand firm' (*G.S.*, VII, 280). When we analyse even an apparently stable period, like the *Aufklärung*, we find that the stability is only a façade behind which living forces move and interact. But there are also points in history where even the appearance of stability is absent, and we are face to face with a process of change, a gradual movement, it may be, or a sudden revolution. Such movements, as well as periods of seeming calm, can be and are made the objects of enquiry in the human studies, and about them also Dilthey has something to say.

Historical changes may be classified according as they are sharp and sudden, or take a long time to develop; or according as they affect only a single cultural system, or all the cultural systems and institutions of one or more nations. In every case, the primary difficulty with them, as with historical periods, is that of delimitation. The change to be studied must not be any segment of the historical process, arbitrarily selected, it must be an individual dynamic system with an inner unity. Such a dynamic system is e.g. the French Revolution, or the establishment of the German *Reich*. But how is such a dynamic system marked off? How are we to conceive its inner unity? Not in purely causal terms. 'For in themselves all changes are causally bound together in the same way; from the point of view of cause and effect, the foundation of the German Empire or the French Revolution is not separate from what happened before or after in the sphere in question.' Nor can we find a unity in the contents, viz. the results aimed at and achieved in such changes, so long as these are considered 'in their purely factual relations'; for these, again, are continuous with the contents of earlier and later processes, and give us, merely as contents, no ground for selection. The only possible ground must lie in a unity of meaning (*Bedeutungseinheit*) subsisting between a certain group of events.

The fragment in which Dilthey undertakes to elucidate this unity of meaning breaks off, before coming to the point, in the middle of an attempt to analyse that particular type of historical changes which we call revolutions. The common character of all revolutions, he says, is that a movement of discontent, which has long been repressed by law and the established institutions, suddenly bursts the barrier and spreads its influence as widely as its inherent force can carry it. The significance of the revolution is heightened if the movement in question is not merely a group of selfish interests, but is associated with a system of disinterested ideas of fairly long standing; for then its influence spreads, beyond the circle of the particular interests which set it going, wherever the ideas which it champions make an appeal. It takes its place as a stage in the development of civilisation. It awakens a pure disinterested enthusiasm, and exercises wide dominion over the minds and hearts of men (*G.S.*, VII, 269–70, and cf. 165).

And now we come to the last step in Dilthey's analysis of the human studies. Cultural systems, organisations, nations, historical periods and revolutions, do not stand in the historical sequence in a merely external juxtaposition; they interpenetrate and belong to one another, and, though our analysis may show each of them to be itself a whole with a distinctive character and meaning, yet they are all parts of one complex whole which is the history of the world. It has been the ambition of historians from the beginning to obtain an understanding of this whole, whether they confined their study to the interaction of all the historical factors within some limited space of time, or whether they boldly claimed to deal with the whole of the recorded past. In either case, they make one presupposition, viz. that the historical process is by nature capable of being understood; this implies that events in history have meaning (*Bedeutung*), and that history as a whole has a sense (*Sinn*). In recent times, the sense of history has been sought in 'progress', by which is meant a gradual increase in the extent to which the major values are realised in human life (*G.S.*, VII, 287). Dilthey now asks, in what sense can we find a meaning in history at all, and in what sense does progress really take place?

The most notable theory on this subject in modern times is certainly Hegel's, and Dilthey, in many of his remarks, has obviously Hegel in mind. Indeed, he openly refers in various places to some of the salient Hegelian doctrines. The whole historical process, according to Hegel, is directed towards a single end, which is the self-expression of the Absolute; and the means by which the Absolute comes to be expressed is the·life of reason as lived by human beings. Reason is the essence of the human mind, its inner substance and the deepest motive of all its activities. With this clue in his hand, Hegel undertakes to classify and arrange in a logical order the stages through which the human mind passes towards its goal. The relations between these stages are not merely temporal, but dialectical. Each of them is in its measure a revelation of the Absolute; but each is abstract, one-sided, and therefore in the long run leads to a contradiction. The human mind, exercised by this latent contradiction in its life, tries to mend it by rushing to an opposite extreme; but this only makes the contradiction explicit, and it is not solved until both extremes are synthesised in a richer form of life, which in turn develops an inner contradiction of its own. Under this constant pressure the human race advances to higher and higher degrees of truth and freedom; and in this advance Hegel finds the meaning of history.

Now, there is no doubt that Dilthey in his later years greatly admired this theory. He singles it out, in his *Jugendgeschichte Hegels* (1904), as the greatest achievement of that philosopher, vindicates Hegel's claim to be its sole originator, and illustrates in detail the applications which Hegel himself was able to make of it. True, he quarrels with the exalted faith in reason which pervades this and every other part of Hegel's philosophy, and which makes him treat the movement of historical life as if it were wholly an expression of ideal principles. But he is at pains to show that this is a comparatively late development in Hegel, who had reached his dialectical conception of history some years before the theory of the Absolute as pure Reason entered his mind. This later development he ascribes to the influence of Schelling, while in the historical dialectic, before it was crushed into a pseudo-logical form, he claims to find the expression of Hegel's own peculiar genius. For the greatness of that philosopher lay in his unique understanding of historical movements, and his power of coining concepts in which the living process of mind comes to expression. His attempt to represent this living process as one of logical development led him in the end to do violence to logic itself, to abandon the principle of contradiction in an effort to express conflict and change.[1] But this is not an essential part of Hegel's historical theory, and to the real essence of that theory Dilthey gives an admiring approval.

In the first place, he admits that every state of human affairs is somehow unsatisfactory, and that this unsatisfactoriness is the motive force which drives us to change (*G.S.*, VII, 187, 271, 288). But, he goes on, the unsatisfactoriness is not wholly due to conditions inherent in the developing human mind itself. A great deal of it is due to the natural environment, which Hegel leaves out of account. Men live in the midst of a physical world, and every attempt which they make to realise an ideal is conditioned and distorted by the pressure of physical facts. It is true that the history of mankind is the history of an increasing control over their environment; but, on the other hand, even this con-

---

[1] This is a misrepresentation of Hegel. See p. 266 n.

trol can only be reached by the adoption of certain habits and attitudes of mind, so that man, even in his conquest of nature, is still conditioned by her. We can distinguish three main factors in the historical process. *First*, there are the 'dead factual necessities' and the struggle for bare life. *Next*, there is the 'highest life of the mind', the recognition and pursuit of ideals. *Lastly*, there is the work of the intelligence (*Verstand*), which forges tools for the furtherance of human effort. Such tools may be purely material, e.g. railways and factories, or may consist in forms of human association, e.g. armies, social organisations, political constitutions; and they are all at the service both of the struggle for life itself, and of the attempt to realise the ideal in life. These three factors are never found separate; and, as the realisation of ideals is conditioned by the means at our disposal, the machinery and the social institutions, so these in turn are conditioned by the irrational factor of the physical environment itself. From this environment, by means of our constant struggle with it, has proceeded the differentiation of mankind according to race, nationality, temperament, and custom, and it is on these factors, materially conditioned as they are, that the realisation of ideas and ideals in this or that period of history depends. 'The Middle Age contains a system of related ideas, ruling in the various spheres. Ideas of fealty in feudalism, imitation of Christ, conceived as an obedience whose content is the otherworldly attitude of mind in face of nature by virtue of the fact of abnegation. Teleological hierarchy in science. But it must be acknowledged that the background of these ideas is the force which this higher world has no power to overcome. And this is everywhere the case. Factuality of race, locality, or balance of forces are everywhere the foundation, which can never be made spiritual. It is a dream of Hegel's that the periods represent a stage in the development of reason. The description of a period always presupposes the clear eye for this factuality' (*G.S.*, VII, 287–8, cf. 271).

We may add that, in so far as men do strive for and achieve the realisation of ideals, their motives and ideals differ, not only from time to time, but from group to group among contemporaries in the same society. There is no single end, or complex of ends, in which the spring of all human idealism may be found. No table of *a priori* values will serve to account for it. The fact

301

behind it is the great fact of life, the inexhaustible potentialities of the structural system, which cannot be reduced to a formula. If we are to understand this life, we must seek it in its objective manifestations, the cultural systems and social institutions, which form a wider structural system in the historical process itself. We shall find it very various. The ruling motive is a desire for the enjoyment of present value, wherever this value may be found. To this are superadded an impulse to obtain control over nature, or 'freedom', and a delight in effort and progressive achievement for its own sake. Under the guidance of these motives arises, in every society, *first* of all a system of ideas about the universe, which, when methodically worked out, develops into science; *secondly*, a reflection or turning inward of the self upon itself, and a continual effort to grasp the meaning of life and the world, which finds its vehicles in religion, art, and philosophy; *thirdly*, a sustained attempt to achieve objective goods, which gives rise to economic organisation, to the social structure, and to the machinery of the State, viz. administration, army, and law.

Progress of a sort takes place in all these spheres, but in each one it aims at a different goal. (1) Progress in science lies in the growth of knowledge, which is made swift and easy by the fact that what one generation knows can be transmitted entire and without misunderstanding to the next; and it is used to further our control over nature and over social development. (2) Progress in the world of religion, art, and philosophy lies rather in the deepening of human consciousness, the enrichment of our experience and the growing realisation of the inexhaustibility of life; it is conditioned by an ever-increasing complexity in our modes of expression, and a clearer correlation of the present with the past and the future. In art, at any rate, there is no continuous advance as there is in science; but in this sphere of life generally Dilthey finds that two notable steps have been taken in recent times, viz. a fuller recognition of the importance of individuality, and a heightening of the historical consciousness. (3) Progress in the economic field lies in our increasing technical mastery over nature, and in the social and political world it lies in the diffusion of freedom and culture over all classes of the community.

In all these spheres, Dilthey notes that progress is not a matter of the history of individuals; the subjects of which progress is predicated are the cultural systems and social organisations. The nature of it is as various as the spheres in which it obtains, which have hardly anything in common except that they all belong to the structural system of human life. If we are to have a formula at all, Hegel's will do well enough, viz. that progress is an 'advance towards freedom'; but then the phrase must be given a very vague and un-Hegelian sense, if it is to cover all the details of the process in question. It is a complex process, in which knowledge, reflective consciousness, organisation, and accumulation of wealth all play their part. And in all these spheres it is open to interruption, and even to retrograde movements from time to time (*G.S.*, VII, 372–4).

Let us now return to the original question, from which this discussion arose. The historian is inevitably led to think and write as if history were a real whole, having a sense or meaning which he could at least partially understand; and he tends in modern times to seek this meaning of history in human progress. Dilthey agrees that, if there is a meaning in history, it must lie in human progress, and we have now seen in what sense, and with what limitations, he admits that progress takes place. It remains for us to ask, in the light of this, whether or how far he can admit a meaning in history.

Since there is no single line of progress in history, it follows that there can be no single meaning, such as Comte or Hegel would affirm. We can indeed discern a meaning in history in a certain sense, but only by breaking it up into the individual lives and dynamic systems which are its components. Every such dynamic system is, as we have seen, centred in itself, and has therefore a meaning of its own, which flows from its specific character. Every event within a dynamic system has a meaning by virtue of the contribution which it makes to the whole, and the immanent meaning of the whole system lies in its coherent and self-developing nature, and the progress which it makes towards its peculiar end. While, however, there is thus a meaning in every cultural system, every historical period or movement, there is no similar meaning of the historical process as a whole. All the meaning or sense we can find here lies in the structural relations which regularly prevail at all times between the components of this whole. These structural relations are enough to give the whole its general character of life and historicity, but not to give it a determinate character as *this* whole. There is no clearly formulable end to which it all progresses, and therefore no ultimate meaning to which the particular systems all contribute (*G.S.*, VII, 172, 185–6).

As there is no single meaning in the process, so also its driving force is not simple, not e.g. the pursuit of a supreme value, or even of some coherent group of more or less independent values. The driving force in history, which settles from time to time the direction of its movement, is nothing less than the whole complex structural system of the human mind, with all its possibilities of confusion, and all its capacities for evil as well as for good. History is not merely the unfolding of the rational nature of men and their inherent virtue, but is also a continual battle of selfish forces. 'Relations of power can never be eliminated from the communal life of psychophysical beings. As the autocracy of the *Aufklärung* produced not only the effort after a rational development of human powers, but also cabinet struggles, and exploitation of the subject for the sake of the life of enjoyment in the courts, so every other arrangement of power-relations in turn includes a similar duality of effects. And the sense of history can only be sought in the meaning-relation of all the forces which were bound together in the system of the ages' (*G.S.*, VII, 187). The progress towards ideal ends is never the only factor in determining the course of history, and 'the whole formulation of the question which looks to an aim (*Ziel*) in history is thoroughly one-sided' (*G.S.*, VII, 172, and cf. 166).

Having thus determined in what sense progress is real or history meaningful, Dilthey goes on to describe briefly the stages by which the true nature of the historical process has come to be recognised, or, in other words, to sketch the history of historiography. This he does in two passages, one in the published *Aufbau* (*G.S.*, VII, 163–4) and one in Plan A (*G.S.*, VII, 272–5). He points out that historiography, properly conducted, is a very complicated task. 'It has for its presupposition autobiography, biography, history of nations, of cultural systems, of organisations. Each of these histories has a peculiar centre to which the processes are related, and therefore values, ends, a significance, which result from this relation. On the combination of these moments with one another rests the possibility of an approach to objective world history.' This approach has actually been made through four stages. (1) The first stage was that of pure narrative for narrative's sake, exemplified in Herodotus. (2) Then came the attempt to explain events, to record not a mere succession of happenings, but a causal process; this appears in Thucydides. (3) In the third stage, the results of reflection upon certain particular systems, e.g. in political theory, in economics, in the theory of strategy and tactics, were brought to bear upon the narrative, which at the same time concerned itself not with isolated and local processes such as the struggle between Athens and Sparta, but with the rise and fall of world powers. This was the work of Polybius. No further progress was made in ancient times, and it was on the same basis that the Christian scheme of world history came in due course to be built, in which the teleological metaphysic of Aristotle, his political theory, the idea of the Roman Empire and of the Kingdom of God, were all welded together into a single meaningful system. The work of Machiavelli and of Guicciardini, in whom historiography begins to move once more independently of theological influences, is still on the same level as that of Polybius. (4) But then came the final stage. Particular systems such as art, religion, economics, science, were singled out and seen to have each a history and an inner life of its own. The interactions between these particular systems were made an object of study, and history thus ceased to be wholly or mainly a record of political events, but became a history of civilisation (*Kulturgeschichte*). Lastly, the idea of development was introduced, which made possible the discovery of lines of progress in the various realms of human activity, and the formulation of the true causes of historical change.

We have now come to the end of Dilthey's methodological and categorial analysis of the human studies, which occupies by far the greater part of the *Kritik der historischen Vernunft*, and is the real kernel of that work. It is, in fact, the *Grundlegung der Geisteswissenschaften*, so long promised as the completion of the *Einleitung in die Geisteswissenschaften*. What shall be our comment upon it?

We may begin by extracting from it Dilthey's answer to Rickert on the four points which we listed in Chapter Eight (pp. 247–8). These points represent four issues on which Rickert has taken up a position, and which are so important that no one should denounce Rickert's attitude upon them unless he has one of his own to offer instead. Dilthey's answers may be set down as follows:

(1) The differentia of the human studies lies in their concern with all those phenomena in the universe which are expressions of mind, and must be understood (*verstanden*) before they can be explained (*erklärt*).

(2) The categories of the human studies are not derived from the concept of value, nor from any *a priori* principle, but from lived experience. They are not capable of precise formulation, but the chief of them have been described above. They are all summed up in the concept of a dynamic system (*Wirkungszusammenhang*), and one of the most important of them is the category of meaning (*Bedeutung*).

(3) The test by which the relatively self-contained wholes, into which history is analysed for purposes of study, are discriminated and delimited, is that every such whole is a dynamic system with a peculiar structure, and all of them together form one comprehensive dynamic system.

(4) The meaning of history is the system of structural relations in which the particular dynamic systems stand to one another in the historical process. Apart from this there is no meaning in history, but each particular system has a meaning of its own, which follows from its determinate structure.

These results are solid, but unexciting, and some readers may feel that the title which Dilthey gave to his work promised something more adventurous. When Kant wrote his *Kritik*, he gave small space in it to methodology, and concentrated rather upon the deeper issues concerning the nature and range of human knowledge. His conclusions on these points are no doubt open to serious question, but at least they made the *Kritik* a contribution to philosophy in the grand style, and enabled it to cover almost as much ground, in its own way, as the metaphysical systems which it claims to overthrow. Dilthey's *Kritik* is conceived in a different vein. It is governed by the modest spirit of the empirical philosophy, content to elicit facts about our ways of thinking and working, without speculating about the alleged deeper implications of these facts. Dilthey does not let himself go as deep into speculation as Kant did. He never forgets that the question he is asking is the question which was asked by the fathers of positivism. Kant is his model only in so far as he gave us a warning against being drawn into metaphysics; the things which Kant actually said on points of detail are viewed with reserve, because in spite of his exhortations to criticism he was not critical enough. And when Dilthey borrows a point from Fichte or Hegel, he always makes a clean cut between their insights into the nature of history and historiography, and the metaphysical systems for which they have become notorious.

Yet it is a fact, and Dilthey as a student of ideas could not fail to note it, that the theory of knowledge constantly tends to go beyond these positivistic limits. In his own lifetime he had seen the Kantian critique transformed by the Marburg school into an idealist system, and the critique of historical knowledge in the hands of Windelband and Rickert absorbed into that same system. Moreover, in *Das Wesen der Philosophie* and elsewhere Dilthey shows that he understands the motive behind such developments. He understands that the activity commonly called 'philosophy' is compounded of two quite distinct activities. On the one hand there is the critical endeavour, which works itself out in the analysis of the foundations of knowledge; and to this the main body of Dilthey's own *Kritik* is a contribution. But there is also the drive towards the formulation and speculative development of *Weltanschauungen*, which is no less original and no less indestructible than the other. The two tendencies in philosophy are in mutual conflict, for the critical tendency, now fully developed through the work of Kant, has undermined the foundations of all those metaphysical constructions in which the *Weltanschauung*-building tendency seeks its fulfilment. But Kant himself, after showing that metaphysics is impossible as a science, had to recognise that it is indestructible as a tendency of thought, and did not think his philosophy complete until he had said something positive about it. On the one hand he made his *Kritik* end with a systematic exposure of the pseudo-science of metaphysics; but on the other hand he went on to indicate the sources from which the metaphysical consciousness takes its origin, and the way in which it can obtain a legitimate satisfaction. Dilthey likewise ends his *Kritik* with a section which is devoted to this purpose, and to that section we must now turn.

The materials from which this last section of the *Kritik* is to be reconstructed are, as usual, very disjointed, but they are fairly full and explicit. They comprise the last section of Plan A, a good deal of Plan B, and several passages among the fragments inserted by Dilthey's editor into Plan A at an earlier point. The arrangement of them, however, must be entirely our own. This is the only point in the *Kritik* where, in the matter of arrangement, Dilthey himself gives us no help whatever.

We may begin with a passage where he asks himself what is the use of his *Kritik*, now that he has made it. How does the philosophical analysis of the human studies contribute to the solution of 'present-day problems'? (*G.S.*, VII, 276). The 'problems' which he means are really one problem, that of finding a tenable outlook upon life in an age when it is no longer possible to take one ready-made from a metaphysical system. 'For the systems of the metaphysicians are fallen, and yet the will has an ever-new desire for stable ends to direct the life of the individual and to guide society' (*G.S.*, V, 11). Dilthey thinks to meet this desire by means of the human studies themselves, treated from a 'philosophic' or comprehensive point of view. As early as 1859 we find him writing: 'it would not be worth while to be a historian, if it were not one way of comprehending the world' (*Der junge Dilthey*,[1] p. 81), and this remained his attitude to the end. The world of mind which the human studies disclose to us is a world of free meaningful activity, and in it we experience and know reality—not 'reality' as the metaphysicians conceive it, not 'pure being' or 'the thing in itself' or 'the Absolute' or any such thing, but the reality of our own life, and we experience and know it as it truly is. The epistemological *Grundlegung* which assures us of this is not merely the logical prolegomenon to historiography, but the basis for a genuinely philosophical superstructure in the form of a reasoned *Weltanschauungslehre*. The closing section of Dilthey's *Kritik* is meant to lead us in this direction.

It seems at first sight as if the human studies are not a sufficient basis for our philosophical superstructure. Surely we must bring in the natural sciences as well. 'From both together arises the problem of philosophy, what practicable life-attitude results from the truth of life, so apprehended. The answer depends on taking the natural sciences and the human studies together. My

[1] *Der junge Dilthey: ein Lebensbild in Briefen u. Tagebüchern, 1852–1870*; edited by Clara Misch-Dilthey (Leipzig and Berlin, 1933).

book therefore cannot dispense with such a combination, if it is to have any result for the present time. But that requires only a discussion in broad principle. It has nothing to do with a system' (*G.S.*, VII, 276).

These words come at the end of Plan A. At the beginning of Plan B comes a hint of how the 'discussion in broad principle' should go. Here Dilthey raises the old problem of mind and nature, which in its speculative form has given so much trouble to the metaphysicians. Dilthey proposes to show us that the metaphysical approach to it is a waste of time, but that the problem can be reformulated in a more modest and more manageable form, which brings it nearer home to life.

The problem, he says, is really a practical one; it arises from the situation in which we find ourselves in life, and is necessarily involved in the work of the human studies. 'The meaning of the human studies and the theory of them can only lie in helping us to see what we have to do in the world, what we can make of ourselves, what we can hope to do with the world and it with us. . . . Natural science, by means of its categories, creates a world, the human studies create another. The mind cannot possibly rest in their duality. The philosophical systems seek to overcome it, in vain. Their essence lies in this, that they either, as since Descartes, construct nature and proceed thence to determine the essence of mind, . . . or we start with ourselves, in the shape, since Kant, of an ego etc.' Dilthey argues that neither line of approach can lead to anything. If we begin with nature, we shall see in mind merely an incident in the course of nature. We shall be unable to account for just that in the mind's life which is distinctive of it, and makes it a world in itself, self-creating and self-understood. But if on the other hand we try to explain it in terms of a transcendental ego, the result is as bad; the transcendental self is conceived formally, abstractly, and cannot serve to account for the actual content which fills the existence of 'the historical being, man'. Neither way does justice to the experience of life which we have in ourselves, conscious as we are of ourselves partly as 'dark, full of instincts, earth-bound', and partly as creators of cultural values.

What we really need, he says, is to see how the two worlds are related, not in absolute reality, but in ourselves. But the whole tenor of Dilthey's teaching is that this is something we must learn from history itself, by ranging widely and penetrating deeply into the experience recorded there. The primary thing that philosophy has to do for us is simply to tell us how historical and social life can be understood, by what methods we can penetrate into it, and how deep we can go. It is in fact the work which the *Kritik* has been doing all this time. As for the natural world, all that we need to know about that has already been set forth above. We have seen that the meaning of the physical world for human life lies not in its own inner constitution, but in the impact which it makes on our minds and wills. We have seen at what point the natural sciences make a contribution to our understanding of life, viz. where they inform us about the physical conditions by which our activities are stimulated and governed. But all this is absorbed into the comprehensive study of human life and consciousness, which the human studies together carry out. It is here that the relation between mind and nature comes home to us, where we feel it on our pulses, and it is here, from this understanding of life, and not from philosophical systems, that our practical attitudes and *Weltanschauungen* take shape.

They take shape in the values which we recognise, the ends which we set before ourselves, and the sense which we have of the meaning of life. But this is just where the shoe pinches, and where we are tempted to ask of philosophy something more than a simple theory of knowledge. For when we come to values and the meaning of life, we find ourselves in a region of doubt and debate, and the question which we address to philosophy is: can any foundation for our value-judgments be found outside our own feelings and desires? And if not, is there any way in which we can reach 'objective' or universally valid standards of judgment? In the course of the *Kritik* we have seen indications of what Dilthey's answer is likely to be; but now is the time for him to speak out fully and openly.

He gives full recognition to the demand for universally valid principles *as a tendency of the mind*; that is, he recognises that we have an ineradicable tendency to seek universally valid principles and to regard the principles which we actually hold as being such. This is true both of individuals, and of peoples and periods of history. 'In a period there develop universal norms, values, ends, in relation to which the meaning of actions is

310

primarily to be seen.' Such principles may be thought of as the law of God, or of reason, or as some kind of cosmic purpose; but, in one guise or another, they are always conceived by those who hold them as universally valid (*G.S.*, VII, 289, 173).

The more, however, we penetrate into human history, the less we can believe that the principles supposed to be universally valid are really so. 'For history knows indeed of the assertion of something unconditional as a value, norm, or good. . . . But historical experience knows only the process, so important for it, of these assertions: of itself, however, it knows nothing as to their universal validity. . . . It notices the unreconciled conflict of these unconditional assertions among themselves' (*G.S.*, VII, 173). If we compare nations and periods, e.g. the Roman Empire, mediaeval Christendom, the *Aufklärung*, it is evident that there is no ideal which is acknowledged by all of them. Sometimes it looks as if even a single nation were divided against itself about values; and this leads us deeper to the Hegelian truth, that the development of such ideas moves through opposition and conflict to ever wider and freer syntheses. It is clear, then, that every standard of judgment which we apply to historical events is itself a historical product: 'history is itself the productive force which generates the value-determinations, ideals, ends, by which the meaning of men and events is measured'. And there are always two standards, by both of which the meaning of any event or person comes to be judged; first, that of his own age, and then that of the contribution he makes to human progress (*G.S.*, VII, 289–90). There is no value-determination which stands outside the flow of events, and is not merely a product of and a factor in this flow. Dilthey's final conclusion is 'the complete recognition, in the historical consciousness, of the immanence of even those values and norms which appear as unconditional' (*G.S.*, VII, 290).

Dilthey is firm in his acceptance of this conclusion. But he is also aware of the problems which it raises. For hundreds and thousands of years we have lived in the faith that there are unconditional principles which we can know and by which we must live. The impulse to seek such principles is as lively to-day as it ever was. If philosophy and history now combine to show that the search is vain, must they not do something to allay the resulting bewilderment?

Dilthey accepts the responsibility; but the clearest account of how he tried to meet it is not in the *Kritik*. It is found in two unfinished sketches which he wrote in 1903–4, ostensibly describing a dream which he had and a conversation in which he took part some ten years before, while visiting his friend von Wartenburg at his castle in Silesia.

In the first, Dilthey tells how one night, after a long philosophical discussion, he went to sleep in a room which contained a copy of Raphael's *School of Athens*, and had a dream in which the picture came to life. The philosophers of post-Renaissance times came in and joined the ancients and mediaevals who were already there, and then the whole company began to sort themselves out into homogeneous groups. First the naturalistic and positivistic thinkers came together around Archimedes and Ptolemy; then the philosophers of freedom gathered around Socrates and Plato; and the objective idealists formed a group around Pythagoras and Heraclitus. Descartes and Kant, who were at first among the mathematicians and scientists, left that group and joined the idealists of freedom. Then the three groups began to recede from one another, great fissures appeared in the ground between them, 'a dreadful hostile alienation seemed to separate them—I was seized by a strange anxiety, that philosophy seemed to exist in three or possibly more different forms —the unity of my own being seemed to be rent, as I was longingly drawn now to this group, now to that, and I struggled to retain it.'

Here the dream ends, and Dilthey continues with his own reflections upon it. 'Every *Weltanschauung* is historically conditioned, and therefore limited, relative. A dreadful anarchy of thought seems to result from this. But the same historical consciousness, which has given rise to this absolute doubt, can also set limits to it. First of all: the *Weltanschauungen* have separated from one another according to an inner law. . . . These types of *Weltanschauung* maintain themselves side by side in the course of centuries. And then the second, the liberating thought: the *Weltanschauungen* are grounded in the nature of the universe and the relation of the finite knowing mind to it. So each of them expresses one side of the universe within the limits of our thought. Each is herein true. But each is one-sided. It is not granted to us to see these sides all at once. The pure light of truth can be seen by us only in variously broken rays' (*G.S.*, VII, 222).

What this means is illustrated by the second sketch, which describes a conversation between Dilthey and several others on the evening of the day after his dream. Dilthey begins by saying that the one great fact before which all scepticism is reduced to silence or silliness is the fact of the natural sciences, which reveal to us, albeit in 'the symbol-language of qualities, movements, spatial relations', a reality independent of ourselves. The point is taken up by a neurologist, who asserts his faith in the mechanical interpretation of nature and in the possibility of reducing psychological processes to terms of physiology. Von Wartenburg replies that natural science is merely an abstraction from the totality of experience; it discovers empirical connections, but knows nothing of the metaphysical reality which may lie behind them. The neurologist retorts that personal idealism, with its attempt to understand that reality, is a leap into speculation, which he himself feels no desire to make. 'It is a matter of our subjective energy, our habits, the objects we think about, whether we are naturalists or idealists. In that case we must live and let live. That is, we cannot refute one another. For in the field of the experiences which control and condition each of us, we are sovereign. . . . And if that is so, then I have a right within my world of experience to think consistently as, in that world, I must.' 'Yes,' says von Wartenburg, 'if the different realms of experience are of equal worth.'

The next speaker is a painter, who is full of the contemplation of the unity of nature. For him there is no antithesis between matter and mind; in the human face, the soul speaks through the body, and in the fields the soil is inseparable from the horses which plough it and the life which grows out of it. The impression is strengthened by a drive through the ripe cornfields and a walk through the garden in the early twilight. Dilthey himself speaks: 'How irresistible, if we do not reflect or draw distinctions, is the unity of nature, her meaning and essential coherence. It exists on a level beyond our reflection, its life was in myth and in language. And what a dialectic arises if man attempts to put this objective idealism into words.' But the sun goes down and the glow of nature dies away. 'Stern and solemn the broad plain now spread out before us.' And then von Wartenburg speaks: 'So vanishes the harmonious beauty . . . the harmony is broken in face of the will which surrenders itself

313

—then the necessity of nature is overcome, her harmony is dissolved—*we are more than all nature.*' The stars begin to appear, and their distant glory is to the two friends a kind of visible symbol of the spiritual transcendence of the human will over nature; and Dilthey thinks how well this is exemplified in his friend, who in the consciousness of the near approach of death has, through his Christian faith, transcended himself, and become 'a proof of that which breaks through nature and her necessity'.

Dilthey goes to his room full of admiration for this spiritual power, and asks himself: 'Is not my own historical standpoint a fruitless scepticism, if I measure it against such a life? We must endure and conquer this world, we must act upon it. How victoriously my friend does so. Where in my *Weltanschauung* is there a like power?' He envies the power which comes from religious faith, but cannot honestly share that faith. 'If historical and psychological relativism were the last word, it would touch the religions first of all.' What then is to be done? According to Dilthey, the solution lies in a 'philosophy of philosophy', i.e. a comparative *Weltanschauungslehre*. But he does not clearly state, in this conversation piece, the conclusion to which that will lead us. For that, we must return to the fragments of the *Kritik*. In the final section of Plan B comes a paragraph, with the quotation of which we may fittingly close.

'The historical consciousness', he writes, 'of the finitude of every historical phenomenon, every human or social state, of the relativity of every sort of belief, is the last step towards the liberation of man. With it, man attains the sovereign power to wring from every experience its content, to surrender wholly to it, without prepossession, as if there were no system of philosophy and no faith which could bind men. Life becomes free from knowledge by concepts; mind becomes sovereign in face of all tissues of dogmatic thought. Every beauty, every sanctity, every sacrifice, relived and expounded, opens up perspectives which disclose a reality. And in the same way we take up into ourselves the evil, the frightful, the ugly, as occupying a place in the world, as enfolding in itself a reality to which justice must be done in the world order. Something which cannot be conjured away. And, in contrast with the relativity, the continuity of the creative force makes itself felt as the central historical fact' (*G.S.*, VII, 290–1).

CHAPTER TEN

THE purpose of this book has been mainly expository: to set before the reader the facts about Dilthey's philosophy, with just so much comment and discussion as might serve to bring out the main points and to clear up obscurities. It would be out of place, at this late stage, to begin discussing his philosophy on its merits. There is no room here for an extended critique of him, and still less is there room for a declaration of my own views on the matters which he raises. My purpose in this final chapter is a limited one: to single out, from among the great mass of his contentions, those which seem to be of abiding significance. A great deal of what he writes is *zeitbedingt*, explicable by the intellectual situation in which he found himself, but of no lasting significance. Setting this aside, what have we left? What is there in his philosophy which deserves further consideration and development?

It would hardly be possible for any philosopher in England to develop Dilthey's themes without being led into a comparison of Dilthey with Collingwood. The likenesses between the two men are so obvious that the comparison imposes itself inevitably; and the differences between them are such that the working out of the comparison must prove instructive. In dealing with Dilthey, point by point, I shall have Collingwood in mind, and shall make such comparisons as may serve to throw light on each philosopher by contrast with the other.

We can begin by dismissing from consideration one whole range of questions. Wherever the living point of Dilthey's philosophy may be, it is not in his theories about sense-perception and the external world. To him this was always a secondary interest, and the views which are summarised in our Chapter Two have little intrinsic value, though they serve to throw light on the ruling motives of Dilthey's thinking. It is clear that his standpoint is anti-metaphysical. He is determined to reject any kind of apriorism, any kind of idealism, or any theory which claims to know the 'inner nature' of things 'behind' the phenomena of perception. He can claim the merit of having seen that the question of the 'real existence' of the 'external world' is largely a question of definitions—what do we *mean* by such words as 'object', 'real', 'external' and so on? However, he does not work out the remoter implications of this, and what little he does say is not free from obscurities.

Much the same must be said of his treatment of the wider issues of logic and epistemology. His approach to philosophy was not logical, and to logic proper he made no contribution whatever. He is more at home in exploring the prelogical levels of experience, whether in sense-perception or in our awareness of our own and other selves. His aim is to make a descriptive analysis of the field of consciousness—an aim which philosophers have often enough set before themselves, and which brings him into line with Kantians, Hegelians, and phenomenologists. But if we accept the fact that this was his aim, we cannot be impressed by his achievement. We need not dwell on his remarks about 'contents' and 'attitudes', or on the triplicity of cognitive, affective, and conative attitudes which runs through his work. These are the tribute which he paid to contemporary habits of thought and speech. He does not take them too seriously in detail himself. There are only two points on which he is immovable. The first is that mental processes are predominantly purposive or, as he says, 'structural', and tend towards the building up of an integrated mind and character. The second is that thought is not an independent source of truth, but exists merely to 'clarify' what is implicit in feeling or 'lived experience'. He can claim to have done what few in his generation were able to do: to be whole-heartedly empiricist in epistemology without being associationist or behaviourist in psychology; to do justice to the movement of life and experience without being led off by it into metaphysical speculation as Bergson was. This is to his credit, and may serve as a model for us too, but not in any matter of detail.

Experience as a self-integrating whole; dependence of all thought upon prelogical forms of experience; fruitlessness of all ontological or metaphysical speculations: these three points contain most of what is sound and living in Dilthey's general theory of knowledge. Let us keep them in mind as we carry our examination of him a stage further.

Perhaps the fact most widely known about Dilthey is that he was a philosopher who concerned himself with history. This is true, but will be deceptive if it leads us to rank him as just one more among those who have devoted themselves to something called the 'philosophy of history', just one more in a group which includes such already well-known members as Croce and Collingwood. The points in which he diverges from that group are as important and instructive as those in which he agrees with them. If we add that he also concerned himself with fine art, music, and literature, and that this brings him into renewed contact with Croce and Collingwood in their capacity as aestheticians, again it must be said that the differences are as important as the likenesses.

One difference arises from the fact that Croce and Collingwood, like many other philosophers, treat art and history not only as forms of experience which are interesting and important in themselves, but also as units in the edifice of a system. The plan of Croce's philosophy is well known; it claims to bring all the activities of the human 'spirit' under four main heads, and so to give a comprehensive view of the mind's life—which turns out also, on Croce's idealist principles, to be a view of all reality. Collingwood's philosophy is true to the spirit of his master, diverging from Croce only where it reverts to a position more like Hegel's, and reintroducing a form of dialectical transition which Croce had abandoned as unsound. The system which he constructed in *Speculum Mentis* will have to be brought under examination before we have done; for the present it is enough to recognise that this kind of system-building is altogether alien to Dilthey.

I do not make it a grievance against Collingwood that he thought he found an ordered system in experience. There is certainly some degree of order in things, and what is thinking for, but to detect as much of it as we honestly can? I think however that Collingwood, like others, has accepted too easily a simple formula as expressing the structure of experience, and has allowed this to determine *a priori* his approach to particular realms of experience. He cannot look straight at art, because he

317

has decided beforehand that it must somehow be correlated with 'imagination' in the Kantian sense of that word. He cannot see the real relation between natural science and historical thinking, because he has decided beforehand that they must represent two rungs in a dialectical ladder. The post-Kantian mirror of the mind, in this its latest configuration, does not result from honest examination of the several activities of civilised man and the relations between them. It is a prefabricated framework into which these activities are fitted by force. By contrast with this, Dilthey's rejection of the post-Kantian systems sets him free from their dogmatic assumptions. It enables him to consult other sources, and to look freely at experience itself. He has not Collingwood's crispness of expression, nor his power of reasoned analysis and ordered presentation; but he has a greater sensitivity to the facts of experience, and a greater humility before them.

This is not to say that Dilthey has not an ordered system of his own. He has, but it is not an all-comprehending one like Collingwood's; the all-comprehending system is just what his rejection of metaphysics is meant to exclude. He too exhibits art and history as elements in a wider whole; but that whole is simply the human studies. It is not even the whole of human knowledge, for the natural sciences remain outside it, a realm whose frontier Dilthey traces, but whose interior he does not venture to explore. And just for this reason, because the human studies are not seen as a link in a chain which must somehow reach from sense-perception, through natural science and history, to a final term in philosophy, but are taken as a province relatively complete in itself, something of their distinctive character becomes visible to Dilthey, which more ambitious systems may miss.

It is to this, I believe, that we must attribute Dilthey's firm refusal to separate historical knowledge from the other disciplines, so diverse in character, which make up the *Geisteswissenschaften*. If we are arranging the sciences dialectically, or by degrees of approximation to some logically determined norm of truth, we are sure to divide them on grounds of method and principle, and the presence of experimental methods and generalising theories in psychology or in economics is sure to lead us to classify them with the natural sciences, while historiography remains separate, distinguished by its individuating

318

or idiographic character. That is the principle on which Croce and Collingwood have worked. It is also, as we have seen, the principle followed by Rickert and the Neo-Kantians, and for the same reason: because their philosophy too is governed by distinctions of logical form. Dilthey's is not, though he recognises these distinctions when he meets them. The central factor in the human studies is not, as he sees it, their interest in the particular and the individual. It is the presence in them all of some element of 'understanding'.

Dilthey's philosophy is not a *philosophy of history*, if that means a theory of historical thinking simply as such. It is a *philosophy of understanding*, and because it is that it is also a *philosophy of culture*. It is one of the marks of civilised men that they can enjoy a community of life and experience. They do not merely 'come to an understanding'; they 'understand' one another. Dilthey knows this, and it is not too much to say that a passion for understanding pervades all his thought. It is here that he finds the meaning and value of history itself; not that it enlarges our knowledge of events, nor even that it gives us individual fact where natural science gives us general law, but that it makes the historian's mind a mirror in which are reflected the minds and experiences of other men. History is a vehicle of understanding. It is 'life embracing life', in a phrase of Dilthey's own. So, in a measure, are all the human studies; for understanding is present throughout the study of human behaviour, as distinct from the anatomy and physiology of the human body. Art too is a sphere of understanding; the artist is one who understands, and we understand him. This is the theme which runs through the *Kritik der historischen Vernunft*, and governs the selection and arrangement of its contents.

'Life embracing life.' This does not mean that all minds are One Mind, and that the Absolute becomes self-conscious in and through the historical self-consciousness of mankind. That kind of fustian may be left to Hegel and his imitators, including the author of *Speculum Mentis*. What Dilthey means is that individual human beings understand individual human beings, and he means no more. But how much that is! It is the basis of all social life, and of all cultural activity. In particular, it is the explanation and justification of Dilthey's own life as a scholar and humanist; he is one who contains in himself, and helps to foster

319

in others, this most essential human capacity of understanding. And in his philosophy, as distinct from his historical and critical writings, a leading aim is to discover what we do, and what it is that we know, when we understand people.

A leading aim in his philosophy—but it is not the sole aim. If we were to ask Dilthey what are the fundamental aims of his philosophy, he would answer that there are two. The first is to dig down to the roots of human knowledge, to discover on what basis it rests, whence it derives its content, its principles, and its authority. This is the aim of epistemology, and of course the enquiry into the nature and basis of understanding is merely one part of this wider enquiry, though it is a part which particularly interests Dilthey. The second aim which he sets before himself is to enquire into what he calls the metaphysical consciousness—what it is in our nature which impels us to raise speculative questions of the kind which traditional metaphysics was supposed to answer, and which Kant and the positivists say cannot be answered. This is a wider enquiry than epistemology, since it concerns not only our intellectual processes and capacities but also our value-judgments, our conscience, our hopes and aspirations. All these play a part in generating and shaping a *Weltanschauung*, and a *Weltanschauung* must assign to each of them its proper place in the picture.

In these enquiries we are led to an idea which is even more fundamental in Dilthey's thought than that of understanding—to the idea of *life* (*das Leben*). Both *Weltanschauungslehre* and epistemology come round to this at last. It is not from the intellect that *Weltanschauungen* arise, and it is not by merely logical analysis that we can discover what they mean. They spring from human life in the 'totality' of its powers and impulses, and must be understood in terms of that totality. But even in the narrower field of epistemology Dilthey finds that the same is true. Life appears here on both sides of the epistemological relation. It is one of the objects—to us the most interesting and important object—which we cognise, and it is also the subject by which the cognising is done; for here too it is not merely the mind or intellect, but the whole living man in the totality of his powers, who perceives and thinks.

Dilthey gives a pregnant sense of his own to this word *life*. With him it is not a biological term. His philosophy is not a variety of vitalism, like Bergson's. Nor is it a psychological term, if by psychology we mean primarily the science of human behaviour; for that science studies people with a detachment which Dilthey, the humanist, does not attain or seek. *Life* to him means human experience as known from within, as known by the poet and the autobiographer. Philosopher as he is, and therefore familiar with the rational activities of the mind, he has also a keen sense of the non-rational side of human nature, of its instinctive and especially of its intuitive aspects, and his philosophy is meant to include an account of all these. Especially noticeable is his keen sense of the action and reaction in which the human being is perpetually involved with all that is around him. We are all the time at grips with our surrounding world, and perceiving and thinking are to be accounted for only in this context of stimulus and response, which is an integral part of what Dilthey means by *life*.

It is in these terms too that we shall understand what he means by *reality* (*Wirklichkeit*), and how he can claim that his philosophy is a recall to reality and objectivity, in spite of the obvious elements of subjectivism in it. He has nothing in the nature of an ontology. He makes it abundantly clear that what we know in nature is not a thing in itself, but an ordered system of appearances, impinging upon us in sensation and interpreted by our thinking. But it is not against an uncritical realism that he directs his controversial shafts. It is against various philosophies of recent times, whose account of knowledge and the knowing subject Dilthey thinks is abstract and formal. It is against the timeless transcendental self of Kant and Kantianism, against the ditch dug between sensory material and *a priori* forms (whereby both are robbed of their objectivity), and against the superstition that knowledge can be analysed exclusively in terms of sense-data and logical relationships. Experience, he says, is not a panorama which unrolls itself before a detached observer, nor is it an imaginative and intellectual construction put together by a transcendental self, or even by many such selves in concert. It is a matter of 'life-relations', of stimulus and response, of action and reaction, of a living conscious organism at grips with its environment. It is here that we are to find the archetypal 'reality'; and it is because Dilthey recognises this that he justly claims to be a true empiricist, while many who claim that title have no conception of what experience actually is.

An English reader may sometimes be reminded of Bradley's recoil from Kantian and Hegelian epistemology, which seemed to him to reduce the world to a 'spectral woof of impalpable abstractions'—his insistence that 'reality' must mean 'feeling' or 'sentient experience'—his criticism of the conception of the timeless self—his insistence that a proper account of 'reality' must include the witness of all modes of experience, of feeling and volition as well as of cognition. Bradley's 'feeling' or 'sentient experience' has much in common with Dilthey's 'lived experience', not least in the intensity with which Bradley himself obviously experienced it; but Dilthey's sense of action and reaction, his belief that the not-self is somehow 'given' in lived experience as acting upon me, is absent from Bradley.

What applies to knowledge applies *a fortiori* to a *Weltanschauung*: it springs not from pure reason, but from the whole of life. It is true that metaphysics has constantly pretended otherwise, and striven to present *Weltanschauungen* under the guise of purely rational speculations; involving itself thereby, as Dilthey says, in a 'labour of Sisyphus' in the attempt to rationalise what cannot be rationalised. It was Kant, Dilthey continues, who half-unknowingly exposed the illusion, and directed our attention to the real roots of the metaphysical consciousness in the moral and religious life. 'What Kant examines is not the living metaphysical outlook, as it draws nourishment and blood from all the forces of its mother earth, which is the totality of human nature, the human heart itself, and so strides along through history as an indestructible reality. What he examines, attacks, and annihilates is a shadow, the dead conceptual science of metaphysics. And so arises a curious drama. He looks for the analytical elements of metaphysics in the sphere of the isolated intelligence, led on by the analogy of logic and mathematics, and under the influence of the metaphysics actually created on that basis by Wolff; he shows that no metaphysics can be erected on the basis of these elements, and finally relegates the origin, power, and evidence of a metaphysical outlook to the place where he should have sought it from the beginning; he arrests the vagabond Metaphysics in the place where she had lately been residing, and sends her back to her home. For that is the great work of his practical philosophy and Critique of Judgment' (quoted in *G.S.*, V, lxv f.).

It does not follow from this that philosophy has no concern with *Weltanschauungen*. It may have a very important concern with them. Like the aesthetic, moral, and religious valuations on which they so largely depend, they spring from sources in human nature which cannot be eradicated. Even if we regard them as pure fantasy, they are yet a perpetually recurring fantasy, and philosophy will have the duty which Kant assigned to it, of exposing the illusion anew to each generation as it grows up. But that is not the whole of the matter. Like value-judgments, again, *Weltanschauungen* play a great part in the formation of personality, and in generating and sustaining the life of social groups. Even if they are all false when taken literally, as theories of the universe, we usually feel that some are more healthy and stimulating to the mind and character than others. The question, for instance, whether Christianity has been a good influence in European life and thought is a real question, even if we assume that the Christian beliefs about God and the universe are not true in the sense in which Christians are supposed to hold them. This is a type of question which has a great deal of philosophical interest. Admitting that a *Weltanschauung* has an influence on life and thought, that is already a matter which will interest the moral philosopher and the philosopher of history. If we then ask how such influence is exerted, and how a set of ideas which are not true in the sense in which they are consciously held can yet exert a good and healthy influence, we are led to deeper questions about truth and meaning. Can a set of formulae which is consciously intended to convey one meaning, a false one, nevertheless have unconsciously another meaning which is in some sense true? The problem of the value and influence of *Weltanschauungen* leads in this way to the problem of their interpretation, and that takes us into difficult questions of symbolism and language. Thus the demonstration that metaphysics as a science of pure reason is impossible is not necessarily the end of our interest in metaphysics. When that demonstration has been given, the *Critique of Metaphysical Symbolism* may find that its work is just beginning.

Such a critique is foreshadowed in Fichte and Hegel and their followers, but with important limitations. In them it is only a critique of other people's religious and metaphysical utterances. For themselves, they let it be seen that they have found the one true metaphysic, of which all the rest are imperfect reflections; and this one true metaphysic is after all a science of reason, indeed it is Absolute Reason becoming self-conscious. To Dilthey, who is in earnest about not having a science of pure reason, not even a 'critical' or 'transcendental' one, this position must appear half-hearted. He must go further. In particular, he must make clear that metaphysical symbols are not imperfect formulations of an intellectually apprehensible truth, but expressions of 'life' in his sense of the word. In so far as they contain something that can be called 'truth', it is not reason becoming self-conscious, but 'life embracing life'; and the function of philosophy in relation to them is to sharpen the symbolism and make clearer what it is that they express. 'Philosophy', he says, 'is an *action* by which *life*, i.e. the *subject* in its *relationships* as *living activity*, is *raised to consciousness and thought through to the end*' (*Briefwechsel Dilthey-Yorck*, p. 247). The understanding and interpretation of metaphysical symbolism is an important element in this task.

Conceiving the task of a *Weltanschauungslehre* in this way, Dilthey might still find his way to the view that one particular set of symbols is the best and truest, because the total attitude to life which finds expression in it is the fullest and healthiest. Then he would be like the Hegelians, understanding and evaluating other people's views of life while yet giving a primacy to his own. We can see what his chosen view would be: a kind of contemplative humanism, closely approximating to Goethe and Novalis. Something of this kind shows through his work as it is; no man can wholly conceal his personal tendencies and enthusiasms; but something else has entered in and prevented him from openly adopting and propagating it. That something is the breadth of his historical and psychological understanding, together with his scrupulous honesty in face of opposing views. These factors together explain why Dilthey, instead of working out a philosophical expression of his own *Weltanschauung* and leaving the matter there, ends on a note of relativism with his three rival types.

In so doing he has in a manner 'transcended himself' (as he says of von Wartenburg), and recognised his own outlook and

standpoint as only one of several which are plausible and legitimate. But he has bequeathed to philosophy a serious problem.
How that problem should be dealt with is a question which we
must discuss shortly. Meanwhile let us notice how, in this cul-
minating section of Dilthey's philosophy, his two leading conceptions of *life* and *understanding* come together. Let us notice
too how the task of philosophy, thus modestly conceived, ap-
proximates to that of history. He said so himself at the outset of
his career, in words which all his later work serves only to
illustrate and confirm. 'It would not be worth while to be a
historian, if it were not also a way of comprehending the world.
. . . What is worth knowing? To what end this planet was
formed, towards the realisation of what purposes we are carried
during the half-century of intelligent life which we live on its
surface: weightier questions than these, questions arising more
out of the depths of human need, I could not name. But if historical knowledge is to be what it ought to be, it will—answer
these questions? That would be foolish presumption, but from
the whole development of mankind it will be able to extract
convincing reflections. . . . When a man studies history with such
an eye for the forms of human existence, the laws which govern
it, the tendencies which arise out of its nature, in his mind
there comes to life, after his own manner, no less a portion of
such truth as is vouchsafed to us than in the mind of the
philosopher' (*Der junge Dilthey*, p. 81).

After these general considerations, it will be convenient to
proceed to a detailed confrontation of Dilthey with Collingwood. We shall find their philosophies running parallel, but at
a noticeable distance from one another. They run parallel, in
that they deal very largely with the same issues, and with a
somewhat similar background of experience. They are kept
apart by the fact that their fundamental assumptions and guiding
principles are different. Dilthey's ruling conceptions of *understanding* and *life* belong to a different world from the Hegelian
conceptions which control Collingwood's thinking.

Collingwood himself has begun the confrontation by giving
us (in *The Idea of History*) his views on Dilthey. We shall have to
examine these views, which throw more light on their author
himself than on Dilthey. Yet, before we are too brusque with
Collingwood, we shall do well to consult the chapter on Dilthey

in *Filosofi del Novecento*, by de Ruggiero, whom Collingwood describes as 'my friend' (*An Autobiography*, p. 99). Allowing for differences of date and purpose, the two men treat Dilthey in a strikingly similar way. Both are prompt to recognise his breadth of learning and his power of historical understanding. De Ruggiero says that his work on the Reformation period is the best that had been written, down to that time, in Germany; and Collingwood writes of him as a 'lonely and neglected genius'. But both draw a picture of him as one who struggled in vain to make his understanding articulate in philosophical analysis. It is the same view of him which we also find in Rickert's disciples (cf. Arthur Stein, *Der Begriff des Verstehens bei Dilthey*). It seems to be impossible for Hegelians and Neo-Kantians to enter understandingly into Dilthey's point of view, or to treat it seriously as a legitimate alternative to their own. In the case of de Ruggiero and Collingwood, it must be confessed, another factor is certainly at work, viz. an insufficient acquaintance with what Dilthey actually wrote.

I shall make the confrontation by taking successively a number of issues, following roughly the order in which they arise in Dilthey's *Kritik*, and examining in each case what Dilthey and Collingwood have to say.

Feeling and imagination

Dilthey and Collingwood are both keenly interested in the subintellectual forms of experience, and in the prelogical forms of expression to which they give rise. Both emphasise the dependence of thought on these lower forms of experience, and the part played by expression in making them accessible to reflective examination. Here is an extensive and important field of enquiry which they have in common. How far do they agree in their treatment of it?

There is one topic on which neither of them shines, viz. the distinctions to be drawn between cognitive and non-cognitive types of experience. Dilthey has his threefold scheme of cognitive, affective, and volitional experiences; but he has obviously taken it over from earlier writers such as Kant, and we have seen how in the end he became sceptical of clear-cut distinctions in this field, and admitted that his terminology was merely a workable approximation. Somewhere behind the 'feelings' and 'volitions' lurk the 'instincts', which are said to constitute the core of the mind's life; but it is not made clear how they are related to 'feelings' and 'volitions'. Collingwood for his part finds little occasion to talk of instinct, desire, or will. It is in his aesthetic writings that his psychology is most fully stated, and there everything which is not a sensation or image or thought appears to be an 'emotion'. What a psychologist would say to this use of the word, I forbear to guess. Collingwood is like too many philosophers in not being really interested in any forms of experience but the cognitive, and not really trained in intro-specting such forms; so to him they are all 'emotions', and there an end.

What really interests Collingwood is the vertical division which he makes between feeling, imagination, and thought. 'Feeling' here includes both sensation and 'emotion': it answers to what Croce calls *impressioni* and *sentimenti*. It is the primary form of conscious experience, and it is characterised by extreme fluidity and obscurity. A feeling is transient, a 'perishing exis-tence', no sooner come than gone; it is not clearly appreciated as to its own character, nor related to other feelings and the ex-periencing subject. It is the function of *imagination* to clarify feelings, and so make them fit objects for knowledge. This is done by focusing attention upon them. By attending to a feeling I single it out from among my other feelings, give it a degree of permanence, and consciously appreciate its quality. I can then go on to think about it, i.e. to detect likenesses and other kinds of relation between it and other things; and so I come to know-ledge of an objective world.

What Collingwood here calls *imagination* is the same as what Croce calls *intuizione*, and it is Kant's *Einbildungskraft*, the 'blind but indispensable faculty' which mediates between sensibility and thought. The analysis certainly indicates something which is real, and can be verified in experience. By means of it Colling-wood is able to throw light on several important aspects of mental and moral life. It is all the more important to him because he, like Croce and all his school, defines art in terms of imagination, and therefore the relation between imagination and thought defines for him the relation between art and science. Even if we do not put the word 'imagination' into the definition of art, we may go with him so far as to agree that imagination, in the sense here in question, plays a very important part in aesthetic contemplation and in artistic creation.

What is there in Dilthey to compare with this?

Dilthey does not approach the analysis of experience with the same preoccupations as Collingwood. He is concerned to stress those characteristics of mental life which show it to be a system and yet not a mechanical system. He describes in vivid phrases the flowing, changeful character of consciousness, the interpenetration of past, present, and future, of memory, perception, and expectation; also the 'structural' relations between different aspects of mental activity, whereby cognitive and conative processes are combined and fused together to make a living whole. All this is reminiscent of Bergson, who is also concerned to make the same points, rather than of Collingwood, who takes them for granted. Collingwood paints on a smaller canvas; he is primarily concerned to distinguish the three grades (sensory, imaginative, intellective) in cognitive experience. There is nothing in Dilthey to conflict with what he says about this; but does Dilthey himself say it or something like it? He does not use the word *Einbildungskraft* in the same way as Collingwood uses *imagination*. Does he convey the same meaning in another way?

Like Collingwood, he is aware of the fluidity of our experience on the lowest level of feeling, and he too sees that this raises a problem. How are feelings made clear enough and stable enough to provide a foundation for thought? Like Collingwood, again, he says that we begin by selective attention; by focussing on one element in experience and isolating it from others we become more vividly aware of it. This allows other images, called up by memory or association, to cluster round it and build up that amplified sensory complex which he calls a *Totalvorstellung*. The process so far is pretty exactly what Collingwood means by 'imagination'. Why then does not Dilthey use that word, and emphasise the importance of this process in similar terms to Collingwood? Because he always sees it as part of a wider process, and never finds any need to single it out to be named and studied by itself. The building up of clear imagery is never separated, in his accounts of the matter, from the elementary unconscious operations of distinguishing, comparing, combining, etc., which he calls 'silent thought'. These too contribute to 'clarify' the given, and to give us a 'distinct consciousness' of it. All this is prior to discursive thought and its expression in language; but still it is something more than what Collingwood means by 'imagination'. The resulting experience is not merely an imaginative intuition, but a perception; and the principle of the 'intellectuality' of perception is one which Dilthey often asserts.

It seems to me that Dilthey's point is just as important as Collingwood's. What Collingwood calls 'imagination' is certainly a real factor in experience, but he isolates it too sharply from the other factors with which it is bound up. We often perceive without speaking or thinking in words; but I doubt whether we ever intuit without perceiving, without 'silent' or unconscious thinking, at any rate in ordinary waking life. (Something of the kind does seem to happen rarely in half-waking states, or under the influence of a drug.) And the same applies to the creative work of the artist, which in popular language is often called 'imagination'. Certainly the artist is characterised by a copious flow of vivid imagery, both in perception and in invention. Dilthey gives examples to illustrate this from the testimony of artists themselves. Certainly also he has a high capacity for selective attention. But he uses this power, as Dilthey says, to bring out what is 'typical' or characteristic in what he sees or portrays; and that is impossible without a great deal of 'silent' comparing and distinguishing, i.e. thinking. Aesthetic contemplation and artistic creation are as 'intellectual', as shot through with elementary thought-activity, as is ordinary perception. They are distinguished from it not by the absence of thought, but by differences of quite another kind. Dilthey is prepared to use the word *Einbildungskraft* in the titles of his two essays on aesthetics, but he uses it in its popular sense and not as a technical term enshrining a doctrine. He does not take the word in Collingwood's sense and use it to define the essence of art.

Expression

Other divergences appear between our two writers when they turn from experience to its expression.

They agree on a number of fundamental points. Both recognise that expression is not something external and superadded to experience, but grows out of experience naturally, continually,

329

inevitably. Both recognise that expression often reacts upon the experience expressed, giving definiteness and a degree of permanence to what might otherwise be a vague passing feeling. Both recognise, again, that expression is a powerful aid to self-knowledge, that (as Dilthey sees it) we learn little about ourselves by direct introspection, but a great deal by understanding our own expressions. This is a point on which Dilthey dwells increasingly in his later years. Collingwood takes us a stage further by showing how expression, by giving self-knowledge, also makes possible self-control and moral freedom.

These are important agreements. But there are also differences.

Dilthey distinguishes three types of expression, one of which consists of human actions; not, that is to say, mere physical motions or gestures, or elementary reflexes, but considered actions and courses of action entered upon deliberately for the fulfilment of a purpose. Collingwood does not recognise actions in this sense as a species of expression at all. The difference here is apparently one of standpoint and purpose. Collingwood in *The Principles of Art* discusses expression primarily from a genetic point of view, describing how it arises out of experience, and how one form of expression develops out of another. From this psychological point of view, an action is something different in kind from an expression; it is one thing to give utterance to one's resolves, and quite another thing to carry them into execution. Dilthey on the other hand takes the point of view of the interpreter, the critic, and the historian; he thinks of expression primarily as that which makes life accessible to understanding. Now, to a historian a man's actions do 'express' his purposes and ultimately his character, in the sense that they make them visible; and Collingwood recognises this in *The Idea of History*, as he could not help doing, though he does not bring in the word 'expression'. Presumably he would have had to raise the point in passing in *The Principles of Art* as well, if he had there been writing less from the genetic point of view and more from the standpoint of the interpreter; for in narrative art, in epic and drama and the novel, we are meant to take the actions of the characters described as 'expressing' something of their minds and souls.[1]

[1] Here, of course, we are not understanding the artist, who has expressed himself in his work; we are understanding the imaginary characters whom

330

A second difference arises from the same fact, that Collingwood's approach to the subject is genetic or psychological, while Dilthey's is hermeneutic. What is it that an expression expresses? Dilthey is content to say that anything which is in the mind may be expressed. Hence he can recognise one type of expression which expresses ideas, another which expresses purposes, and a third (the *Erlebnisausdruck*) which expresses total states of mind, with the emotional element predominating. In his view a thought can quite well find expression on its own account, independently of any emotional aura which may cling about it, and this does in fact happen in strictly scientific statements and in strictly pragmatic communications, like the example he gives of the signal which announces the approach of a train. This is not to deny that many expressions which are meant to convey ideas do in fact, whether intentionally or not, convey also the speaker's or writer's emotional attitude to what he is saying. When that happens, we have two kinds of expression blended in a single utterance. Here we have in effect the theory of the two uses of language, which is expounded by Richards, and is the target of a vigorous attack by Collingwood. He claims to see deeper into the matter than this, and says that what is expressed is always *primarily* an emotion. Sensations, perceptions, ideas are expressed indirectly, in and through the expression of the emotion which they arouse. *All* intellectual expression is emotionally coloured, and it is only through the emotion that the idea comes to be expressed at all. Whether this is true or not, we need not here try to judge. It is irrelevant from the strictly hermeneutic point of view which is Dilthey's, and which (incidentally) Richards largely shares.

A third difference flows from Collingwood's distinction between feeling and imagination; for this gives rise to a parallel distinction between two kinds of expression. All emotion, says Collingwood, has a tendency to find overt expression, but the expression is of a different character according as the emotion expressed is or is not attended to and imaginatively apperceived. If it is crude and unselfconscious emotion, the expression too is

---

he sets before us, whom he describes as acting in ways which 'express' their characters. It is the kind of 'expression' and understanding which belong to history, not to art, though in certain cases they appear in the realm of art because the work of art takes the form of a history.

331

crude, unselfconscious, and involuntary; while the expression arising from an imaginative experience is itself imaginative, the conscious and deliberate utterance of one who knows what he is expressing. It is this imaginative type of expression which makes self-knowledge possible. We are then told that language is the same thing as imaginative expression; and we are shown how, though it is essentially the expression of imaginative experience, it can be modified and developed to give expression to intellective experiences—how it is not strictly an expression of the thought, but of the imaginatively apperceived emotion accompanying the thought.

This distinction between 'psychic' and 'imaginative' expressions is undoubtedly a description of something which is real and important. It is a defect in Dilthey that he gives no place to it. As I indicated in Chapter Five, the 'psychic' and 'imaginative' expressions of Collingwood's theory are both included in Dilthey's class of *Erlebnisausdrücke*. I have tried to show that Dilthey's analysis of experience includes something which is roughly equivalent to Collingwood's 'imagination', and may even be a more accurate or at least a more adequate account of what happens. In terms of his theory of the 'clarification' of experience by selective attention and silent thought it would presumably be possible for him to draw a distinction between two types of expression which would answer to the distinction here drawn by Collingwood; and his aesthetic, if not his theory of historical knowledge, would be the clearer and stronger for it. However, he does not do so.

Understanding and historical knowledge

To understand, says Dilthey, is to relive (*nacherleben*) or reproduce (*nachbilden*) someone else's experience in my own. Confronted by the expression of someone else's experience, I enact that same experience in my own consciousness, and yet at the same time 'project' or 'transpose' it into him whose experience it properly is. I am able thus to re-enact his experience because I have a mental structure like his, and the experiences which are actual in him are potential in me. In understanding, these potentialities are actualised. That, Dilthey adds, is why understanding, in art and in history, is an enlargement and enrichment of life for the understanding subject. He enjoys, through

332

understanding of others, experiences which could never come to him in his own person.

Collingwood says much the same. We can understand an artist, he says, because he is expressing ideas and emotions which are present, at least potentially, in ourselves, and what serves to express these ideas and emotions when he has them serves also to arouse them in us. We understand him by 're-constructing' in our own consciousness the experience which he has expressed, recognising as we do so that it is really his experience, not our own. Similarly the historian understands people's actions by rethinking their thoughts, 're-enacting' or 'reliving' their experiences, and, while distinguishing the persons whom he studies from himself, 'making their experience his own'.

Collingwood's position is thus fundamentally the same as Dilthey's; nevertheless he, in company with de Ruggiero, finds ground for adverse comments on Dilthey. The point of attack is the same which is chosen by Rickert and the Neo-Kantians— the use of the word *nacherleben* in Dilthey's account of understanding. Like the Neo-Kantians, de Ruggiero suspects, and Collingwood assumes, that *Erlebnis* means 'feeling' in their sense of the word, a sub-logical and even sub-imaginative level of experience; and it needs no argument to show that *nacherleben* in that acceptation is not genuine understanding.

De Ruggiero puts his criticism in the form of a question: does Dilthey mean by *Erlebnis* an immediate feeling, or 'a true and proper intuition', i.e. an imaginative experience? It ought to be the latter, for Dilthey is analysing historical knowledge on Kantian lines, and *Erlebnis* is meant to be to *Verstehen* what 'spatio-temporal intuition' is to the scientific concept. But most of what Dilthey says about *Erlebnis* suggests the other meaning. De Ruggiero concludes that Dilthey wavered between the two interpretations, and never clearly distinguished them in his own mind.

I have tried in the last section but one to show how much truth there is in the allegation that Dilthey overlooks the intuitional level of experience. If he does not emphasise it as Croce and his followers do, it is not because he is wallowing in immediate experience; it is because he is anxious to emphasise rather the 'intellectuality' of our experience at a lower level than is

333

often realised. De Ruggiero himself recognises that *Verstehen* is meant to be a conceptual operation, and goes on in connection with it to discuss some of Dilthey's 'categories of life'.

Collingwood's criticism is more drastic. He has no doubt that by *Erlebnis* Dilthey means 'immediate experience, as distinct from reflection or knowledge', something which is 'merely private and personal, . . . not objective'; and he says that this immediate experience, without any intellectual superstructure at all, is what Dilthey means by historical understanding. To understand someone is to *nacherleben* his experience, and that means simply to re-feel his feelings. Collingwood rightly says that this will not do. If I merely make Julius Caesar's feelings my own, that means that I merely feel as he felt; I do not thereby know Caesar, or myself, or anything at all. But Dilthey, he says, cannot envisage an intellectual knowledge of human life and experience in any form but that of psychological explanation; and so, since historical knowledge is not psychological explanation, he has to say that it is mere *Erlebnis*. Collingwood goes on to describe what historical knowledge really is, and how it grows out of a kind of thinking which is interwoven with ordinary experience. Suppose I am disturbed by an emotional discomfort, and pause to reflect upon it. At once I am led to trace its connections with previous events which have helped to cause or condition it, and I come to see my present state as part of a wider process of life. This is knowledge of myself, not as an instance of a general law, but as this unique individual in this unique context of events. It is true historical knowledge; and historical knowledge of other persons is of the same logical type as this.

The best comment to make on this is to point to the passage in Dilthey's *Kritik* where he describes the 'onward trend' of lived experience, how it passes of its own accord into a train of reflection, of memories and expectations, which lead to a vision of myself in my present context in the stream of events; and where he goes on to show how, from such reflection as this, auto-biography and biography and historical writing arise. Collingwood's account of what Dilthey did not know would do very well as a summary of what Dilthey actually said.

I have tried to show in Chapter Five where the weakness of these Hegelian and Neo-Kantian critics lies. Because Dilthey does not accept their mythology of reason, they think he ascribes too much to mere feeling. But 'feeling' as a chaos, devoid of form and meaning, is their conception, not his. His conception is of a stream of experience possessing structural unity on every level, and illuminated by the continual work of silent thought. In his view Julius Caesar's experience, which the historian relives, was the experience of a self-conscious person, shot through with silent thought and accompanied by a running commentary of discursive reflection on himself. Because Caesar's experience was thus a self-knowledge, to relive his experience is to know him. If *Erlebnis* is highly intellectual, so is *das Nacherleben*. We have seen how Dilthey explains this in detail, and ends by saying that 'understanding is an intellectual process involving the highest concentration'.

Dilthey does not underestimate the part played by thought in life and in the understanding of life. On the other hand, it might well be argued that Collingwood overestimates it. For in *The Idea of History* he says that thought is the only proper subject-matter of historical knowledge. History, he says, is not a record of sensations and feelings, of dreams and fancies, of emotions and desires which men have had, nor even of their actions simply as actions, but only of their thoughts. 'All history is the history of thought.' And, of course, the only way to understand thought is to rethink it. Historical knowledge, therefore, appears to be a wholly intellectual performance. It is not 'life embracing life', but thought apprehending thought.

If this meant that a historian must never talk about anything but ideas, it would be too silly for anyone to maintain. The practice of any historian, including Collingwood's own practice, would refute it at once. A true historian is potentially interested in anything that can occur in human experience; *nihil humani a se alienum putat. Nihil humani*—but there is the clue to what Collingwood is saying. History is not merely the story of life, it is the story of human life, and that means intelligent life. Sensations and perceptions, emotions, desires and resolves and actions, these are indeed the substance of life; but what makes it human life, and therefore historical, is that all this is illuminated and directed by thought. Experience without thought would be a mere sequence of events, a tale told by an idiot, signifying nothing. It is thought that puts meaning into life. Take, for

335

example, an action, say Brutus' action in stabbing Caesar. The mere knowledge that he did it is not history, it is only material for history. What the historian wants to know is what was in Brutus' mind that led him to do it, i.e. what thought was behind the physical act. All human action, in so far forth as human, is deliberate action in pursuance of a known end. Different departments of human action are marked out by their respective ends: economic, political, military, ethical, scientific, religious, and so on. The one apparent exception is art; for, according to Collingwood, the artist as distinct from the craftsman does not know what he is going to do before he does it. But even he knows that he is going to engage in artistic creation in order to find expression for something which is obscurely haunting his mind, and to that extent he too acts for a known end.

Here we have the typical Hegelian and Neo-Kantian dualism. Experience is cut in two, with a meaningless chaos on one side, and on the other side thought, the only source of meaning. What should be said of it from the Diltheian point of view?

Collingwood says that action is made human and historical by having a known purpose. Now, the *knowledge* of our purposes is evidently a result of thought. But, we may ask, whence come the purposes themselves? Are they also from thought? How can they be? In the economic sphere, for instance, although no doubt our aims are differently shaped because our actions are self-conscious and deliberate, is not the ultimate driving force behind them the force of instinctive desires? Or is Collingwood's point that all such desires are transmuted, and raised to a new level of significance, by being integrated into the unity of a life which is governed by moral principles? And is he adopting the Neo-Kantian position, which makes life derive all its meaning from principles or norms of pure reason? He does not say so; and if he did say so, could it be true? How can reason be a source of motives? It cannot, if reason is the same as thought. διανοία αὐτή οὐθὲν κινεῖ. The conception of reason as a moral principle can only make sense, as Dilthey argues in his moral theory, if by 'reason' we mean not thought, but the shaping and self-organising power which is inherent in the structural system of the mind.

Life is a self-organising process, and the teleological unity which is manifest on the higher levels of life is continuous with what we find on the lower levels. It is true that man is man because he not only lives and acts, but knows the pattern of his actions. But the thought which knows that pattern does not create it; it only makes it conscious, and so raises it to a higher level of integration. Meaning is not imparted to life by thought, but is inherent in life and is merely revealed and enhanced by thought. And, while it is impossible to understand life without thinking, it is equally impossible to understand it by thinking alone. We must relive the other person's experience, re-enact his sensations and his emotions and his desires, or else there will be nothing for our historical thinking to think about. And our thinking, when we come to do it, will not be governed by abstract principles of reason, but by concepts which derive directly from life, such as the 'categories of life' of which Dilthey gives us a rough list. It is only a rough list, and we need not take it too seriously in detail; but the underlying principle, that thought does not bring meaning to life, but finds it there, is fundamental to Dilthey's philosophy.

A further problem. Whether we speak of reliving or of re-thinking it seems to be agreed that understanding involves the building up of a pattern in the understanding mind, on the basis of certain experiences which that mind has had, together with the assertion that this pattern is really the pattern of someone else's experience, which the understanding mind somehow re-enacts. How can we ever really know that it is so? How can the other mind ever be more than an inaccessible thing in itself? Or how can we avoid an ultimate solipsism? Collingwood and Dilthey both face this problem, and they agree that it can only be solved if minds are not cut off from one another, but can live and work in one another. My life is in a real sense continuous with other lives with which I come into contact, including lives belonging to the historical past, and my understanding of other persons grows out of this continuity. But Collingwood and Dilthey do not conceive this continuity in the same way.

Collingwood, as might be expected, states the problem in terms of thought, and asks how I, by an act of thought occurring now in my own mind, can understand a thought which occurred in a quite different mind, perhaps a long time ago. He develops an argument to show that it is possible for a thought to be one and the same thought even when it is thought on different occa-

337

sions and by different persons. In that case I can understand another person's thinking because the self-same thought which he has had enters into my mind and is now re-enacted or re-thought by me. This involves attributing to acts of thought a certain independence of date, a certain super-temporal identity. Collingwood in *The Idea of History* does not press on very far into the metaphysical consequences of this; but it is clear that that way lies the doctrine of the ultimate unity of all minds in the One Mind, which he undoubtedly held when he wrote *Speculum Mentis*, and never expressly repudiated.

Dilthey on the other hand sees the question as one of influences, a dynamic question rather than a logical one. We can reconstruct other people's experience correctly because we are continually being stimulated and moulded by their influence. Historical knowledge is possible because the knower is himself a product of history. The historical personages whom I study have shaped the conditions in which I now live; I am surrounded by the effect of their actions, and feel the impact of them continually. They also influence me directly through my understanding of their words and other self-expressions; and I know that this is not merely my fantasy, because these expressions set up in me a pattern of experience which is not native to me, and which acts upon my own life as an independent power.

History and the human studies

Here again we have to deal with criticisms brought against Dilthey by Collingwood and de Ruggiero.

Collingwood accuses him of simply not knowing what historical knowledge is, nor what is the object that it knows. Dilthey, according to him, begins rightly by saying that historical knowledge is knowledge of the concrete individual, as distinct from natural science, which is knowledge of abstract general laws; but he wholly fails to see under what conditions such knowledge is possible, and what form it must take. Thus in the *Einleitung* he treats the individual as an 'isolated past fact', torn away from his historical context, and therefore robbed of all historical character and meaning. De Ruggiero makes the same complaint about the *Einleitung*. According to de Ruggiero, however, Dilthey rectified the error at least as early as the *Ideen*, and came to see that it is impossible in the long run to understand an individual without his historical context; 'because in the formation of the individual the whole historical environment is involved, and, through it, the whole of past history'. Collingwood does not recognise this improvement in Dilthey's later work. On the contrary, according to him, it is precisely 'in later essays' that Dilthey asks himself how knowledge of the individual is possible, and gives the wrong answer. For Dilthey is too much the positivist to be able to think of any answer except by appealing to psychological analysis and explanation. That is his only way to self-knowledge or knowledge of others; and it is generalised knowledge, not knowledge of the individual in his individuality at all.

In Chapter Six I have quoted passages from the *Einleitung* which expressly deny that the individual can be understood as an 'isolated fact', and insist that he is only what social and historical influences make him. In Chapter One I have quoted other passages which show that Dilthey was aware of this as much as twenty years earlier than the *Einleitung*, and was using it as an argument against Schleiermacher. Yet there is some excuse for Collingwood's and de Ruggiero's misconception. The early history of Dilthey's ideas is not recounted in the *Einleitung*, nor in any of his major works. The *Einleitung* itself was written at a time when the positivist side of him was strongly to the fore. It is largely positivist in language and thought, and the presence of Goethe and Novalis and Schleiermacher in its author's mind is not obvious to a reader who does not know the 1867 inaugural lecture, or the *Leben Schleiermachers*, or the early essays on Goethe, Novalis, and Hölderlin. What is obvious at the first glance is the order in which the human studies are dealt with, and the amount of space allotted to each. Psychology comes first, and is treated as a principal study, of which biography is a kind of outlier. Much more space is given to the social studies and the normative disciplines than to historical enquiry proper, though the book makes brief and tardy amends by saying that it is in history, not in sociology, that the synthesis of all the sectional human studies is to be found. There is an incongruity between the initial insistence on psychology and the final exaltation of history; we feel the presence of a divided mind. It is different in the *Kritik* of 1910. There Dilthey begins with his analysis of lived experience, expression, and understanding, and shows how from lived experience, through memory, we pass to reflection on the past, and so to autobiography, biography, and history. There is a long account of the aims and methods of historical enquiry; the generalising social studies come in only incidentally in the course of this, and psychology is not formally included at all. More space is given to art as a vehicle of insight than to psychology.

This is clear evidence that, as Dilthey grew older, the sociologist in him grew weaker and the historian grew stronger. The sociologist in him never died. He never wavered in his belief that the generalising sciences have their legitimate place and indispensable function in the body of the human studies. Even psychology, in spite of great difficulties, was never formally excluded. But historical enquiry came to have in his mind a clear primacy over the rest, which survive as ancillary to it.[1]

Should he have excluded the generalising sciences altogether? That is the Neo-Kantian and Hegelian view, and we are familiar by now with the reasons for it. But we should also be familiar with Dilthey's reasons against it. They are good empirical reasons. The generalising sciences are in real life very much mixed up with the historical studies. It is paradoxical to drive a wedge between economic theory and economic history, or between sociology and social history, or between aesthetics, art criticism, and the history of art. Though distinct, these studies form a group by natural affinity. The gap is perhaps greatest in the case of psychology, if we concentrate our attention mainly on the experimental studies of stimulus and reaction which play so large a part in that science. But such studies are not the whole of psychology. And, like the other generalising sciences, psychology draws its data from historical records (case-histories) and

[1] De Ruggiero says that the *Einleitung* was meant to be a study of historical knowledge as contrasted with natural science, history being idiographic in method and natural science being nomothetic. Later the conception of historical knowledge was widened and adulterated by the introduction of generalising sciences, which on the score of their nomothetic method should have been regarded as natural sciences; hence 'a certain positivistic hybridism' in Dilthey's work. In other words, Dilthey is a Neo-Kantian who deviated into positivism. This is a complete travesty of the course of events. The 'positivistic hybridism' was there from the beginning, and found clear expression in the essay of 1875. Later development weakened rather than strengthened it.

340

finds its application in advice and guidance to individuals in actual historical situations. Dilthey does not pretend that all the human studies are branches of history. What he says is that, in and through their very diversity, their differences of method and aim, the human studies form a single body, and work together for common ends in the advancement of knowledge and in practical application to life. This unity of the human studies is an intellectual and social fact which invites philosophical examination; and if philosophy is, as Dilthey believes, not so much a critique of thought as of life, the Critique of Historical Reason will inevitably widen out into a Critique of the Human Studies, which is what Dilthey's work really is.

Philosophy as the mirror of mind

Collingwood and Dilthey are agreed that there can be no metaphysics in the ancient style, no ontology or science of absolute being. The age-long ambition of philosophy, to complete the system of the sciences and set it on a firm foundation, is not to be fulfilled in the traditional way, by a general science of being. Instead, philosophy must become a critical study of the principal modes of experience, showing how, and on what basis, the edifice of knowledge is built.

In Collingwood this analysis leads to the construction of what he himself calls a 'scale of forms', i.e. a rising scale of truth and reality, from mere feeling at the bottom up to philosophy at the top. The scale is set forth in full in *Speculum Mentis*, a work which won high praise from de Ruggiero as a powerful and original contribution to idealist theory. In Collingwood's latest writings, from 1937 onwards, many details of the scheme are revised and restated, but it is obvious that the general plan of it still controls his thinking. It was woven of too many strands to be easily unmade.

The system of *Speculum Mentis* requires to be considered under two aspects.

(1) It may be taken as a theory of knowledge, a study of the various factors which are involved in cognition, and the successive stages by which we advance towards truth. From this point of view the initial stage is crude feeling, the lowliest type of experience, formless and meaningless, where there is neither truth nor falsity, because there is no critical judgment and no asser-

341

tion or denial. The stage above this is imaginative experience, where we have clear and distinct vision, though we do not yet apply objective tests to our imagery in order to sift truth from fantasy. There is a kind of truth here, but it is imaginative and not logical truth, i.e. it is not knowledge of an objective reality. The first stage in reality-thinking is that in which we affirm or deny what we have imagined, without caring to analyse or define or to weigh reasons; it is figurative and mythological thinking, characterised by dogmatic assertion and uncritical faith. Critical thinking comes in when we begin to have a precise terminology and some rigour of method, i.e. to think scientifically. The argument goes on to show how we advance through the stage of abstract thinking, concerned with universal laws and principles, to a knowledge of individual facts and their inter-relations. The final stage, however, is that in which thought turns round and reflects upon itself, and this of course is the stage of philosophical thinking. Philosophy's business is to recognise all the stages and processes here enumerated, and the relations between them, and to see them all together as the activity of the mind knowing its world and itself. Philosophy, in short, is an account of how we come from feeling to knowing, and ultimately to philosophy itself as the critique of knowledge.

(2) Presented in this way, Collingwood's philosophy is a theory of knowledge, built up in a way of his own from elements drawn from various sources: Kant, Hegel, Croce, and others. But then this somewhat dull analysis is given a wholly new significance by a series of bold identifications, which transform it from a theory of knowledge into a philosophy of culture. The most important cultural activities of mankind are equated with the rungs of Collingwood's epistemological ladder. Art is identified with imagination, and religion with mythological thinking and uncritical faith. Mathematics and natural science are presented as abstract thinking, intent on generalisations, in contrast with historical thinking, which is concrete and apprehends the individual. Philosophy itself is the civilised mind reflecting on all its varied activities and the relations between them, and discovering the true meaning of life. Nor is the practical side of life left out. To each level of the cultural ladder corresponds an appropriate type of ethic. Thus interpreted and elaborated, Collingwood's scheme becomes a rival to the Neo-Kantian culture-

philosophy, of which we have heard so much in earlier chapters; though the influence behind it is rather Hegel's than Kant's.

If Dilthey were criticising the scheme, he would probably begin here. Collingwood's identifications are all open to challenge. (1) Of course the imagination plays a decisive part in aesthetic experience; but it does not follow that art can be simply identified with imagination. Dilthey finds in art a greater degree of objectivity, a greater intellectuality, a closer affinity with knowledge, than Collingwood's formula allows. (2) As for the relation between natural science and history, of course it is true that natural science is more abstract than historical thinking; but Dilthey points to the idiographic aspect of natural science, and on the other hand to the affinity between history and the nomothetic human studies, to show that the distinction is not absolute. Natural science cannot be identified outright with abstract thinking, nor history with concrete apprehension of the individual. Besides, there are important differences between them which are not matters of logical form, but lie in the nature of their objects and the attitudes which they evoke in us. History and the human studies have a moral aspect, by virtue of dealing with persons and personal relations, which natural science has not. (3) Religion shares this moral aspect. Moreover, it claims to be concerned with God; and God is not merely a symbol for the objects which we know in science and history, but takes us into another realm, the realm of absolutes, which is of higher import than anything which science or history can disclose. It can therefore claim a very high rank among our activities, not less than the highest; and this is true, however figurative and mythological its language may be. (4) Philosophy too has this moral aspect, which links it with the human studies; we saw in Chapter Six how Dilthey proposes to include moral and political theory and aesthetics among the empirical human studies, and everywhere he shows himself conscious of a closer affinity between philosophy and the human studies than between it and natural science or mathematics. All this apart from the question of metaphysics, which, for what it is worth, brings philosophy into the same field of operation as religion. Hegel's view, that religion and philosophy have the same object and differ only in their way of apprehending it, would be correct if metaphysics as a philosophical discipline were really possible.

In a word, Collingwood's whole scheme is constructed by isolating one aspect of experience, the aspect of logical form, and arranging the various departments of knowledge by reference only to that. But a more critical culture-philosophy must bring in the factors which he leaves out, even though it should mean breaking up the neat pattern of *Speculum Mentis*. Dilthey does bring in these other factors. He judges the various cultural activities not by their logical form alone, but by their whole *Sitz im Leben*; and from this there results a wholly different pattern from anything in Collingwood.

Dilthey's culture-philosophy is based on the three types of conscious attitude to things, and the three types of expression to which these attitudes give rise. (1) Natural science is as nearly as possible a purely cognitive construction. True, there can be no apprehension of an independent reality except through the affective and volitional experience of frustrated effort. To that extent all cognition is bound up with elements of the other two attitudes. But, once granted the conception of an independently existing world, natural science proceeds to make a purely factual study of it, deliberately excluding all value-judgments and norms. (2) The human studies give a factual account of their subject-matter, the world of human experience and activity, but they also do much more. They make, and are expected to make, judgments of value. The type-concept, so important in all the human studies, is not merely a symbol of what is usual, it is also a norm of what is good and healthy, and the historian and the sociologist, the economist and the psychologist, inevitably use such norms, even if they pretend not to do so. From this point of view there is no distinction between history and the other human studies; it is only from the narrowly logical and formalistic point of view that the distinction arises. (3) The same combination of factual knowledge with value-judgment and typology appears in art, which is therefore closely associated with the human studies. We have seen how Dilthey emphasises this association. But whereas the human studies are always tied to objective facts which they must describe, explain, or evaluate, art can move more freely into a world of imagination, where it serves no master but the need for emotional balance and satisfaction. In achieving this it becomes a vehicle for the expression of the artist's *Weltanschauung*, and takes rank with religion and

344

philosophy. Yet the difference between these and the human studies is only a matter of manner and degree. We have seen how Dilthey insists that historical enquiry is itself a way of forming and expressing a *Weltanschauung*, and has thus a genuinely philosophical quality in itself. The only difference is that, in history and the other human studies, these wider issues are handled incidentally, or by implication, through our treatment of the historical and social facts, whereas in art and religion and philosophy it is the wider and more fundamental issues which take the centre of the stage. (4) It is the peculiar business of philosophy as theory of knowledge to examine the three types of expression, the cognitive statement, the value-judgment, the command or precept, to trace them to their roots in the three types of attitude, and so to lay bare the true relations between them. In this way philosophy is the *Grundlegung* of natural science and the human studies, and throws light on the significance of art and religion too.

Metaphysics

Is the critique of knowledge, or of the modes of experience, the whole work of philosophy? Has philosophy no loftier aim than this? The traditional view has been that it has, and the critical work of philosophy has often been overshadowed and all but lost in the more ambitious enterprise of metaphysical speculation. Metaphysics has been variously defined, and has taken many forms; but a common feature of them all is its claim to give knowledge of the existence and character of a super-empirical reality. This claim was raised by the old-style ontology or science of being, which began by laying down propositions which were supposed to be true of all possible finite beings, and ended by inferring the existence of an infinite being, or God. The transcendental philosophy, which began as a study not of being but of experience, ultimately took the same road. For, in making their critique of experience, the post-Kantians came to the conclusion that experience and reality are coextensive; with the result that what began as a theory of knowledge was transformed into a theory of reality. Even God was reintroduced in the guise of the transcendental self or Absolute Spirit. This is the characteristic teaching of all idealist philosophers, including Dilthey's Neo-Kantian rivals and Collingwood's Italian friends.

345

Dilthey himself would have no dealings with metaphysics, whether in the ancient or in the post-Kantian form. His attitude on the point was clear from the start and never wavered. With Collingwood the case is not so clear. In *Speculum Mentis* he appears to put forward an idealist metaphysic; it reads like the work of a Hegelian who has been strongly influenced, but not wholly converted, by Croce. Most readers have taken it so. Collingwood in his last years denied that that was its meaning (*An Autobiography*, p. 56). Perhaps he wrote it with reserves and qualifications in mind which did not find clear expression in the text. If so, they found expression later. In his latest works, such as the *Autobiography* and the *Essay on Metaphysics*, he comes forward with a more carefully guarded position, which challenges comparison with that of Dilthey. In these later works he still speaks as a believer in 'metaphysics', and himself a 'metaphysician'; but he quite firmly abolishes the old-style science of being, and gives the name of 'metaphysics' to something quite different—in fact, an epistemological enquiry.

Metaphysical statements, he now tells us, are not statements about being, but about the fundamental principles or 'absolute presuppositions' by which, consciously or unconsciously, our thinking is governed. These absolute presuppositions are, in effect, Kant's '*a priori* synthetic judgments', provided that by *a priori* we understand not that they are undeniably true, but merely that they are not derived as generalisations from experience. They are principles of interpretation which we bring with us to experience, and it is only because we bring them, or presuppose them, that coherent thinking is possible. Philosophy does not originate these presuppositions; they are made, and operate, and find expression in various ways, e.g. in religious symbolism, independently of the philosopher's activities. What the philosopher has to do is to draw them out into the light of consciousness and formulate them clearly and unambiguously. In so doing the philosopher is indeed discovering truth, but not the truth about being. What he discovers is the truth about the principles by which he and his contemporaries think and live. The function which Collingwood ascribes to him is analogous to that which he ascribes, in *The Principles of Art*, to the artist. Whereas the artist, by an act of imaginative creation, finds adequate expression for his own and his contemporaries' feelings, the philosopher, by a process of logical analysis, finds adequate expression for his and their fundamental principles. This enquiry, which is obviously epistemological, is what Collingwood calls 'metaphysics'.

In carrying it out, he seems determined to get rid of every trace of a transcendent (i.e. in principle unexperienceable) reality. The idea of such a reality, he seems to say, does not arise within experience itself; it is a ghost conjured up by misguided reflection upon experience. Metaphysics arose originally out of the recognition that there is an element in knowledge which is not empirical. Wrongly interpreted, this becomes the theory that there exists a world of real entities which we do not experience, but which through metaphysics we can come to know. The right interpretation finds the non-empirical aspect of knowledge in the absolute presuppositions on which our experience depends. These are not derived from experience, but they are bound up with it. They exist to make science, or the systematic exploration of experience, possible. They trace the lineaments not of a 'reality' beyond experience, accessible only to pure thought, but of the world which our thought, working on the data of sense-experience, is able to construct. If therefore an absolute presupposition is expressed in a form of words which seems at first sight to refer to a transcendent reality, it cannot really mean that. It must be translated into terms which refer plainly to the structure of the experienceable world. Collingwood himself makes some remarkable translations of the Christian creeds in this spirit. Presumably too he would wish his own apparently idealist utterances in *Speculum Mentis* to be interpreted in this way.

Dilthey traces the origin of metaphysics to a similar cause, but with characteristic differences.

He sees clearly that sense-data alone yield no experience. We have to bring with us the principles by which an ordered world can be constructed. He has a good deal to say about these principles in various places. But, whereas Collingwood says much about the absolute presuppositions of science and much less about moral principles, or about the relation between principles of scientific explanation and principles of value-judgment, Dilthey makes this a central issue. He was always more interested in principles of value, especially in moral, legal, and

347

political principles, than in those of natural science. This attitude was forced upon him by his keen sense of the valuational aspect of history and the human studies generally, as well as by the pressure of the Neo-Kantian philosophy of values. He was always sensitive to the difference between a statement of fact, a judgment of value, and a command or precept, and he found that there are principles in each of these kinds. For him, therefore, the relation between fact and value must be a central problem; and it is from this problem that he traces the origin of metaphysics.

The problem is dimly felt, if not clearly seen, by everyone, and a man's *Weltanschauung* is nothing but the solution which he finds for it—a working solution in terms of life, if not a reasoned one in terms of thought. Life demands a solution, and a thought-out solution is desirable. We can see, too, according to Dilthey, that in principle there can only be one solution: fact and value, the actual and the ideal, must be shown to spring somehow from a common root, or to be aspects of the same thing. Metaphysics is an attempt to perform this necessary task. Unfortunately, it goes about it in the wrong way, seeking the common ground and ultimate unity of fact and value in something which transcends experience. Dilthey undertakes to show that all alleged transcendent realities are in fact projections from within experience, and it is only by recognising this that we can understand what real sense is concealed under the time-honoured metaphysical formulae. The independently existing reality, *ens in se*, is a symbol of that in experience which is independent of the experiencing subject's will. The divine Reason from which, variously conceived, metaphysicians deduce the principles of truth and goodness, is a symbol of our own self-organising, self-disciplining, ideal-forming power. The problem of the relation between God and the world is a reflection of the problem of the relation between the higher and lower worlds within ourselves, between our ideal aspirations and our animal nature. In short, all the elements of the problem lie within experience, and all the elements of the solution are to be found there also.

Collingwood and Dilthey are thus agreed in what they reject, and in the main principle on which they reject it. The differences between them are the characteristic ones with which we should by now be familiar. Collingwood concentrates mainly on an analysis of knowledge, and the enquiry which he calls 'metaphysics' is an enquiry into the conditions for progressive discovery. Dilthey's range is wider. For him the fundamental fact, behind which we cannot go, is the total human being at grips with his environment, perceiving, thinking, feeling, desiring. All the intellectual and linguistic structures which philosophers study, and from whose complexities and obscurities the problems of philosophy arise, are incidents in this interaction between man and his world. Dilthey's picture, in fact, is the whole, of which Collingwood has taken up and developed one part.

Relativity

Our difficulties are not yet over. In fact, they are only now approaching their climax. Collingwood and Dilthey agree that philosophy has no higher task than the critique of first principles, and that everything in metaphysics which is not merely a disguised form of this critique must be set aside. But we have still to ask what the scope of the critique itself may be. Up to a point it is obvious. The critique must elicit and formulate clearly the principles of thought and judgment by which we are in fact guided, but of which we are not always fully conscious. It must show how they are related to experience, and what is their function in thought and life. But has it also to decide between rival versions of them? Has it the duty, or even the power, to tell us where our principles are wrong, and to show us the right ones?

Kant would have had no doubt of the answer. In his view there is only one set of absolute presuppositions and moral principles which is valid, and the transcendental argument shows what that set is. Of course he had not the knowledge which Collingwood and Dilthey have of the history of thought. He did not know the full extent to which the fundamental principles accepted in one age or civilisation can differ from those of another. Collingwood and Dilthey both know this and stress it; Dilthey adds to it his own recognition of a psychological relativity inherent in the structure of human consciousness. Yet it may be doubted whether these considerations are enough in themselves to shake Kant's position. Hegel, who knew a great deal about the history of thought, did not therefore think it impossible to say what principles and thought-patterns are the true ones. He held that philosophy can establish the norm by which they are all to be judged, and to which they approximate in varying degrees. His *Logic* is in fact his version of the norm, combined with a running critique of many thought-patterns in common use, which fall short of it. All his other philosophical works, except the *Naturphilosophie*, are meant to show how far in actual life, under varying psychological, social, and historical conditions, human thinking succeeds in its search for truth. Why should not Collingwood and Dilthey do something analogous to this?

Collingwood did so in *Speculum Mentis*. Whatever may be said about the metaphysical aspect of that work, its logical significance is plain: it sets up a norm of truth and judges different thought-patterns by means of it. And when, in *The Idea of Nature*, we are invited to recognise that nature can only be truly seen if it is seen as dependent on something else, and that natural science cannot be thought through to the end without leading us beyond itself to history, it is evident that the same procedure is being followed here, in one of Collingwood's latest writings.

It is true that the *Autobiography* and the *Essay on Metaphysics* contain remarks which seem at first sight to deny the legitimacy of this procedure. Collingwood there says that we cannot properly speak of one set of absolute presuppositions as being truer than another. For, since it is the very function of absolute presuppositions to make coherent thinking and enquiry possible, it follows that they themselves cannot be established or overthrown by any enquiry. Investigation can never furnish evidence for or against them. And therefore, Collingwood argues, they cannot be judged to be true or false. That question does not arise in connection with them, for there is no conceivable means of answering it. The only enquiry which can be made concerning absolute presuppositions is the enquiry, what presuppositions are actually made at a given time by a given group of thinkers. That is a historical question; and if metaphysics is by definition the science of absolute presuppositions, it must be the history of absolute presuppositions, for a historical science is the only science of them which is possible.

This looks at first sight like uncompromising relativism. It seems to say that absolute presuppositions are something which just happens, and may perhaps be explained by historical causes, but that there can be no ground for a reasoned preference as between one set of presuppositions and another. I do not believe, however, that this conclusion really follows from what Collingwood says.

History is not merely a factual study, because it is not merely a record of events. It is a record of men's actions, and of their success or failure in carrying out their purposes. History therefore has in itself a principle by which it can and does judge the actions which it describes. It follows the principle of *Wertbeziehung*, not of *Wertung* (above, p. 241); that is, it judges actions not by an extraneous standard, but by one which is intrinsic to them, viz. the end to which they were directed. Now, 'actions' for the present purpose include not only physical actions, but all purposive activities. They include all coherent and systematic thinking, which has for its purpose the finding of answers to questions. They include also the making of presuppositions, and the 'faith' or 'loyalty' with which men adhere to their absolute presuppositions when once made. These are purposive activities, and their purpose is 'to reduce such experience as (we) enjoy to such science as (we) can compass' (*Essay on Metaphysics*, p. 198). A set of absolute presuppositions, in short, is a contrivance to make science possible, and can be judged by its success or failure in producing that result.

Collingwood himself writes the history of European thought in this way. He makes clear that the Graeco-Roman world was frustrated in its attempts at scientific thinking by defects in its absolute presuppositions, and that the Christian *Weltanschauung* which replaced the Hellenic contained the possibility of overcoming this frustration. He believes that Europe since the Renaissance has been more successful in science than any previous civilised community. Does that not mean that the absolute presuppositions of post-Renaissance Europe have proved themselves more 'logically efficacious' than any previously held, and more efficient in the fulfilment of the purpose to which all such presuppositions are dedicated? And that is an intellectual purpose, the promotion of knowledge. What is the difference between 'efficient in promoting knowledge' and 'true' or 'right' or 'valid', whichever word we prefer to use? We have here a criterion by which the truth (or rightness, or validity) of absolute presuppositions can be assessed. It is therefore not the case that the only question which can properly be asked about them is the question of fact, who presupposes what. The science of absolute presuppositions may be a historical science, if it judges absolute presuppositions by their proven efficiency or inefficiency in action instead of by purely theoretical considerations; but that only means that it will be using the evidence of historical fact to determine what remains in itself a question of value.

I do not see how Collingwood could deny this, nor indeed why he should wish to do so—unless he thought that the intellectual ideal itself changes, so that what one civilisation regards as progress towards a more efficient type of scientific thinking will not necessarily be recognised as such by some later civilisation. To take that suggestion seriously, however, would be the suicide of history. It would mean that one age could never be sure that it understood another; for understanding is possible only on the basis of a common thought-structure underlying all differences of detail. Scepticism on this scale is of course a real possibility in itself, but it is not to be attributed to Collingwood. On the contrary, as a historian he clung consciously and deliberately to the absolute presuppositions which make historical thinking possible. It is just because he was so sure of historical knowledge that he thought he could rescue metaphysics from discredit by showing it to be a branch of history. But it appears that the absolute presuppositions which are required for historical knowledge include one—the fundamental invariance of the ideal of thought—which makes possible also a solution of the metaphysical problem as he conceives it.

It is easy to see how a parallel argument could be built up to set a norm for moral and social principles, once granted the presupposition that the ultimate ideal of practical life is unchanging.

Let us now turn to Dilthey. He meets us at first with the appearance of a thoroughgoing relativism, proclaiming that there are no absolute first principles, and working out his theory of the three types of outlook which he says cannot be synthesised. Yet on examination it will be found that his relativism, like Collingwood's, is not as drastic as it seems.

So far as concerns the principles of science, his view is essentially the same as Collingwood's. He too has studied the history

352

of science, he too is aware of the defects of Graeco-Roman thought, and the distinctive principles which make modern science so much more successful than that of previous ages. What is true of Collingwood is true also of Dilthey: his account of the history of science has implicit in it a principle by which one set of principles can be judged to be better founded than another. At the same time he says a great deal about principles in other spheres of thought, in morality, in art, in education, etc.; and in each of these spheres he thinks that there are principles which are firmly established and can be the object of scientific exposition. Such principles are not *a priori* edicts of a legislative Reason. They represent, in each sphere where they occur, the conditions which our thought or action must satisfy if it is to succeed in its basic aim; and so long as man is what he is, and the world is what it is, these conditions will be what they are.

Of course there is an element of historical relativity. No one can fail to see that. Since the conditions in which a civilised community has to be maintained are not the same in detail from one time or place to another, the rules which govern thought and action will also differ from one time or place to another. But these are differences of detail and application. The fundamental factors of the problem of life do not change.

There is a psychological relativity also, and this is independent of historical conditions. The three basic psychological types occur in any and every society; and whatever the historically conditioned aims and problems of that society may be, different types of people will confront them in different ways. This factor of psychological relativity is discernible in many spheres of life, in art, in religion, in morality, and it means that at any given time and place different people will acknowledge different principles in these fields.

There is nothing in this which need cause uneasiness. Different ideals in art or moral character may represent alternative possibilities of human development; and provided that the adherents of different ideals have the sense to live and let live, that may be welcomed as an enrichment of experience. From a slightly different point of view, Dilthey's three ethical principles may be taken to represent the conditions of the good life as they appear when regarded from three different standpoints. Each sees truly as far as its vision goes, but none sees all that there is to see. It is a question of different perspectives in which an object—in this case the good life—may be seen. Each perspective is a real perspective, but no perspective is the entire object.

Relativity of perspectives is familiar to us in perception. There, however, we have been able, by a system of abstractions and syntheses, to construct an 'object' which is the same for all observers, and a language in which they can talk about it without serious ambiguity. This has not been achieved to anything like the same extent in respect of minds and their experiences, and still less in respect of moral values and ideals. Here our ways of looking at things differ so widely, and our feelings and attitudes vary so subtly from one person to another, that misunderstandings and disagreements are a regular feature of ethical discussion. Yet the difficulty which we find in correlating our several perspectives does not imply that they are all false perspectives, still less that the object itself is illusory. It only means that we must accept the hitherto irreducible diversity of views as our starting-point, as Dilthey in fact does. He then shows how all the various moral attitudes and principles arise naturally out of life, how all of them develop under the influence of changing social and intellectual conditions, and how they interact, intersect, and fuse to form the moral consciousness of individuals and communities. They cannot be brought under one formula, nor can one point of view so develop as to eliminate its rivals; but they are one in their origin (the structure of life) and one in their joint operations and interactions. Need we ask for more?

A different kind of relativity appears when we pass to consider *Weltanschauungen* and metaphysical theories. These, when taken at their face value as descriptions of the real order of things, are not merely different, but irreconcilable. To a believer in metaphysics this fact is an embarrassment; to Dilthey it is merely one of his strongest reasons for not believing in metaphysics. He believes that, if we go behind the *Weltanschauungen* to their respective foundations in experience, we shall once again find ourselves dealing with different but not irreconcilable perspectives. Life is varied and experience is vast. No one can be expected to give conscious recognition to all its aspects and to find a clear and balanced expression for them all. Each must see as widely and as clearly as he can, and abstain from erecting

354

what he sees into a system which claims complete and exclusive truth. If he so abstains, he will be free to enlarge his own vision by the progressive understanding of other people's vision, and so to approximate to that full and balanced view of things which is, after all, our infinitely distant goal. To desire this and to strive consciously for it is the mark of a cultured man; and philosophy, history, art, and the human studies generally are the means by which he will come as near to his goal as is possible for man.

Collingwood in *The Idea of History* (p. 173) launches an attack upon Dilthey's *Weltanschauungslehre*. According to him, Dilthey reduces the history of philosophy to a study in the psychology of philosophers, and by so doing 'makes nonsense of it'. For 'the only question that matters about a philosophy is whether it is right or wrong. If a given philosopher thinks as he does because, being that kind of man, he cannot help thinking like that, this question does not arise. Philosophy handled from this psychological point of view ceases to be philosophy at all.'

Let us be sure that we understand the point of this criticism. Everyone knows that there are some factors, conditioning a man's thought, over which he has no control, because they are there before he begins to think at all. One such factor is the state of scientific and historical knowledge at the time and place where he is working. Another is the 'constellation' of absolute presuppositions in which he has been brought up, and which have entered into the very substance of his thinking. Collingwood recognises both these factors; he would be no historian if he did not. But he feels that to add a man's psychological disposition to the list is to introduce a new and vicious principle. It is easy to see why. The two factors mentioned above constitute, in brief, a man's style of thinking and the data he has available to start from. They are, in a sense, factors native and intrinsic to the thought-process. Moreover, they are or may be progressively modified by the process itself; as a man gains fresh knowledge, and perhaps comes to a fresh formulation of his presuppositions, he transcends the limiting conditions under which he began. Thought is free, is its own master, and can find its way step by step towards truth. But to say that a man's thinking is governed by his psychological disposition, and to treat such dispositions as fixed and unchangeable, is to say that reason is

355

the prisoner of the irrational—a suggestion against which Collingwood always revolts with violence.

His reaction is intelligible, but is it just to Dilthey? The influence of psychological disposition upon thought as well as action is surely a fact, and Dilthey is right to recognise it. A man's thinking is not determined exclusively by the factors which Collingwood recognises, his absolute presuppositions and the state of his knowledge. It is affected also by his interests. He may hold, consciously or unconsciously, presuppositions which lead logically to the asking of a certain question, but unless that question has to do with matters in which he takes an interest he will not trouble to ask it. Temperament and disposition, therefore, lead their possessors in the direction of some observations and discoveries, and away from others. It is therefore not unreasonable to expect that recurrent psychological types, if such there are, will give rise to recurrent types of philosophy. Dilthey is to be congratulated on having explored this line of investigation.

Of course it is not itself a philosophical enquiry. It is a psychological one. But it gives rise to a philosophical question as soon as we ask whether the psychological determination of our thought makes it impossible for us to attain truth. Collingwood writes as if Dilthey had never raised that question, and his criticism is wide of the mark because Dilthey did raise it and answer it—rightly or wrongly—in the way we have seen. The situation is a repetition of what we have found before. Collingwood is a rationalist, moved by an exaggerated fear of irrationalism, hostile to any mention of psychology in philosophy or the human studies, and giving an excessively intellectualistic account of history and philosophy. Dilthey on the other hand sees thought as one activity among others which all together make up life; he tries to do justice to them all, and especially to the interaction between thought and the non-cognitive aspects of experience, without concealing the epistemological problems which arise, but also without exaggerating them. Collingwood's philosophy, in spite of his aesthetic, is on the whole a philosophy of thought and discovery; Dilthey's is a philosophy of life and understanding.

Both Dilthey and Collingwood have acquired a name for philosophical relativism, and up to a point they deserve it.

There is a kind of relativism in their writings. I have tried to show what kind of relativism it is, and how narrow is its range. For both of them it arises incidentally, almost casually, in the course of their reflections on history and the human studies. In neither does it represent a fundamental attitude of scepticism, and neither has seriously faced the possibility of such an attitude. Their dismissal of speculative metaphysics does not indicate any doubt about the solidity of human knowledge in general. On the contrary, it is axiomatic for both that we have knowledge, and are able to make discoveries, both in natural science and in the human studies. The experience of seeking and finding in the sphere of history is a fundamental experience for them both, and they accept without doubt the presuppositions which seem necessary to account for it, viz. the fundamental invariance of the structure of human nature and especially of the ideals of thought and action. This is of course an assumption, and they both know that it is so; but neither is troubled about it, or takes seriously the possibility that it might be unjustified. They seem to feel that the success of historical enquiry, which is for them an undeniable fact, is enough to vindicate its basic assumptions.

This confidence in knowledge, which characterises them both, is symptomatic of their background and experience. Both speak as citizens of the academic world, that world of universities and learned institutions in which scholarship is an accepted ideal and a pervading fact, and the worthwhileness of the scholar's life and activities is not questioned. Dilthey especially is the German scholar and humanist, after the pattern of the age of Goethe and Humboldt, a man of insatiable curiosity, inexhaustible learning, and all-embracing imaginative sympathy. He aspires to unite in himself, through historical study and understanding, all the achievements of European culture, whose intrinsic value and essential unity he does not question. Collingwood too is a scholar, conscious of achievement in the promotion of archaeological studies, conscious of having taken part in a methodological revolution in that field, and anxious to apply its lessons to philosophy. Writing a generation and more after Dilthey, having witnessed 1914 and 1933 and much more of which those dates are symbolic, he is conscious that standards of scholarship, and indeed of civilisation, can be attacked and repudiated, or can perish of neglect; and in his last years we see

357

him trying to diagnose the nature of barbarism and to rouse resistance against it in our threatened world. But though he sees the cultural tradition of Europe threatened, he has himself no doubt of its value or of its essential unity.

Yet even in Dilthey's time these things were being questioned. Today the questioning has become insistent, and has found expression in organised revolutionary movements.

Dilthey confesses that there are things in Christianity which stretch his power of understanding to the breaking-point. That is indeed obvious from what he writes about it. Collingwood would have been wise if he had made the same admission. This points to the first deep cleavage in Europe. Those whose reading of history jumps gaily over from Hadrian to the Medici, as if nothing had happened between, may manage not to see it; but in fact the Christian *Weltanschauung*, taken seriously in its own terms, puts a question mark against all the achievements of civilisation, ancient or modern. Catholicism has never quite let the world forget this, and Protestantism wakes up to it from time to time with a start. It gave one such start in Dilthey's youth, in the person of Kierkegaard; but Dilthey was no more awake to the meaning of Kierkegaard than were the majority of his contemporaries.

But Dilthey's contemporaries also included Marx, and Marx of course is far more than a mere political leader; he is also a ruthless critic of the inherited intellectual and cultural capital of Europe. Implicit in his teaching is a sociology which presents a radical challenge to the assumptions with which Dilthey approaches the human studies. How far is it possible for a liberal and a Marxist to agree in their view of history? How much understanding is there in general between a convinced and instructed Marxist and a liberal humanist such as Dilthey and Collingwood both were? How far are we from having here an instance of two *Weltanschauungen* which are not merely incompatible, but mutually unintelligible?

Then, too, one of Dilthey's contemporaries was Nietzsche, whose criticism of the European tradition, both Greek and Christian, was drastic and dangerous. Perhaps in his lifetime academic persons thought they could safely ignore him. Today only a human ostrich could think so. What is the meaning for our humanist tradition of a man, himself bred in that tradition, who declares that Socrates was truly a corrupter of men, and that the principles of classical Hellenism, of Christianity, and of modern liberalism alike must be rejected?

Other names might be added, but these three will suffice. They show that, if there is a basic identity of structure in all human minds, it is on a level which allows of deep and irreconcilable conflicts in actual life. If these conflicts are due to misunderstanding, it is not misunderstanding at a level where historical study can be relied upon to remove it. On the contrary, it is so deep-seated and intractable that it calls in question the possibility of objective historical understanding itself. Nor can it be resolved by a mere epistemological analysis, however good and necessary that may be in its place; for our *Weltanschauungen* affect our theory of knowledge, as well as being affected by it, and the enquiry which Dilthey calls *Selbstbesinnung* and Collingwood calls 'metaphysics' is the sport of our disagreements, rather than their conqueror.

Dilthey says at the beginning of the *Einleitung* that it is 'a vital question for our civilisation' to understand the cause and cure of the prevailing social unrest. He wrote that in 1883; it is incomparably more true in 1950. But the recipe which he offers in the *Einleitung* is the human studies, especially of course history and the social sciences. Does this go deep enough? Can economic or sociological theories, however profound, suffice to show us our way past what is evidently one of the turning-points of history? Later Dilthey gave us the *Weltanschauungslehre*. That helps us to diagnose some of our cultural divisions, but not the most serious ones; a theory of permanent types cannot solve problems which are peculiar to one age, but only those which are common to all. Collingwood wrote when things were getting worse, but he actually offers us less than Dilthey; only a perpetual exhortation to be honest with ourselves and to think scientifically. Excellent: but the refashioning of a civilisation calls for more than that. It lays upon us an imperious demand for decision and clear purpose in a changing world, while at the same time it threatens us with a scepticism far deeper than anything that is touched by Dilthey. Collingwood may have felt the need of the time, but he was never able to meet it. Dilthey lived too early to see it at all in its present dimensions.

Here we come to the term of our enquiry. Dilthey cannot

solve for us the problems which have become actual since his time. But the mind of an age is made what it is very largely by its memories of previous ages, and we go about our present tasks with minds that are shaped by the thoughts and discoveries of the nineteenth century. In the rich heritage of that century, Dilthey's work occupies and will continue to occupy a distinguished place, interesting as it is in itself, and full of suggestion for us who come after.

SUBJECT INDEX

Acquired system (of mental life), 111–12, 202, 206–7, 209, 280
act (*Akt*) and content (*Inhalt*), xxi, 35–40, 316
three types of act, 37–8, 41–3, 78, 216–17, 272–3, 316, 326–7
aesthetics, 74, 107–9, 114–15, 171, 176–7, 183, 197, 205, 250, 343
anthropology (= descriptive psychology), *see under* psychology
anthropology (= ethnology), *see* ethnology
a priori, the, xviii, 2, 3, 27, 30, 31, 58, 65, 70, 73, 74, 76, 95, 168, 255, 257–8, 306, 316, 321, 346
art, 87–8, 120 n., 132–3, 135–6, 176, 233–5, 284–5, 317–19, 327, 329, 330, 332, 336, 340, 342–6, 355
association of ideas, 17, 44, 151
associationism, 22, 199–201
attitudes—
(=acts as distinct from contents), 37, 64, 78–9, 216–19, 316, 344–5
(=basic life-attitudes), xxi, xxii, 18, 95, 101, 107, 111, 123
Aufbau der geschichtlichen Welt, Der, 155, 182 n., 219, 222, 251, 254–70, 285, 291, 297, 304
autobiography, 125, 201, 217, 228, 274–5, 281, 340

Biography, 172, 281–3, 287, 339, 340

Categories—·
their derivation, 24, 30, 65, 68–70
formal and real categories, 68–9, 92, 127, 230
categories of life, 127, 142, 219, 270–3, 275, 277–81, 289–90, 334, 337
historical categories, 296–7
practical categories, 101, 103–4

causality, 2, 60, 70, 200, 207, 218
in the world of mind, 123, 145, 165, 199–200, 267–9
consciousness, 28–30, 36–44, 49–51, 53–4, 58, 206–7, 270, 316
facts of consciousness, 29, 35, 36, 40, 51
cultural studies (*Kulturwissenschaften*), 75, 149–50, 211–12, 242 n., 244
cultural systems, 157, 176–8, 180–3, 206–7, 268, 288, 291–3, 295–6, 302–3, 304

Dialectic, 13, 202, 265–6, 299–301, 317
dynamic systems (*Wirkungszusammenhänge*), 267–9, 281, 283, 286, 289, 291, 295, 298, 303, 306

Economics, 19–20, 183, 205, 229, 318, 340
Einleitung in die Geisteswissenschaften, xxiv, 20, 60, 85, 97, 104, 157, 161, 168–95, 199, 222, 231, 246, 248, 253, 254, 259, 267, 291, 305, 338, 339, 340 n., 359
empiricism—
British, xviii, 1, 2, 16, 17, 26, 160
Dilthey's, xviii–xx, xxi–xxii, 2, 20, 21, 23–4, 28, 76, 95, 97, 104 n.. 150, 259, 306, 316, 321–2
epistemology, 31–3, 35, 50, 62, 65, 66, 71, 116, 159, 164, 168, 192, 194, 245, 246, 249, 253, 258–9, 276, 316, 320, 359
its relation to psychology, 31–3, 197, 222
ethnology, xxii, 7, 19, 175, 188, 290–1

2B*

SUBJECT INDEX

255, 257–8, 260, 261–2, 268, 270, 276, 279–83, 286–7, 288–290, 291, 308, 309, 310, 318, 338–9
individuality, 9–10, 13–14, 202, 206, 209–11, 227, 232–6, 276, 280
inner perception, 39–40, 124, 200, 205, 207, 226
interpretation, xxv, 9, 12–13, 115, 129, 137–42, 236–8
logical circle in, 138
element of divination in, 12, 141
introspection, xxi, 2, 38, 132, 163, 200, 206, 212, 215–16

Jurisprudence, 21, 27, 81, 97, 176, 183, 184–5, 232, 249–51

Kritik der historischen Vernunft, xiii, xv, xvii, xviii, xxiii, xxv, 1, 97, 155, 159, 166, 167, 192, 194, 222, 245, 248, 251, 252, 253, 254, 265, 297, 305, 306, 307, 308, 319, 334

Law, 103, 177, 180–1, 183, 184, 204–5, 250
natural law, 162, 181, 184, 193
life (*das Leben*), 82, 83, 142–3, 144–5, 147, 214, 218, 265–7, 270–1, 273, 284–5, 302, 320–1, 324–5, 336–7
thought and life, 126–8, 265–7
meaning of life, 87–8, 147, 220, 225, 227, 280, 284, 310
lived experience (*das Erlebnis*), xix, 38–41, 45, 47–52, 65–6, 83, 116, 120, 123–6, 150–2, 202, 207, 213, 215, 217, 219, 249, 262, 278, 306, 316, 333–5, 339–40
erleben and *vorstellen*, 38–40
erleben as immediate awareness, 38–40, 51, 126, 218
its 'reality', 51–2, 206
its relation to time, 45–6, 48–9, 213
its relation to thought, 51, 65–7, 83, 126–8, 150, 207, 259, 316, 333–5
amplified by understanding, 125–6
the *Erlebnis* as unit of experience, 40–1, 47–8, 151

logic, 15, 66, 74, 316

Mathematics, xiii, xiv, xx, 1, 16, 21–2, 26–7, 33, 69, 126, 127, 208, 255, 266, 342
meaning (*Bedeutung*) (= significa-tion), 118, 133, 139, 142–3
meaning (*Bedeutung, Sinn*) (= intel-ligible unity), xv, 86, 113, 116, 142–7, 151, 187, 218, 243 *n.*, 250, 272–4, 278–80, 286–7, 289–90, 296, 298, 299, 306. 308, 336–7
memory, 42, 46–8, 68, 79, 143, 203, 213, 271, 272–4, 279, 281, 290, 340; *see also* presentness (*Präsenz*)
metaphysics, xvi, xviii, xix-xx, 1, 9, 15, 16, 18, 26, 61–2, 81, 84, 91–4, 104, 167, 202, 307–11, 316, 322–4, 341, 343, 345–50, 352, 354–5, 359
m. and the human studies, 168, 192–4, 305
moral theory, xvii, 8, 16–17, 19–20, 81, 89, 96–8, 158, 161, 164–6, 176, 183–4, 197, 347, 352
in Kant, 24, 73, 99–100, 349
in Schleiermacher, 9–10
in the utilitarians, 104–5
morality, xxii, 10, 11, 20, 73–4, 76–7, 98–103, 105–7, 183–4, 353

Nation, the, 6, 7, 175–6, 255–6, 268–9, 293–5
national consciousness, 175, 293–4
natural sciences, xiii, xiv-xv, xvi, xvii, xxiii, 1, 3, 5, 16, 18, 20, 21, 22, 26, 33, 45, 60–2, 70, 75, 91, 124, 127, 139, 148, 160, 162–5, 168–70, 188, 192, 199–201, 203–4, 211–12, 225–7, 229–30, 233, 235–6, 240, 249, 254–5, 259, 260, 269–70, 271–2, 308–9, 310, 313, 318, 338, 340 *n.*, 342–5, 350
their architectonic, 162–5, 169, 188, 254–5, 262
naturalism, 89, 90, 92, 104, 312–313
nomothetic studies, 226–7, 229–30, 240, 246, 340 *n.*, 343

363

INDEX OF PERSONS

367